T0235356

Lecture Notes in Computer Science   9344

Commenced Publication in 1973
Founding and Former Series Editors:
Gerhard Goos, Juris Hartmanis, and Jan van Leeuwen

More information about this series at http://www.springer.com/series/7408

Ladjel Bellatreche · Yannis Manolopoulos (Eds.)

Model and Data Engineering

5th International Conference, MEDI 2015
Rhodes, Greece, September 26–28, 2015
Proceedings

 Springer

Editors
Ladjel Bellatreche
National Engineering School for Mechanics
 and Aerotechnics
Poitiers
France

Yannis Manolopoulos
University of Thessaloniki
Thessaloniki
Greece

ISSN 0302-9743   ISSN 1611-3349 (electronic)
Lecture Notes in Computer Science
ISBN 978-3-319-23780-0   ISBN 978-3-319-23781-7 (eBook)
DOI 10.1007/978-3-319-23781-7

Library of Congress Control Number: 2015947934

Springer Cham Heidelberg New York Dordrecht London

Springer International Publishing AG Switzerland is part of Springer Science+Business Media
(www.springer.com)

Preface

The 5th event of the International Conference on Model Engineering and Data Engineering series (MEDI) took place on Rhodes, Greece during September 26–28, 2015. The main objective of the conference is to bridge the gap between model engineering and data engineering and allow researchers to discuss the recent trends in model and data engineering. It follows the success of the Obidos (Portugal, 2011), Poitiers (France, 2012), Armantea (Italy, 2013), and Larnaca (Cyprus, 2014) events.

For MEDI 2015, two internationally recognized researchers were invited to give a talk. Prof. Christian Jensen from the University of Aalborg, Denmark, gave a talk entitled "Keyword-Based Querying of Geo-Tagged Web Content", whereas Prof. Oscar Pastor Lopez of the Universidad Politecnica de Valencia, Spain, delivered a talk on "Using Conceptual Model Technologies for Understanding the Human Genome: From "Homo Sapiens" to "Homo Genius." We would like to thank the two invited speakers for their contributions to the success of MEDI 2015.

MEDI 2015 received 55 submissions covering both model and data engineering activities. These papers focus on a wide spectrum of topics, covering fundamental contributions, applications, and tool developments and improvements. Each paper was reviewed by three reviewers. The Program Committee accepted 18 regular papers and 9 short papers leading to an attractive scientific program. The authors came from many different countries from all over Europe, e.g., Austria, Estonia, France, Germany, Greece, Ireland, Italy, Poland, Portugal, Spain, as well as from Australia, Algeria, Japan, and Tunisia.

MEDI 2015 would not have succeeded without the deep investment and involvement of the Program Committee members and the external reviewers, who contributed to reviewing (149 reviews) and selecting the best contributions. This event would not exist if authors and contributors did not submit their proposals. We address our special thanks to all authors, reviewers, session chairs, and all Program Committee and Organization Committee members involved in the success of MEDI 2015.

The EasyChair system was set up for the management of MEDI 2015 supporting submission, review, and volume preparation processes. It proved to be a powerful framework. In this respect, special thanks are due to Yannis Karydis for his timely technical support.

We hope that these proceedings will help researchers worldwide to understand and to be aware of recent issues related to model and data engineering. We do believe that they will be of major interest to scientists over the globe and that they will stimulate further research in these domains.

September 2015

Ladjel Bellatreche
Yannis Manolopoulos

Organization

Organizing Committee

General Co-chairs

Yamine Ait Ameur   ENSEEIHT/IRIT, France
Athena Vakali   Aristotle University of Thessaloniki, Greece

Program Chairs

Ladjel Bellatreche   University of Poitiers, France
Yannis   Aristotle University of Thessaloniki, Greece
   Manolopoulos

Organizing Chair

Lazaros Iliadis   Democritus University of Thrace, Greece

Website and Advertising chair

Ioannis Karydis   Ionian University, Greece

Program Committee

Alberto Abello   Universitat Politècnica de Catalunya, Spain
Idir Ait Sadoune   E3S-SUPELEC, France
Abdelmalek Amine   Tahar Moulay University of Saida, Algeria
Kamel Barkaoui   Cedric-CNAM, France
Alberto Belussi   Verona University, Italy
Sadok Ben Yahia   Université de Tunis El Manar, Tunisia
Alexander Borusan   Technische Universität Berlin, Germany
Frederic Boulanger   Supelec, France
Nieves R. Brisaboa   Universidade da Coruña, Spain
Francesco Buccafurri   Università Mediterranea di Reggio Calabria, Italy
Antonio Corral   University of Almeria, Spain
Alfredo Cuzzocrea   University of Calabria, Italy
Florian Daniel   University of Trento, Italy
Remi Delmas   ONERA, France

Robert Wrembel   Poznan University of Technology, Poland
Demetrios   University of Cyprus, Cyprus
  Zeinalipour-Yazti
Bin Zhou   University of Maryland, USA

External Reviewers

Pavlos Basaras   Selma Khouri
Nick Bassiliades   Yassine Ouhammou
Besim Bilalli   Nafees Qamar
Selma Bouarar   Panagiotis Symeonidis
Xiahong Chen   Vasileios Theodorou
Hariton Efstathiades   Demetris Trihinas
Zoé Faget   Theodoros Tzouramanis
Flavio Ferrarotti   Jovan Varga
Olga Gkountouna   Vassilios Verykios
Dimitrios Karapiperis   Qing Wang
Panagiotis Katsaros   Hao Wang

Invited Talks

Keyword-Based Querying of Geo-Tagged Web Content

Christian S. Jensen

Aalborg University, Denmark

Abstract. The web is being accessed increasingly by users for which an accurate geo-location is available, and increasing volumes of geo-tagged content are available on the web, including web pages, points of interest, and microblog posts. Studies suggest that each week, several billions of keyword-based queries are issued that have some form of local intent and that target geo-tagged web content with textual descriptions. This state of affairs gives prominence to spatial web data management, and it opens to a research area full of new and exciting opportunities and challenges. A prototypical spatial web query takes a user location and user-supplied keywords as arguments, and it returns content that is spatially and textually relevant to these arguments. Due perhaps to the rich semantics of geographical space and its importance to our daily lives, many different kinds of relevant spatial web query functionality may be envisioned. Based on recent and ongoing work by the speaker and his colleagues, the talk presents key functionality, concepts, and techniques relating to spatial web querying; it presents functionality that addresses different kinds of user intent; and it outlines directions for the future development of keyword-based spatial web querying.

Bio. Christian S. Jensen is Obel Professor of Computer Science at Aalborg University, Denmark, and he was previously with Aarhus University for three years and spent a one-year sabbatical at Google Inc., Mountain View. His research concerns data management and data-intensive systems, and its focus is on temporal and spatio-temporal data management. Christian is an ACM and an IEEE Fellow, and he is a member of Academia Europaea, the Royal Danish Academy of Sciences and Letters, and the Danish Academy of Technical Sciences. He has received several national and international awards for his research. He is Editor-in-Chief of ACM Transactions on Database Systems.

Using Conceptual Model Technologies for Understanding the Human Genome: From an "Homo Sapiens" to an "Homo Genius"

Oscar Pastor Lopez

Universidad Politecnica de Valencia, Spain

Abstract. Everybody accepts that understanding the Human Genome is a big challenge for the humanity. It will take at the very least decades to achieve such a goal reasonably well. But new advances that are showing promising results come continuously. Day after day new data is provided and new information is derived from them. As DNA sequencing technologies improve and evolve, it is evident that the rate of data generation at a local level is increasing dramatically. In this scenario, assuring the interoperability and consistence of data at the global level becomes both a challenge and a need. To face these problems adequately, the most advanced Information Systems design technologies are strongly required, to cover the needs of better data capture, organization and storage, improved data analysis and interoperability, and more efficient data standardization with the support of foundational ontologies. This principle is in the "Genome" of this keynote. Using Advanced Conceptual Model and Data Technologies, there is an opportunity to understand the secrets of life that the Genome Code hides. More and more data that relate genotype and phenotype are available, with especially attractive clinical applications. These ideas will be approached in the keynote, showing that the challenge of understanding the human genome can suppose a conceptual revolution: understanding the genome could allow improving human being features, something never before in the hand of we, humans. This is the idea of the title: Homo Sapiens becoming Homo Genius being able to understand and manage the principles of life, and subsequently improve then.

Bio. Full Professor and Director of the Research Center on "Metodos de Produccion de Software (PROS)" at the Universidad Politecnica de Valencia (Spain). He received his Ph.D. in 1992. He was a researcher at HP Labs, Bristol, UK. He has published more than two hundred research papers in conference proceedings, journals and books, received numerous research grants from public institutions and private industry, and been keynote speaker at several conferences and workshops. Chair of the ER Steering Committee, and member of the SC of conferences as CAiSE, ESEM, ICWE, CIbSE or RCIS, his research activities focus on conceptual modeling, web engineering, requirements engineering, information systems, and model-based software production. He created the object-oriented, formal specification language OASIS and the corresponding software production method OO-METHOD. He led the research and development underlying CARE Technologies that was formed in 1996. CARE Technologies has created an advanced MDA-based Conceptual Model Compiler called Integra Nova, a tool that produces a final software product starting from a conceptual schema that represents system requirements. He is currently leading a multidisciplinary project linking Information Systems and Bioinformatics notions, oriented to designing and implementing tools for Conceptual Modeling-based interpretation of the Human Genome information.

Contents

Context Modeling and Model Transformation

Data Mining

Query Processing

Modeling Activities and Inference

Prediction and Recommendation

Requirement and Systems Engineering

Modeling and Meta Modeling

Semi-automated Generation of DSL Meta Models from Formal Domain Ontologies

Andres Ojamaa, Hele-Mai Haav[(⊠)], and Jaan Penjam

Institute of Cybernetics, Laboratory of Software Science,
Tallinn University of Technology, Tallinn, Estonia
{andres.ojamaa,helemai,jaan}@cs.ioc.ee

Abstract. This paper addresses the problem of alignment of domain ontologies and meta-models of Domain Specific Languages (DSL) in order to facilitate the DSL development process by formal methods. The solution presented in this paper automatically generates design templates of a DSL meta-model that are consistent with a given domain ontology represented in OWL DL. Consistency of alignment is ensured by predefined mapping rules between constructs of ontology modelling language OWL DL and a modelling language used for representing DSL meta-models. The approach is implemented as an extension to the CoCoViLa system and the CoCoViLa modelling language is used for representing DSL meta-models. The evaluation of the provided method is carried out by developing the DSL for the IT risk analysis and management domain.

Keywords: Model-driven software engineering · Ontology-based modelling · Model transformations · DSL meta-models

1 Introduction

In recent years, several approaches to incorporate ontologies into general frameworks of Model Driven Software Engineering (MDSE) have been proposed [1, 9, 16, 19]. In addition, an effort is put to using ontologies in the field of DSL engineering [5, 17–20]. However, in order to facilitate the DSL development process by utilization of formal methods more attention needs to be paid to alignment of domain ontologies as formal domain models with DSL meta-models. This creates a new challenging task for software engineers not well supported by existing traditional and ontology-driven MDSE methods. This paper provides a method and tools to perform this task.

The main contribution of the paper is an approach that focuses to partial automation of the design and implementation phases of the DSL development process by introduction of formal domain ontologies into this process and automatic generation of design templates of a DSL meta-model from a given domain ontology. Ontology Web Language (OWL) [14] is used for representing formal domain ontologies. The approach is implemented as an extension to the CoCoViLa system [10] and the CoCoViLa modelling language is used for representing meta-models of DSLs. The CoCoViLa system enables automatic generation of executable Java programs according to the given DSL meta-model. The evaluation of the provided method is carried out by developing the DSL for the IT risk analysis domain.

© Springer International Publishing Switzerland 2015
L. Bellatreche and Y. Manolopoulos (Eds.): MEDI 2015, LNCS 9344, pp. 3–15, 2015.
DOI: 10.1007/978-3-319-23781-7_1

Novelty of our approach comparing to other ontology-driven software development methodologies lies in using formal domain ontologies as a basis for automatic generation of design templates of a DSL meta-model that are consistent with the given domain ontology. This makes a DSL closely aligned with the domain for what it is designed for. Consistency of alignment is ensured by predefined mapping rules between constructs of the ontology modelling language OWL and a modelling language for DSL meta-models (i.e. the CoCoViLa modelling language in our case).

The development of this new approach was motivated by practical needs of using the CoCoViLa modelling tool for the development of different DSLs in the domains of simulation of hydraulic systems as well as simulations of security measures for banking and communication networks [10]. From these experiences we have learned that tighter integration of domain knowledge with the corresponding DSL will create advantages in achieving consistency of the DSL with domain knowledge and will ease maintenance of applications developed by using the DSL.

The rest of the paper is structured as follows. Section 2 is devoted to related work and Sect. 3 provides an overview of the CoCoViLa modelling language and the system giving background knowledge for our approach. In Sect. 4, our approach for domain ontology driven DSL engineering is presented. Section 5 is devoted to the evaluation of the provided method by implementation of a prototype of the DSL for the IT security risk analysis and management field. Section 6 concludes the paper.

2   Related Work

Ontologies in computer science represent computer-usable specifications of basic concepts in a domain and relationships among them. Ontologies are usually expressed in a logic-based language. There are several ontology languages available, but the most widely used are the W3C standards OWL DL and OWL2 [14].

In software engineering, domain analysis plays an important role in understanding the domain of interest. Nowadays, many researchers propose to use ontology engineering methods in the domain analysis process [1, 4, 19, 20] and some of them suggest to represent resulting model of domain analysis by domain ontology [4, 7, 20]. In these works, domain models are considered as descriptive models consisting of a set of domain instances (ABox in Description Logics (DL) [2]) and a set of classes for classifying these instances (TBox in DL). Comparing to traditional analysis models formal ontologies have additional useful features like reasoning based on DL [2].

Most of existing ontology driven MDSE methodologies use ontological services for performing model consistency checking and model transformations [16, 19]. Some of the approaches use domain ontologies (e.g. represented in UML) as a part of Computation Independent Models (CIM) [18]. Few works address also semantic search and composition of models of software components [9].

Several proposals [1, 19, 20] are about integrating ontologies to the OMG meta-pyramid of Model Driven Architecture (MDA) [15]. For example, in [1] ontology-aware mega-model is provided for ontology integration to MDA. Another approach in [19] shows that the Ecore meta-meta-model of the Eclipse Modelling Framework [6] and OWL2 meta-model can be integrated in order to provide a meta-meta-model for modelling DSLs. In [20] OWL2 ontologies are integrated into the meta-meta-model level in order to support joint DSL and domain engineering.

Similarly to these works, we also introduce ontologies to the meta-meta-model level but we are focused to partial automation of creation of DSL meta-models.

There are frameworks that examine domain ontologies as domain models that can be automatically transformed to a DSL grammar [4, 5]. We were inspired by these works but our approach uses predefined mapping rules.

3   The CoCoViLa Modelling Language and System Overview

The approach presented in this paper is developed as an extension to the CoCoViLa modelling system[1] that is implemented in Java. The CoCoViLa modelling language consists of visual and textual declarative languages for developing DSLs for engineering fields, where scientific and engineering computations play a crucial role. Intended users of the CoCoViLa modelling language are DSL designers (together with domain experts), who create meta-models and a DSL for a particular domain. DSL designers can create textual and/or visual DSLs.

The most important construct of the textual declarative modelling language is a concept specification that represents a collection of instances. Concept specifications can be arranged into taxonomy. Concept specifications include descriptions of structural components of a concept as declarations of variables. In addition, they may include relations that are specifications showing how to derive values of some variables from the values of other variables. Relations are divided to equations and axioms. Equations define dependencies between variables bound by the equation. Axioms describe functional dependencies between variables and they differ from equations in that they have realizations as Java methods.

Important feature of the modelling language is its grounding with a subset of Intuitionistic Propositional Calculus (IPC) [13] that is used as a logical language for representation of domain specific axioms. From the given concept specifications and the task specification the CoCoViLa system automatically constructs the algorithm of the program and generates the Java program that solves the computational problem given by the task specification. The latter is a statement of a computational problem that specifies what outputs are to be computed from given inputs. It does not have a given realization but its realization is attempted to generate automatically from the constructive proof of the corresponding theorem in IPC according to the inference rules of Structural Synthesis of Programs (SSP) [12].

When using the CoCoViLa modelling language we distinguish between the DSL meta-modelling and application specific modelling levels. In our terminology, a DSL meta-model consists of a set of concept specifications and an application specific model consists of a task specification and a set of valuations of variables. We explain the main idea behind the language using a simplistic example from the geometry domain. The geometry DSL may contain specifications of the Square and the Circle concepts including all necessary variables and equations. If we are interested in calculating the

---

[1] http://cocovila.github.io/.

area that is difference of areas of a square and a circle where diagonal of a square is equal to diameter of a circle, then we need to create a new concept specification (e.g. SquareWithinCircle) as depicted in the following Fig. 1.

```
specification SquareWithinCircle {
            double area_difference;
            Square S;
            Circle C;
            C.diameter=S.diagonal;
            area_difference = C.area-S.area; }
```

Fig. 1. An example of the CoCoViLa modelling language

Dot notation is used to refer to inner concept specifications. As a result, the geometry DSL is composed from the following concept specifications: Square, Circle, and SquareWithinCircle.

On the application specific modelling level, we can use this DSL and specify different task specifications (e.g. ->area_difference), which specify computational problems that need to be solved. Values of inputs are assumed to be given (e.g. S.hasHeight = 10) or computable on the basis of the specification. If output variables of a task are computable from (possibly empty) list of inputs, the task is solved and the Java program is automatically generated. Besides equations, a Java method could be declared to be as a realization of a given functional dependency. For example, instead of the equation area_difference = C.area-S.area we may write axiom C.area, S.area ->area_difference {<JavaMethod>}.

The syntax of the full CoCoViLa modelling language is presented in [10]. Using the current system, DSL meta-models are created manually by DSL developers. In practice, informal methods are used for representation of domain models.

4   An Approach to Domain Ontology-Driven DSL Engineering

4.1   Introducing Formal Ontologies to the DSL Development Process

For improvement of the workflow of DSL development we introduce two types of ontologies into the DSL development process: domain and system ontologies.

Purpose of *domain ontology* is to provide specification of conceptualization of domain knowledge. Formal domain ontology could be seen as a static part of a meta-model of a DSL, particularly a part of a CIM. Using formal ontologies as a part of a CIM makes connections from CIM to Platform Independent Model (PIM) transparent and methodical. We automate creation and maintenance of connections between CIM and PIM by automatic generation of design templates of DSL meta-models from formal domain ontologies. In our case (i.e. the CoCoViLa system extension), design templates of a DSL meta-model are concept specifications that do not include specifications of dynamic parts of a meta-model like axioms and equations (except binding, e.g. see Table 1). These need to be added manually to the template.

▼ ● Thing
  ► ● Variable
  ▼ ● Relation
    ► ● Axiom
    ► ● Equation
    ● Constant
  ► ● DiagramElement
  ▼ ● JavaClass
    ▼ ● Metaclass
      ► ● VisualClass

Fig. 2. A fragment of system ontology (a screen shot of the Protégé ontology editor)

Purpose of *system ontology* is formally describing the modelling language and the system concepts (see Fig. 2 for a part of a class hierarchy).

We utilize the CoCoViLa system ontology in the implementation phase of a DSL. Individuals of the system ontology classes together with their property values are used to store knowledge about a particular DSL meta-model. It is important to notice that domain ontology and the system ontology are linked to each other for this purpose.

4.2 Mapping Formal Domain Ontologies to DSL Meta-Models

For automatic transformation of formal domain ontologies to DSL meta-models corresponding mappings between a set of ontology representation language constructs and a DSL modelling language constructs need to be defined. As depicted in Fig. 3, in our case we need to provide mappings between a subset of OWL DL constructs and a subset of the CoCoViLa modelling language constructs.

Both languages are declarative languages intended to be used for knowledge representation. OWL DL semantics is given by DL [2] and the CoCoViLa modelling language semantics is based on a subset of IPC [13]. DL enables to reason whether domain ontology is consistent and complete. Expressive power of SSP used for deciding about computational correctness of a program automatically generated from a given specification is equivalent to IPC [13].

Since semantical basis of both languages is different, then some restrictive conditions must be placed on domain ontology structure in order to ensure that it can be properly transformed into a set of constructs of the CoCoViLa modelling language. These restrictions mainly concern OWL constructs for object property characteristics, property restrictions and complex classes that cannot be mapped to the CoCoViLa language.

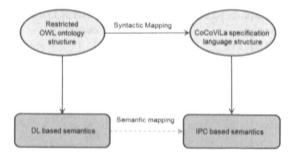

Fig. 3. Mapping formal domain ontology to the CoCoViLa language

Table 1. Mappings between OWL and the CoCoViLa modelling language constructs

Acceptable OWL constructs of formal domain ontology (i.e. the CoCoViLa compatible OWL ontology)	The CoCoViLa modelling language statements generated from corresponding OWL constructs

A class is a set of individuals with similar properties. Classes should be disjoint.
 	
`owl:Class`
e.g.
`<owl:Class rdf:ID="Square"/>`
`</owl:Class>`
	A concept specification is a specification of conceptualization of a domain represented in the CoCoViLa textual modelling language. A concept specification represents a collection of instances.
	
	specification `<name> {}`
	e.g.
	specification `Square {}`

Datatype properties represent relations between instances of classes and RDF literals and XML Schema datatypes
 	
`owl:DataTypeProperty,`
`rdfs:domain, XML Schema`
`datatypes`
e.g.
`<owl:DatatypeProperty`
`rdf:ID="hasHeight">`
`<rdfs:domain`
`rdf:resource="#Square" />`
`<rdfs:range`
`rdf:resource="&xsd;double"/>`
`</owl:DatatypeProperty>`
	Each concept specification has an associated collection of attributes (represented by concept specification variables in textual specification) which can be filled by values of a given Java type or other concept specifications.
	
	`<Java type> < attribute name>`
	e.g.
	specification `Square`
	`{`**double** `hasHeight;}`

Object properties represent relationships between instances of two classes.
 	
`owl:ObjectProperty`
e.g.
`<owl:ObjectProperty`
`rdf:ID="compS"> <rdfs:domain`
`rdf:resource="#SquareWithinCir`
`cle"/> <rdfs:range`
`rdf:resource="#Square"/> …`
	Attributes associated with concept specification can be filled by a concept specification.
	
	`<concept specification name>`
	`<attribute name>`
	e.g.
	specification
	`SquareWithinCircle {`
	`Square compS;}`

(Continued)

Table 1. (*Continued.*)

Two properties may be stated to be the same by using property equivalence.
 	
`owl:equivalentProperty`
`e.g.`
`rdf:about="#hasHeight">`
`<rdfs:domain`
`rdf:resource="#Square"/>`
`<owl:equivalentProperty`
`rdf:resource="#hasWidth"/>`
`<rdfs:range`
`rdf:resource="&xsd;double"/>`
	A binding represents an equality relation (equation) between two variables. It could be used for representation of data and object property equivalences.
	
	`<variable name> = < variable name>`
	`e.g.`
	`specification` `Square {`
	`double` `hasHeight;`
	`double` `hasWidth;`
	`hasHeight=hasWidth; }`

Taxonomic constructor of class hierarchies.
 	
`rdfs:subClassOf`
`e.g.`
`<owl:Class rdf:ID="Square">`
`  <rdfs:subClassOf`
`rdf:resource="#Rectangle" />`
`   ...`
`</owl:Class>`
	The assertion of concept specification taxonomy. Concept specification associated with a Java class B can inherit concept specification of class associated with a Java class A iff A is a superclass of B in Java, i.e. B is declared as class B extends A. No multiple inheritances are allowed.
	
	`specification` `Square` **`super`**
	`Rectangle {... }`

Individuals with values of datatype properties.
 	
`<owl:NamedIndividual`
`rdf:about="#MySquare">`
`<rdf:type`
`rdf:resource="#Square"/>`
`<hasHeight`
`rdf:datatype="&xsd;double">5.0`
`</hasHeight>`
`</owl:NamedIndividual>`
	The CoCoViLa modelling language does not distinguish between classes and individuals on the specification level. Instances will be created during the code generation of the program for specific problem solving as Java class instances.
	The created instance will be initialized by a declared value.
	
	`<variable name> = <value>`
	`e.g.`
	`MySquare.hasHeight = 5.0;`

Semantic correspondence of mappings is given only indirectly via syntactic mappings in Table 1. Providing semantic mappings and a proof of the corresponding theorem are out of scope of this paper. In Table 1, OWL constructs that are allowed in the CoCoViLa compatible ontologies are listed and mapping rules are provided. The given mappings are used to automatically generate design templates of a DSL meta-model. OWL constructs for what mappings are not defined are not allowed and the corresponding OWL constructs are ignored in the automated model generation process.

4.3   Implementation of the Approach

The approach takes into account important DSL development phases as follows: domain analysis, design, implementation, deployment, testing and maintenance [11]. We suggest using the iterative (agile) DSL development process that starts with building a core of domain ontology by taking into account requirements of domain and a DSL. Domain ontology is created according to an expert centric agile ontology development methodology [8]. DSL design and implementation stages are supported by the tool that is an extension to the existing CoCoViLa system and is also implemented in Java. The implementation is designed to fit into general architecture of the CoCoViLa system. An overall view of the structure of the extension is provided in Fig. 4.

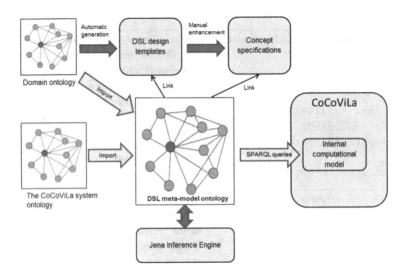

Fig. 4. A general view of the implementation of the approach

Automatically generated templates of a DSL meta-model are implemented as Java classes. For each concept specification from a template, the corresponding Java class is generated. Java classes including concept specifications can be manually enhanced with necessary equations and axioms. In addition, these Java classes may contain Java methods that are the realizations of axioms described in the concept specification. Currently, for each DSL its meta-model ontology is created that imports the CoCoViLa system and domain ontologies. It also contains the DSL specific instances (ABox). Consistency of the DSL meta-model ontology is checked by using OWL DL inference provided by Apache Jena.[2] When loading the DSL, its meta-model ontology is dynamically loaded and SPARQL[3] queries are used to find definitions of elements of

---

[2] https://jena.apache.org/.

[3] http://www.w3.org/TR/sparql11-query/.

the diagrammatical language and other DSL components in order to insert information about them to the internal computational model of CoCoViLa. After that, the visual part of the DSL is shown in the CoCoViLa DSL window and the DSL is ready to be used by application developers.

5   Evaluation

5.1   A Problem: IT Security Risk Analysis

In order to solve IT security risk analysis problems, a threat modelling tool could be useful. One of the ways to build a threat modelling tool is to develop a DSL for creation of attack simulations using ontological modelling of security knowledge, dynamic attack tree generation techniques and probabilistic models of threat agent behavior. In order to build a particular threat modelling tool following the DSL development approach presented in this paper, we adapted the multi-parameter attack tree method proposed in [3]. Attack trees according to this method are used to estimate the cost and the success probability of attacks. Elementary game theory is used to decide whether the system under protection is a realistic target for gain-oriented attackers.

In the following example that is adapted from [3] a threat analysis for forestalling release is considered. This threat is related to the situation where a competitor of an IT company steals the developed source code and completes it to own product.

5.2   Development of a DSL for the IT Security Risk Analysis Domain

A visual DSL was developed for IT security risk analysis with attack trees methodology. The DSL consists of components to model attack trees and to perform computations on the trees. An attack tree is basically an AND-OR tree that consists of three types of components (nodes) – leaves (atomic threats where there are estimated values for attack parameters), AND-nodes representing complex attacks that are considered successful when all sub-trees are successful, and OR-nodes representing complex attacks that are considered successful when any of the sub-attacks is successful. In addition to the components used for specifying attack trees, there are two additional components required as follows: a simulator component that performs computations on the attack tree models and a visualized component for displaying results.

Formal Ontology of IT Risk Analysis for the Forestalling Release Domain. There are several events necessary for a forestalling release that we consider as domain knowledge. By the attack analysis method that we use, an attack is seen as a game played by the rational attackers and the game is to be profitable for them. In order to decide about the profitability, there are several characteristics related to threat events to be taken into account by the attack game. These constitute domain knowledge related to the particular threat analysis method. Both types of domain knowledge are captured in formal domain ontology of IT security risk analysis. As a result, domain ontology of the forestalling release domain consists of taxonomy of disjoint classes of threat events.

Threat events have associated characteristics needed for the attack game. These are described by data properties which domain is the `Threat_event` class. Main direct subclasses of the `Threat_event` class and data properties that are inherited by its subclasses are shown in Fig. 5.

Fig. 5. The forestalling release domain ontology (a screen shot of the Protégé ontology editor)

Generation of DSL Design Templates. According to the given domain ontology and the transformations given in Table 1, the DSL design templates are automatically generated (see a fragment of automatically generated code in Fig. 6).

```
specification Threat_event {
                      string hasDescription;
                      double
                      hasAverage_Penalty_Failure,hasCost,
                      ...; }
specification Bribe_a_programmer super Threat_event { }
specification Forestalling_release super Threat_event { }
specification Stealing_the_code super Threat_event { }
...
```

Fig. 6. A fragment of generated DSL meta-model in the CoCoViLa modelling language

Enhancement of DSL Design Templates and DSL Meta-model Ontology. The DSL implementation involves an enhancement of design templates, if necessary. For example, equations used for calculating parameters of an attack game are added to the `Threat_event` specification.

In the DSL meta-model ontology, `Threat_event` is declared as a subclass of the class `Metaclass` from the system ontology. For each subclass of the `Threat_event` class an instance and links to the corresponding `VisualClass` instances are created for capturing diagrammatical part of the DSL. Instances of the `VisualClass` class become components of the attack tree diagram. The DSL is implemented so that the same threat analysis method can be used for different IT risk analysis domains by importing different domain ontologies to the DSL meta-model ontology. The DSL will then be automatically aligned with new domain ontology.

5.3   Analysis of the Evaluation of the Approach

According to the evaluation of the approach by developing a DSL for the IT security risk analysis domain, we identify the following advantages of the approach:

- Since domain analysis is done by developing formal domain ontology, then DL reasoning services can be used for validation of domain models.
- Alignment of formal domain ontologies with DSL meta-models makes it possible to automatically propagate changes in ontology to a DSL i.e. capture the evolution of a domain. It also allows detecting and avoiding errors.
- Formal consistency checking of domain knowledge and a DSL meta-model ontology using DL inference. This is also useful for debugging DSL meta-models. In addition, other resources (e.g. images, multi-media, linked data etc.) could be linked to a DSL meta-model and used as components of a DSL.
- Separation of different kinds of knowledge about the system, domain and a DSL into modular OWL ontologies makes the knowledge more reusable.

However, as our approach is implemented as an extension to the existing Co-CoViLa system only partial automation of mapping domain ontology to a DSL meta-model can be provided. Another issue is related to productivity of the DSL development process. We did not provide any productivity analysis yet. We think that there might be problems of creation of formal domain ontologies as ontology engineering techniques do not constitute a part of existing traditional software development methodologies. This may create initial complexity.

6   Conclusion

In this paper, we presented an approach that introduces formal domain ontologies into the DSL development process and allows to automatically generate design templates of a DSL meta-model that are consistent with a given domain ontology represented in OWL DL. The approach was implemented as an extension to the CoCoViLa system. The provided method was tested by developing the DSL for IT risk analysis domain.

Our approach creates the following benefits: formal consistency checking of domain knowledge and a DSL meta-model ontology, automatic generation of design templates of a DSL meta-model and capture of evolution of the domain in a DSL.

Our future work will be related to integrating rules represented in Semantic Web Rule Language (SWRL)[4] to the framework. Rules combined with ontology will allow us to model behavioral aspects (e.g. equations) of a domain and perform corresponding transformations from SWRL to the CoCoViLa modelling language.

Acknowledgements. This research was supported by Estonian Research Council institutional research grant no. IUT33-13, and by the ERDF through the ITC project MBJSDT and Estonian national CoE project EXCS.

---

[4] http://www.w3.org/Submission/SWRL/.

References

1. Aßmann, U., Zschaler, S.: Ontologies, meta-models, and the model-driven paradigm. In: Calero, C., Ruiz, F., Piattini, M. (eds.) Ontologies for Software Engineering and Software Technology, pp. 249–273. Springer, Heidelberg (2006)
2. Baader, F., Calvanese, D., McGuiness, D., Nardi, D., Patel-Schneider, P.: The Description Logic Handbook: Theory, Implementation and Applications. Cambridge University Press, Cambridge (2003)
3. Buldas, A., Laud, P., Priisalu, J., Saarepera, M., Willemson, J.: Rational choice of security measures via multi-parameter attack trees. In: López, J. (ed.) CRITIS 2006. LNCS, vol. 4347, pp. 235–248. Springer, Heidelberg (2006)
4. Čeh, I., Črepinšek, M., Kosar, T., Mernik, M.: Ontology driven development of domain-specific languages. ComSIS 8(2), 317–342 (2011)
5. Fonseca, J.M.S., Pereira, M.J.V., Henriques, P.R.: Converting ontologies into DSLs. In: Pereira, M.J.V., Leal, J.P., Simões, A. (eds.) 3rd Symposium on Languages, Applications and Technologies (SLATE'14), pp. 85–92. Dagstuhl Publishing, Germany (2014)
6. Gronback, R.: Eclipse Modeling Project: a Domain-Specific Language (DSL) Toolkit. Addison-Wesley Professional, Boston (2009)
7. Guizzardi, G.: Ontology-based evaluation and design of visual conceptual modelling languages. In: Reinhartz-Berger, I., Sturm, A., Clark, T., Bettin, J., Cohe, S. (eds.) Domain Engineering. Product Lines, Languages, and Conceptual Models, pp. 317–347. Springer, Heidelberg (2013)
8. Haav, H.-M.: A practical methodology for development of a network of e-government domain ontologies. In: Skersys, T., Butleris, R., Nemuraite, L., Suomi, R. (eds.) Building the e-World Ecosystem. IFIP AICT, vol. 353, pp. 1–13. Springer, Heidelberg (2011)
9. Katasanov, A.: Ontology-driven software engineering: beyond model checking and transformations. Int. J. Semant. Comput. 06, 205–242 (2012)
10. Kotkas, V., Ojamaa, A., Grigorenko, P., Maigre, R., Harf, M., Tyugu, E.: CoCoViLa as a multifunctional simulation platform. In: Proceedings of the 4th International ICST Conference on Simulation Tools and Techniques (SIMUTools 2011), pp. 198–205. ICST, Brussels (2011)
11. Mernik, M., Heering, J., Sloane, A.M.: When and how to develop domain-specific languages. ACM Comput. Surv. 37(4), 316–344 (2005)
12. Mints, G., Tyugu, E.: Justification of the structural synthesis of programs. Sci. Comput. Program. 2(3), 215–240 (1982)
13. Mints, G., Tyugu, E.: Propositional logic programming and the PRIZ system. J. Log. Program. 9(2&3), 179–193 (1990)
14. Motik, B., Patel-Schneider, P.F., Horrocks, I.: OWL 2 Web Ontology Language: Structural Specification and Functional-Style Syntax. http://www.w3.org/TR/owl2-syntax
15. OMG. MDA Guide 1.0.1. http://www.omg.org/mda June 2003
16. Roser, S., Bauer, B.: Automatic generation and evolution of model transformations using ontology engineering space. In: Spaccapietra, S., Pan, J.Z., Thiran, P., Halpin, T., Staab, S., Svatek, V., Shvaiko, P., Roddick, J. (eds.) Journal on Data Semantics XI. LNCS, vol. 5383, pp. 32–64. Springer, Heidelberg (2008)
17. Tairas, R., Mernik, M., Gray, J.: Using ontologies in the domain analysis of domain-specific languages. In: Chaudron, M.R.V. (ed.) MODELS 2008. LNCS, vol. 5421, pp. 332–342. Springer, Heidelberg (2009)

18. Vanden Bossche, M., Ross, P., MacLarty, I., Van Nuffelen, B., Pelov, N.: Ontology driven software engineering for real life applications. In: Proceedings of the 3rd International Workshop on Semantic Web Enabled Software Engineering, Innsbruck, Austria (2007)
19. Walter, T., Parreiras, F.S., Staab, S.: An ontology-based framework for domain-specific modeling. Softw. Syst. Model. **13**, 83–108 (2014)
20. Walter, T., Parreiras, F.S., Staab, S., Ebert, J.: Joint language and domain engineering. In: Kühne, T., Selic, B., Gervais, M.-P., Terrier, F. (eds.) ECMFA 2010. LNCS, vol. 6138, pp. 321–336. Springer, Heidelberg (2010)

Extension and Utilization of a Design Framework to Model Integrated Modular Avionic Architecture

Yassine Ouhammou[1]([⊠]), Emmanuel Grolleau[1], and Pascal Richard[2]

[1] LIAS - Futuroscope, ENSMA, Poitiers, France
{ouhammoy,grolleau}@ensma.fr
[2] LIAS - Futuroscope, Université de Poitiers, Poitiers, France
pascal.richard@univ-poitiers.fr

Abstract. Embedded avionics systems often involve hard real-time constraints intended to ensure full system correctness. Avionics software development costs can be sharply impacted by wrong design choices made in the early stages of development, but often detected after implementation. By using temporal scheduling analysis, designers could detect infeasible real-time architectures, and prevent costly design mistakes. Recently, model-driven engineering paradigm facilitates the use of several analysis tools with standards modeling languages (e.g. SysML, AADL, UML-MARTE, etc.) to get a complete design cycle ranging from modeling up to verification and validation. However, only few model-based researches have studied the difficulty that designers face while seeking appropriate analysis tests which match their designs. MoSaRT (Modeling Oriented Scheduling Analysis of Real-Time systems) framework is one of these researches. It provides various facilities to help designers to model and analyze traditional real-time systems. In this paper, we propose the extension and the utilization of the MoSaRT framework to support avionics architectures. An analysis tool has also been developed and added in line with this kind of architectures. The proposed research is illustrated by discussing a real case study.

1 Introduction

On-board avionic systems are real-time systems which should meet strict temporal requirements. The architecture of these systems is based on the Integrated Modular Avionics (IMA) architecture instead of the traditional federated approach. Only few analysis tools have been dedicated to IMA systems. The integration of these tools with existing design languages, in order to get a model-based process combining modeling and analysis, is error prone. This integration requires a deep knowledge in both the modeling and the temporal analysis of real-time systems. In other words, the temporal analysis test chosen to validate a specific architecture has to be very appropriate to this latter. On the one hand, the test should be conservative because of the safety and the criticality of the system. On the other hand, the test should not be too pessimistic, otherwise

© Springer International Publishing Switzerland 2015
L. Bellatreche and Y. Manolopoulos (Eds.): MEDI 2015, LNCS 9344, pp. 16–27, 2015.
DOI: 10.1007/978-3-319-23781-7_2

the developed system can be costly in terms of equipments and wiring. A design framework called MoSaRT has been developed [16,17] to help designers to choose the most suitable temporal analysis tools referring to the system architecture conceived. Since the MoSaRT framework is based on model-driven engineering facilities, it is extensible and re-utilizable. This paper highlights the extension of the MoSaRT design language to support IMA architectures and shows how to enrich the framework by a prototype analysis tool helping designers to check the temporal requirements.

In order to make this paper self-contained, we introduce the main concepts related to IMA architectures and the MoSaRT framework. Then, the remainder of this paper is organized as follows. Section 2 discusses the specificities of IMA architectures. Section 3 introduces MoSaRT framework concepts and describes the way the framework can be used to ease the design of real-time architecture. Section 4 presents our proposition to extend the MoSaRT design language to support IMA architectures and the utilization of an analysis advisor which leads the temporal analysis process independently from the designer knowledge. A case study showing the significance of such model-based framework is also presented throughout Sect. 4. Finally, Sect. 5 drafts our conclusions and final remarks.

2   Partitioned Scheduling in Integrated Modular Avionics

Processor partitioning is a mean used in Integrated Modular Avionics (IMA) to insure freedom from interference between applications, which may be of different Design Assurance Level (DAL), but sharing the same physical resources. Freedom from interference, as defined in the standard ISO 26262 [7], insures that the failure of a piece of software will not create the failure of another piece of software. It also insures that the interference of two software independent parts is bounded. Moreover, an application can be studied independently from another application, even if they share the same processing resources.

The classic way to arbitrate the computing resources in a partitioned system is to use a hierarchical scheduler. In the IMA standard ARINC 653 [1], a two level scheduler is used: a low level cyclic scheduler is statically assigning the computing resources to the partitions, using a pre-defined table. Then, in each partition, a real-time operating system is assigning the processor to the tasks, using its own scheduling policy. On a timing behavior point of view, freedom from interference means that the interference of a partition on another one should be null or bounded. In most models, like it is the case in this paper, absence of interference is assumed. Nevertheless, cache related preemption delays may occur and create a bounded interference between one partition and other partitions of the same computing resource.

The seminal research on partitioned scheduling of Deng et al. [5] proposes two hierarchical levels. Later, Feng and Mok [6] proposed the resource partitioning model and schedulability analysis based on the supply bound function (sbf), which is an elegant mathematical way to extend non-hierarchical schedulability analysis to hierarchical scheduling. Shin and Lee [14] introduced the concepts of temporal interface with the periodic resource model. For applications containing Fixed-Task Priority (FTP) schedulers, Kuo and Li [9] and Saewong et al. [13] proposed dedicated hierarchical schedulers. In the context of server based temporal partitioning, numerous techniques have been proposed. Lipari and Bini [11] used the abstraction of a periodic server in order to solve the problem of creating a partitioning such that the system is schedulable. Davis and Burns [4] proposed an upper bound on the response time of the tasks when the partitions are scheduled by an FTP. An exact worst-case response-time can also be obtained [2,3].

In the rest of this section, we present a scheduling model for hierarchical scheduling fitting with the ARINC 653 standard, and techniques allowing to compute the worst-case response times of the tasks.

2.1   Analysis Model

A (temporal) partition can be defined as a collection of time intervals defining statically the allocation of the CPU to a partition.

Definition: a resource partition is noted $\Pi = (\Gamma, P)$ where:

- $\Gamma = \{(S_1, E_1), (S_2, E_2), ..., (S_N, E_N)\}$ is a set time intervals, where S_i is the offset of a time interval allocated to the resource partition, related to the starting time of the period of the partition. E_i is the ending date of the time interval. The size of the ith time interval is given by $E_i - S_i$.
- The size of the period of the resource partition is P.

A resource partition on a single CPU processing resource must obviously satisfy non-overlapping property: $0 \leq S_1 < E_1 \leq S_2 < E_2... \leq S_N < E_N \leq P$. For simplicity, we suppose that P is common to every partition of a CPU, corresponding to the MAF (MAjor Frame) in ARINC 653. A simple algebraic transformation using greatest common divisor and lest common multiple could be used to transform a classic ARINC 653 partition using MIF (MInor Frames) into a resource partition model.

An IMA application is a set of tasks, allocated to a resource partition on a CPU. In the sequel, we consider sets of sporadic independent tasks. Each application has its own fixed-task priority scheduler, which is scheduling its tasks in its resource partition.

Definition: an application j contains n_j sporadic tasks $\tau_i^j, i = 1..n_j$. A task τ_i^j is defined by (C_i^j, D_i^j, T_i^j) where:

- C_i^j is the task's Worst-Case Execution Time (WCET),
- D_i^j is the relative deadline of the task, i.e., the maximum allowed interval of time for the task to be completed after each of its activation,
- T_i^j is the period of the task, i.e., the minimum interval of time between two successive activations of the task.

Since we consider that every task τ_i^j is scheduled by a fixed-task priority scheduler, we order the tasks by priority order in each application. The task τ_1^j has the highest priority while $\tau_{n_j}^j$ has the lowest priority.

2.2   Response Time Analysis

In this paper, we consider a simple test tool that will be developed for the case of IMA applications. This tool will compute the worst-case response time of each task in each application. Since we consider the system application per application, for the sake of simplicity, in the sequel, we will drop the exponent j of the application number. Response-time analysis (RTA) in the IMA context is an extension of the classic RTA, which is based on the request bound function (rbf) [8]. When considering a sporadic task τ_i, released at time 0, its worst-case response time cannot be lower than its own WCET C_i.

Classic Non Hierarchical RTA

1. Therefore, we know that the processor will be busy at least in the time interval $[0, C_i)$. Let's denote rbf_i^1 the value of the end of this interval. In this time interval, any release of a higher priority task $\tau_k, k < i$ is postponing the end of the execution of τ_i. The amount of releases of higher priority tasks in the interval $[0, rbf_i^1)$ occurs if all the higher priority tasks are released at the time 0, and execute with their shortest period (they are sporadic). This is called the **critical instant**. Each task $\tau_k, k < i$ can postpone the end of τ_i by up to $\left\lceil \frac{rbf_i^1}{T_k} \right\rceil C_k$.

2. The processor will be busy with tasks whose priority is at least the priority of τ_i at least in the time interval $\left[0, rbf_i^2 = C_i + \sum_{k=1}^{i-1} \left\lceil \frac{rbf_i^1}{T_k} \right\rceil C_k \right)$. In this time interval, the amount of times every higher priority task can postpone the end of τ_i may be higher, and given, for each task $\tau_k, k < i$ by $\left\lceil \frac{rbf_i^2}{T_k} \right\rceil C_k$

3. Going back to point 1, substituting rbf_i^1 by rbf_i^2, we obtain at the smallest fixed point of rbf_i^* the worst-case response time of τ_i as long as it is not greater than its period (because if it was greater than its period, then τ_i may delay itself and the formula should be adapted like in [10].

   We therefore consider the classic RTA test stating that:

– the worst-case execution time of a constrained deadline task $(D_i \leq T_i)$ is obtained as the smallest fixed-point rbf_i^* of the equation $rbf_i^* = C_i + \sum_{k=1}^{i-1} \left\lceil \frac{rbf_i^*}{T_k} \right\rceil C_k$ if $rbf_i^* \leq T_i$. If $rbf_i^* > T_i$ then τ_i will miss its deadline.

RTA for IMA. The main difference between hierarchical and classical RTA is that, in classical RTA, the processor dedicates on time unit of its time every time unit, while in hierarchical scheduling, the processor dedicates one time unit every time unit to the elected processor partition only. This phenomenon is accounted for by using a supply function of the processor.

   The supply function is depending on the beginning of the MAF. Since there is no information concerning the offset between a considered instant for a task under analysis, and the beginning of the MAF, we have to consider any offset between the tasks critical instant to study and the offset in the MAF. The lowest amount of processor supplied to a processor partition $\Gamma = \{(S_1, E_1), (S_2, E_2), ..., (S_N, E_N)\}$ is given, in an interval of length t, by considering the minimal supply function assuming the critical instant of the tasks coincides with $E_1, E_2, ...,$ or E_N [6]. These points are called **critical points**.

Definition: the supply function of the processor in a time interval $[0, t]$, depends on the critical point $E_1, E_2, ...,$ or E_N coinciding with the critical instant at the date 0. It is denoted $sf(E_i, t)$.

When computing the time required by the processor to compute the workload given by the rbf, we need to consider how long, in the worst case, is necessary for the processor partition to be supplied with enough processor time to compute the rbf. This is given by the reverse supply function sf^{-1} (see [6] for the way to compute this function).

Theorem [6]: the worst-case execution time of the first job of a task τ_i of an application scheduled in a processor partition $\Gamma = \{(S_1, E_1), (S_2, E_2), ..., (S_N, E_N)\}$ is given by the maximal for $E_j, j = 1..N$ of the smallest fixed-point $rbf_i^*(E_j) = C_i + \sum_{k=1}^{i-1} \left\lceil \frac{sf^{-1}(rbf_i^*(E_j))}{T_k} \right\rceil C_k$. If this value is not greater than the task's period T_i, then it is giving the worst-case response time of the task.

3   MoSaRT Framework in a Nutshell

The objective behind the MoSaRT framework is to benefit from analysts/researchers skills and modelers/architects skills in order to unify their efforts, then to avoid wrong design choices at an early design phase. MoSaRT framework plays a dual role aiming (i) to help designers to cope with the scheduling analysis and to be more autonomous during the analysis stage, and (ii) to help analysts to alleviate their efforts related to the analysis of design models.

Figure 1 shows the general architecture of the framework, which contains two parts: front-end and back-end as described in the following paragraphs.

Front-End of MoSaRT Framework is based on a design language. It provides a set of concepts to model different architectures of real-time systems characterized by temporal extra-functional properties (e.g. execution times, deadlines, periods). The MoSaRT design language is a graphical language developed using Ecore [15] and Object Constraint Language [12] (OCL, which is a textual language fitting with Ecore and enabling to express invariants). The modeling editor provides different model views such as hardware architecture diagram, software architecture diagram and behavioral diagram.

Back-End Part of MoSaRT Framework is based on a meta-model of an analysis repository enabling researchers and analysts to share their analysis models and tests. Every instantiation of the meta-model leads to obtain a repository

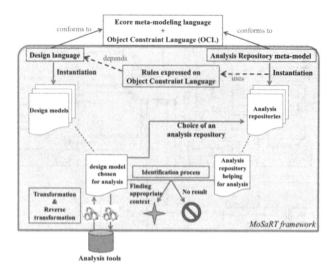

Fig. 1. General MoSaRT framework architecture and excerpt of the main workflow

playing the role of an advisor during its utilization with a model conforming to MoSaRT design language. The utilization of a repository with a model consists on the running an identification process in order to check if the repository contains a context (a set of architectural and timing behavioral characteristics) corresponding the model needs analysis. Once a context is found, the designer can use the proposed analysis tool. This latter can be reached thanks to a transformation process (which can be model-to-model or model-to-text) provided by the framework. The definition of contexts inside an instance of the analysis repository is based on the utilization of OCL and MoSaRT design language in order to express the characteristics.

4   Extension and Enrichment of MoSaRT Framework

This section presents our proposition to deal with IMA systems, which consists in extending the MoSaRT design language. Moreover, we highlight the analysis model of the developed prototype, then the rules a design (expressed using the extended MoSaRT language) has to conform to in order to be correctly analyzed.

4.1   Extension of MoSaRT Design Language

Figure 2 shows an overview of the proposed extension. We have designed this extension using the eclipse modeling framework [15], which is also used for the MoSaRT design language core. The elements added are those whose name are prefixed by "*Ima*". In the following, we detail each element.

— *ImaPartition* class represents the temporal partition. It has been added as an element of software architecture. A partition is related to a process (instance of *SoSpaceProcess* class), which can contain several partitions. Moreover, inside

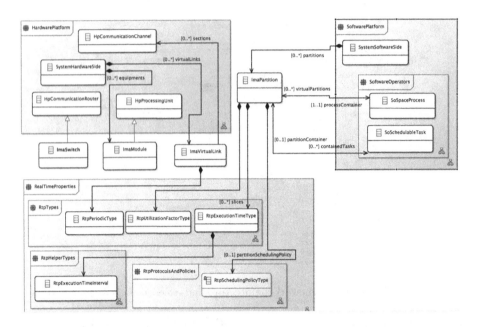

Fig. 2. Overview of the extended MoSaRT language meta-model

a partition, a set of tasks (instances of *SoSchedulableResource* class) can be executed. Thanks to the way MoSaRT design language has been implemented, we can notice that all the temporal properties needed have been meta-modeled as concept, then the enrichment of the *ImaPartition* class has been done easily. For instance, the execution time of a partition is a set of time intervals, which are instances of *RtpExecutionTimeInterval* class (Fig. 2).

– *ImaModule* class represents the module which executes a set of partitions through their container process. It has been added as an element of Hardware architecture. The *ImaModule* class inherits from the *HpProcessingUnit* class. This latter can be uniprocessor or multiprocessor.

– *ImaVirtualLink* and *ImaSwitch* classes have been added as elements of the hardware architecture. Those elements are dedicated to design distributed architectures, which is not presented in this paper due to space limitation.

The extension also consists of adding a set of structural rules which have to be verified in order to have a coherent system design. For instance, the time intervals of a partition may not overlap. The structural rules have been implemented on OCL and can be checked automatically via MoSaRT editor.

4.2 Example: Utilization of the MoSaRT Design Language After Extension

Thanks to the extension added to the MoSaRT language an architecture like the one shown in Fig. 3 can be totally designed. The architecture represents

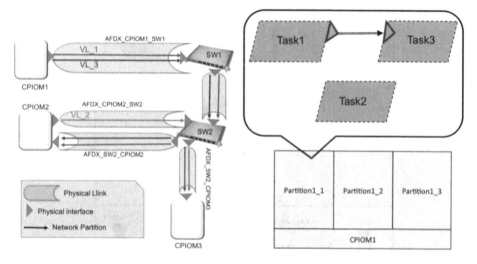

Fig. 3. Distributed architecture   **Fig. 4.** Content of CPIOM1

Table 1. Timing properties of the task-set

Tasks	Priority	Period (ms)	Deadline (ms)	Execution time (ms)
Task1	15	8	8	1
Task2	10	14	14	2
Task3	5	30	30	4

a communication between a set of tasks executed in different CPIOMs (Core Processor Input/output Module) communicating through an AFDX network (Avionics Full DupleX). The networking is based on various switches and physical links. Therefore, via the extended design language we can model:

- physical links as instances of HpCommunicationChannel;
- switches as instances of ImaSwitch;
- CPIOMs as instances of ImaModule;
- network partitions as instances of ImaVirtualLink;

This paper does not discuss the distributed architecture, then we only focus on the software content of CPIOM1 of Fig. 3. Figure 4 shows a hierarchical architecture composed of three partitions where the first partition contains three independent tasks.

Table 1 presents the timing properties related to tasks and partitions. Moreover, the period of the partition *Partition1_1* is 30 ms and the time slices (i.e. time intervals) allocated to it are (0,5), (10,15) and (20,25).

Figure 5 represents a part of a MoSaRT model compliant with the software architecture of the example. The model highlights the software structure (i.e. tasks and partition) and temporal behavior of tasks (i.e. task activities and triggers).

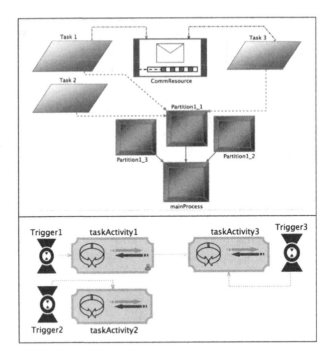

Fig. 5. Excerpt of a model expressed using the extended MoSaRT language

4.3   Implementing a Prototype of the Test

To the best of our knowledge, the test presented in Sect. 2.2 could not be found in any freely available schedulability analysis toolset. It is easy to implement, and the most time consuming part of a tool implementing this test would be to connect it to a design framework in order to call it when necessary, as well as to check if an input model fits with the underlying hypothesis of this test: independent tasks, IMA hierarchical scheduler, sporadic constrained deadlines tasks, uni-processor CPU. Using MoSaRT framework, we show how it is easily possible to connect such a tool to a design language, as well as to check if an input model can be handled by the developed tool. Hereafter, we show how the analysis repository can be instantiated to lead designers to this tool for analysis.

4.4   Example: Instantiation and Utilization of MoSaRT Analysis Repository

In order to assist designers to analyze models compliant with IMA architecture specifications, we have used the analysis repository of MoSaRT back-end. We can create a new repository or enrich an existing one. Due to the lack of space we prefer the first way, because using an existing repository requires to explain its content. Therefore, the new created repository is based on the context Feng analysis model [6], which is defined by a set of characteristics, such that:

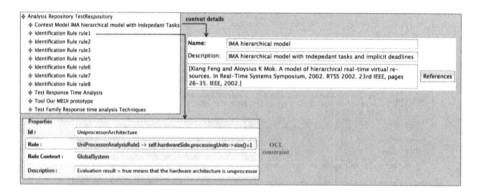

Fig. 6. Excerpt of a repository containing the analysis context related to hierarchical scheduling

- The architecture of CPOM is uniprocessor;
- Tasks are independant;
- No network used in the hardware architecture;
- Fixed priotity scheduling policy is used in partition level;
- etc.

If a design does not respect these characteristics, it does not mean that the structure of the design is incorrect. However, when all characteristics are respected we can conclude that the analysis context of the design is the one presented in Sect. 2. Figure 6 is our instance of the MoSaRT analysis repository. This instance contains several characteristics equivalent to a set of identification rules, where each rule is an OCL constraint (e.g. rule1 on Fig. 6). We also link the implemented analysis test to the context in order to check the schedulability of the design by calculating the response times of the tasks.

Once the new instance of the repository is ready to be used, we can connect it to a design expressed using MoSaRT language. For example, if we launch the MoSaRT identification process from the design of the example treated in Sect. 4.2, the design will be checked if it is compliant with the context added in the new repository. Moreover, the identification process of MoSaRT presents the result of this step. Figure 7 shows the analysis test corresponding to the characteristics of the design. The result window recapitulates the rules that are verified by the design and also the suitable analysis model. References related to tests and models are also presented in case when designers need more details.

Note that if the designer agrees with the proposed tests, this latter can be performed from the MoSaRT framework by doing a transformation to the input formalism of the analysis tools. Indeed, the worst-case response times of our case study are presented in Table 2.

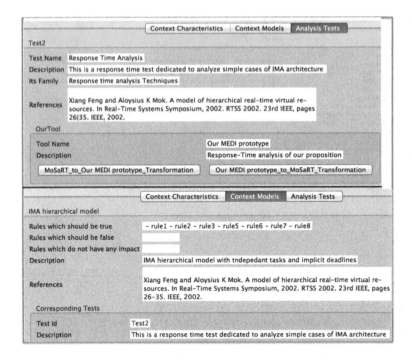

Fig. 7. Result of a MoSaRT identification process

Table 2. Analysis result

Task	Response Time (ms)	Schedulable
Task1	6	Yes
Task2	8	Yes
Task3	27	Yes

5   Conclusion

Numerous analysis tests have been proposed, but their utilization requires a colossal background related to identify the exact underlying hypothesis of each test, and the certainty of the analysis results depends on the context of each analyzed system. We underlined the advantages of having a framework such as MoSaRT framework, which facilitates the analysis phase of designers. Since MoSaRT framework is mainly based on model-driven engineering techniques, we had easily extended it in order to support the design of IMA architectures and ease their analysis. In our ongoing research, we will be interested in distributed avionics architectures by taking AFDX networks into considerations. Moreover, we will add various analysis tools to compare and discuss the output results.

References

1. ARINC. Avionics application software standard interface: Arinc specification 653 part 0. Arinc, Aeronautical Radio Inc. (2013)
2. Balbastre, P., Ripoll, I., Crespo, A.: Exact response time analysis of hierarchical fixed-priority scheduling. In: 15th IEEE International Conference on Embedded and Real-Time Computing Systems and Applications, RTCSA 2009, pp. 315–320. IEEE (2009)
3. Bril, R.J., Cuijpers, P.JL.: Analysis of hierarchical fixed-priority pre-emptive scheduling revisited. Technische Universiteit Eindhoven (TU/e) CS-Report, pp. 06–36 (2006)
4. Davis, R.I., Burns, A.: Hierarchical fixed priority pre-emptive scheduling. In: 26th IEEE International Real-Time Systems Symposium, RTSS 2005, p. 10. IEEE (2005)
5. Deng, Z., Liu, JWS., Sun, J.: A scheme for scheduling hard real-time applications in open system environment. In: Proceedings, Ninth Euromicro Workshop on Real-Time Systems, pp. 191–199. IEEE (1997)
6. Feng, X., Mok, A.K.: A model of hierarchical real-time virtual resources. In: 23rd IEEE Real-Time Systems Symposium, RTSS 2002, pp. 26–35. IEEE (2002)
7. ISO. ISO 26262–1:2011 road vehicles functional safety. ISO, International Organization for Standardization, Geneva, Switzerland (2011)
8. Joseph, M., Pandya, P.: Finding response times in a real-time system. Comput. J. **29**(5), 390–395 (1986)
9. Kuo, T.-W., Li, C.-H.: A fixed-priority-driven open environment for real-time applications. In: Proceedings, The 20th IEEE Real-Time Systems Symposium, pp. 256–267. IEEE (1999)
10. Lehoczky, J.P.: Fixed priority scheduling of periodic task sets with arbitrary deadlines. In: RTSS, vol. 90, pp. 201–209 (1990)
11. Lipari, G., Bini, E.: A methodology for designing hierarchical scheduling systems. J. Embed. Comput. **1**(2), 257–269 (2005)
12. OMG. Object constraint language, OMG available specification, version 2.0 (2006). www.omg.org/spec/OCL/2.0/
13. Saewong, S., Rajkumar, R.R., Lehoczky, J.P., Klein, M.H.: Analysis of hierarchical fixed-priority scheduling. In: Euromicro Conference on Real-Time Systems, pp. 173–173. IEEE Computer Society (2002)
14. Shin, I., Lee, I.: Periodic resource model for compositional real-time guarantees. In: 24th IEEE Real-Time Systems Symposium, RTSS 2003, pp. 2–13. IEEE (2003)
15. Steinberg, D., Budinsky, F., Paternostro, M., Merks, E.: EMF: Eclipse Modeling Framework. Pearson Education, Boston (2008)
16. Yassine, O.: Model-based framework for using advanced scheduling theory in real-time systems design. Ph.D. thesis, ISAE-ENSMA (2013)
17. Yassine, O., Emmanuel, G., Michael, R., Pascal, R., Frdric, M.: Mosart framework: a collaborative tool for modeling and analyzing embedded real-time systems. In: Boulanger, F., Krob, D., Morel, G., Roussel, J.-C. (eds.) CSDM, p. 12. Springer, Switzerland (2014)

Extending the MOF for the Adaptation of Hooks, Aspects, Plug-Ins and Add-Ons

Richard Braun[(⊠)] and Werner Esswein

Technische Universität Dresden, Chair of Wirtschaftsinformatik, esp. Systems Development, 01062 Dresden, Germany
{richard.braun,werner.esswein}@tu-dresden.de

Abstract. Conceptual modeling languages are valuable means for analyzing, designing and controlling information systems. In recent years, some languages became de facto standards in their particular field of application, which simultaneously leads to an increasing demand for domain-specific extensions in order to both benefit from dissemination and apposite concepts. However, recent studies reveal a remarkable lack of methodical support for language extensibility, which hampers systematic extension design, comprehensibility and interoperability. This research article therefore aims to outline different meta model extension mechanisms based on an analogy to extension principles from the field of Software Engineering. The techniques of hooking, aspects, plug-ins and add-ons are presented and their adaptation is elaborated by the definition of additional extension packages within the Meta Object Facility (MOF) in order to provide constructs for the definition of extensible meta models.

Keywords: Meta meta modeling · Meta model extensions · Conceptual languages · Abstract syntax · Meta object facility

1 Introduction

Conceptual modeling languages are valuable means for the management of enterprise information systems and constitute as one of the most essential research objects within the Information Systems discipline [1,2]. During the last decade, a few languages became de facto standards in their particular fields of application (e.g., BPMN for business process modeling [3]). Prevalence and dissemination of those languages imply several benefits such as a common understanding of syntax and semantics and a certain level of quality management. Moreover, it seems to be promising to focus on a few stable, prevalent and mature standard languages and the design of language dialects, instead of expensively building domain-specific modeling language (DSML) from scratch[1]. However, the emergence of commonly used artifacts also entails an increasing demand for their

---

[1] Indeed, DSMLs are worthwhile and powerful methods for solving very specific tasks within a limited project scope.

© Springer International Publishing Switzerland 2015
L. Bellatreche and Y. Manolopoulos (Eds.): MEDI 2015, LNCS 9344, pp. 28–38, 2015.
DOI: 10.1007/978-3-319-23781-7_3

extension. This situation can be also observed for conceptual modeling languages [4–8], which are extended due to different reasons like extending the language vocabulary [8], facilitating model analysis or enabling model interoperability [4].

Despite these promising benefits, current language specifications reveal a remarkable lack in terms of both syntactical concepts and methodical support for extension design (cf. [4,9]). This lack provokes the unguided ad-hoc alteration of existing meta models, which hampers extension exchange, tool integration and general comprehensibility. The stated issue is mainly caused by the limited capabilities of meta modeling languages like MOF in terms of structured meta model extensibility [4,10]. We therefore aim to examine possibly adaptable mechanisms from Software Engineering in order to provide syntactical constructs on the meta meta model layer. Instantiating those constructs should then lead to extensible meta models of particular languages, which could facilitate more systematic extension design. The analogy to Software Engineering is driven by the similarity of conceptual modeling languages and programming languages regarding to their well-defined, formal syntax[2]. Although modeling languages and programming languages differ in terms of semantics (informal versus formal [1,12]), we argue that the adaptation of extension mechanisms can enhance the systematic design of the abstract syntax of meta model extensions. Consequently, the research paper primarily addresses the abstract syntax in order to set a base for further investigation in terms of semantics and pragmatics [1]. The adaptation is exemplarily implemented in the Meta Object Facility (MOF), as MOF is the prevailing meta modeling language and the base for numerous languages (e.g., BPMN, CMMN or KDM).

The remainder of this article is as follows: Sect. 2 provides some fundamentals regarding extensibility. Section 3 elaborates the adaptation of four extension techniques, namely hooking, aspects, add-ons and plug-ins. The article ends with a brief conclusion and an outlook in Sect. 4.

2   Fundamentals

2.1   Extensibility in Conceptual Modeling Languages

In a wider sense, an *extension* is understood as enhancement of the expressiveness of a conceptual modeling language by introducing new constructs, properties or by specifying existing elements in order to represent purpose-specific concepts. In the narrower sense, an extension must follow the extension mechanism of a modeling language in order to ensure meta model conformity. Generally, an extension is neither useful nor functional on its own (referring to [7]). The extended modeling language is denoted as *host language* [8]. An *extension mechanism* is understood as the specification of elements, rules and constraints within a language meta model as well as the provision of methodical support

---

[2] This article only considers conceptual modeling languages in the understanding of semi-formal modeling languages having a formal syntax definition and informal semantics [1,11,12].

for their application. Only very few research articles explicitly address the issue of extending languages. BRAUN (2015) outlines the current state of the art and provides a classification for mechanisms and the underlying purposes [9]. ATKINSON ET AL. (2013) discuss the topic against the background of enterprise modeling, present some extension design principles and introduce a multi-level modeling approach [8]. BRAUN & ESSWEIN (2014) examine BPMN extensions and found that only few extensions are compliant to the meta model [5]. KOPP ET AL. (2011) present an extensive analysis of BPEL extensions [7] and PARDILLO (2010) analyzes published UML profiles [6]. None of these articles tackles the issue on the meta meta model level.

2.2   Extensibility in Software Engineering

Motivation for program extensions comes mainly from elementary software principles like modularization (separation of concern [13]), scalability [14], maintenance [15,16] or dependency inversion [17]. The consideration of unforeseen program extensions is perceived as important but non-trivial task within Software Engineering [14,18]. An extensible program is defined as program that can be adapted to new tasks without altering the original source code [15,18]. An extensible program should provide explicit concepts and mechanisms for customization on the one side, but needs to ensure high cohesion within an extension and low coupling between extension and the host software on the other side [17,19]. Although PARNAS (1979) emphasized the importance of extensible software already in the beginnings of Software Engineering [14], explicit literature on this topic is rather scarce: ZENGER (2002) elaborates assessment aspects for software extensions like level of independence [20]. KLATT & KROGMANN (2008) propose more technical extension attributes like execution strategy and evolution [21]. HEINLEIN (2003) introduces vertical and horizontal extensions (vertical extensions enhance the type hierarchy, whereas horizontal extensions aim to provide the additional operations for specify types [22]).

3   Adapted Extension Techniques

Our examination addresses the techniques of *hooking*, *aspects*, *plug-ins* and *add-ons* as those techniques are frequently considered in Software Engineering literature. Each techniques is briefly introduced and its possible adaptation to meta models is elaborated. As stated in Sect. 1, the adaptation is exemplarily applied to the meta meta model layer of the Essential MOF (EMOF) by proposing three additional packages and particular constructs (cf. Fig. 1). Both syntax and semantics are described for each technique in order to outline their application to language definitions on the meta model layer.

3.1   Hooking

Concept and Adaptation: The concept of *hooking* is understood as leaving open parts of a program in order to define and specify those parts later in

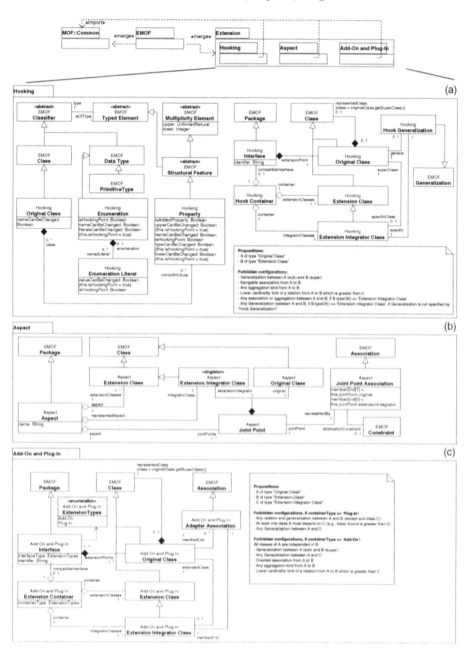

Fig. 1. Overview of all meta meta model packages for defining extensible modeling languages. Constraints are expressed by informal annotations instead of OCL statements in order to enhance readability at this point.

accordance with specific requirements. Hooks[3] can be implemented by abstract classes, interfaces or methods, which need to be concretized for the situational injection of individual code [23], while other parts of the software remain fixed (referred as *frozen spots* in [24]). Hooking is adapted in the sense of defining and formulating open points in meta models for their later concretization. The skeleton of a meta model remains rather fixed and only single aspects need to be specified in accordance to a domain. This intention is generally similar to the reference modeling approach, especially to the *instantiation* technique and the *specification* technique [25,26]. A hook consists of exactly one meta model element and new meta model elements can be hooked into a meta model in two kinds: Firstly, meta model elements may act as placeholders and their specific structure is *left open*. Secondly, meta model elements can be specified as abstract for reasons of later *specification*, which covers the creation of sub types.

We propose the following *hooking points* according to the level of detail in the meta model: On the *model level*, single meta model classes are left open for filling in specific constructs. A hook thereby always relates to one original meta model element. Original meta classes can only be referenced; extensions in the form of new dependencies or existential constraints are not permitted. On the *level of concepts*, single meta model classes can be specialized by domain-specific subtypes. On the *level of attributes*, several hooks are possible: Firstly, the entire attribute body can remain open for individual attributes. Further, it should be possible to specify the types of attributes (e.g., specific enumeration values). Addressing the *constraint level* of meta models, hooks can be also applied to constraints of single elements like multiplicities (lower and upper bounds) or complex constraint statements (e.g., OCL expressions). It is also allowed to rename a model element in order to adjust it to a particular context (cf. [25]).

Abstract Syntax and Semantics: The left side of Fig. 1a defines the meta meta model for renaming concepts and specifying attributes. The property *name-CanBeChanged* indicates, whether the name of a particular meta model element can be customized. Then it has to start with a $_ prefix. *IsHookingPoint* indicates whether the property acts as hooking point and *IsAddedProperty* reveals whether a property was added by a hook. *TypeCanBeChanged* represents the opportunity of altering a property type. The properties *lowerCanBeChanged* and *upperCanBeChanged* stand for a possible change of the cardinality values (cf. the *Multiplicity Element* class from EMOF). The *Enumeration* class from EMOF is also extended with the property *isHookingPoint*. *LiteralsCanBeChanged* indicates that literals can be changed or added at all. The right side of Fig. 1a covers constructs for concretization. *Original Class* represents the point of the host meta model that can be refined (hooking point). The *Interface* class is introduced as an adapter for hooking points and consists of exactly one class and one *Hook Container*, which is a used for encapsulating added *Extension Classes*. These classes represent new concepts in order to fulfill the defined hook. The *Extension Integrator Class* facilitates the logical integration between the hook component and the single meta model class that is extended.

---

[3] Alternatively referred as *extension points* [23] or *hot spots* [24].

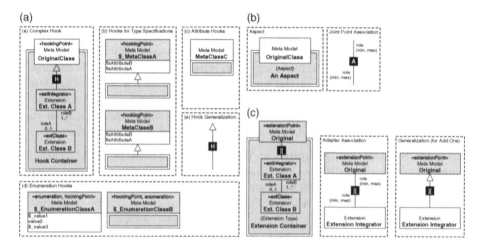

Fig. 2. Overview of introduced notational elements for the graphical representation of the respective meta meta model concepts within language definitions.

Therefore, a generalization between the integrator class and the original class is used (*Hook Generalization*).

Concrete Syntax: Figure 2a represents the proposed notational supplements for the meta meta model layer in order to explicate hooking concepts. Generally, extensible parts have a grey background. *Hook Containers* are represented as grey filled rectangles with a double lined border and the particular *extension-Class* is positioned at their border. Open attribute bodies are also depicted by a grey attribute background. Renamings of class names (e.g., *$_MetaClass*) and attribute values (e.g., *$_value1*) are indicated by the required prefix.

3.2   Aspects

Concept and Adaptation: Functions for logging, transactions control or security are typically needed at numerous points within a program hierarchy, but an integration of those rather analytical functions to the class structure of the business logic would cause class overloading, complication and violation of separation of concern. Aspect-oriented programming (AOP) aims to centralize those *cross-cutting concerns* and provide them dynamically in requested spots [24, 27]. An *Aspect* consists of *Joint Points*, *Point Cuts* and *Advices* [27]. A *Joint Point* serves as specified intrusion point for an *Aspect* (e.g., exceptions or method calls). A *Point Cut* consists of different *Joint Points* and summarizes them with boolean statements. An *Advice* is the code which has to be executed, if a particular *Point Cut* is reached during program execution [27]. The principle behind AOP can be abstracted and adapted to the case of meta model extensions as follows: Cross-cutting concerns are adapted as domain-unspecific model information, which can be used by several parts of the meta model (e.g., for model analysis). The AOP program structure (class hierarchy) is adapted in the sense of a host meta model. Thereby, specializations (sub classes of host meta classes) are not permitted due to the additive kind. An *Aspect* is understood as extension, which contains particular extension classes. The inner logic and structure of these extension classes can be reflected as *Advices* in the sense of the actual added value. The *Joint Point* concept is adapted for the integration of original classes and extension classes. This means, that if a particular original class is instantiated, then the aspect can also be instantiated. The *Point Cut* concept is not applied.

Abstract Syntax and Semantics: Within Fig. 1b, the *Aspect* meta class is composed of at least one *Extension Class*, at least one *Joint Point* and one *Extension Integrator Class*. *Extension Classes* are used for the creation of the actual extension content (*Advice*). A *Joint Point* consists of one *Extension Integrator Class* and one *Original Class*. The dependency of both elements is represented by a special association, the *Joint Point Association*. The *Extension Integrator Class* is typed as singleton in order the emphasize that only one instance per aspect package is created. The *Constraint* meta class from EMOF can be used for the specification of constraints in order to specify particular *Advices*.

Concrete Syntax: Figure 2b represents the graphical representation of aspects for meta model definitions.

3.3   Plug-Ins

Concept and Adaptation: Plug-ins are functional extensions of a host system through well-defined interfaces [28,29]. Plug-ins constitute as applications for specific business problems instead of providing generic functionality [29] and are usually able to exist on their own [23]. A plug-in interface is realized by the definition of several *extension points*, which are code spots where the executing program asks a central registration unit for plug-ins which want to execute own code. A meta model plug-in is hence understood as consistent, coherent and independent model, which can enhance the expressiveness of a modeling language.

A meta model plug-in is characterized by an ample level of complexity in regard of its concepts and interdependencies. On the meta model level, a *plug-in interface* is adapted in the form of one or more original classes, which are connected to a contextually related interface, to which a plug-in must be compliant. At this point, model integration techniques are required in order to map concepts of the intended plug-in to the defined interface (e.g., [30,31]). The plug-in technique is appropriate for enhancement and augmentation of a host meta model as it adds conceptually new elements [4,8].

Abstract Syntax and Semantics: Figure 1c depicts required meta meta model concepts for plug-ins within the *Add-On and Plug-In* package. The *Interface* class defines the interface between the host (meta model) and the extension (plug-in). An interface consists of at least one original class which constitutes as extension point (cf. *Original Classes*). The de facto copy of a particular meta class is required for separating the original meta model from its extensions. An original class can be assigned to multiple interfaces. *Extension Containers* group plug-in concepts and can be compatible to an interface. The *Extension Class* is used for the definition of plug-in concepts, which represent the actual content of a plug-in. *Extension Integrator Classes* facilitate the logical integration by linking the extension point and the extension content. The *Adapter Association* class is a special association for the representation of this essential linkage and aims to support the analysis of particular dependencies. An adapter association is assessed as *dependent*, if the lower bound is greater than 0 or if the relation constitutes as aggregation or composition. If all adapter associations are dependent, then the influence of the plug-in is perceived as very strong. If all adapter associations are independent, then the influence is weak and the plug-in adaptation remains rather optional. Additionally, relations and generalizations between original classes and plug-in classes are forbidden (except the relation to integrator classes), as plug-ins are understood as separated components.

Concrete Syntax: Figure 2c depicts notational elements the specification of plug-in extension points in meta models. *Extension Containers* is represented in the same kind as a *Hook Containers*, whereby the extension type is represented at the top. *Adapter Associations* are depicted as associations with a special icon in the middle.

3.4   Add-Ons

Concept and Adaptation: Although add-ons are similar to plug-ins, they possess rather limited capabilities and have a smaller conceptual scope. Their existence depends strictly on the host system and add-ons cannot be executed separately. Add-ons merely provide optional features, which are not that important for the host system. Add-ons have the same basal architecture as plug-ins, excepting two points: The inner complexity of add-ons is limited and an add-on cannot be instantiated or executed alone. The adaptation of the add-on mechanism corresponds largely to the adaptation of plug-ins which is outlined in Sect. 3.3. With regard to meta models, we propose add-ons as primarily incremental, attribute-wise extensions of host meta classes. Thereby, new attributes and concepts have a strong dependency on original concepts, while the original meta class is never dependent on any extension class. Add-ons can further specify original classes. Both aspects are neither possible nor reasonable with plug-ins. Consequently, add-ons are appropriate for model analysis, specification and minimal augmentation [4,8].

Abstract Syntax and Semantics: Meta model add-ons can be designed by applying concepts of the previously introduced *Add-On and Plug-In* package. In order to distinguish add-ons logic from plug-ins logic, specific constraints are defined for *Original Classes*, *Extension Classes* and *Extension Integrator Classes*. These constraints are required to ensure that each original class is independent of each extension class. However it is allowed to refer to original classes by extension classes (which is forbidden within plug-ins as they are isolated model components). Also respective sub class building is feasible.

Concrete Syntax: Figure 2c already introduced the graphical notation for new elements of the *Add-On and Plug-In* package. Add-on definitions might use the specified generalization edge for representing generalizations between *Original Classes* (super types) and *Extension Classes* (sub types).

4   Conclusion and Outlook

Figure 3 summarizes the basic syntactical architecture of each considered approach. Especially, the dependencies between original classes (extension points) and extension integrator classes are focussed in order to emphasize the difference between plug-ins and add-ons, for instance. It is further important to keep in mind, that hooks and add-ons are rather weaved with an original meta model, whereas plug-ins constitute as isolated, separately defined model components.

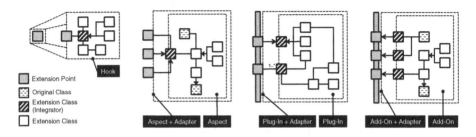

Fig. 3. Comparison of the basic architecture of each proposed extension technique. Respective dependencies are presented as directed edges with an unfilled arrow head.

Figure 4 summarizes the general procedure for applying the presented approaches. Some mechanisms require the definition of specific interfaces or the declaration of extensible elements. This declaration is realized in the first step and enables extensibility of the meta model at all. In the next step, the concrete extension content is applied to the meta model. In the last step, host classes and extension classes have to be merged (e.g., hooking) or simply connected (e.g., plug-ins) in order to shape a unified meta model version, which constitutes the language extension.

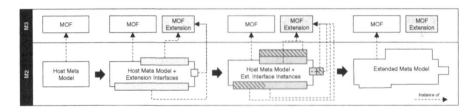

Fig. 4. General procedure for applying the introduced mechanisms.

This position paper tackles the under-investigated field of meta model extensibility and is motivated by the potential benefits of adapting software extension techniques in order to facilitate the definition of extensible meta models. We therefore examined four techniques and elaborated their adaptation through appropriate analogies and concretization. The stated adaptations are implemented as additional meta meta model packages within the EMOF in order to enable an integration and implementation within the prevalent MOF environment. This facilitates the straightforward application on the meta model layer of any MOF-based conceptual modeling language. Currently, the proposed architecture is prototypically implemented in the Eclipse Modeling Framework (EMF) and its usefulness is evaluated in the context of enterprise modeling languages. Results on that will be published in a separate research report. Due to the limited space of this paper, we refrain from the presentation of detailed applications on the meta model layer. However, exemplarily instantiations of the proposed mechanisms were applied to the business process modeling language BPMN and will be available in an upcoming publication (cf. [32]).

As this article focusses the abstract syntax, it is important to investigate semantical aspects of extension design. For instance, there is only little research on the semantic description of language extensions and their distinction from original concepts. It seems to be reasonable to conduct semantical check routines in order to avoid contradictions between meta models and added extensions. It is also required to provide better integrated guidance for the creation of single extension based on specific domain requirements.

Acknowledgements. This research was funded by the German Research Foundation (DFG) within the research project *SFB Transregio 96*.

References

1. Wand, Y., Weber, R.: Research commentar: information systems and conceptual modeling - a research agenda. Inf. Syst. Res. **13**(4), 363–376 (2002)
2. Frank, U.: Conceptual modelling as the core of the information systems discipline-perspectives and epistemological challenges. In: AMCIS 1999. Proceedings (1999)
3. OMG: business process model and notation (BPMN) - version 2.0. Object Management Group (OMG) (2011)
4. Braun, R.: Towards the state of the art of extending enterprise modeling languages. In: Proceedings of the 3rd International Conference on Model-Driven Engineering and Software Development (2015)
5. Braun, R., Esswein, W.: Classification of domain-specific BPMN extensions. Lect. Notes Bus. Inf. Process. **147**, 42–57 (2014)
6. Pardillo, J.: A systematic review on the definition of UML profiles. In: Petriu, D.C., Rouquette, N., Haugen, Ø. (eds.) MODELS 2010, Part I. LNCS, vol. 6394, pp. 407–422. Springer, Heidelberg (2010)
7. Kopp, O., Görlach, K., Karastoyanova, D., Leymann, F., Reiter, M., Schumm, D., Sonntag, M., Strauch, S., Unger, T., Wieland, M., et al.: A classification of BPEL extensions. J. Syst. Integr. **2**(4), 3–28 (2011)

8. Atkinson, C., Gerbig, R., Fritzsche, M.: Modeling language extension in the enterprise systems domain. In: Proceedings of the 17th IEEE EDOC, pp. 49–58 (2013)
9. Braun, R.: Behind the scenes of the BPMN extension mechanism - principles, problems and options for improvement. In: Proceedings of the 3rd International Conference on Model-Driven Engineering and Software Development (2015)
10. OMG: meta object facility (MOF) core specification, version 2.4.2 (2014)
11. Clark, T., Evans, A., Caskurlu, B.: Engineering modelling languages: a precise meta-modelling approach. In: Kutsche, R.-D., Weber, H. (eds.) FASE 2002. LNCS, vol. 2306, pp. 159–173. Springer, Heidelberg (2002)
12. Pfeiffer, D., Gehlert, A.: A framework for comparing conceptual models. In: Proceedings of the EMISA Workshop, pp. 108–122 (2005)
13. Booch, G.: Object Oriented Analysis and Design with Application. Pearson Education, India (2006)
14. Parnas, D.L.: Designing software for ease of extension and contraction. IEEE Trans. Softw. Eng. 2, 128–138 (1979)
15. Krishnamurthi, S., Felleisen, M.: Toward a formal theory of extensible software. In: ACM SIGSOFT Software Engineering Notes, vol. 23, pp. 88–98. ACM (1998)
16. Sommerville, I.: Software Engineering, 6th edn. Pearson, Boston (2001)
17. Martin, R.C.: Design principles and design patterns. Object Mentor 1, 34 (2000)
18. Rytter, M., Jørgensen, B.N.: Independently extensibile contexts. In: Babar, M.A., Gorton, I. (eds.) ECSA 2010. LNCS, vol. 6285, pp. 327–334. Springer, Heidelberg (2010)
19. Bass, L.: Software Architecture in Practice. Pearson Education, India (2007)
20. Zenger, M.: Evolving software with extensible modules. In: Proceedings of the International Workshop on Unanticipated Software Evolution (2002)
21. Klatt, B., Krogmann, K.: Software extension mechanisms. TH Karlsruhe, Research report (2008)
22. Heinlein, C.: Vertical, horizontal, and behavioural extensibility of software systems. Universität Ulm, Fakultät für Informatik (2003)
23. Birsan, D.: On plug-ins and extensible architectures. Queue 3(2), 40–46 (2005)
24. Kulesza, U., Alves, V., Garcia, A., de Lucena, C.J.P., Borba, P.: Improving extensibility of object-oriented frameworks with aspect-oriented programming. In: Morisio, M. (ed.) ICSR 2006. LNCS, vol. 4039, pp. 231–245. Springer, Heidelberg (2006)
25. Becker, J., Delfmann, P., Knackstedt, R.: Adaptive reference modeling: integrating configurative and generic adaptation techniques for information models. In: Becker, J., Delfmann, P. (eds.) Reference Modeling, pp. 27–58. Springer, Heidelberg (2007)
26. Becker, J., Delfmann, P.: Reference Modeling. Springer, Heidelberg (2007)
27. Kiczales, G., Lamping, J., Mendhekar, A., Maeda, C., Lopes, C., Loingtier, J.M., Irwin, J.: Aspect-oriented programming. In: Akşit, M., Matsuoka, S. (eds.) ECOOP 1997. LNCS, vol. 1241, pp. 220–242. Springer, Heidelberg (1997)
28. Wolfinger, R.: Plug-in architecture and design guidelines for customizable enterprise applications. In: Companion to the 23rd ACM Conference on Object-Oriented Programming Systems Languages and Applications, pp. 893–894. ACM (2008)
29. Marquardt, K.: Patterns for plug-ins. In: EuroPLoP, pp. 203–232 (1999)
30. Kühn, H., Bayer, F., Junginger, S., Karagiannis, D.: Enterprise model integration. In: Bauknecht, K., Tjoa, A.M., Quirchmayr, G. (eds.) EC-Web 2003. LNCS, vol. 2738, pp. 379–392. Springer, Heidelberg (2003)
31. Zivkovic, S., Kuhn, H., Karagiannis, D.: Facilitate modelling using method integration: an approach using mappings and integration rules. In: Proceedings of the ECIS, pp. 2038–2049 (2007)
32. Braun, R.: Meta model extensibility of BPMN - current limitations and proposed improvements. In: Communications in Computer and Information Science. Springer, Heidelberg (2015)

Ontology-based Modeling, Reasoning and Reuse

Repairing Errors in PRISM Programs Using Probabilistic Abduction Reasoning

Mustapha Bourahla$^{(\boxtimes)}$

Laboratory of Pure and Applied Mathematics (LMPA),
Computer Science Department, University of M'sila,
BP 166 Ichebilia, 28000 M'sila, Algeria
mbourahla@hotmail.com

Abstract. This paper presents a technique to diagnose probabilistic counterexamples that are generated when model checking probabilistic systems against probabilistic properties. In probabilistic model checking (PMC), a counterexample is a set of paths in which a path formula holds, and their cumulative probability mass violates the probability bound. The diagnosis is to repair errors in probabilistic PRISM programs using the probabilistic abduction reasoning on Independent Choice Logic (ICL) programs describing the generated probabilistic counterexamples.

Keywords: Stochastic systems · Probabilistic model checking · Independent choice logic · Probabilistic abduction reasoning

1 Introduction

Probabilistic model checking has appeared as an extension of model checking for analysing systems that exhibit stochastic behaviour [11]. Several case studies in several domains have been addressed from randomized distributed algorithms and network protocols to biological systems and cloud computing environments. These systems are described usually using Discrete-Time Markov Chains (DTMCs), Continuous-Time Markov Chains (CTMCs) or Markov Decision Processes (MDPs), and verified against properties specified in Probabilistic Computation Tree Logic (PCTL) [8] or Continuous Stochastic Logic (CSL) [3]. If the model does not satisfy such specification, it generates an error trace (counterexample); by analysing it we can locate the source of the error.

The counterexample in PMC is a set of evidences or diagnosis paths that satisfy path formula and their probability mass violates the probability threshold. As it is in conventional model checking, in PMC the generated counterexample should be small and most indicative to be easy for analysing [2,7,9]. In PMC, this task is more challenging since the counterexample consists of multiple paths. However, generating small and indicative counterexamples only is not enough for understanding the error. Therefore, counterexamples diagnosis is inevitable. Many works in conventional model checking have addressed the diagnosis of counterexamples to better understand the error. As it was done in conventional model

© Springer International Publishing Switzerland 2015
L. Bellatreche and Y. Manolopoulos (Eds.): MEDI 2015, LNCS 9344, pp. 41–52, 2015.
DOI: 10.1007/978-3-319-23781-7_4

checking, addressing the error explanation in the probabilistic model checking is highly required, especially that probabilistic counterexample consists of multiple paths instead of single path, and it is probabilistic.

In this work, we present a technique for the diagnosis of the probabilistic counterexample generated when model checking probabilistic systems. This technique is based on Independent Choice Logic (ICL) [15] which combines logic programming and probability into a coherent framework. The idea of the Independent Choice Logic is straightforward: there is a set of independent choices with a probability distribution over each choice, and a logic program that gives the consequences of the choices. There is a measure over possible worlds (models) that are defined by the probabilities of the independent choices, and what is true in each possible world is given by choices made in that world and the logic program. The idea of this work is to create ICL programs that are descriptions of generated probabilistic counterexamples. These ICL programs are inputs to a diagnosis system which is defined at Meta level for analysing the equivalent ICL programs where many Meta level reasoning operations are defined. These Meta level diagnosis operations are based on reasoning by probabilistic Horn abduction [14] which allowed for probabilistically independent choices and a logic program to give the consequences of the choices. The diagnosis reasoning can detect spurious behaviours that should be eliminated by a process of refinement.

Related Works. There are several works that have used the definition of causality in the context of model checking [5,6]. In our previous work [6], we have proposed an aided-diagnosis method for probabilistic counterexamples based on the notions of causality paths and responsibility. The definition of causality has also been used by the authors of [10]. They adopt the definition of causality to event orders for generating fault trees from probabilistic counterexamples. They extended their approach by integrating causality in the model checking algorithm itself [13]. The authors of the work in [4] have developed an approach to reduce the problem of probabilistic model repair to a nonlinear optimisation problem of a minimal-cost objective function using a new version of parametric probabilistic model checking.

This paper is organized as follows. In Sect. 2, we present the theoretical aspect of diagnosing the probabilistic counterexamples; we begin by presenting a simple stochastic program as an example for generating probabilistic counterexample which will be used for explaining the idea of this diagnosis approach. In Sect. 3, we review the Independent Choice Logic and we explain how we can generate ICL programs from probabilistic counterexamples. Section 4 presents the computing aspect of this technique using probabilistic abduction reasoning. At the end, we give conclusions and future works.

2   Diagnosing Probabilistic Counterexamples

To explain this approach for diagnosing probabilistic counterexamples, we need to present an example of a stochastic system. Its model is written with the

```
 1:  dtmc //Discrete-Time Markov Chain
 2:  module Example
 3:    f0 : bool init true ;
 4:    f1 : bool init false ;
 5:    f2 : bool init false ;
 6:
 7:    [a] f0 & !f1 -> 0.4 : (f0' = false) +
 8:                    0.6 : (f1' = true) ;
 9:    [b] !f0 -> 0.3 : (f1' = true) & (f2' = false) +
10:                0.7 : (f1' = false) & (f2' = true) ;
11: endmodule
```

Fig. 1. Example program

language used by the model checker PRISM [12]. Consider a probabilistic system composed of one process. The set of system states S is $\{f_0, f_1, f_2\}^2$, the variables f_0, f_1, and f_2 are Boolean variables. An element $\langle f_0, f_1, f_2 \rangle \in S$ represents the state of the process. The initial state s_0 is $\langle f_0, \neg f_1, \neg f_2 \rangle$ (a state is a tuple of formulas, each one should be true, for example f_0 means $f_0 = true$, $\neg f_1$ means $f_1 = false$ and $\neg f_2$ means $f_2 = false$), and the probabilistic finite state-transition program is defined in Fig. 1.

This model program can now be subjected to detailed quantitative analysis. Thus the key idea of this analysis process is to perform a series of experiments on the resulting model for a range of stochastic properties. A property can be expressed as the probability that the process will reach a state where f_2 becomes $true$ is less than or equal 0.25 and the formula $f_0 \vee f_1$ is true in all the preceding states. This is expressed by the PCTL [8] formula

$$\mathbf{P}_{\leq 0.25}\left[(f_0 \vee f_1)\mathbf{U}f_2\right].$$

The probabilistic model checking can confirm the satisfaction of this property. In the case of the non-satisfaction of the property, and since probabilistic model checkers as PRISM [12] do not offer the possibility to generate counterexamples, then using tools like DiPro [1] to generate counterexamples explaining the non-satisfaction of the property is necessary. DiPro (Directed Probabilistic Counterexample Generation) is a tool used for generating counterexamples from DTMC, CTMC and MDPs models, and it is used jointly with the model checker PRISM to render the counterexamples in text or XML formats as well as in graphical mode. Figure 2 shows a probabilistic counterexample generated by the tool DiPro, which demonstrates that the property is unsatisfied by the model where an intentional error is introduced (the colored underlined text in line number 7 is removed from the program). The counterexample is composed of two finite paths aab and $aaab$, where a and b are transition labels and its probability is 0.2688 which exceeds the property threshold (0.25). The initial state (the cubic node) is encoded by $f_0 \wedge \neg f_1 \wedge \neg f_2$, the second state (the big circle node) is encoded by the formula $f_0 \wedge f_1 \wedge \neg f_2$, the third state (the small circle node) is encoded by $\neg f_0 \wedge f_1 \wedge \neg f_2$ and the last state in the counterexample (the diamond node) is encoded by $\neg f_0 \wedge \neg f_1 \wedge f_2$.

Fig. 2. Graphical representation of the probabilistic counterexample

However, generating probabilistic counterexamples as a set of finite paths [7,9] demonstrating the non-satisfaction is not enough for understanding the error. Therefore, counterexamples diagnosis is inevitable. In this paper, we will present a work to diagnose the probabilistic counterexamples to identify causes of errors. Due to our experience, addressing the error explanation in the probabilistic model checking is highly required.

The probabilistic property with upper threshold $\phi = \mathbf{P}_{\leq p}[\varphi]$ (the properties with lower threshold can be easily transformed to properties with upper threshold [2,7]) is refuted when the probability mass of the paths (probabilistic behaviours) satisfying φ exceeds the bound p. Therefore, a probabilistic counterexample for the property ϕ is formed by a set of infinite paths starting at state s_0 and satisfying the path formula φ. We denote these paths by $Paths(s_0 \models \phi)$. The counterexample can be formed of set of finite paths where each finite path $\omega = s_0 (P(s_0, s_1)) s_1...s_n$ is the smallest prefix of infinite paths from $Paths(s_0 \models \phi)$ satisfying the formula φ. Where, s_i, $0 \leq i \leq n$ are states from the set S of the program model states and $P(s_i, s_{i+1})$ is a transition probability. We denote these finite paths by $FinitePaths(s_0 \models \phi)$.

It is clear that we can get a set of probabilistic counterexamples, noted $PCX(s_0 \models \phi)$, which is a set of any combination from $FinitePaths(s_0 \models \phi)$ that their probability mass exceeds the bound p. Among all these probabilistic counterexamples, we are interested in the most indicative one. The most indicative counterexample is minimal counterexample (has the least number of paths from $FinitePaths(s_0 \models \phi)$) and its probability mass is the highest among all other minimal counterexamples. We denote the most indicative probabilistic counterexample by $MIPCX(s_0 \models \phi)$. We should note that the most indicative probabilistic counterexample may not be unique.

2.1 Diagnosis Approach

For PCTL/CSL properties of the form $\phi = \mathbf{P}_{\leq p}[\varphi]$, explaining the violation reduces to the explanation of exceeding the probability bound p over the DTMC, CTMC or MDP models. A path in the probabilistic counterexample can represent a spurious (false positive) probabilistic behaviour of the model under verification. A false probabilistic behaviour is caused by at least one false transition from a source state to a target state that is caused by the abstraction level used for formulating transition guards or false probability/rate expression associated with it. As a consequence, the model program should be modified by refining transitions guards or correcting probability/rate expressions to eliminate these spurious transitions. Thus, the diagnosis approach is to detect these transitions causing the unsatisfaction of the PCTL (CSL) property. As it will be explained, it is possible to get different possibilities (alternatives) for diagnosing a most indicative counterexample which they are called possible diagnoses.

Definition 1. *A most indicative counterexample $MIPCX(s_0 \models \phi)$ is considered as a tuple $(\mathcal{V}, Q, q_0, \Omega)$ where $\mathcal{V} = \{v_1, v_2, \cdots, v_n\}$ is the set of program variables, $Q \subseteq S$ is a subset of states from the set of model states S, $q_0 = s_0$ is the initial state, Ω is the set of probabilistic finite paths $(\omega = q_0 (p_1) q_1 (p_2) q_2 \cdots q_n)$ in $MIPCX(s_0 \models \phi)$, where $q_i \in Q$ and $p_i \in \mathbb{R}_{>0}$ for $i > 0$, p_i is probability/rate value associated with the model transitions. We note by $L_Q = lastStates(\Omega)$ $(L_Q \subseteq Q)$ the last states of the finite paths in $MIPCX(s_0 \models \phi)$.*

A false probabilistic counterexample transition $\tau_m = q_i (p_{i+1}) q_{i+1}$ from a probabilistic finite path $\omega \in \Omega$ is a probabilistic model transition built from a program transition expression (τ_p) that has a weak abstract guard formula and then, it should be strengthened by extra condition on variables from $\mathcal{V}$ to get rid of this false model transition or to correct its probability/rate program expression. Each guard ψ of probabilistic program transition, as specified with the PRISM language, is a formula that may represent a superset of states from the program model states S. This means the abstract probabilistic program transition guarded by ψ represents a superset of probabilistic model transitions. Consequently, certain counterexample states from Q may be the cause of spurious probabilistic behaviours (due to abstraction, we have more probabilistic behaviours than the concrete set of probabilistic behaviours). Thus, the diagnosis approach is to detect these spurious probabilistic behaviours modulo the property specification and then eliminating them by a process of refinement of false program transition guards or correction of false program probability or rate expressions.

To detect the spurious probabilistic behaviours modulo the property specification $\phi = \mathbf{P}_{\leq p}[\varphi_1 \mathbf{U}^{\leq n} \varphi_2]$, we begin by creating from the path formula $\varphi = \varphi_1 \mathbf{U}^{\leq n} \varphi_2$ the set of simple formulas SF_ϕ that are responsible of its truth. We call a formula sf a simple formula which satisfies φ, if any formula sf' simpler than sf doesn't satisfy φ. We define a simple proposition sp to be an atomic proposition or negation of an atomic proposition that is used for specifying the formula φ (it is possible to transform the formula φ to a negative normal form, where the negation appears only before an atomic proposition). The set of all simple propositions in the property ϕ is denoted by SP_ϕ. A simple formula sf can be either a simple proposition sp (noted by $sf = \{sp\}$) or a disjunction of simple propositions $sf \equiv sp_1 \vee sp_2 \vee \cdots \vee sp_n$, where $n > 1$ which can be also represented as a set $sf = \{sp_1, sp_2, \cdots, sp_n\}$. A simple proposition sp can belong to many simple formulas.

A simple formula sf of the path formula φ should verify the condition: if Q is the set of states in the most indicative probabilistic counterexample and L_Q is its last states then $\forall q \in Q \backslash L_Q \models sf \vee \forall q \in L_Q \models sf$. We define the degree of responsibility of a probabilistic counterexample state $q \in Q$ to satisfy the path property φ with respect to a simple proposition $sp \in SP_\phi$ from a simple formula sf by, if q doesn't satisfy sp then $dr(q, sf[sp]) = 0$ else $dr(q, sf[sp]) = 1/|sf'|$, where $sf' \subseteq sf$ is defined by $\forall sp \in sf \wedge q \models sp \Rightarrow sp \in sf'$. The notation $sf[sp]$ means we take the simple proposition sp from the simple formula sf. Thus, the degree of responsibility of a probabilistic counterexample state $q \in Q$ to satisfy the path property φ with respect to a simple proposition $sp \in SP_\phi$ from any simple formula $sf \in SF_\phi$ is

$$dr(q, sp) = \max \{ dr(q, sf[sp]) \,|\, sf \in SF_\phi \}.$$

For example, from the property $\phi = \mathbf{P}_{\leq 0.25}[(f_0 \vee f_1) \mathbf{U} (f_2)]$ we can create the set of simple propositions $SP_\phi = \{f_0, f_1, f_2\}$. The simple formulas are $sf_1 = f_2$ and $sf_2 = f_0 \vee f_1$ (that is represented by $SF_\phi = \{\{f_2\}, \{f_0, f_1\}\}$). If $q \in Q$ is defined by $q = \{f_0, f_1, f_2\}$, then $dr(q, sf_2[f_0]) = 0.5$, $dr(q, sf_2[f_1]) = 0.5$, and $dr(q, sf_1[f_2]) = 1$. We should remark that $\forall sf \in SF_\phi$, $dr(q, sf)$ equals to one $(\forall sf \in SF_\phi : \exists sp \in sf : q \models sp)$.

Let ω be a finite path in the most indicative counterexample $MIPCX(s_0 \models \phi) = (\mathcal{V}, Q, q_0, \Omega)$; $\tau_m \equiv [v_1 = x_1 \wedge \cdots \wedge v_n = x_n] (p) [v_1 = y_1 \wedge \cdots \wedge v_n = y_n]$ is a model transition from the finite path ω where $v_i \in \mathcal{V}, x_i, y_i \in dom(v_i)$, for $1 \leq i \leq n$. We note the source and target states of τ_m (that are represented as conjunctions of simple propositions) by the sets $\tau_S = \{v_i(x_i)\}$ and $\tau_T = \{v_i(y_i)\}$ for $i = 1, \cdots, n$, respectively. Then $\tau_m \equiv \tau_S (p) \tau_T$.

Definition 2. *Let $\tau_p \equiv \psi \wedge (A (px))$ be a PRISM program transition where ψ and A are the guard and target (assignments of the update) formulas of τ_p, respectively and px is its associated probability/rate expression (it can be a constant). Let $\tau_m \equiv \tau_S (p) \tau_T$ be a model transition from the most indicative counterexample. We say τ_m is strongly associated with τ_p (denoted by $\tau_m \Subset \tau_p$) if*

$$(\tau_S \models \psi \wedge \tau_T \models A) \wedge (\exists m \in \mathbb{N}_+ : m \times p = px(x_1, \cdots, x_n)).$$

where $\mathbb{N}_+$ is the set of the positive natural numbers. We will have a weak association denoted by $\tau_m \subset \tau_p$, if the condition $\exists m \in \mathbb{N}_+$ such that $m \times p = px(x_1, \cdots, x_n)$ is not verified.

We check the satisfaction relations $\tau_S \models \psi$ (or $\tau_T \models A$) by valuating the expression ψ (or A) over values from the set $\tau_S = \{v_i(x_i)\}$ (or $\tau_T = \{v_i(y_i)\}$). The expression $px(x_1, \cdots, x_n)$ is valuated using the variables values from the set $\tau_S = \{v_i(x_i)\}$ (the current model state). We define the function $spSet : S \rightarrow 2^{SP_\phi}$ to return a subset $spSet(s)$ from the simple propositions set SP_ϕ verified in a state $s \in S$ (i.e. $spSet(s) = \{sp \in SP_\phi | s \models sp\}$).

Definition 3. *Let $\tau_m \Subset \tau_p$ be a strong transition association where $\tau_m \equiv \tau_S (p) \tau_T$ is a model transition and $\tau_p \equiv \psi \wedge (A (px))$ a program transition. We define the set of simple propositions candidates for eliminating spurious behaviours caused by the transition τ_p by $SP_c = spSet(\tau_S) \backslash spSet(\psi)$. We say a program $\mathcal{P}' = \mathcal{P} \cup (\mathcal{P} \backslash \tau_p) \cup (\psi \wedge \neg sp \wedge (A (px)))$ is a refinement of the program $\mathcal{P}$ by the simple proposition sp of the property specification ϕ, if*

$$sp \in SP_c \wedge \forall sp' \in SP_c : dr(\tau_S, sp) \leq dr(\tau_S, sp')$$

If SP_c is empty then the spurious behaviours may be caused by probability/rate expressions in strongly/weakly associated program transitions. In this case the refined program is

$$\mathcal{P}' = \mathcal{P} \cup (\mathcal{P} \backslash \tau_p) \cup (\psi \wedge (A (px')))$$

Where px in $\tau_p \equiv (\psi \wedge (A (px)))$ is modified by a new probability/rate expression px'. This new expression should reduce the probability/rate of the model transition by a sufficient amount to verify the condition $\tau_S(px') < p$ if $\tau_m \Subset \tau_p$ (strong association) and/or it should increase the probability/rate of the model transition to verify $\tau_S(px') > p$ if $\tau_m \subset \tau_p$ (weak association). The expression $\tau_S(px')$ means valuation of px' in the state τ_S.

If the model of $\mathcal{P}'$ satisfies the property ϕ then the used simple proposition sp for refinement (or modified probability/rate expression) is a possible diagnose else the refinement/correction process continues by the same way with other simple propositions from the set SP_c (or other probability/rate expressions) if it is not empty else we investigate with other probabilistic counterexample transitions. The process of model-checking-refinement/correction will continue until the property is satisfied (there is no counterexample) or there is no possible refinement/correction (there is no diagnose).

3   Generating ICL Diagnosis Models

To diagnose the generated most indicative counterexamples against the program of stochastic system model modulo the property specification, we need to build diagnosis models to be used as inputs for reasoning operations. In our approach we have used the Independent Choice Logic [15] where the diagnosis is based on probabilistic abduction reasoning [14]. The Independent Choice Logic (ICL) is logic for adding independent stochastic inputs to a logic program.

An ICL theory is a triple (F, C, P) which consists of a set of facts F representing an acyclic logic program, a choice space $C = \{A_1, A_2, \cdots, A_n\}$, which is a set of sets of atoms. The elements of the choice space are called alternatives. The elements of the alternatives are called atomic choices $A_i = \{c_1^i, c_2^i, \cdots, c_n^i\}$. Atomic choices in the same or different alternatives cannot unify with each other. Atomic choices cannot unify with the head of any clause in the set of facts F. The element P is a probability distribution over the alternatives in C. That is $P : \cup C \rightarrow [0, 1]$ such that $\forall A_i \in C : \sum_{c \in A_i} P(c) = 1$. The restrictions on the unification of atomic choices are there to enable a free choice of an atomic choice from each alternative.

With respect to the definition of ICL, the logic program of the diagnosis model for the most indicative probabilistic counterexample $MIPCX(s_0 \models \phi) = (V, Q, q_0, \Omega)$ is a tuple $DM = (F_r, F_t, C, P)$, where F_r is the set of facts asserting the satisfaction of simple propositions of property specification ϕ, F_t is the set of facts asserting the different transitions in the probabilistic counterexample, C is the choice space and P is a probability distribution over C. First, from the property $\phi = P_{\leq p}[\varphi_1 U^{\leq n} \varphi_2]$, we create the set of simple formulas SF_ϕ containing simple propositions as defined before. Then, the produced set SF_ϕ is used for generating the set of facts F_r defining the degree of responsibility for each state from the counterexample states to satisfy the path formula $\varphi_1 \mathbf{U}^{\leq n} \varphi_2$ with respect to each simple proposition from the set SP_ϕ.

Each fact is a predicate of the form $fdr(s(q), L)$, where the predicate $s(\ldots)$ is used to assert that its argument is a counterexample state, q is a counterexample state from Q and L is a list of sub-lists. Each sub-list element is the set of simple propositions where the sum of responsibility degrees of the state $q \in Q$ according to these simple propositions is one (we recall the responsibility degree of a probabilistic counterexample state to satisfy the path formula φ according to each simple formula sf is one). For example, if we have $sf_1 = \{sp_1\}$, $sf_2 = \{sp_2, sp_3\}$, $dr(q, sf_1[sp_1]) = 1$, $dr(q, sf_2[sp_2]) = 0.5$ and $dr(q, sf_2[sp_3]) = 0.5$ then the responsibility degree fact of the state q according to all these simple formulas is $fdr(s(q), [[sp_1], [sp_2, sp_3]]) = 1$. If the state doesn't satisfy a simple proposition from the set SP_φ then it will not be present in the list (its degree of responsibility with respect to this simple proposition is zero). A simple proposition can be listed more than one if it is an element of many simple formulas. By this way, we define only one responsibility degree fact for each probabilistic counterexample state.

For each transition $q(p)q'$ from the finite path $\omega \in \Omega$, we create a clause of the form $s(q') <- s(q) \ \& \ fdr(s(q), X)=D \ \& \ p1qq'(D)$., where $fdr(s(q), X)=D$ is the responsibility degree of the source state on satisfying the path formula with respect to simple propositions X. In the case of a cycle transition and as the ICL programs are acyclic; we create a copy of the source state of each transition. The set of choice alternatives $Alt = \{A_0, \cdots, A_n\}$ is created for each source state in addition to their copies where n is its number, for example, the logic choice $p1qq'(D)$ is inserted to the choice alternative of the state q'. By this way, we create the choices space C. At the end, the probability distribution P is generated from the list of alternatives Alt and the probability distribution over the initial states, for example as we have only one initial state the probability distribution is $prob \ s(q_0) : 1$.

For example, the counterexample $MIPCX(s_0 \models \phi = \mathbf{P}_{\leq 0.25}[(f_0 \vee f_1)\mathbf{U}(f_2)]) = (\mathcal{V}, Q, q_0, \Omega)$ generated when model checking the example program (Fig. 1), against the property ϕ is defined by $\mathcal{V} = \{f_0, f_1, f_2\}$, $Q = \{q_0, q_1, q_2, q_3\}$, $q_0 = s_0$ and $\Omega = \{q_0 (0.6) \ q_1 (0.4) \ q_2 (0.7) \ q_3, q_0 (0.6) \ q_1 (0.6) \ q_1 (0.4) \ q_2 (0.7) \ q_3\}$ is composed of two finite paths. The set of finite paths contains a cycle $(q_1 (0.6) \ q_1)$, then a copy q_1^c of q_1 should be created. The model counterexample states are defined as follows. $q_0 = f_0 \wedge \neg f_1 \wedge \neg f_2$, $q_1 = q_1^c = f_0 \wedge f_1 \wedge \neg f_2$, $q_2 = \neg f_0 \wedge f_1 \wedge \neg f_2$ and $q_3 = \neg f_0 \wedge \neg f_1 \wedge f_2$. The set of simple formulas $SF_\phi = \{\{f_0, f_1\}, \{f_2\}\}$ is constructed from the set of simple propositions $SP_\phi = \{f_0, f_1, f_2\}$. The responsibility degrees are $dr(q_0, f_0) = 1$, $dr(q_1, f_0) = 0.5$, $dr(q_1, f_1) = 0.5$, $dr(q_1^c, f_0) = 0.5$, $dr(q_1^c, f_1) = 0.5$, $dr(q_2, f_1) = 1$ and $dr(q_3, f_2) = 1$. The responsibility degrees of all other cases are zero. The ICL program generated from this counterexample is defined by the tuple (F_r, F_t, C, P), where

$$F_r = \begin{cases} fdr(s(q_0), [[f_0]]) = 1 ., fdr(s(q_1), [[f_0, f_1]]) = 1 ., fdr(s(q_1^c), [[f_0, f_1]]) = 1 ., \\ fdr(s(q_2), [[f_1]]) = 1 ., fdr(s(q_3), [[f_2]]) = 1 . \end{cases}$$

$$F_t = \begin{cases} s(q_1) < -s(q_0) \ \& \ fdr(s(q_0), X) = D \ \& \ p_1 c_{01}(D) ., \\ s(q_1^c) < -s(q_1) \ \& \ fdr(s(q_1), X) = D \ \& \ p_2 c_{11^c}(D) ., \\ s(q_2) < -s(q_1) \ \& \ fdr(s(q_1), X) = D \ \& \ p_1 c_{12}(D) ., \\ s(q_2) < -s(q_1^c) \ \& \ fdr(s(q_1^c), X) = D \ \& \ p_2 c_{1^c 2}(D) ., \\ s(q_3) < -s(q_2) \ \& \ fdr(s(q_2), X) = D \ \& \ p_1 c_{12}(D) . \end{cases}$$

$$C = \begin{cases} A_0 = \{p_1 c_{01}(D)\}, A_1 = \{p_1 c_{12}(D), p_2 c_{11^c}(D)\}, \\ A_2 = \{p_2 c_{1^c 2}(D)\}, A_3 = \{p_1 c_{23}(D)\} \end{cases}$$

$$P = \begin{cases} prop \ s(q_0) \ : \ 1.0 ., prop \ p_1 c_{01}(D) \ : \ D * 0.6 ., \\ prop \ p_2 c_{11^c}(D) \ : \ D * 0.6 , \ p_1 c_{12}(D) \ : \ D * 0.4 ., \\ prop \ p_2 c_{1^c 2}(D) \ : \ D * 0.4 ., prop \ p_1 c_{23}(D) \ : \ D * 0.7 . \end{cases}$$

The counterexample contains a cycle transition $(q_1 \ (0.6) \ q_1)$. To make the corresponding logic program acyclic, we create a copy q_1^c of the state then the transition becomes $q_1 \ (0.6) \ q_1^c$. This syntax is based on the ICL language syntax which is a meta-language of Prolog (Prolog extra-logical predicates).

4   Reasoning on ICL Diagnosis Models

A total choice for choice space C of a diagnosis model $DM = (F_r, F_t, C, P)$ is a selection of exactly one atomic choice from each grounding of each alternative in C, in the example, we have two total choices: $\{c_{01}(1), c_{12}(1), c_{23}(1), s(q_0)\}$ and $\{c_{01}(1), c_{11^c}(1), c_{1^c 2}(1), c_{23}(1), s(q_0)\}$. A stable model (called possible world) is an interpretation associated with a total choice where each atom in the logic program has a truth value. The semantics of ICL is defined in terms of possible worlds and there is at most one possible world for each total choice. For example, for the total choices, we have the interpretations:

$$W(\{c_{01}(1), c_{12}(1), c_{23}(1), s(q_0)\}) \triangleq c_{01}(1) \wedge c_{12}(1) \wedge c_{23}(1) \wedge s(q_0)$$
$$W(\{c_{01}(1), c_{11^c}, c_{1^c 2}(1), c_{23}(1), s(q_0)\}) \triangleq c_{01}(1) \wedge c_{11^c}(1) \wedge c_{1^c 2}(1) \wedge c_{23}(1) \wedge s(q_0)$$

The probability for a possible world is the product of the probabilities of the atomic choices that make up the possible world. The probability of any proposition is the sum of the probabilities of the possible worlds in which the proposition is true. For example,

$$P(s(q_3)) = \mu(\{W(\{c_{01}(1), c_{12}(1), c_{23}(1), s(q_0)\}), W(\{c_{01}(1), c_{11^c}(1), c_{1^c 1}(1), c_{23}(1), s(q_0)\})\})$$
$$= 0.6 \times 0.4 \times 0.7 \times 1.0 + 0.6 \times 0.6 \times 0.4 \times 0.7 \times 1.0 = 0.2688 > 0.25$$

A simple proposition sp extracted from the property ϕ which is associated with a state q from the most indicative counterexample, is true in a possible world W if q is true in W. A state q is true in a possible world if the atomic choices set of the possible world covers the atomic choices for satisfying the state q. The idea of the diagnosis technique is to find possible worlds in which simple propositions are true. Then with these simple propositions, we try to refine program transitions guards (or probability/rate expressions) associated with counterexample transitions whose source states having true simple propositions in such possible world. For example, the state q_1^c which is the source of the model transition $\tau_m \equiv q_1^c (0.4) q_2$ ($\tau_S = q_1^c = f_0 \wedge f_1 \wedge \neg f_2$ and $\tau_T = q_2 = \neg f_0 \wedge f_1 \wedge \neg f_2$) is true in the possible world $W(\{c_{01}(1), c_{11^c}(1), c_{1^c2}(1), c_{23}(1), s(q_0)\})$, because the atomic choices of this possible world cover the atomic choices ($\{p_1 c_{01}(1), p_1 c_{11^c}(1), s(q_0)\}$) for satisfying the state q_1^c. Consequently, its simple propositions $\{f_0, f_1\}$ are true in this possible world.

The transition τ_m is strongly associated with the program guarded transition $\tau_p \equiv \psi \wedge (A(px))$ of line number 7 (Fig. 1), where $\psi = f_0$ and $A(px) = (f_0' = false)(0.4)$. The conditions for this strong association, $\tau_m \Subset \tau_p$ ($\tau_S = f_0 \wedge f_1 \wedge \neg f_2 \models \psi = f_0$, $\tau_T = q_2 = \neg f_0 \wedge f_1 \wedge \neg f_2 \models A = (f_0' = false)$ and $\exists m \in \mathbb{N}_+ : m \times p = px = 0.4$, where $m = 1$) are verified. Thus, the set of simple propositions candidates for the refinement is computed by the expression $SP_c = spSet(\tau_S) \setminus spSet(\psi) = \{f_0, f_1\} \setminus \{f_0\}$ and the result is $SP_c = \{f_1\}$. Now, it is possible to refine the program using one simple proposition from the set SP_c. Each refinement according to a simple proposition is called diagnose. Thus, we have $|SP_c|$ diagnoses with different degrees of responsibility. The selected simple proposition sp for refinement, should verify the conditions in Definition 3. Now it is possible to refine the program by the expression $\neg sp_1 = \neg f_1$ as it is the unique candidate expression, thus the new refined program is

$$\mathcal{P}' = \mathcal{P} \cup (\mathcal{P} \setminus (f_0 \wedge ((f_0' = false))(0.4))) \cup (f_0 \wedge \neg f_1 \wedge ((f_0' = false))(0.4))$$

As a consequence of this refinement, the old model transition will not occur in the new model of the new program. Then the spurious world (behaviour) $W(\{c_{01}(1), c_{11^c}(1), c_{1^c2}(1), c_{23}(1), s(q_0)\})$ is eliminated and the property is satisfied.

This diagnosis technique uses reasoning by abduction coupled with probabilistic reasoning. The reasoning by abduction is a powerful reasoning framework [14]. The basic idea of abduction is to make assumptions to prove a goal. The ICL is a language for abduction where the atomic choices are assumable (they are abducibles or possible hypotheses) and they are all probabilistic atoms that can be used by the probabilistic reasoning for measuring the probability of a proof by abduction. Abduction is used to derive those atomic choices over which the measure is defined. For example, the explanations of observing $\neg s(q_1^c)$ are, the first assumption is $\neg c_{01}(1)$ with probability equals to 0.4, the second assumption is $c_{12}(1)$ with probability equals to 0.4 and the third assumptions is $\neg s(q_0)$ with a probability 0. To compute its probability we should observe the dual, where $P(\neg s(q_1^c)) = 1 - P(s(q_1^c))$. The observation of the proposition $s(q_1^c)$ gives the unique explanation $c_{01}(1) \wedge c_{11^c}(1) \wedge s(q_0)$ with the probability $0.6 \times 0.6 \times 1.0 = 0.36$. Thus, the probability $P(\neg s(q_1^c)) = 1 - P(s(q_1^c))$ equals to 0.64. The predication of the query $\neg s(q_1^c) \wedge s(q_3)$ is explained by assuming the following atoms $c_{01}(1) \wedge c_{12}(1) \wedge c_{23}(1) \wedge s(q_0)$ where the probability is

$$P(\neg s(q_1^c) \wedge s(q_3)) = P(c_{01}(1)) \times P(c_{12}(1)) \times P(c_{23}(1)) \times P(s_0)$$
$$= 0.6 \times 0.4 \times 0.7 \times 1.0 = 0.168$$

The idea of this technique to diagnose $MIPCX(s_0 \models \phi = \mathbf{P}_{\leq p}[\varphi]) = (\mathcal{V}, Q, q_0, \Omega)$ is to find spurious possible worlds (spurious behaviours) by first computing the probability $P_{\max} = \sum_{q \in lastStates(\Omega)} P(s(q))$ by predicting the last states in the set of finite paths Ω ($P_{\max}$ is greater than the property threshold p). Then, we begin by observing queries expressed as propositions representing states from $Q \backslash lastStates(\Omega)$ (for example, $s(q_1^c)$). The probability of this observation is given to compute the probability of observing the dual to analyse its effect over the counterexample behaviours. This last observation of the dual will be used to compute the probability of predicting queries expressing states from the set $lastStates(\Omega)$ (conditioned only by the last observation of the dual). For example, the probability of predicting $s(q_3)$ conditioned by observing $\neg s(q_1^c)$ is $P(s(q_3)|\neg s(q_1^c))$ which equals to 0.2625. Now we can compute $P(\neg s(q_1^c) \wedge s(q_3))$ whose formula is $P(\neg s(q_1^c)) \times P(s(q_3)|\neg s(q_1^c))$ (its value is 0.168). The corresponding possible world of the diagnosis query $\neg s(q_1^c) \wedge s(q_3)$ is a spurious behaviour if $P_{\max} - P(\neg s(q_1^c) \wedge s(q_3)) \leq p$. In this example, $P_{\max} = 0.2688$ then $0.2688 - 0.168 = 0.1008$ is less than 0.25. This confirms that the corresponding possible world $\{c_{01}(1), c_{11^c}(1), c_{1^c2}(1), c_{23}(1), s(q_0)\}$ is a spurious behaviour. If this is the case, we search possible associations between model transitions that has as source or target the states used for expressing the diagnosis queries (for example, $s(q_1^c)$) and equivalent abstract program transitions for possible refinement as explained before.

5   Conclusions and Perspectives

A probabilistic counterexamples guided technique for repairing PRISM program modulo property specification is presented. It is based on transition guards' refinement or transition probabilities/rates correction. The property specification involving more program variables will conduct to an efficient program refinement. The strategy of refinement is based on selecting the spurious behaviour with less probability using the responsibility degrees when selecting the states and their associated simple propositions. As a future work, we want to realise compositional diagnosis by which we can analyse probabilistic counterexamples composed of large numbers of finite paths.

References

1. Aljazzar, H., Leitner-Fischer, F., Leue, S., Simeonov, D.: DiPro - a tool for probabilistic counterexample generation. In: Groce, A., Musuvathi, M. (eds.) SPIN Workshops 2011. LNCS, vol. 6823, pp. 183–187. Springer, Heidelberg (2011)
2. Aljazzar, H., Leue, S.: Directed explicit state-space search in the generation of counterexamples for stochastic model checking. IEEE Trans. Softw. Eng. **36**(1), 37–60 (2010)
3. Baier, C., Haverkort, B.R., Hermanns, H., Katoen, J.: Model-checking algorithms for continuous-time markov chains. IEEE Trans. Softw. Eng. **29**(6), 524–541 (2003)

4. Bartocci, E., Grosu, R., Katsaros, P., Ramakrishnan, C.R., Smolka, S.A.: Model repair for probabilistic systems. In: Abdulla, P.A., Leino, K.R.M. (eds.) TACAS 2011. LNCS, vol. 6605, pp. 326–340. Springer, Heidelberg (2011)
5. Beer, I., Ben-David, S., Chockler, H., Orni, A., Trefler, R.J.: Explaining counterexamples using causality. Formal Methods Syst. Des. **40**(1), 20–40 (2012)
6. Debbi, H., Bourahla, M.: Causal analysis of probabilistic counterexamples. In: 11th ACM/IEEE International Conference on Formal Methods and Models for Codesign, MEMCODE 2013, 18–20 October 2013, Portland, OR, USA, pp. 77–86 (2013)
7. Han, T., Katoen, J., Damman, B.: Counterexample generation in probabilistic model checking. IEEE Trans. Software Eng. **35**(2), 241–257 (2009)
8. Hansson, H., Jonsson, B.: A logic for reasoning about time and reliability. Formal Asp. Comput. **6**(5), 512–535 (1994)
9. Jansen, N., Wimmer, R., Ábrahám, E., Zajzon, B., Katoen, J., Becker, B., Schuster, J.: Symbolic counterexample generation for large discrete-time markov chains. Sci. Comput. Program. **91**, 90–114 (2014)
10. Kuntz, M., Leitner-Fischer, F., Leue, S.: From probabilistic counterexamples via causality to fault trees. In: Flammini, F., Bologna, S., Vittorini, V. (eds.) SAFE-COMP 2011. LNCS, vol. 6894, pp. 71–84. Springer, Heidelberg (2011)
11. Kwiatkowska, M., Norman, G., Parker, D.: Stochastic model checking. In: Bernardo, M., Hillston, J. (eds.) SFM 2007. LNCS, vol. 4486, pp. 220–270. Springer, Heidelberg (2007)
12. Kwiatkowska, M., Norman, G., Parker, D.: PRISM 4.0: verification of probabilistic real-time systems. In: Gopalakrishnan, G., Qadeer, S. (eds.) CAV 2011. LNCS, vol. 6806, pp. 585–591. Springer, Heidelberg (2011)
13. Leitner-Fischer, F., Leue, S.: Causality checking for complex system models. In: Giacobazzi, R., Berdine, J., Mastroeni, I. (eds.) VMCAI 2013. LNCS, vol. 7737, pp. 248–267. Springer, Heidelberg (2013)
14. Poole, D.: Logic programming, abduction and probability - A top-down anytime algorithm for estimating prior and posterior probabilities. New Gener. Comput. **11**(3), 377–400 (1993)
15. Poole, D.: The independent choice logic and beyond. In: De Raedt, L., Frasconi, P., Kersting, K., Muggleton, S.H. (eds.) Probabilistic Inductive Logic Programming. LNCS (LNAI), vol. 4911, pp. 222–243. Springer, Heidelberg (2008)

Semantic of Data Dependencies to Improve the Data Quality

Houda Zaidi[1,3](✉), Yann Pollet[1], Faouzi Boufarès[2], and Naoufel Kraiem[3]

[1] Laboratory CEDRIC, CNAM, 75003 Paris, France
{houda.zaidi,yann.Pollet}@cnam.fr
[2] Laboratory LIPN, University Sorbonne Paris Cité, 93430 Villetaneuse, France
faouzi.boufares@lipn.univ-paris13.fr
[3] Laboratory RIADI, University Manouba, Manouba, Tunisia
naoufel@squ.edu.om

Abstract. Data quality in databases is a critical challenge because the cost of anomalies may be very high, especially for large databases. Therefore, the correction of these anomalies represents an issue that has become more and more important both in enterprises and in academia. In this work, we address the problems of intra-column and inter-columns anomalies in big data. We propose a new approach for data cleaning that takes into account the semantic dependencies between the columns of a data source. The novelty of our proposal is the reduction of the size of the search space in the process of functional dependency discovery based on data semantics. In this paper, we present the first steps of our work. They allow recognizing the semantics of data and correct intra-column anomalies.

Keywords: Data quality · Big data · Functional dependencies · Semantic dependencies · Data structure · Data cleaning

1 Introduction

The improvement of data quality in data sources represents a major challenge, especially for large organisations which need to exchange information between systems and integrate large amounts of data. There are many types of data anomalies [11,14] such as duplicates, similar data (non-strict duplicates), obsolete data, inconsistencies and missing values. The cost of the difficulties caused by these anomalies can be very high. Therefore, they have a great influence on the activity of organizations. Anomalies in the data sources may be due to the poverty of the description of data semantic. Using of a priori knowledge to improve the data semantic should contribute to the improvement of quality. In this paper, we propose a new approach to guide the detection and the correction of intra-column (e.g. missing values, incorrect values) and inter-columns anomalies (e.g. functional dependencies violation). We focus on the verification of functional dependencies and the correction of anomalies in large quantities of data. Our approach is based on a priori knowledge which is called data dictionary.

© Springer International Publishing Switzerland 2015
L. Bellatreche and Y. Manolopoulos (Eds.): MEDI 2015, LNCS 9344, pp. 53–61, 2015.
DOI: 10.1007/978-3-319-23781-7_5

This paper is organized as follows: Sect. 2 explains the context of our work. In Sect. 3, we present the related work. In the fourth section, we present our proposition. An overview of our future work is given at the end.

2   Problematic

In the literature, various existing studies have been carried on the anomalies related to the same column. Generally, they are based on a preliminary step of standardization of values before processing the anomalies. However, little research has addressed the problem of semantic links that may exist between the columns. In our work, we study the constraints of dependencies between the different columns of a given data source. We focus on anomalies caused by the violation of these constraints. In addition, we assume that the data source is present under the form of set of tuples without any additional information about metadata.

Example 1: Let 's consider a CSV file (Patient.csv). S is a data source. It contains j columns and m rows.

The file bellow (see Fig. 1) contains several anomalies, such as incorrect Email of the patient 1097, the information about patients 33333 and 10992 contains missing values, the values of columns 6 and 7 are heterogeneous (e.g. many date formats are used) and the columns 9, 10 and 11 contain incorrect values (e.g. Parisss, Franc, Eurape). In order to correct these anomalies, there are many issues: (1) How to infer the semantic of data? (2) How to discover the semantic dependencies between columns? (3) How to correct anomalies in large quantities of data?

```
100101;175099943272264;-;-;M;M;-;Fb@lipn.univparis13.fr;Parisss;France;-
100203;180089987976564;CRI;-;Mme;F;-;yp@cnam.fr;Paris;Franc;-
100388;165037895642322;AGRR;-;M;F;15-mars-65;w@cnam.fr;Loiret;France;Europe
100407;180046378965464;CRP;Martin;-;M;-;03-avr-80;ben. w@lip6.fr;Paris;Fr;Europe
100530;171038976542322;MGEN;Anne; Mlle;1;12/03/1971;-;Beijing;Chine;Asie
584;278025125874563;-;Karine;Mlle;1;-;stephane.a@@gmail.com;-;China;Afrique
710;157054725912564;OTC;Robert;M;0;-;b-i@irit.fr;Pari;Frence;Europe
729;177125915879625;IPECA;Simon;M;0;-;Nick.Tous@loria.fr;Bruxelle;France;-
1097;174046784763822;CRI;Djamel;M;-;12/04/1974;sb fe@irisa.fr; Paris;-;Eurape
1213;283068794585464;IPECA;Katia;Mlle;Femme;24/06/1983;-;Calvados;-;-
33333;275478784581464;-;Houda;-;-;-;-;Vill;Pai;Conti
10992;285099935116964;-;Adem;M;0;-;-;Beijing;Pai;Asia
```

Fig. 1. Patient.csv File extraction (from a data source S)

3   Related Work

Many methods and tools exist to solve data quality problems. We have performed a study of ETL (Extract-Transform-Load) tools (Talend Data Quality [13], Pentaho Data Integration [10]). We studied several features such as transformation, elimination of redundant data and functional dependencies verification. We concluded that these tools are too manual and require the knowledge of the structure and constraints of data.

Dallachiesa et al. are presented in [6] NADEEF a data cleaning system. The users need to specify quality rules such us conditional functional constraints, deduplication rules and customized ones.

We have studied several algorithms to discover functional dependencies such as FUN [9], CFun [8] and AFD-DYNAMICUPDATE [12]. These approaches require user knowledge of the structure and semantics of the data. Furthermore, they do not detect all valid dependencies especially for heterogeneous data or data which contains anomalies. Furthermore, the dependency discovery problem has an exponential search space to the number of attributes, and the runtime of the proposed algorithms is linear to the number of tuples. Consequently, they do not allow the treatment on functional dependencies in large databases. The originality of our proposal is the reduction of the size of the search space in the process of the functional dependency discovery based on the data semantics. We eliminate the invalid semantic dependencies.

As part of the data quality management project in collaboration with Talend company [13], we have developed several deduplication algorithms [4,5]. A draft of data categorisation was started in [1,2]. We propose a new approach which allows to guide the detection and correction of anomalies from the constraints analysis of dependencies between the different columns of the same data source. Our approach does not require user knowledge of the structure and semantics of the data handled from the sources. We focus on large data sets. We are implementing a massive, parallel and distributed processing based on mapreduce concept [7]. In this paper, we present the first steps of our proposition.

4   Semantic Recognition of Data Structure

Our proposition is to detect and correct anomalies related to a column or the anomalies caused by the violation of dependencies constraints between different columns from a source. The cleaning process is based on the knowledge and reference data (called repository or data dictionary). This data dictionary represents information about countries, cities, sex and gender in several languages. This knowledge will be used to infer the semantics and data structure which represents the first step of our proposition. Using of our data dictionary, we can infer probable category of each column.

4.1   Data Dictionary

The data dictionary contains two types of knowledge [2]: (i) Elements defined by extension (Cat_{Ext}). This consists of a set of a priori data such as the names of cities, countries, companies, organizations. (ii) Elements defined by intention (Cat_{Int}). This type of knowledge contains data values that verify a given model,

Table 1. An example of Data Dictionary DDVS (by extension)

Category	Subcategory	ValidString
City	English	Beijing, Brussels
	French	Pékin, Bruxelles
Country	English	Tunisia, France
	French	Tunisie, France
Civility	English	Mrs, Mr
	French	Mme, M
FirstName		France, Houda

Table 2. An example of Data Dictionary DDKW (by extension)

Category	Subcategory	KeyWord
Adress	English	Street, St
	French	Rue, Avenue, Place
Health_Organization	English	Hospital
	French	Hopital, clinique

or they verify such properties of regular expressions (e.g. an Email or URL) or they belong to a range of values.

So, our data dictionary is composed of a set of tuples. It is described by:

(1) categories (Cat_{Ext} and Cat_{Int}), each category can have subcategories such as languages (English, French) and (2) information. These information are the correct values of categories (valid strings) or key words (a set of keywords which define a category) for Cat_{Ext} (Table 1) and a regular expressions for Cat_{Int} (Table 2).

Let us now introduce some notations: Cat = $Cat_{Ext} \cup Cat_{Int}$.

The set of categories is Cat = $\{Cat_r, r = 1...p\}$, p is the total number of categories. For instance $Cat_{Ext} = \{$City, Country, Civility, FirstName, Adress,...$\}$, $Cat_{Int} = \{$Email, Temperature,...$\}$.

We will consider that the flowing three sets DDVS, DDKW and DDRE are disjoint. DDVS $\cap$ $DDKW$ $\cap$ $DDRE = \emptyset$.

For instance, the category FirstName defined by extension has not to be defined using a regular expression. An Email can not be defined by extension DDVS = $\{(Category, Subcategory, ValidString)_a, a = 1, n_1\}$ (see Table 1).

Table 3. Examples of data dictionary DDER (by intention)

Category	Subcategory	RegularExpression
Email		^[a-zA-Z0-9.._%]+@[a-zA-Z0-9.-]+ \.[a-zA-Z]2,4$
Temperature		^(-?[0-9]\d*(.\d+)?)?(°C|°F)$

DDKW = {(Category, Subcategory, KeyWord)$_b$, b =1,n_2} (see Table 2).

DDRE = {(Category, Subcategory, RegularExpression)$_c$, c =1, n_3} (see Table 3). n1 (respect. n2 and n3) is the total number of valid strings (respect. keywords and regular expressions). With n_1 (respectively n_2 and n_3) is the cardinality of the set DDVS (respectively DDKW and DDRE)

Let C be the set of columns of S: C = {Col_k, k = 1..j}. One note that the data structure of S is: S(Col_1,Col_2,..Col_j) or S(C). Each column is defined on a syntactic domain such as Strings, Numbres or Dates.

Let us call [Col_k] the set of values belonging to S. [Col_k] = {v_{1k} , ..., v_{mk}}.

Example 2: if Col_k means Cities, [Col_k] may contain the set of values {Paris, Parisss, Brussels, Pekyn, Beijing, Bruxelles, Adem, Eve, abc}.

We can easily see that Parisss and Pekyn are invalid syntactic values, while Bruxelles and Brussels are valid strings. Note that Paris, Brussels and Beijing are given in english. The other valid strings are given in french.

Example 3: the set of valid strings for the category City is {Beiging, Brussels, Paris, Pékin, Bruxelles, Paris}

Let us consider V the set of all valid strings and valid key words: V = $\Pi_{[ValidString]}(DDVS) \cup \Pi_{[KeyWord]}(DDKW)$.

Definition 1 (Syntactically Correct Value): v_{ik} is a syntactically correct value iff $v_{ik} \in V$ or v_{ik} verifies at least one regular expression belonging to DDRE. One note that: (i) $v_{ik} \in V$ ($v_{ik} \in V$ or $\exists w \in V /v_{ik} \approx w$). v_{ik} and w are similar using an algorithm of similarity distance (Levenshtein, Jaro-Winkler). (ii) v_{ik} can belong to several categories.

Example 4: Paris $\in$ V; $Pari \approx Paris$; $Beijing \in V$; $houda@cnam.fr \in DDRE$.

Definition 2 (Dominant Category (Cat_d) (Respect. Dominant Subcategory $SubCat_d$)): Let us consider that β_r is the empirical probability that the column Col_k is to be of category Cat_r, r = 1..p. β_d = Max(β_r) since a column can belong to several categories.

The dominant category for a column Col_k is the category that has the probability β_d. Note that β_r is calculated using Hypergeometric distribution [3] as follows.

Let α_r the number of $v_{ik} \in Cat_r$; m = number of rows of S; S' $\subseteq$ S; m' = number of rows of S'; x = number of $v_{ij} \in Cat_r$ in S'; y a threshold The probability of y values belong to Cat_r in S' is defined by: β_r = P(x = y) = $(C_{\alpha_r}{}^y C_{m-\alpha_r}{}^{m'-y})/C_m^{m'}$.

Example 5: The values of [Col_k] = {Paris, Parisss, Brussels, Pekyn, Beijing, Bruxelles, Adem, Eve, abc}, m = 9; {Paris, Parisss, Brussels, Pekyn, Beijing, Bruxelles} $\subseteq$ City, α_1 = 6; {Paris, Parisss, Adem, Eve} $\subseteq$ FirstName, α_2 = 4; Col_k can belong to City or FirstName; m' = 3; y = 2. City: β_1 = P(x=2) = 0,53. FirstName: β_1 = P(x=2) = 0,35.

Cat_d = Dominant Category(Col_k) = City.

Definition 3 (Semantically Correct Value): v_{ik} is a semantically correct value iff $v_{ik} \in \text{Cat}_d$ and $v_{ik} \in \text{SubCat}_d$.

Example 6: "Beijing" is a semantically invalid value while "Pékin" is semantically correct, because the dominant category is City and the dominant subcategory is French.

4.2   Algorithm

We propose a data categorization algorithm which determines the domain, the category and the subcategory (the dominant language) of each column of a given data source. In this step, a data sample is created, using the data source, and then it is analyzed. We extract several samples to infer a set of valid categories. First, we create a sample by column of the source S. Then, we search the dominant category (respectively subcategory) for each column. Finally, we use a set of measures M to validate the choice of the dominant category and the dominant subcategory. These measures are applied to each column.

M = {M1:Number of rows of the source, M2: Number of nulls values, M3: Number of valid syntactic values, M4: Number of invalid syntactic values, M5: Number of values semantically correct, M6: Number of categories, M7: Number of subcategories}.

A set of rules is deduced from the various measures. We present below examples of rules.

Rule1: a dominant category is valid iff $r_1 \geq \epsilon_1$ ($r_1 = \text{M2}/\text{M1}$, ϵ_1 is a threshold).

Rule2: a dominant category is valid iff $r_2 \geq \epsilon_2$ ($r_2 = \text{M5}/\text{M1}$, ϵ_2 is a threshold).

4.3   Results of Data Categorization

Below are the results of the experimentation on the file Patient.csv (Table 4). From a CSV file we can determine the syntactic domain, the category and the subcategory of each column. We use the concepts Dominant Category and Dominant Subcategory. The treatments of unknown categories may allow the enrichment of the dictionary. Some lexical databases such as WordNet and WOLF can be used. Enrichment of dictionaries will be part of our future work. The categorization step consists to recognize the semantic of data. This allows to correct, first, intra-column values and then inter-columns anomalies.

5   Data Cleaning

After discovering of the semantic category and subcategory of each column, we use the methods of similarity distance calculation to correct the syntactically and the semantically incorrect values which are similar to values that exist in Cat_{Ext} (Table 5). We call this step the data standardization. It consists to homogenize the heterogeneous data. On the one hand, we replace the data that does not

Table 4. Results of data categorization

ID$_column$	Syntactic Domain	Category	SubCategory
Col1	Integer	Unknown	Unknown
Col2	Double	Unknown	Unknown
Col3	String	Mutual	French
Col4	String	FirstName	*
Col5	String	Civility	French
Col6	String	Sex	French
Col7	Date	Date	French
Col8	String	Email	*
Col9	String	City	French
Col10	String	Country	French
Col11	String	Continent	French

belong to the dominant Category with the nearest values in our data dictionary using a method of similarity distance calculation. In the other hand, we replace the data that does not belong to the dominant subcategory with their synonyms in the dominant language. In addition, we try to guide the user in the process of transformation such as the transformation of values in one until of measurement and the unification of the date formats.

Therefore, we can correct intra-column anomalies.

The correction of intra-column anomalies facilitates the verification of semantic links between columns which is our ultimate goal. Since, the verification of functional dependencies (FDs) in data that contains errors can give incorrect results. Knowledge are stored in metaBase such us invalid semantic dependencies (functional dependencies, inclusions...) to guide the user in the verification process of semantic links between the columns of a source.

Note that our semantic approach very considerably reduces the search space functional dependencies to check.

Indeed, when the cardinality of X is much less than that of Y, then X does not determine semantically Y. One can easily see that in the case where the syntactic domains of X and Y are not compatible, the semantic dependency is rather invalid. For example, if the syntactic domain of X is of type Date, the following semantic dependencies are improbable: $X \rightarrow Sex$, $X \rightarrow FirstName$, $X \rightarrow Civility$, $Sex \rightarrow City$, $Sex \rightarrow Continent$, $FirstName \rightarrow Civility$.

The data domains (data types) may be useful for targeting the valid functional dependencies. The number of FDs can be elevated and each test requires a very large number of computations. Then, some FDs must be eliminated from the set of dependencies constraints to be verified according to the data type. Consequently, we verify only the valid DFs in our analyse. Hence, we can facilitate the treatments in Big Data.

Table 5. Data cleaning

Source schemaless	⇒	New Semantic schema
Col9; Col10; Col11		Col9; Col10; Col11
		City; Country; Continent
Old invalid values		New valid values
Parisss; France; -		Paris; France; -
Paris; Franc; Europe		Paris; France; Europe
Pari; Frence; Europe		Paris; France; Europe
Beijing; China; Asia		Pékin; Chine; Asie
Vill;Pai; Conti		Vill; Pai; Conti
Beijing; -; Asia		Pékin; -; Asie
Paris; Fr; Eurape		Paris; Fr; Europe

In our case, we propose to verify only the following set of dependencies: City → Country, City → Continent, Country → Continent, Civility → Sex. For instance the dependency Sex→ Email has not to be verified. It has no semantic meaning.

6   Conclusion and Future Work

The existing ETL tools are too manual and require the knowledge of the structure and constraints of data. Therefore, we interested on the concept of semantic repository to store the necessary knowledge. We try to contribute to the development of new tools that do not require the user knowledge of the structure and semantic of the handled data from the source. They allow to assist the correction of anomalies. The data collected and merged should have more sense.

We propose a data cleaning approach based on the analysis of dependencies constraints in large databases. We have presented in this paper the first step of our work. It consisted to recognize the semantics and structure of data. Then, we started the standardization of heterogeneous data. These steps are preliminary steps before beginning the process of FDs verification and the correction of inter-columns anomalies. We stock in our repository a semantic knowledge about links between the columns of a source. For example, this knowledge represents a set of insignificant FDs to reduce the number of FDs to be verified. The user is thus assisted in determining dependency cheking The next step is to verify FDs from large quantities of data [7]. We focus on the concepts of Mapreduce in order to assist the processes of this step. Our ultimate goal is to correct the anomalies caused by the violation of the dependencies constraints.

References

1. Ben Salem, A., Boufarès, F., Correia, S.: Semantic recogonition of a data structure in Big-data. In: 6th International Conference on Computational Intelligence and software Engineering, Beijing, pp. 93–103 (2014)
2. Ben Salem, A.: Qualité contextuelle des données: Détection et nettoyage guidés par la sémantique des données. Thèse de doctorat, de l'université Sorbonne Paris cité, Paris (2015)
3. Berkopec, A.: HyperQuick algorithm for discrete hypergeometric distribution. J. Discrete Algorithms. **5**(2), 341–347 (2007)
4. Boufarès, F., Ben Salem, A., Correia, S.: Qualité de données dans les entrepôts de données: élimination des similaires. In: 8èmes Journées francophones sur les Entrepôts de Données et l'Analyse en ligne, Bordeaux, France, pp. 32–41 (2012)
5. Boufarès, F., Ben Salem, A., Rehab, M., Correia, S.: Similar elimination data: MFB algorithm. In: IEEE-2013 International Conference on Control, Decision and Information Technologies, Hammamet, Tunisie, pp. 289–293 (2013)
6. Dallachiesay, M., Ebaidz, A., Eldawy, A., Elmagarmid, A, Ilyas, I.F., Ouzzani, M., Tang, N.: NADEEF: a commodity data cleaning system. In: 2013 ACM SIG-MOD International Conference on Management of Data, pp. 541–552. IEEE Press, New York (2013)
7. Dean, J., Ghemawat, S.: MapReduce: simplified data processing on large clusters. In: 6th Conference on Symposium on Operating System Design and Implementation, California, pp. 137–150 (2004)
8. Diallo, T., Novelli, N.: Découverte des dépendances fonctionnelles conditionnelles. In: 10th conférence internationale sur l'extraction et la gestion des connaissances, Hammamet, Tunisie, pp. 315–326 (2010)
9. Novelli, N., Cicchetti, R.: FUN: an efficient algorithm for mining functional and embedded dependencies. In: Van den Bussche, J., Vianu, V. (eds.) ICDT 2001. LNCS, vol. 1973, pp. 189–203. Springer, Heidelberg (2000)
10. PentahoDataIntegration. http://www.pentaho.fr/explore/pentaho-data-integration
11. Raman, V., Hellerstein J.M.: Potter's wheel: an interactive data cleaning system. In: 27th International Conference on Very Large Data Bases, Rome, Italy, pp. 381–390 (2001)
12. Simonenko, E., Novelli, N.: Extraction de dépendances fonctionnelles approximatives: une approche incrémentale. In: 12th Conférence Internationale Francophone sur l'Extraction et la Gestion des Connaissances, Bordeaux, France, pp. 95–100 (2012)
13. Talend. https://www.talend.com/
14. Vassiliadis, P., Simitsis A., Georgantas, P., Terrovitis, M.: A framework for the design of ETL scenarios. In: 15th Conference on Advanced Information Systems Engineering, Klagenfurt, Austria, pp. 520–535 (2003)

A Cloud-Based Reusable Design
for Mobile Data Sharing

Nadir Guetmi[1][✉] and Imine Abdessamad[2]

[1] LIAS/ISAE-ENSMA, Poitiers University, Chasseneuil, France
nadir.guetmi@ensma.fr
[2] Université de Lorraine and INRIA-LORIA Grand Est, Nancy, France
abdessamad.imine@loria.fr

Abstract. Mobile devices have experienced a huge progress in computing capacity, storage and visualization of data. They are becoming the device of choice for operating a large variety of applications while supporting real-time collaboration of people and their mobility. Despite this progress, the energy consumption and the network coverage remain a serious problem against an efficient and continuous use of these mobile collaborative applications and a great challenge for their designers and developers. To address these issues, this paper describes design patterns that help modeling mobile collaborative applications enabling real-time data sharing through the cloud. Our design model consists of two levels: the first one provides self-protocol to create clones of mobile devices, manage users' groups and recover failed clones in the cloud. As for the second level, it supports group collaboration mechanisms for data sharing between mobile users via their clones. Our patterns have been used as a basis for the design of SOCIALVPN, a cloud-based platform enabling mobile users to build and exploit their own virtual social networks.

Keywords: Pattern design · Mobile data sharing · Collaboration · Cloning middleware · Consistency preservation · Synchronization

1 Introduction

Nowadays, mobile devices are increasingly part of our everyday lives, taking on more and more tasks. A variety of services (such as real-time data streaming, mobile commerce, social networking and ad hoc collaboration) are available through mobile applications that take benefit of the increasing availability of built-in communication network and better data exchange capabilities of mobile devices. In addition, in terms of flexibility and mobility, mobile devices provide the tool of choice for people to collaborate with family members, friends and business colleagues in order to achieve a common goal.

However, even though mobile devices hardware and network modules continue to evolve and improve, mobile devices will always be resource-poor, less secure, with unstable connectivity, and with constrained battery life. Resource deficiency is a main issue for many applications, and as a result, computation on

© Springer International Publishing Switzerland 2015
L. Bellatreche and Y. Manolopoulos (Eds.): MEDI 2015, LNCS 9344, pp. 62–73, 2015.
DOI: 10.1007/978-3-319-23781-7_6

mobile devices will always involve a compromise [14]. More precisely, managing collaborative works (e.g. editing a shared document or a friend list) in real-time through ad-hoc peer-to-peer mobile networks is often costly in terms of energy consumption and network traffic and it may lead to the congestion of mobile devices [5,10]. Moreover, it is not possible to ensure a continuous collaboration due to frequent disconnections.

To deal with the mobile resources limitation, one straightforward solution is to delegate the majority of mobile intensive computations to the cloud. Thus, enjoying the benefits of the virtualization in the cloud enables us to extend the mobile device resources by offloading execution from the mobile to the cloud where a *clone* (or *virtual machine*) of the mobile is running. Cloud computing allows users to build virtual networks "à la peer-to-peer" where a mobile device may be continuously connected to other mobiles to achieve a common task. The goal of this cloning is to provide self-configuration capabilities such as on-demand resources provisioning (e.g. memory size) without requiring user intervention.

Defining reusable designs is more challenging in new collaborative applications for cloud-supported mobile data sharing services, because the combination of mobile and cloud environments raises many design issues such as the management of real-time data synchronization. These mobile collaborative applications require suitable design patterns for modeling communication and synchronization services that are intended to be deployed in the cloud and several mobile devices, while delegating the majority of inherent tasks to the cloud. In addition, other processes such as installation, deployment, configuration, monitoring and management of software modules must be well modeled to fully provide the collaborative service to mobile users in the cloud.

In this paper, we present a new cloud-based reusable design for mobile data sharing. We provide an extensible model for implementing purely decentralized synchronization mechanisms in order to preserve the consistency of the shared resources under constraints of mobile applications, namely the short-life battery and the connection instability. Accordingly, design solutions are illustrated for addressing the challenge of modeling the cloning and collaboration services in the cloud. The proposed design patterns are for two main levels: the first one provides self-control for creating clones of mobiles, managing users' groups and ensuring the smooth functioning in the cloud platform. The second level presents group collaboration mechanisms for data synchronization in real-time, without any central role. As proof-of-concept, we use our design patterns as a basis for devising SOCIALVPN, a cloud-based platform enabling mobile users to build and exploit their own virtual social networks. To our knowledge, this is the first effort aimed at defining reusable designs for cloud-supported mobile collaborative applications.

The remainder of this paper is organized as follows: Sect. 2 presents the global model and its requirements. Section 3 presents design patterns of the proposed architecture. In Sect. 4, we describe an example for applying the proposed architecture. We discuss the related work in Sect. 5 and conclude in Sect. 6.

2   Requirements for Enhancing Mobile Data Sharing

Model Presentation. To enhance mobile data sharing under limited mobile resources constraints, we present a new cloud-based model. For dealing with these limitations, our solution consists in offloading the most of the mobile intense tasks (computation and communication) to the clone (i.e. virtual machine) in the cloud. With this model, users can expect to benefit from the cloud computing advantages for properly managing their uninterrupted collaborative works. This is done through virtual private networks (VPNs) formed of clones of their mobile devices. Thus, each user owns two copies of the shared data (e.g. text or friend list) where the first copy is stored on the mobile device whereas the second one is on its clone (at the cloud level). The user modifies the mobile copy and then sends local modifications to the clone in order to update the second copy and propagate these modifications to other clones (i.e. other mobile devices). Moreover, the user can work even during disconnection (in offline mode) by means of the mobile device's copy.

Model Requirements. Given the particularity of mobile applications constrained by limited resources and connection availability, enhancing mobile data sharing is tightly related to a specific requirements list such as: user's interaction flexibility (or scalability), user's interaction protection[1], communication, heterogeneity and interoperability, autonomous interaction-support services, user awareness, and data consistency [8]. Moreover, we must add another important requirement, namely the fault tolerance for managing recovery from failures. In the following, we enumerate requirements related to the proposed cloud-based design for enhancing mobile data sharing over distributed mobile collaborative applications:

- *Data consistency.* The collaborative application should be responsive in online and offline works. This means that frequent disconnections should not affect the consistency and availability of the shared data. Therefore, lightweight and decentralized synchronization mechanisms (based on explicit data replication between mobiles and their clones) must be used.
- *Communication.* Synchronization for maintaining data consistency is mainly based on communication. However, ad-hoc peer to peer networks are expensive and suffer from frequent disconnections. To overcome this problem, intense communication tasks are pushed to the cloud. Our cloud-based model allows a direct communication for each mobile with its clone. On the other hand, clones form virtual networks and perform the most of communication tasks.
- *Scalability.* Shared data availability and integrity should not be affected by the dynamic aspect of collaboration environments where users can create, join or leave groups and participate on-demand to collaborative work sessions. As we will see in the next sections, our proposed cloud-based model is well suited for transparently achieving highly scalable mobile collaborative applications.

---

[1] Due to space limitation, we do not consider here the user's interaction protection.

- *User awareness.* Collaborators must be able to share their real-time status information. Like [7], we use the following mechanisms: user's reachability (i.e. connected/disconnected) and user's availability (i.e. available/busy) in which each user is notified via the clone of its real mobile device on the presence/availability of other users.
- *Heterogeneity.* Diversity of mobile devices and their operating systems is considered one of the major obstacles for the mobile data sharing. Our model is based on a cloning middleware composed of web services for creating mobiles' clones with a unified operating system (i.e. Android OS). In this case, the clone/clone heterogeneity problem is eliminated. On the other hand, the mobile/clone heterogeneity problem is solved using communication based on standard SOAP (Simple Object Access Protocol) through the cloning middleware. But, this is an exception, as android devices can directly communicate with their clones. It should be noted that, at present, our cloning middleware does not consider data backup from non-Android devices.
- *Failure recovery.* Users have to recover easily all shared data when technical hitch (e.g. crash, theft or loss of mobile device, or clone failure) happens, and continue seamlessly the collaboration. To tackle this problem, a manager of the complete life cycle of clones is necessary. This manager will detect failed clones and restore their states without affecting collaborative tasks.

3   Design Patterns of the Proposed Architecture

This section presents a reusable cloud-based model for the mobile data sharing. First, as shown in Fig. 1, a global layered architecture is given. Next, design patterns for both main layers, cloning and collaboration, are described.

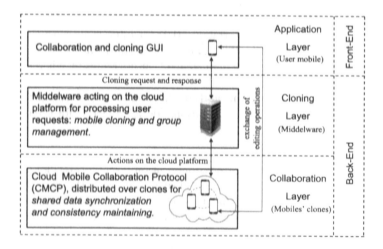

Fig. 1. Architecture for mobile data sharing on the cloud

3.1 Context and Problem

For resource limitation and frequent disconnection (e.g. leading to the collaboration interruption) problems, the cloud is considered as a good solution to relieve mobile devices and ensure permanent bonds between collaborators. However, automating actions of a middleware for: (i) creating clones, (ii) managing dynamic groups through virtual networks deployed in the cloud and (iii) transparently dealing with failures is not a simple task. The problem raised at this stage is: how to devise an interface (Back-end) that implements a self-cloning mechanism to achieve these objectives. To deal with these issues, cloning solution is presented in the next section.

After creating a new clone, it must be able to perform a self-initialization for beginning the collaboration phase. This clone must autonomously act for acquiring the required parameters (detailed below) to: (i) integrate the collaborative group and (ii) exchange (communicate) with its mobile device and other clones. Note that during the collaboration phase, concurrent access to shared data between clones can result in inconsistent views. Furthermore, an offset for applying requests between the clone and the real device is unavoidable; this is another concern for maintaining consistency of shared data. Therefore, the collaboration protocol (distributed over clones) must offer fully decentralized synchronization (clone/clone and mobile/clone) mechanisms without any central role for avoiding a central point of failure. On the other hand, the proposed model should be reusable for supporting any shared data type (e.g. document, video, table, ...).

3.2 Our Solution

To deal with problems previously mentioned, Fig. 1 presents services that are grouped in different layers where three main layers are considered. The application layer provides Graphical User Interfaces (GUI) for interacting with the remaining two layers. Interaction with cloning layer (the cloning middleware) allows for processing the "cloning and group management" users requests, whereas interaction with the collaboration layer enables user to start a synchronization between the mobile and its clone. The cloning and collaboration layers represent the "Back-End" part of the system and include solutions (detailed below) for the previously raised problems.

Cloning Pattern. The cloning solution consists of a middleware based on web services acting on the cloud platform (collaboration layer) for: (i) cloning mobile devices, (ii) managing virtual networks and (iii) supervising the smooth running of the clones. It should be noted that this solution is reusable in the sense that developers can redefine interfaces methods for adapting the cloning middleware to any virtualization environment (e.g. VirtualBox[2] and XEN[3]). Figure 2 shows our design pattern of the Cloning Middleware that is described as follows:

---

[2] https://www.virtualbox.org/.
[3] http://www.xenproject.org/.

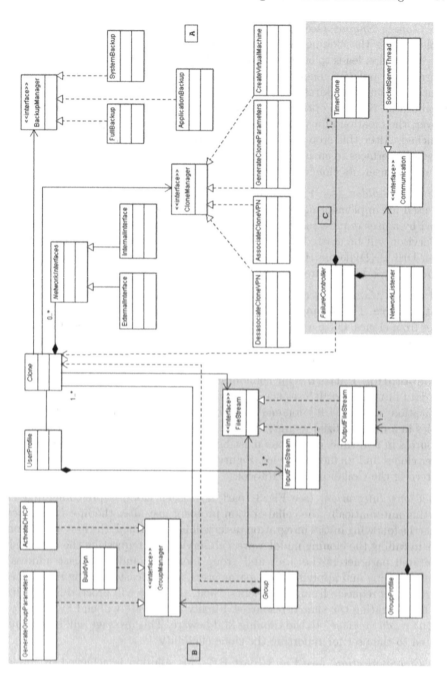

Fig. 2. Cloning diagram class.

(A) Cloning Engine. (see Fig. 2 (part A)). The proposed solution consists in implementing the cloning engine as web service for encapsulating its actions. The first action leads to creating a user profile by: (i) saving the introduced user information and (ii) generating the required clone parameters (i.e. the clone identifier, clone IP address and the group identifier where the user intends to collaborate). Next, an optional backup is proposed to the user. Once this backup is over, the creation of a virtual machine based on Android operating system is launched. After this step it is necessary to configure the internal and external network interfaces to ensure an efficient and continuous communication between the mobile user, its clone and the remaining members of the group.

(B) VPN Builder. (see Fig. 2 (part B)). Like the cloning engine, web services are used for implementing this solution. The VPN builder process will be triggered by a user request in order to create a new group. Then, the virtualization hypervisor will be started for: (i) building a new virtual network, (ii) activating a DHCP (Dynamic Host Configuration Protocol) server and (iii) assigning a specific broadcast address to this VPN.

(C) Failure Manager. (see Fig. 2 (part B)). This solution is based on the heartbeat principle. The cloning middleware uses listeners for receiving periodic messages from clones. Once a timer expires, the repair process is triggered by calling the cloning engine for creating a new clone and restoring all saved parameters related to the failed clone.

Collaboration Pattern. Our collaboration solution offers a protocol for sharing data in the cloud. It uses synchronization mechanisms (based on optimistic replication scheme [4,9]) for enabling the reconciliation of divergent resource copies in a decentralized manner. For maintaining the consistency of the shared resources in real time, each clone must be simultaneously synchronized with the other clones and its mobile device. Figure 3 shows the following described design pattern of the Collaboration Protocol:

(A) Clone Integration. (see Fig. 3 (part A)). Each clone is pre-configured for starting automatically the collaboration protocol just after the first clone boot. Thus the following initial integration tasks will be performed: the first action consists in calling the cloning middleware web services for requesting the previously generated parameters (i.e. user and group identifiers and broadcast address). After receiving and applying these parameters, a broadcast listening is launched for receiving requests from other clones. Next, the clone will proceed in initializing and updating the shared resources. Finally, this phase will end by sending a *"clone ready message"* to the Cloning Middleware. This message will be retransmitted to the user for reporting the clone eligibility.

(B) Communication. (see Fig. 3 (part B)) This solution is achieved by implementing network primitives for simultaneously listening and sending messages. It should be noted that these network primitives are provided in two modes: (i) the unicast mode for receiving/sending messages from/to mobile devices and (ii) the broadcast mode for receiving/broadcasting messages from/to other clones.

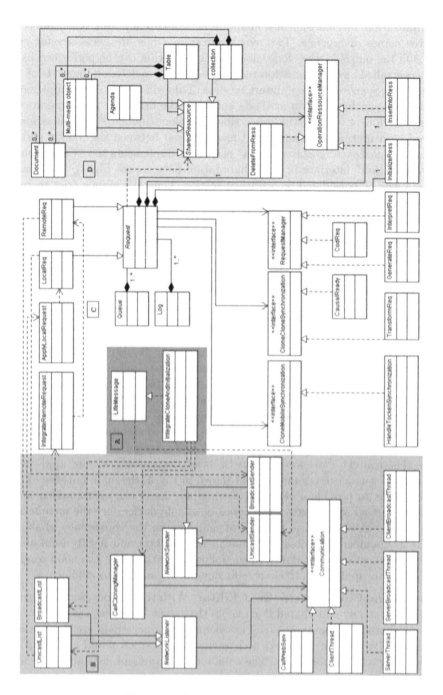

Fig. 3. Collaboration diagram class.

(C) Synchronization. (see Fig. 3 (part C)) This solution offers decentralized synchronization mechanisms for maintaining consistency and reconciling the resource copies divergence. Two synchronization steps are necessary for each clone. On the one side, the clone/clone synchronization can be performed using any decentralized synchronization technique [4,9] by redefining methods of the *"CloneCloneSynchronization"* interface class. This will enable us for implementing different synchronization methods known in the literature (e.g. Operational Transformation [4,9]). On the other side, the clone/mobile synchronization is ensured by a mutual exclusion-based method used between the mobile and its clone (*"HandleTokenSynchronization"* class that implements the *"CloneMobile-Synchronization"* interface in the collaboration pattern, see Fig. 3). The shared resource will be considered as a critical section when the mobile tries to commit/synchronize w.r.t its clone. Only one of them will have the exclusive right to access in synchronizing mode to its resource copy.

(D) Resource Management. (see Fig. 3 (part D)) This solution allows for creating and editing multiple types of simple or compound data resources (e.g. documents, images, tables, collections). Developers can redefine the interface methods to adapt them with any type of data.

4   Case Study: SocialVPN

Most of existing social networks are based on a centralized (client/server) architecture, where providers have the control on the user data. Nevertheless, this architecture suffers from server failures and particularly privacy problems: user might generally not want his/her data to be known by a central entity, and it is not guaranteed the providers will not disclose this data. It is clear that users are confident in social networks based on decentralized architecture as their data are not concentrated in a central point, and hence, user privacy is improved.

In this context, we present here a brief description of our application SocialVPN (under development). As shown in Fig. 4, the main purpose of this application is to provide a cloud platform where users can create and manage their own virtual social networks. Clones of mobile devices are the members of these social VPNs and have the role of maintaining the consistency of shared data (e.g. documents, photos and multimedia objects) and notify users about any new publications or updates. In the following, we describe two main services offered by this application to share/edit documents and photo albums:

A Real-Time Collaborative Text Editor. With this editor, users can create and collaboratively edit shared documents that owns linear data structure (e.g. a list of characters, paragraphs). Two elementary operations are the basis of this editor: (i) $Ins(p,c)$ to insert a character c at position p and (ii) $Del(p)$ to delete a character at position p. The collaboration protocol distributed through the clones is inspired from Optic protocol [9]. It uses operational transformation approach to preserve the consistency of the replicated document [4,9]. To better understand the role of operational transformation, consider the following example: given two clones, CLONE1 and CLONE2, starting from a common state of the document "XYZ". At CLONE1, a mobile user executes op-CLONE1 $=$ $Ins(2, A)$ to insert the character 'A' at position 2 and end up with "XAYZ". Concurrently, a user at CLONE2 performs op-CLONE2 $= Del(1)$ to remove the character 'X' at position 1 and obtain the state "YZ". After the operations are exchanged among CLONE1 and CLONE2, if they are applied naively both clones get inconsistent states: CLONE1 with "AYZ" and CLONE2 with "YAZ". Operational transformation is considered as safe and efficient method for consistency maintenance. In general, it consists of application-dependent transformation algorithm, called IT, such that for every possible pair of concurrent operations, the application programmer has to specify how to integrate these operations regardless of reception order. Thus, at CLONE2, operation op-CLONE1 needs to be transformed to include the effect of op-CLONE2: op-CLONE1' $=$ IT(op-CLONE1, op-CLONE2) $= Ins(1, A)$. As for CLONE1, operation op-CLONE2 is left unchanged. Accordingly, both get the same state "AYZ".

A Photo Album Editor. This service allows for creating, sharing and editing photo albums. Thus, each user can create a photo album referring to a particular event and invite other users to enrich it. Adding a photo can be done by a capture through the application or from a photo library. On the other hand, this application offers a collaborative personalization tool. Users can concurrently edit shared photos by changing their formats, applying a variety of proposed themes and adding captions. Therefore, the users' applied actions will be translated into operations and sent to the clones in the cloud. Clones exchange the received operations and transform them to have a consistent state of their replicated album.

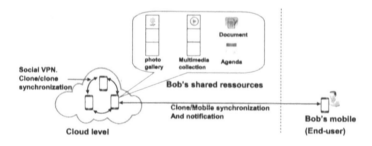

Fig. 4. Architecture of SOCIALVPN

5   Related Work

The area related to the mobile data sharing has experienced several research works but few works have presented a reusable model. In [12], a reusable structural design for mobile collaborative applications was presented. This model is mainly based on coordination and communication services. However, mobile constraints previously described (i.e. short-life battery and connection instability) were not considered by this design. This may negatively impact on such collaboration systems that are not intended for cloud environments. Furthermore, to our knowledge, there is no work that proposed a reusable model specifically designed for mobile data sharing in the cloud. In the following, we review works around two main axes: cloud offloading and real time collaboration.

Cloud Offloading. Treating classic problems related to limited mobile resources was the subject of multiple research works. Solutions presented in [1, 2, 13, 15, 16] are based on offloading techniques of intense computing tasks to the cloud. In [6] a Mobile Cloud Middleware (MCM) is proposed in order to perform dynamic resource allocation mechanisms for asynchronously migrating mobile tasks to heterogeneous cloud platforms. However, offloading techniques are based on monitoring process of the mobile resources use. Background monitoring processes and cloud workload can be as costly for mobile devices in time and energy consumptions [3]. Moreover, these approaches do not support the cloud mobile data sharing, since they require constant mobile/cloud connection. In contrast, our proposed cloning middleware enables static offloading of computing tasks.

Real Time Collaboration. Several research works have proposed collaboration systems specifically designed for editing shared documents in cloud environments. System SPORC [5] is a collaborative system that offers several users to edit shared documents. To maintain their consistency, SPORC relies on a technique based on Operational Transformation (OT) approach and the use of a single server to give global order to concurrent user updates. As the synchronization logic is based on one server, this leads to bottleneck and a single point of failure. Indeed, a large number of messages are exchanged between users and the server. Based on this analysis, we can conclude that SPORC is not well-suited for mobile devices constrained by their limit battery life. System CloneDoc [11] enables (like SPORC) a centralized collaboration for mobile devices that are cloned in the cloud in order to alleviate the burden of collaborative editing works on mobile devices. Unfortunately, a server failure could stop the collaboration between mobile devices. Moreover, as mobile and its clone are two entities physically separated, a delay when executing the same operations on both sides is possible. This may cause inconsistencies of the shared documents. Clonedoc addresses this problem through additional processing of OT on the mobile side. But this will cause supplementary energy consumption.

6   Conclusion

Modeling data sharing systems through mobile applications is considered as a challenge, since it must take into consideration the resource deficiency. However, recent research works on design models for mobile applications are not intended for data sharing in the cloud. Furthermore, other solutions are supported by the cloud environments, but without providing a reusable design. In this paper, we presented design patterns for mobile data sharing in the cloud under resource limitation constraints. The designed system makes abstraction of two main levels. The first one is the cloning middleware that allows for preparing a platform of mobile clones. This protocol offers web services, where end users can create and control clones of their mobile devices and manage their collaborative groups.

The second level is the collaboration protocol that provides decentralized mechanisms for mobile data synchronization in the cloud. As future work, we plan to provide a reusable design for security within mobile data sharing applications in the cloud.

References

1. Chun, B.G., Ihm, S., Maniatis, P., Naik, M., Patti, A.: Clonecloud: elastic execution between mobile device and cloud. In: Proceedings of the Sixth Conference on Computer Systems, pp. 301–314. ACM (2011)
2. Cuervo, E., Balasubramanian, A., Cho, D.K., Wolman, A., Saroiu, S., Chandra, R., Bahl, P.: MAUI: making smartphones last longer with code offload. In: Proceedings of the 8th International Conference on Mobile Systems, Applications, and Services, pp. 49–62. ACM (2010)
3. Dinh, H.T., Lee, C., Niyato, D., Wang, P.: A survey of mobile cloud computing: architecture, applications, and approaches. Wirel. Commun. Mob. Comput. **13**(18), 1587–1611 (2013)
4. Ellis, C.A., Gibbs, S.J.: Concurrency control in groupware systems. In: Proceedings of the ACM SIGMOD Record, vol. 18, pp. 399–407. ACM (1989)
5. Feldman, A.J., Zeller, W.P., Freedman, M.J., Felten, E.W.: SPORC: group collaboration using untrusted cloud resources. In: OSDI, vol. 10, pp. 337–350 (2010)
6. Flores, H., Srirama, S.N.: Mobile cloud middleware. J. Syst. Softw. **92**, 82–94 (2014)
7. Herskovic, V., Ochoa, S.F., Pino, J.A.: Modeling groupware for mobile collaborative work. In: Computer Supported Cooperative Work in Design, CSCWD 2009. 13th International Conference on IEEE, pp. 384–389 (2009)
8. Herskovic, V., Ochoa, S.F., Pino, J.A., Neyem, H.A.: The iceberg effect: behind the user interface of mobile collaborative systems. J. UCS **17**(2), 183–201 (2011)
9. Imine, A.: Coordination model for real-time collaborative editors. In: Field, J., Vasconcelos, V.T. (eds.) COORDINATION 2009. LNCS, vol. 5521, pp. 225–246. Springer, Heidelberg (2009)
10. Kosta, S., Perta, V.C., Stefa, J., Hui, P., Mei, A.: Clone2clone (c2c): peer-to-peer networking of smartphones on the cloud. In: 5th USENIX Workshop on Hot Topics in Cloud Computing (HotCloud13) (2013)
11. Kosta, S., Perta, V., Stefa, J., Hui, P., Mei, A.: CloneDoc: exploiting the cloud to leverage secure group collaboration mechanisms for smartphones. In: Computer Communications Workshops (INFOCOM WKSHPS), 2013 IEEE Conference on IEEE, pp. 19–20 (2013)
12. Neyem, A., Ochoa, S.F., Pino, J.A., Franco, R.D.: A reusable structural design for mobile collaborative applications. J. Syst. Softw. **85**(3), 511–524 (2012)
13. Park, S., Chen, Q., Han, H., Yeom, H.Y.: Design and evaluation of mobile offloading system for web-centric devices. J. Netw. Comput. Appl. **40**, 105–115 (2014)
14. Satyanarayanan, M., Bahl, P., Caceres, R., Davies, N.: The case for vm-based cloudlets in mobile computing. IEEE Pervasive Comput. **8**(4), 14–23 (2009)
15. Shiraz, M., Gani, A.: A lightweight active service migration framework for computational offloading in mobile cloud computing. J. Supercomputing **68**(2), 978–995 (2014)
16. Xia, F., Ding, F., Li, J., Kong, X., Yang, L.T., Ma, J.: Phone2Cloud: exploiting computation offloading for energy saving on smartphones in mobile cloud computing. Inf. Syst. Front. **16**(1), 95–111 (2014)

Event-B and Modeling Languages

Deriving Event-B Models from Mealy Machines: Application to an Auction System

Christian Attiogbé[✉]

LINA - UMR CNRS 6241, University of Nantes, Nantes, France
Christian.Attiogbe@univ-nantes.fr

Abstract. Formal methods still lack guidelines to construct models. We propose a systematic modelling approach to derive an event-based model of a system from the process-oriented models of its components. An extension of Mealy machines called *polyadic Mealy machine* is proposed, formalised and used to support the process-oriented view of local models that describe the components of a system. We show how event-based models can be derived from the process-oriented Mealy machines. The local process models are composed to build a global process-oriented model of the intended initial system, i.e., we derive systematically an event-based model from the composed system. The method is illustrated through the example of an auction system which is representative of a system without a static architecture: an evolving system. The resulting specification is augmented with desired properties and then analysed using the Event-B/Rodin framework. This method is well-suited to build Event-B models in general but also models with evolving architectures.

Keywords: Event-B · Multiparadigm modelling · Mealy machine · Rodin

1 Introduction

Modelling, design and analysis of software intensive systems are difficult engineering tasks. They still raise challenging questions, especially the lack of methods to combine and reuse the analysis and specification practices. Specific methods and tools to guide the use of formal methods may help in mastering these challenges. The motivation of our work is the need of practical methods, techniques and tools to help the developers in specifying and analysing asynchronous software systems, using an event-based approach. These systems are made of several processes interacting to achieve the functionalities defined at a more general level. However, even using a formal method one can build a formal model which is proved correct with given properties but which does not meet the desired behaviour.

One difficulty of using without guidance, an event-based approach like the Event-B one, is that the structure of the behaviours of involved components is not explicitly stated. The modeller has to focus on the description of the events

© Springer International Publishing Switzerland 2015
L. Bellatreche and Y. Manolopoulos (Eds.): MEDI 2015, LNCS 9344, pp. 77–88, 2015.
DOI: 10.1007/978-3-319-23781-7_7

of the system at hand, by considering the conditions of their occurrence and their effect. But, the structuring of the system components behaviour according to these events is not straightforward and is often left implicit, i.e. it is not effectively given. This is error-prone.

In the case of the modelling of large complex systems, it is tedious to conduct the modelling only with implicit behaviours of the system components, their elicitation can considerably help in avoiding mistakes in the modelling process. However it is not easy to build an exhaustive explicit behaviour of the system. In this work we focus on a modelling method: a systematic approach to capture and build the formal model of the behaviour of the global system at hand. The method is based on the construction of an explicit process-based behaviour at the level of local components. Event-based models are derived from the process models of the components and then the overall system is built by composing the event-based models of the components. For the experimentation purpose we use Event-B[1] as the support of event-based model construction; an auction system is modelled using the presented approach.

The contribution of this work is twofold: *(i)* a multiparadigm specification approach[2] to capture and construct a global model which will be the starting point from which the developper will perform a complete Event-B development chain; a formal treatment of the multiparadigm aspect is considered; *(ii)* a complete experimentation which may serve as a cookbook for further case studies.

The remainder of the article is organised as follows: in Sect. 2 we present the materials used to conduct this work. Section 3 is devoted to the core of the specification approach. Section 4 introduces the modelling of the auction system which illustrates the method. Finally Sect. 5 concludes the article.

2 Background

Polyadic Mealy Machines. A Mealy state machine [9] describes the evolution of a process; the process is in a given state of the machine at any time. Assume we have several processes whose evolutions are supported by the same Mealy machine; we could have built the product of the state machines in order to compose the processes, but it is better to use their free product in order to have less constraints on the number of the processes to be composed. For that purpose, we extend the (monadic) Mealy machine to a *Polyadic Mealy Machine*. This is introduced in order to define very simply, how several processes can simultaneously share the same behaviour, using only one specific Mealy machine.

Definition 1. *A Polyadic Mealy Machine is a Mealy machine extended so as to simultaneously support the behaviour of several processes. The extension consists in labelling each state by a set containing the identifiers of the processes that are currently in this state.*

A polyadic Mealy machine is defined by a tuple $\langle S, L, \delta, P, \Omega \rangle$ where

---

[1] Rodin http://wiki.event-b.org/index.php/Main_Page.

[2] That combines state-machine and event-based notations.

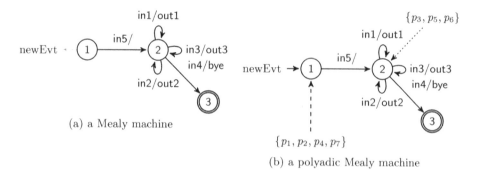

Fig. 1. Polyadic form of a process type

- S is a finite set of states among which an initial state S_0 and possible final states;
- $L = In \times Out$ is a set of labels made of an input from the set In which is the trigger (a guard – a boolean expression) of the labelled transition, an output from the set Out which is the action associated to the transition;
- $\delta : S \times L \to S$ is a partial transition function;
- P is a set of given processes;
- $\Omega : S \to \mathcal{P}(P)$ is the state annotation function.

The function Ω depends on discrete time; it is such that each state s is annotated with the set of processes which have currently reached the state s (see Fig. 1(b)). But at a given instant, a process is in exactly one state; it means that the states of the Mealy machine do not share the processes:

$$\forall s_i, s_j . s_i \in S \wedge s_j \in S \wedge s_i \neq s_j \Rightarrow \Omega(s_i) \cap \Omega(s_j) = \emptyset.$$

Operational Semantics of Polyadic Mealy Machine. While the semantics of a standard Mealy machine is given by the transition relation from the initial state with at each time the information on the current state, the semantics of our polyadic Mealy machine is the *non-deterministic co-evolution* of the processes running the transition relation. Formally, consider a polyadic Mealy machine $pM = \langle S, L, \delta, P, \Omega \rangle$; the behaviour induced by pM is given by the set of transitions enabled by pM (The next state is denoted by pM'). They are formalised by the following operational semantics rules[3].

Initially all the existing processes are in the initial state $S_0 : \Omega(S_0) = P$.

$$\frac{}{pM = \langle S, L, \delta, P, \Omega \rangle \quad \wedge \quad \exists s_0 \in S . \Omega(s_0) = P} \; P_{init}$$

---

[3] We use the set theoretic notation with the standard operators; the operator dom stands for the domain of a relation.

Any process p in a state from which the guard of a label λ is enabled[4], may evolve nondeterministically and reach the target state of the transition labelled by λ.

$$\frac{\begin{array}{c} pM = \langle S, L, \delta, P, \Omega \rangle \quad \wedge \\ ((s, \lambda), t) \in \delta \quad \wedge \quad \mathsf{guard}(\lambda) = true \quad \wedge \quad \exists p \in \Omega(s) \quad \wedge \\ \Omega'(s) = \Omega(s) - \{p\} \quad \wedge \quad \Omega'(t) = \Omega(t) \cup \{p\} \end{array}}{pM' = \langle S, L, \delta, P, \Omega' \rangle} p_{transition}$$

When all the processes reach a final state with no output transition or a state with no enabled transition, there is a deadlock.

$$\frac{\begin{array}{c} pM = \langle S, L, \delta, P, \Omega \rangle \quad \wedge \\ \exists s \mid \Omega(s) = P \wedge (s \notin \mathsf{dom}(\mathsf{dom}(\delta)) \quad \vee \\ (\ s \in \mathsf{dom}(\mathsf{dom}(\delta)) \quad \wedge \quad (\forall \lambda_i \mid (s_i, \lambda_i) \in \mathsf{dom}(\delta) \ . \ \mathsf{guard}(\lambda_i) = false) \ )) \end{array}}{pM' = \langle S, L, \delta, P, \Omega \rangle} p_{deadlock}$$

In the following we use the polyadic Mealy machine to model the components that constitute a system as *process types*[5]. The main interest is that Event-B models can be systematically derived from the polyadic Mealy machine due to the compatibility of events semantics; each transition is viewed as an occurrence of an event. Note that any expressive process-based graphical formalism can be used to sketch the behaviour of the identified processes.

Free Product of Transition Systems. The parallel composition of processes, can be built by the *free product* of the transition systems of the processes. Theoretically, their free product results in a (huge) model where a global state[6] is made of a state of each of the processes, a global transition from a global state is made of the transitions of each of the processes from its state involved in the global state. Practically, the global transitions can be constrained to avoid inconsistency in the access or update of the state variables.

While *synchronous product* is appropriate to dependent processes, free product is more appropriate to the composition of independent processes which may share communication channels. In our work, the global system is asynchronous and its involved processes can be distributed, concurrent and dynamic; wherefrom the relevance of the free product. We use the free product to compose independent processes modelled by Mealy machines; guards are used to constraint the transitions. When several guards are simultaneously true, a non-deterministic choice is made to select the process that evolves, but the other guards remain true for next evaluation.

---

[4] $\mathsf{guard}(\lambda)$ denotes the guard of a label.

[5] A process type is the set of behaviours that characterises a process.

[6] The term *global state* refers to the state of the process composition.

Overview of Event-B/Rodin. Event-B [2,7] is a modelling and development method where components are modelled as abstract machines which are composed and refined into concrete machines. An *abstract machine* describes a mathematical model of a system behaviour[7]. In an Event-B modelling process, abstract machines constitute the dynamic part whereas *Contexts* are used to describe the static part. A *Context* is seen by machines. It is made of carrier sets and constants. It may contain properties (defined on the sets and constants), axioms and theorems. A machine is made of variables and invariant, together with several *event* descriptions. *Proof Obligations* are defined to establish model consistency via invariant preservation. The Rodin[8] tool is an open tool dedicated to building and reasoning on B models.

3   B Model Derivation: The Method

We extend and improve previous results on the *P-B method[9] [3]. The improvement lies on the introduction of polyadic Mealy machines to perform a systematic and rigorous construction of the formal reference model.

3.1   Overview of the *P-B Method

The coarse grains of the steps of the method are as follows:

1. Build a *reference formal model* from the system at hand and state the desired global properties according to this formal model. The reference model is an abstract, multi-process model from which specific models may be built; it may be composed of elementary models. This step is detailed in Sect. 3.2.
2. Perform formal analysis (property verification) with the reference model.
3. Refine gradually, if necessary, the abstract formal model into less abstract ones, and perform (iteratively) formal analysis on the current model.
4. Deal with multifacet aspect if it is necessary; derive specific models in other formalisms which are specific inputs of various analysis techniques and tools; ensure the feedback and the consistency with the reference model.

   In the current article we detail and enhance the specification approach to deal with the first step (1). This step needs methods that are suited to the system at hand, hence several domain-based methods may be appropriate. Steps 2. and 3. are considered in the illustration example.

3.2   Structuring the Reference Model with Processes and Events

The undertaken approach consists in building gradually the reference model of a global system from those of its constituent processes. For this purpose, a set of processes with the same behaviour is characterised by a polyadic Mealy machine, which models the *type of the processes*. Depending on the requirements at hand, several such types may be built.

---

[7] A system behaviour is a discrete transition system.
[8] Rodin http://wiki.event-b.org/index.php/Main_Page.
[9] Multi-process specification using B.

Processes Described as Mealy Machines. We consider first the Mealy machines and then we systematically derive event-based models from the Mealy machines. From the requirements at hand, common state variables and properties are identified and described, some of them will be shared. Besides, elementary processes are identified according to the behaviours which are expressed. Depending on the cases, one can have several processes with the same behaviour hence we deal with *process types* to describe processes. Each process type is described as a polyadic Mealy machine $pM = \langle S, L, \delta, P, \Omega \rangle$ previously introduced (Sect. 2).

The definition of polyadic machine is enriched with the context of the requirements we have to model. Therefore, a process type PT_i is such that $PT_i \triangleq \langle S_i, E_i, Evt_{i_{\langle L_i, \delta_i, P_i, \Omega_i \rangle}} \rangle$ where

- S_i models the state space including the data of the context, using sets and variables;
- E_i is the set of events identified from the requirements. Describing this set meets the requirement capture and design approaches where events are first listed and then described, for example using conditions and actions.
- $Evt_{i_{\langle L_i, \delta_i, P_i, \Omega_i \rangle}}$ is the description of the events in E_i according to the transition relation $\delta_i : S_i \times L_i \rightarrow S_i$ and the state annotation function $\Omega_i : S_i \rightarrow P_i$. Each element e_i of E_i is described with a labelled transition λ_i with $\lambda_i \in L_i$; therefore λ_i is a couple (in_i, out_i) (see Definition 1). We use the form (e_i, λ_i) to denote the element of Evt_i. Consequently $Evt_{i_{\langle L_i, \delta_i, P_i, \Omega_i \rangle}}$ is abstracted as $\langle E_i, \delta_i \rangle$ in the forthcoming algorithms.

In the sequel we use the structure $PT_i \triangleq \langle S_i, E_i, Evt_{i_{\langle L_i, \delta_i, P_i, \Omega_i \rangle}} \rangle$ to describe and to compose the local process types which will form the global model.

Consider for example a process type *buyer* in an *auction application*. Several buyers are there and they have the same behaviour with respect to the auction. But, the current buyers are not always performing the same actions; they are not all in the same states. When some buyers are just registered, some others are already buying or consulting the available items. A polyadic Mealy machine captures easily the situation. In the same way, all other processes (for instance Seller, Manager) identified in the auction application will be described.

Global Model: Composing the Process Types. We build a global formal model by composing the local process types previously built.

Interaction with Abstract Channels. Shared abstract channels are introduced to link the interacting processes and to make them communicate. An abstract channel is modelled as a set; it is used to wait for a message or to deposit it.

For the interaction purpose, the defined process types are linked with the identified common data and abstract channels. The abstract channels are modelled according to the interaction needs; each process type uses, independently from the other processes, the global variables that denote the defined abstract channels and state variables. Hence the interaction between the processes is handled using these shared abstract channels. The communications are achieved in a completely decoupled way to favour dynamic structuring. A process may deposit a message in the channel, other processes may retrieve the message from the channel.

Composition of the Processes. A bottom-up view is adopted where the composition of process types is explicit. Practically the composition by a merging can be implicit during the modelling of the considered processes. The described processes are combined by a *fusion* operation $\uplus$ which merges an undefined number of process types. We build on the existing works [1,11]; the fusion operation merges the state spaces and the events of the processes into a single global system Sys_g which has the conjunction of the invariants, and which in turn can also be involved in other fusion operations. The semantics basis is the use of the free product (see Sect. 2).

$$ Sys_g \;\widehat{=}\; \uplus_i PT_i \;\;=\;\; \uplus_i \langle S_i, E_i, Evt_i \rangle \;\;=\;\; \langle S_g, E_g, Evt_g \rangle $$

When process types are merged, a variable denoting the set of processes of each type is maintained in order to identify the processes of this type. The variable is then used in the guards for distinguishing the events related to each type. Moreover the cardinal of the set of processes can vary, making it easier to model the composition of unbounded number of processes. The processes access the global state and communicate with others processes through their events.

3.3   Derivation of the Event-Based Model from the Process Types

According to the semantics of a polyadic Mealy machine, the transition from a state s to another one is non-deterministically achieved by one of the processes (described with $\Omega(s)$) in the state s. The guards of the events capture this semantics. The event-based model of the machine is then obtained by translating systematically each transition of the polyadic Mealy machine into an event. We get the behaviour of a process type by combining the occurrences of its resulting events. We introduce for this purpose a derivation schema to describe the event of Evt_i. Each element (e_i, λ_i) of Evt_i is expanded as $(e_i, (in_i, out_i))$ and then in the form $e_i \;\widehat{=}\; in_i \;\rightarrow\; out_i$, where in_i represents the guard of the event and out_i the action performed when the event occurs. To generalise, the generic form $evt \;\widehat{=}\; guard \;\rightarrow\; action$ is formatted with the more readable syntactic form:

$$ evt \;\widehat{=}\; \text{when } guard \text{ /* the condition to enable the event */} $$
$$ \text{then } action \text{ /* the action performed by the event */} $$
$$ \text{end} $$

A process type PT is characterised by a list of events e_P which are guarded by the type PT itself[10]; these events will be enabled only for processes of type PT. Accordingly an event without a guard describes a behaviour shared by all processes, whatever its type.

---

[10] As a type is a property, it is safe to write a guard $p \in PT$ to express that p has the property PT.

for each process type $PT_i = \langle S_i, E_i, Evt_i \rangle$:
    for each $(e_i, \lambda_i) \in Evt_i$ with $((s_i, \lambda_i), s_j) \in \delta_i$ where $\lambda_i = (in_i, out_i)$
       Generate an event e_{λ_i} associated to λ as follows:

$$e_{\lambda_i} \;\hat{=}\; \text{ANY } p \text{ WHERE } p \in PT_i \;\wedge$$
$$p \in \Omega(s_i) \;\wedge\; in_i \;\; /^* \; in_i = \mathsf{guard}(\lambda_i) \; ^*/$$

      THEN

$$\Omega(s_i) := \Omega(s_i) - \{p\} \quad /^* \text{ update of } \Omega \; ^*/$$
$$\Omega(s_j) := \Omega(s_j) \cup \{p\} \quad /^* \text{ update of } \Omega \; ^*/$$
$$\text{perform the action } out_i \text{ associated to } \lambda_i$$

      END

Fig. 2. Algorithm to derive events from process type

The derivation of the core event model from the behavioural semantic rules (see Sect. 2) of the polyadic Mealy machine is then achieved with the following algorithm (see Fig. 2). This derivation algorithm is then generalised to several types and extended with the treatment of data specific to the processes.

Generalising the Derivation of Event-Model from Process Types. Consider a process type PT where each process p has the features aa, ff and a behaviour defined by the events e_l, e_g. To deal with several processes of the same type PT we need a subset $thePTs$ of PT; therefore a function is used to distinguish the feature aa or ff of each element p of the subset $thePTs$. More generally, each feature that is modelled with a variable in one process type,

Derivation from S_i ————————————————

USED SETS

PT	/* a given process type */
Da	/* the value domain of feature aa */
Df	/* the value domain of feature ff */
GT	/* a given type */
$ChanT$	/* a channel type */
$\ldots$	

INVARIANT PROPERTIES

$thePTs \subseteq PT$	/* the set of processes of type PT : P */
$aa : thePTs \rightarrow Da$	/* each process has an a */
$ff : thePTs \rightarrow Df$	/* each process has an f */
$gv : GT$	/* a global variable with a given type */
$gChan : ChanT$	/* a global variable modelling a channel */
$\ldots$	

Fig. 3. Global shape of event-based model derived from process type (1)

results in a function from the set of process identifiers to the value domain of the considered feature. A process p may have access to global variables modelling its environment. The guard of each event of p may use global variables gv and also local variables l resulting in an explicit predicate $cond(p, l)$ or $cond(p, gv, l)$. In the same way the action may update global variables. Note that the subset $thePTs$ meets the set P in the definition of polyadic machine, thus the modifications of Ω are achieved via the modification of $thePTs$. The generalised derivation schema for any $PT_i = \langle S_i, E_i, Evt_i \rangle$ is as in Figs. 3 and 4.

Derivation from E_i, Evt_i ———————————
EVENT DESCRIPTIONS
$e_l =$ any p, l /* event depending on local variables l */
         where $p \in thePTs$ /* p is one of the processes */
               $\wedge \ cond_{(p,gv,l)}$ /* with specific conditions $cond_{(p,l)}$ */
         then
                update of $ThePTs$ /* that is update of Ω */
                . . .   /* update of other state variables : out */
         end ;
$e_g =$ any p /* an event with gv a global variable */
         where $p \in thePTs \ \wedge \ cond_{(p,gv)}$
         then
                update of $ThePTs$ /* that is update of Ω */
                . . .   /* update of global variables : out */
         end

Fig. 4. Global shape of event-based model derived from process type (2)

Translation into Event-B. According to the shape and the semantics adopted for the derivation of the event models, the translation into Event-B of the derived event-based model is straightforward. Asynchronous communication is modelled with the interleaved composition of process behaviours viewed as event occurrences. Event-B/Rodin framework is used for the experimention.

4   Illustration: The Auction System

The auction system is a benchmark[11] treated with several approaches [5,6]. It describes a distributed interaction between several processes of different types; they communicate via messages. In the auction system, items are proposed by sellers and bought after bids.

---

[11] (See for example Rubis http://rubis.ow2.org/).

The Auction System (à la eBay). The informal requirements of the auction system are as follows.

"An auction site implements the core functionality of an auction: selling, browsing and bidding. Several sessions are distinguished: visitor sessions, buyer sessions and seller sessions. In a visitor session, users do not need to register but they are only allowed to browse items. Buyer and seller sessions require registration. In addition to the functionality provided during visitor sessions, within a buyer session users can bid on items and consult a summary of their current bids, ratings and comments left by other users. Seller sessions require a fee before a user is allowed to put up an item for sale. An auction starts immediately and lasts for a given delay (typically no more than a week). The seller can specify a reserve (minimum) price for an item."

Capturing the Process Behaviours with Process Types. From the requirements we distinguish three kinds of processes corresponding to the described user sessions: *visitor, buyer and seller*. We introduce a process *manager* to model the orchestration of the bids. Applying the proposed method, we capture the behaviour of each process type, using the extended Mealy machine. A simplified behaviour of the buyer, where the transitions are only labelled by an event name is depicted in Fig. 5. The set of events of the Buyer process is then obtained: $E_b = \{b\_register, b\_start, b\_placeBid, b\_browse, b\_consultItem, b\_pay, b\_waitItem, b\_leave\}$. This step helps to tune quickly the desired behaviour and to correct it in case of mistakes.

We modelled the behaviour of the other processes with extended Mealy machines. The names of the events are prefixed by the initial letter of the process name so as to favour readability. These four Mealy machines are then used to build the four process types.

$$VISITOR \;\widehat{=}\; \langle State_v, E_v, Events_v\rangle; SELLER \;\widehat{=}\; \langle State_s, E_s, Events_s\rangle$$
$$BUYER \;\widehat{=}\; \langle State_b, E_b, Events_b\rangle; MANAGER \;\widehat{=}\; \langle State_m, E_m, Events_m\rangle$$

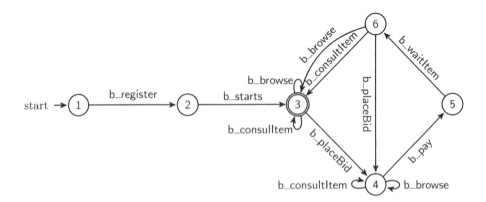

Fig. 5. A simplified (Mealy) view of the buyer's behaviour

Merging the Process Types into a Global Model. The targeted global reference model is the composition of the process models of the four identified processes using the fusion operator. We get a global model $Auction_g$ from which we derive the event-based model of the auction system.

$$Auction_g = \biguplus \{VISITOR, \ SELLER, \ BUYER, \ MANAGER\}.$$

Deriving the Event-Based Model. The event-based model is derived from the process types using the derivation algorithm presented in Sect. 3.3. The obtained event-based model is completed by an invariant stating the required properties. For illustration, the complete Event-Models can be found at our website[12].

Formal Analysis of the Final Event-B Model. To illustrate the use of the obtained reference model we show how preliminary analysis are performed.

Consistency Analysis. Consistency analysis is based on the invariant properties and the proof obligations generated using Rodin.

Reachability Analysis. An example of such property is as follows: *"The received items are those shipped (for some buyers)"*. After analysis and according to the modelling choices, the property is restructured and rephrased as: *When there are some bought items, the items owned by someone as bought items, are those which have been payed and shipped.*

$$boughtItems \neq \emptyset \Rightarrow dom(boughtItems) \subseteq shippedItems \qquad (\mathbf{P}_{ob})$$

The properties are incorporated in the invariant and then analysed. The Rodin tool is used to work out the Event-B model. A total of 85 proof obligations is generated; 100 % of the PO are proved (one PO needs an interactive proof).

5   Conclusion

We proposed a method to systematically capture an event-based global model of a system using a process-oriented model. The process-oriented model is used to derive an event-based model using the semantics of a polyadic Mealy machine which is introduced in this work. The event-model is then translated into Event-B. The method which is proposed to capture the global formal model, is an enhancement of the preliminary step of a methodological approach previously proposed to guide the modelling and analysis of different kinds of software. An auction system is used to illustrate the proposed method. For practical experimentations, the Rodin tool is used to analyse the obtained Event-B model.

---

[12] http://pagesperso.lina.univ-nantes.fr/info/perso/permanents/attiogbe/nabla/
M2BAuction/.

As far as related works are concerned, there are works [4,10] that combine Event-B and process Algebra (CSP); they help to structure the interaction between sub-systems modelled using B; unlike our approach they are not dedicated to help the construction of B components. At a different abstraction level, the synthesis of program codes from finite state machines is close to our work. To the best of our knowledge, there is no similar works which adopt a similar approach to guide the use of event-based methods including Event-B. In [8], the authors propose a translation into Event-B from a formalism combining graphical notation and process algebra. The translation of the behaviours are related, but their focus is on the analysis of information systems, instead of assisting event-based modelling as we done. But, in the category of works dedicated to methods to apply B, the authors of [7] give a methodology of using B patterns to construct B models; this is a complementary approach to fight the problem of lack of methods to build formal models. We plan to mechanise the derivation of events schema, in order to increase the assistance on Event-B modelling.

References

1. Abadi, M., Lamport, L.: Conjoining specifications. ACM Trans. Program. Lang. Syst. **17**(3), 507–535 (1995)
2. Abrial, J.-R.: Modeling in Event-B: System and Software Engineering. Cambridge University Press, New York (2010)
3. Attiogbé, C.: Event-based approach to modeling dynamic architecture: application to mobile adhoc network. In: Margaria, T., Steffen, B. (eds.) Leveraging Applications of Formal Methods, Verification and Validation, ISOLA 2008. CCIS, vol. 17, pp. 769–781. Springer, Heidelberg (2008)
4. Butler, M., Leuschel, M.: Combining CSP and B for specification and property verification. In: Fitzgerald, J.S., Hayes, I.J., Tarlecki, A. (eds.) FM 2005. LNCS, vol. 3582, pp. 221–236. Springer, Heidelberg (2005)
5. Chen, B., Sadaoui, S.: Simulation and verification of a dynamic online auction. In: IASTED Conference on Software Engineering - SEA 2003 (2003)
6. Hillston, J., Kloul, L.: Performance investigation of an on-line auction system. Concurrency Comput. Pract. Experience **13**(1), 23–41 (2001)
7. Hoang, T.S., Kuruma, H., Basin, D.A., Abrial, J.-R.: Developing topology discovery in Event-B. Sci. Comput. Program. **74**(11–12), 879–899 (2009)
8. Milhau, J., Frappier, M., Gervais, F., Laleau, R.: Systematic translation rules from ASTD to Event-B. In: Méry, D., Merz, S. (eds.) IFM 2010. LNCS, vol. 6396, pp. 245–259. Springer, Heidelberg (2010)
9. Roth, C.H., Kinney, L.L.: Fundamentals of Logic Design. Thomson/Brooks/Cole, Belmont (2004)
10. Schneider, S., Treharne, H., Wehrheim, H.: A CSP approach to control in Event-B. In: Méry, D., Merz, S. (eds.) IFM 2010. LNCS, vol. 6396, pp. 260–274. Springer, Heidelberg (2010)
11. Zave, P., Jackson, M.: Conjunction as composition. ACM Trans. Softw. Eng. Methodol. **2**(4), 379–411 (1993)

Integrating Domain-Based Features into Event-B: A Nose Gear Velocity Case Study

Dominique Méry[(⊠)], Rushikesh Sawant, and Anton Tarasyuk

Université de Lorraine, LORIA, BP 239, 54506 Vandœuvre-lès-Nancy, France
`dominique.mery@loria.fr`, `rushikesh.sawant@gmail.com`,
`anton.tarasyuk@abo.fi`

Abstract. This paper presents the formal modelling of a nose gear velocity system, a software-based system for estimating the ground velocity of an aircraft. We employ the Event-B modelling language to conduct this case study. Event-B allows us to construct and verify the formal model of the system using the incremental refinement-based process. The main goal of the case study is to highlight the need for separating and integrating explicit semantics of application domain into the formal development process. Traditionally in Event-B development, domain descriptions of systems containing domain knowledge are treated as second-class citizens, and the modelling is implicit and usually distributed between the requirements model and the system model. In this paper, we highlight the need for explicit modelling of domain contexts as first-class citizens, and we illustrate concepts related to implicit and explicit semantics with the help of an example in Event-B.

Keywords: Modelling · Refinement · Formal method · Event-B · Implicit semantics · Explicit semantics · Nose gear velocity

1 Introduction

Rigorous modelling and verification of software intensive systems is an actively developing area of software engineering that is well supported by variety of methods and tools, e.g., model-checking, automated theorem-provers, simulation and animation tools, satisfiability solvers, etc. Usually, these methods and tools allow the developer to construct a *formal model* of a system under construction and enable verification of critical system properties, such as performance, reliability, safety, etc. One of the goals of rigorous modelling approaches is the support for effective requirements engineering since capturing and structuring valid system requirements remains one of the main challenges in software engineering.

In refinement-based methods, such as Event-B [1], an induction principle is *implicitly* integrated. It is used for proving correctness properties by discharging

This work was supported by grant ANR-13-INSE-0001 (The IMPEX Project http://impex.loria.fr) from the Agence Nationale de la Recherche (ANR) and by a project supported by Région Lorraine Certification des systèmes logiciels médicaux avec une méthode formelle (october 2013–october 2014).

L. Bellatreche and Y. Manolopoulos (Eds.): MEDI 2015, LNCS 9344, pp. 89–102, 2015.
DOI: 10.1007/978-3-319-23781-7_8

proof obligations that are automatically generated. We refer to these features as *implicit semantics*, as they are provided by the underlying theory (in this case, semantics of Event-B). On the other hand, domain knowledges constitute *explicit semantics* as they provide external informations about the domain within which system operates. It has been shown that the domain knowledge [4,5] is crucial and critical to design safe software-based systems which interact with and, or, respond to events originating in environment. For example, consider a data bus ensuring communication among software agents (nodes), and one agent is waiting for data expressed in the *metric unit system*, while another one requires same data in the *imperial unit system*. The data here, for example, can be the speed of some vehicle. In this case, respective unit system for each agent provides critical information for further processing the received data. Another case is the evaluation of the velocity of an aircraft, expressed in miles per hour, whereas some other interacting system or component requires a precision in kilometers per hour. As a one more example, consider the problem of positioning: a vehicle is guided by the control system and has the strong requirement to *know* where it is currently on the route. In this case, it is critical that validation of data on the route should make a clear distinction between an absolute data and a relative data.

Allowing formal methods users and developers to integrate — in a flexible and modular manner — both the implicit semantics, offered by the formal methods, and the explicit semantics, provided by external formal knowledge models (e.g., ontologies), is a major research challenge [3]. In an attempt to tackle this problem, we consider the case study of a *Nose Gear velocity system* [7]. It is a critical function responsible for estimating the ground velocity of an aircraft. We employ the Event-B modelling language and its inherent *refinement* technique to formally derive and verify the model of the system. We use this formal model for identifying and evaluating explicit features involved in this development. The case study has been developed using the Rodin platform – an integrated development environment for Event-B [2].

Related work on integrating domain contexts and formal methods includes notes of MacCarthy [8] proposing *the introduction of contexts as abstract mathematical entities with useful properties for AI*. Here, a context defines the frame related to the domain of the problem. More recently, Schmidtke and Woo [10] studied pervasive computing systems and proposed to formally describe pervasive computing systems as distributed concurrent systems operating on the background of a mereotopological context model. It allows to integrate the operating environment into the model. Finally, Ait-Ameur et al. [3] introduce questions related to the integration of implicit and explicit semantics in proof-based development method.

The paper is organised as follows. Section 2 introduces the *Nose Gear velocity* problem. In Sect. 3, we present an overview of the case study development and the reader can consult the link http://eb2all.loria.fr for obtaining the Event-B archive of the complete *Nose Gear velocity* model. Section 4 discusses the paper contribution and summarises the lessons learnt. Finally, in Sect. 5, we conclude by discussion of future research directions.

2   The Case Study and the Modelling Language

The system under consideration is a *Nose Gear (NG) Velocity Update* function. It is responsible for estimating the velocity of an aircraft while moving on the ground. This case study was first posed as a verification challenge in *Third Workshop on Theorem Proving in Certification* in 2013. We develop this case study since it represents a typical system consisting of multiple heterogeneous components working together to produce the expected output. It also represents components assuming different domain knowledge regarding received data. Hence, it is suitable for our goal of exposing the need for identifying and integrating explicit semantics in formal modelling. We briefly describe the system and introduce the Event-B modelling language in this section.

In the *NG velocity system*, the velocity is estimated by calculating an elapsed time for a complete rotation of a nose gear wheel. These rotations are monitored by an electro-mechanical sensor connected to a computer. Whenever there is a complete rotation of the nose gear wheel, the sensor generates a *click* (also called 'pulse'), which subsequently generates a *hardware interrupt*. An interrupt service routine (ISR) of the system is then responsible for serving these interrupts. The ISR increments a 16-bit counter, *NGRotations*, to capture a complete rotation of the NG wheel, and stores the current time of an update in a 16-bit variable, *NGClickTime*.

The NG velocity system is equipped with a millisecond counter called *Millisecs*. This counter is incremented once every millisecond and provides a read-only access of its current value to all components in the system.

Another component of the system is a real time operating system (RTOS), responsible for *invoking* the update function. The RTOS makes sure that this function is invoked *at least once* every 500 ms. However, the exact time of each invocation relative to a hardware interrupt is *not* predictable.

Finally, the update function is responsible for estimating the current velocity of an aircraft on the ground. This estimation is based on currently available values of accessible counters. Estimated velocity is stored in a variable called *estimatedGroundVelocity*. Update function has a read-only access to *Millisecs* counter along with *NGRotations* counter and a global variable *NGClickTime*. Also, the diameter of the NG wheel is vailable to the function as a compile time constant called, *WHEEL_DIAMETER*. Moreover, the function *can* store all the necessary private data required for calculating an estimation of the ground velocity. These values are protected from invocation to invocation.

There is one explicit requirement for this system, EXFUN-1: *While the aircraft is on the ground, the estimated velocity shall be within 3 km/hr of the true velocity of the aircraft at some moment within the past 3 s.* Along with EXFUN-1, we have systematically extracted several other implicit/derived requirements from this requirements description. In the next section, we present the formal model of the system and address these requirements.

Event-B [1] is a formal modelling language for expressing state-based models of reactive systems. It is supported by two proof-assistant-based environments, namely Rodin [2]. The construction of an Event-B model is based on concepts like sets, constants, axioms, theorems, variables, invariants, events; these syntactic constructions are organised in two kinds of structures, namely *contexts* for modelling static informations and *machines* or expressing *events* modifying *state variables* satisfying *invariants* and *safety* properties. The validity of a context and a machine is achieved by *discharging* generated proof obligations using proof assistants. Proof obligations states conditions derived from the principles for deriving safety and invariance properties. We are not giving details of syntax and semantics of Event-B and we will progressively add more details when developing the case study in the next section.

3   Development of Nose Gear Velocity

In this section, we present our attempt on formal modelling of the NG velocity update function. This development has been performed with a traditional Event-B modelling approach. That is, we do not treat domain features (explicit semantics) differently in this development but rather use it as a starting point for that purpose, and identify them.

The development strategy employed for this modelling is such that we start with a very *unconstrained* view of the system. We introduce all components of the system independently in an incremental fashion, and then, in later refinement steps, we establish relationships between these components as per requirements. As we proceed, we gradually unfold a detailed representation of the system, with an attempt to address a single functionality (or a system component) at each refinement level. Finally, once all necessary relationships between components have been established, we address the main requirement, EXFUN-1.

3.1   Initial Model: Updating Ground Velocity

The initial model is the most abstract specification of the system. It introduces the most fundamental functionality of the system – estimation of the ground velocity – at utmost abstract level. Hence, this model consists of a single event addressing an estimation of the ground velocity, which states *what* is expected of our system and not *how* this estimation is performed.

A state variable *esmt_velocity* stores a current estimated velocity of an aircraft, while event updateGroundVelocity states that *esmt_velocity* holds some value in *MPH* unit. A variable *old_velocity* records an old estimated value when *esmt_velocity* variable is updated with a new estimation. The record of the old velocity is required to specify system properties (for instance, *"estimated velocity is always available"*) later in the development.

INVARIANTS
$inv1 : esmt\_velocity \in MPH$
$inv2 : old\_velocity \in MPH$

```
updateGroundVelocity
begin
  act1 : esmt_velocity :∈ MPH
  act2 : old_velocity := esmt_velocity
end
```

The context for this model introduces new type *MPH* (stands for miles per hour) to model estimated ground velocity. This type is abstractly specified by a set MPH and (constant) injective function $mph \in \mathbb{N} \rightarrowtail MPH$.[1] Note that we make use of *explicit types* to model units in this development. This design decision based on two observations – (1) model is easier to communicate with other stakeholders (designers, developers, etc.), as it becomes explicit regrading manipulations of types and their use; (2) from modelling perspective, assigning types (rather than treating them subsets of $\mathbb{N}$) creates distinct entities which results in more transparent proofs.

3.2 First Refinement: Introducing Time Progression

The *NG velocity system* is primarily constrained by the *time*. Our first refinement introduces a *milliseconds* counter incrementing for each millisecond. With this counter we capture the progression of time for the system. As stated in the system description, we have to model *milliseconds* counter with a 16-bit capacity constraint. We assume that the counter is *unsigned*. Hence, the counter is modelled with a modular semantics.

To model the progressing time, we introduce four new variables *Millisec*, *dummyTick*, *updateTime*, *updateRecords* and one new event MillisecTicks in this refinement.

```
INVARIANTS
    inv1 : dummyTick ∈ ℕ ∧ Millisec ∈ ms[0..MAXBIT]
    inv2 : updateTime ∈ ms[0..MAXBIT] ∧ updateRecords ⊆ ℕ
    inv3 : updateRecords ≠ ∅ ⇒ dummyTick > 0
    inv4 : esmt_velocity ≠ mph(0) ∨ old_velocity ≠ mph(0) ⇒ updateRecords ≠ ∅
```

Context for this refinement introduces a new set $MILLISECOND$ and three constants. The set $MILLISEC$-OND is used as a distinct type to represent the time in milliseconds.

```
AXIOMS
    axm1 : ms ∈ ℕ ↣ MILLISECOND
    axm2 : MAXBIT ∈ ℕ₁
    axm3 : modMaxBit ∈ ℤ ↣ 0..MAXBIT
```

```
MillisecTicks
begin
    act1 : Millisec := ms(modMaxBit(dummyTick + 1))
    act2 : dummyTick := dummyTick + 1
end
```

Event MillisecTicks models the progression of time for the system.

Introduction of the time here is necessary to establish various properties of the system in the later development. As *Millisec* counter has to be 16-bit, the problem is to model and establish properties related to continuous progression of time within Event-B. For this purpose, we introduce a new state variable, *dummyTick*, which is modelled as an *always incrementing* counter and assigned to *Millisec*. Variable *dummyTick* is a *dummy* variable used to establish time related system properties in this model – for example, "*ground velocity update is done at some time in the future*".

---

[1] Axioms listing for each context in this ocument is not complete. Here, we list *typing* axioms so hat relationships between different types are clear to the reader.

Finally, *updateTime* records the last update time for *esmt_velocity*, while set variable *updateRecords* keeps track of all previous ground velocity estimation times.

```
updateGroundVelocity
when
    grd1 : dummyTick > 0
then
    act1 : esmt_velocity :∈ MPH
    act2 : old_velocity := esmt_velocity
    act3 : updateTime := Millisec
    act4 : updateRecords := updateRecords ∪ {dummyTick}
end
```

3.3 Second Refinement: Introducing Interrupt Service Routine

ISR in the *NG velocity system* is responsible for updating rotation counter and records the service request time. As per the system description, *NGRotations* counter is a 16-bit counter. However, it is observed that *NGRotations* counter can be modelled as an *always incrementing* counter– taking into account possible diameters of an aircraft wheel, a 16-bit rotations counter is more than enough for the longest existing runway. To model the ISR functionality, we introduce

```
serviceInterrupt
when
    grd1 : dummyTick > 0
then
    act1 : NGRotations := NGRotations + 1
    act2 : NGClickTime := Millisec
    act3 : interruptRecords := interruptRecords ∪ dummyTick
    act4 : oldRotationCount := NGRotations
end
```

four state variables *NGRotations*, *NGClick Time*, *oldRotation-Count* and *interruptRecords*, as well as one new event serviceInterrupt.

```
INVARIANTS
    inv1 : NGRotations ∈ ℕ ∧ oldRotationCount ∈ ℕ ∧ NGClickTime ∈ ms[0..MAXBIT]
    inv2 : interruptRecords ⊆ ℕ ∧ finite(interruptRecords)
    inv3 : interruptRecords ≠ ∅ ⇒ dummyTick > 0
    inv4 : updateRecords ≠ ∅ ⇒ interruptRecords ≠ ∅
    inv5 : interruptRecords ≠ ∅ ⇒ NGRotations − RotationCount = 1
    inv6 : dummyTick ∈ interruptRecords ⇒ NGClickTime = Millisec
```

As discussed earlier, *NGRotations* is modelled as always incrementing counter that records the number of complete rotations of a nose gear wheel. We increment it by one each time an interrupt is serviced (see event serviceInterrupt below). A new state variable, *oldRotationCount*, is used to record previous value of *NGRotations* after it is updated with a new value. Variable *NGClickTime* is confined automatically to modular semantics as it receives values from *Millisec* counter.

In the same spirit of collecting information about the system states, *interruptRecords* is used as a set for recording time for each invocation of ISR. With the help of this information we can prove that *"NG Velocity system will start estimating ground velocity only after at least one interrupt is serviced"*.

Invariants (3,4,5,6) establish new properties related to serving an interrupt introduced by a serviceInterrupt event. Finally, one more detail is revealed in this refinement – velocity estimations occur only after *at least one* interrupt has been serviced. This is achieved by strengthening guards of updateGroundVelocity: *interruptRecords ≠ ∅*.

3.4   Third Refinement: Introducing an Electro-Mechanical Sensor

The sensor is responsible for generating a *click*. We model it as a hardware interrupt generated after each complete rotation. *click* is represented by either 0 or 1, where 0 indicates that there is no hardware interrupt or a requested interrupt has been served, while 1 indicates that there is a *new* hardware interrupt and it needs to be served. To model this sensor we introduce events for *monitoring rotation progress* and *detection of a complete rotation*. Finally, this refinement also addresses that no false-positive click is generated and each complete rotation takes some time.

To model the sensor, we introduce three new variables *click, rotationAngle, clickRecords* and two new events – one for monitoring rotation progress of a wheel (monitorRotationProgress) and one for generation of a click on a complete rotation (detectRotationComplete). We do not list actions of these events here, but rather discuss them in order to give overall idea. The model invariants are presented below:

```
INVARIANTS
   inv1 : click ∈ {0, 1} ∧ rotationAngle ∈ degree[0..359] ∧ clickRecords ⊆ ℕ
   inv2 : clickRecords ≠ ∅ ⟹ dummyTick > 0
   inv3 : rotationAngle = degree(359) ⟹ dummyTick > 0
   inv4 : rotationAngle = degree(359) ⟹ dummyTick ∉ clickRecords
   inv5 : click = 1 ⟹ dummyTick ∈ clickRecords
   inv6 : click = 1 ⟹ rotationAngle = degree(0)
   inv7 : dummyTick ∈ clickRecords ∧ click = 0 ⟹ Millisec = NGClickTime
   inv8 : click = 0 ∧ dummyTick ∈ interruptRecords ⟹⟹ dummyTick ∈ clickRecords
```

The context for this refinement step defines a new explicit type *DEGREE* to model rotation progress for the NG wheel. As before, we also define a mapping $degree \in \mathbb{N} \rightarrowtail DEGREE$.

Event monitorRotationProgress can be considered as a first part for the required functionality of the sensor. Its action captures the progression of a rotation angle (*rotationAngle*). Event detectRotationComplete then constitutes the second part of the functionality. This event is triggered when a complete rotation is detected. State variable *click* is set to *1* to indicate that there is a new hardware interrupt generated by the sensor. The event monitorRotationProgress is a *non-blocking* event. That is, after reporting a new hardware interrupt, sensor continues its work of monitoring the next rotation. With these two events, we establish four new properties targeted for this refinement step – invariants 3,4,5,6,7,8. Variable *clickRecords* is used for keeping record of all interrupts generated since initialisation.

click establisesh the relationship between the electro-mechanical sensor and the ISR in the previous refinement step – once a hardware interrupt is generated (i.e., *click* := 1), ISR can immediately serve that interrupt – it updates the rotations counter and records that click time. Essentially we model the fact that some time progresses with each rotation of a wheel. Hence, in this refinement step we strengthen the guards of serviceInterrupt event so that it is enabled only when there is a new (unserviced) hardware interrupt.

3.5   Fourth Refinement: Modelling Basic Functionality of RTOS

A real time operating system (RTOS) invokes the update function *at least once* every 500 ms. The case study document [7] explicitly mentions that the exact invocation time relative to a hardware interrupt is not *predictable*. The only assurance we have here is that RTOS will invoke the function once every 500 ms. We also need to model the case that, once invoked, velocity estimation must complete within 500 ms.

INVARIANTS
   $inv1 : invokeTime \in ms[0..MAXBIT]$
   $inv2 : updateInvoked \in BOOL$
   $inv3 : updateInvoked = TRUE \Rightarrow interruptRecords \neq \varnothing$
   $inv4 : Millisec \neq invokeTime \Rightarrow$
        $ms(modMaxBit(ms^{-1}(Millisec) - ms^{-1}(invokeTime))) \in ms[0..500]$
   $inv5 : Millisec = updateTime \Rightarrow$
        $ms(modMaxBit(ms^{-1}(updateTime) - ms^{-1}(invokeTime))) \in ms[0..500]$

We model the basic functionality of RTOS explained above and we introduce two new state variables – a variable *updateInvoked* that flags the invocation of update function, and variable *invokeTime* used to record the exact time at which update function has been invoked. The invocation of the update function is modelled by event invokeUpdate.

---
invokeUpdate
when
   $grd1 : interruptRecords \neq \varnothing$
   $grd2 : updateInvoked = FALSE$
   $grd3 : Millisec \neq updateTime$
then
   $act1 : updateInvoked := TRUE$
   $act2 : invokeTime := Millisec$
end

In this refinement step, we also add constraints on event MillisecTicks to establish following system properties – *"ground velocity function is invoked at least once every 500 ms"* and *"once invoked, update should finish within 500 ms"*.

These properties are totally time dependent, and since we have already introduced the notion of progressing time in our model, these properties are addressed in a straightforward manner at this step (invariants 4 and 5).

The condition (guard) for executing updateGroundVelocity is now changed – it can now be entered when there is an invocation by an RTOS: *updateInvoked = TRUE*. Earlier abstract models had information related to serviced interrupts only, so event could be entered when there is at least one interrupt is serviced, which is ultimately the effect of an invocation by RTOS.

3.6   Fifth Refinement: Modelling the Estimation Process

Now that we have introduced all functional components of the system, in this refinement we model *how* an update function estimates the ground velocity. This step addresses two specific cases – (1) the aircraft travels some distance in a given time interval and an update occurs; (2) zero distance is travelled in a given time interval and an update occurs.

Modelling the estimation process requires to take into account the computation of a travelled distance and an elapsed time before the actual estimation of the current velocity. There are six new variables introduced in this refinement step – *elapsedTime, travldDist, lastRotations, lastClickTime, et_computed* and *td_computed* – as well as three new events for modelling the estimation – update_zeroTravlDist, computeDistance and computeElapsedTime.

```
INVARIANTS
    inv1 : elapsedTime ∈ MILLISECONDS ∧ travldDist ∈ INCH ∧ lastRotations ∈ ℕ
    inv2 : lastClickTime ∈ ms[0..MAXBIT] ∧ et_computed ∈ BOOL ∧ td_computed ∈ BOOL
    inv3 : NGRotations ⩾ lastRotations
    inv4 : et_computed = TRUE ∧ td_computed = TRUE ⇒updateInvoked = TRUE
    inv5 : et_computed = TRUE ⇒ elapsedTime ≠ ms(0)
    inv6 : travldDist = inch(0) ∧ updateInvoked = FALSE ⇒esmt_velocity = old_velocity
    inv7 : et_computed = TRUE ⇒
              ms(modMaxBit(ms⁻¹(Millisec) − ms⁻¹(invokeTime))) ∈ ms[0..500]
    inv8 : td_computed = TRUE ⇒
              ms(modMaxBit(ms⁻¹(Millisec) − ms⁻¹(invokeTime))) ∈ ms[0..500]
```

Context for this refinement introduces three new explicit types – *INCH, MILE, HOUR*. Constructing functions are also introduced for respective explicit types, such as *inch, mile, hour*. These are required for mapping between Event-B supported integer types and our explicit types. Moreover, we define three additional constants *WHEEL_CIRC, cmpElpsdTime* and *mph_velo*. The first one represents the circumference of the aircraft wheel (computed from given wheel diameter), the second one is the abstract function that computes the elapsed time, and the last one is the abstract function that converts estimated velocity form inches per millisecond into miles per hour.

```
AXIOMS
    axm1 : inch ∈ ℕ ↣ INCH ∧ hour ∈ ℕ ↣ HOUR ∧ mile ∈ ℕ ↣ MILE
    axm4 : WHEEL_CIRC ∈ INCH \ {inch(0)}
    axm5 : cmpElspdTime ∈ MILLISECONDS ↠ MILLISECONDS \ {ms(0)}
    axm6 : mph_velo ∈ (INCH × MILLISECONDS) ↠ MPH
```

A new event update_zeroTravlDist is enabled when there is no distance travelled (see guard *travldDist = inch(0)*) and an update process is initiated. With this event we model that even though there is no distance travelled, update is performed for a newly calculated elapsed time. The necessary condition to perform velocity update is that the computation of a travelled distance and an elapsed time must have been performed earlier. That is, new state variables *et_computed* and *td_computed* are set to *TRUE*.

Events computeDistance and computeElapsedTime are modelled as sort of '*sub-states*'. They are indeed part of the overall velocity estimation process. Once there is an invocation by RTOS, either of the two events can be executed. Once both these events have been executed, then, based on the value of travldDist, either event updateGroundVelocity or update_zeroTrvalDist is triggered.

```
update_zeroTravlDist
when
    grad1 : et_computed = TRUE
    grad2 : td_computed = TRUE
    grad3 : travldDist = inch(0)
then
    act1 : old_velocity := esmt_velocity
    act2 : updateTime := Millisec
    act3 : updateRecords :=
              updateRecords ∪ dummyTick
    act4 : updateInvoked := FALSE
    act5 : et_computed := FALSE
    act6 : td_computed := FALSE
end
```

```
computeDistance
when
Update    grad1 : updateInvoked = TRUE
          grad2 : td_computed = FALSE
then
    act1 : travldDist :=
              inch((NGRotations − lastRotations)∗
              inch⁻¹(WHEEL_CIRC))
    act2 : lastRotations := NGRotations
    act3 : td_computed := TRUE
end
```

```
computeElapsedTime
when
    grad1 : updateInvoked = TRUE
    grad2 : et_computed = FALSE
then
    act1 : elapsedTime :=
        cmpElspdTime(ms(modMaxBit(ms⁻¹(NGClickTime) − ms⁻¹(lastClickTime))))
    act2 : lastClickTime, et_computed := NGClickTime, TRUE
end
```

Finally, a new variable *lastClickTime* is used for calculating total elapsed time between two consecutive invocations. Event `computeElapsedTime` updates the value of this variable for each invocation. This updated value is then used for calculating elapsed time for the subsequent invocation. A new state variable *lastRotations* is used in a similar manner but for the calculation of a travelled distance.

3.7 Sixth Refinement: Establishing EXFUN-1

We address the *main* requirement for the system – EXFUN-1: *"Estimated ground velocity of the aircraft is available only if it is within 3 KPH of the true velocity at some moment in within past 3 s"*. However, there is one more important requirement derived from the requirements description – *"published velocity should be available all the time"*. To address these two requirements, we have to consider three different cases here – (1) estimated ground velocity is published if EXFUN-1 is satisfied; (2) old ground velocity is published if the latest velocity is not yet available and the old velocity continues to satisfy EXFUN-1 (update is in progress); (3) *zero* velocity is published if EXFUN-1 is not satisfied.

The property EXFUN-1 adds time constraints on the system's velocity estimation process. Also, this estimated velocity needs to be available all the time. To model these two requirements we have made distinction between the *estimated velocity* and the *published velocity*.

The state flow is such that after an invocation by RTOS (1) velocity estimation is performed (as discussed earlier); (2) once the velocity estimation process is complete, a new velocity is checked against constraints for EXFUN-1; (3.a) if these constraints are satisfied, we publish the new velocity; (3.b) if they are not satisfied, but an old velocity is still valid, we keep publishing the old velocity (3.c) if none of the constraints are satisfied, we publish the zero velocity. With this design we achieve the second requirement of having velocity published all the time.

There are three new variables introduced in this refinement step – *published_ velocity, esmt_velo_avlbl* and *actual_velocity* – and four new events modelling the state flow explained above – `validateVelocity`, `publishZeroVelocity`, `publish Velocity` and `publishOldVelocity`. Moreover, context for this refinement step introduces a new explicit type, *KPH*, in order to address EXFUN-1, which states its constraints in *SI* units system. Here, we also need to handle conversions between *MPH* to *KPH*. For these conversions we introduce a new constructed type, *mphTokph*.[2]

---

[2] $(axm1 : kph \in \mathbb{N} \rightarrowtail KPH, axm2 : mphTokph \in MPH \twoheadrightarrow KPH)$.

INVARIANTS

$inv1 : esmt\_velo\_avlbl \in BOOL \wedge published\_Velocity \in KPH \wedge actual\_velocity \in KPH$

$inv2 : esmt\_velo\_avlbl = TRUE \Rightarrow mphTokph(esmt\_velocity) \in$
$kph[kph^{-1}(actual\_velocity) - 3..kph^{-1}(actual\_velocity) + 3]$

$inv3 : esmt\_velo\_avlbl = TRUE \Rightarrow$
$ms(modMaxBit(ms^{-1}(Millisec) - ms^{-1}(updateTime))) \in ms[0..3000]$

$inv4 : ms(modMaxBit(ms^{-1}(Millisec) - ms^{-1}(updateTime))) \notin ms[0..3000] \Rightarrow$
$published\_Velocity = kph(0)$

$inv5 : actual\_velocity \neq kph(0) \wedge mphTokph(esmt\_velocity) \notin$
$kph[kph^{-1}(actual\_velocity) - 3..kph^{-1}(actual\_velocity) + 3] \Rightarrow$
$published\_Velocity = kph(0)$

$inv6 : actual\_velocity \neq kph(0) \wedge mphTokph(esmt\_velocity) = published\_Velocity \Rightarrow$
$\left(\begin{array}{l} mphTokph(esmt\_velocity) \in kph[kph^{-1}(actual\_velocity) - 3..kph^{-1}(actual\_velocity) + 3] \wedge \\ ms(modMaxBit(ms^{-1}(Millisec) - ms^{-1}(updateTime))) \in ms[0..3000] \end{array} \right)$

Event `validateVelocity` is enabled only when a new estimated velocity is available, and all constraints related to EXFUN-1 are satisfied. A new state variable *esmt_velo_avlbl* is used to flag the availability of a new, valid, velocity for publishing. In this same event, a new state variable *actual_velocity* is assigned a value from a local parameter of the event, which represents true velocity of the aircraft at that instant. Once the *esmt_velo_avlbl* is set to *TRUE*, a new event `publishVelocity` can be executed to update the value of a new state variable *published_Velocity*. We use this variable to denote the published velocity by the *NG velocity system*.

As discussed earlier, we also model the case where a new velocity estimation is not available or invalid, but old velocity is still valid with respect to EXFUN-1. Event `publishOldVelocity` models this case. Finally, when new and old velocities are not valid any more with respect to EXFUN-1, we publish zero velocity. For this, we update *published_velocity* with 0 KPH in a new event `publishZeroVelocity`. These four new events allows us to meet the functional requirement that the published velocity is always available.

---

validateVelocity

any
   $tureVelo$
when
   $grd1 : trueVelo \in KPH$
   $grd2 : mphTokph(esmt\_velocity) \in$
      $kph[kph^{-1}(trueVelo) - 3..$
      $kph^{-1}(trueVelo) + 3]$
   $grd3 :$
      $ms(modMaxBit(ms^{-1}(Millisec) -$
      $ms^{-1}(updateTime))) \in ms[0..3000]$
   $grd4 : esmt\_velo\_avlbl = FALSE$
then
   $act1 : esmt\_velo\_avlbl := TRUE$
   $act2 : actual\_velocity := trueVelo$
end

publishOldVelocity

when
   $grd1 : esmt\_velo\_avlbl = FALSE$
   $grd2 : mphTokph(esmt\_velocity) \in$
      $kph[kph^{-1}(actual\_velocity) - 3..$
      $kph^{-1}(actual\_velocity) + 3]$
   $grd3 :$
      $ms(modMaxBit(ms^{-1}(Millisec) -$
      $ms^{-1}(updateTime))) \in ms[0..3000]$
   $grd4 : esmt\_velo\_avlbl = FALSE$
then
   $act1 : published\_Velocity :=$
      $mphTokph(old\_velocity)$
end

publishVelocity

when
   $grd1 : esmt\_velo\_avlbl = TRUE$
then
   $act1 : published\_Velocity :=$
      $mphTokph(esmt\_velocity)$
end

publishZeroVelocity

when
   $grd1 : mphTokph(esmt\_velocity) \notin$
      $kph[kph^{-1}(actual\_velocity) - 3..$
      $kph^{-1}(actual\_velocity) + 3] \vee$
      $ms(modMaxBit(ms^{-1}(Millisec) -$
      $ms^{-1}(updateTime))) \notin ms[0..3000]$
then
   $act1 : published\_Velocity := kph(0)$
end

We have addressed all requirements (both explicit and derived) that we could extract from the requirements document for the *NG velocity system*. Hence, we can conclude that the development of a formal model for the system (with an adopted refinement strategy) is complete at this stage.

4   Discussion and Lessons Learnt

We make use of explicit types to model units in NG velocity development. Making use of explicit types for numerical units is a design decision based on two observations – (1) model is easier to communicate with other stakeholders (individuals that interact with formal models in some way), as it becomes explicit regarding manipulations of types and their use; (2) from the modelling perspective, assigning types (rather than treating them subsets of $\mathbb{N}$) creates distinct entities which results in clearer proofs.

Our first goal was to develop a case study which would help us to study properties and scenarios we were looking for *implicit and explicit semantics*, and also to evaluate the suitability of Event-B and Rodin platform for that purpose. Even though the development was undertaken by people with significant background in formal verification, the initial modelling attempt was rather unsuccessful. Probably the main reason behind that was the fact that our first model involved too detailed representation of domain entities. Since the *NG velocity system* was a kind of test bed for investigating potentially good ways for incorporating explicit semantics into Event-B, the excessively detailed model soon become too cumbersome for its purpose. As a result, we made a decision that in the *NG velocity model*, we only abstractly define all the required entities, while their complete definitions should be left for the future work. Also, in order to validate our modelling decisions, the development was constantly accompanied by discussions with domain experts. On one hand, such discussions allowed us to reveal new, subtle yet important, properties that our model was lacking in, yet on the other hand, they resulted in multiple redevelopment of the model.

Based on this experience we argue that, even if formal models are less famed in software engineering community (one of the reasons may be of being less indirect in transition from specification to code, which is not a mature area yet), formal models could at least be used for extracting all requiredsy stem properties and requirements correctly and unambiguously, before proceeding to the software design phase. Software and/or hardware systems' clients in this case should ask for proved formalisations of their requirements specification from prime contractors. Finally, we can say that refinement-based modelling method demonstrated a positive impact on requirement traceability and detection of missing and contradicting requirements.

Our second goal was to identify and separate domain descriptions, that is explicit semantics, mixed in the formal model of the *NG velocity system*. After realizing the process of specifying domain descriptions from domain engineering perspective [4,5] (*genericity, extendability, and reusability*), it is clear how a classical formal modelling approach bundles everything together in the same model, with implicit semantics (i.e. semantics of the underlying theory used for modelling). A task similar to reverse engineering was performed to extract probable domain descriptions from the *NG velocity system* Event-B model. As a results, we were able to separate two distinct vocabularies from this model. First vocabulary, describing units and their conversions, is more abstract and relevant to *upper ontology* model. That is, the same vocabulary can be used by many other domain specific vocabularies, such as science and engineering domains. Second vocabulary is specific to aeronautics domain, which essentially sits lower in hierarchy to the first one. Future work in this direction is discussed in detail in the next section.

Our third goal was twofold. We call it *separation* and *integration*. By separation we mean that one should be able to model explicit semantics separately as the first class objects. By integration we mean that one should be able to integrate and (re)use explicit semantics within formal models. Unfortunately, despite all the strengths of Rodin platform, out of the box it does not provide modelling support sufficient for achieving this goal. Theory feature is an external plugin available for Rodin platform and which enables to create reusable components [6]. However, our experiments with the theory plugin have shown that, at the current state, it is also not capable of dealing with the separation aspect. In particular, there is no appropriate way to define inheritance.

Hence, our solution is to employ *ontologies* as formal concept models suitable to tackle the separation problem. After a comparative survey, PLIB ontology model was chosen because of its formal, yet executable representation of concepts, and context-explication mechanisms [9]. Our experiment with PLIB model suggests that it potentially satisfies all criteria for handling the separation aspect of the problem.

5 Conclusion and Future Work

We have made a first important step towards the separation and seamless integration of explicit semantic features into the formal development in Event-B. To explicitly define domain knowledge, we abstractly specified all the required entities (data types) and relationships between them in model's contexts. However, as per the main properties of domain descriptions, these descriptions should be *generic, extendable,* and *reusable.* Therefore, the next important step is to develop an independent Event-B component – *ontology/domain description library* – that will contain formal definitions of data types and functions for *all* (not only fundamental) units of physical quantities related to the *NG velocity* development (i.e., velocity, distance and time) in two most widely used systems of measurement (i.e., metric and imperial). Unlike the definitions presented in contexts of the *NG velocity* development, these new definitions will be fully axiomatised using standard physical metrics, which will allow us to guarantee that each definition in the library is sound and complete. Also, to make our definitions more flexible/usable we aim at redefining some of them as instances of the real numbers and to see whether pre-existing upper ontologies can be re-used for our purpose.

We plan to use PLIB ontology model approach both to create the ontology library and to properly define the set of real numbers. Future research directions would be towards automated and seamless integration of PLIB concept model instances and/or schema into Event-B models. This work involves many criteria to consider, such as automated inferences to discover new logical relationships among modelled entities. This will require changes/extensions to Rodin platform side in order to cope-up with automated integration and support reasoning on explicitly modelled relations in proof obligations. Clearly, once we create, verify and validate the library for time, distance and velocity, it is important to elaborate on this work and extend the library with other physical quantities (e.g., weight, mass, temperature, energy). Future plan also includes more case studies including heterogeneous systems targeting various domains.

References

1. Abrial, J.R.: Modeling in Event-B: System and Software Engineering. Cambridge University Press, New York (2010)
2. Abrial, J.R., Butler, M.J., Hallerstede, S., Hoang, T.S., Mehta, F., Voisin, L.: Rodin: an open toolset for modelling and reasoning in Event-B. STTT **12**(6), 447–466 (2010)
3. Ait-Ameur, Y., Gibson, J.P., Méry, D.: On implicit and explicit semantics: integration issues in proof-based development of systems. In: Margaria, T., Steffen, B. (eds.) ISoLA 2014, Part II. LNCS, vol. 8803, pp. 604–618. Springer, Heidelberg (2014)
4. Bjørner, D.: Software Engineering 1 Abstraction and Modelling. Software Engineering 2 Specification of Systems and Languages; Software Engineering 3 Domains, Requirements, and Software Design. Texts in Theoretical Computer Science. An EATCS Series. Springer, Heidelberg (2006)
5. Bjørner, D.: From domain to requirements. In: Degano, P., De Nicola, R., Meseguer, J. (eds.) Concurrency, Graphs and Models. LNCS, vol. 5065, pp. 278–300. Springer, Heidelberg (2008)
6. Butler, M., Maamria, I.: Practical theory extension in Event-B. In: Liu, Z., Woodcock, J., Zhu, H. (eds.) Theories of Programming and Formal Methods. LNCS, vol. 8051, pp. 67–81. Springer, Heidelberg (2013)
7. Critical Systems Labs Inc: Nose Gear (NG) Velocity Example Version 1.1, September 2011. http://www.cl.cam.ac.uk/mjcg/FMStandardsWorkshop/example.pdf
8. McCarthy, J.: Notes on formalizing context. In: Proceedings of the 13th International Joint Conference on Artifical Intelligence, IJCAI 1993, vol. 1, pp. 555–560. Morgan Kaufmann Publishers Inc. (1993)
9. Pierra, G.: Context representation in domain ontologies and its use for semantic integration of data. In: Spaccapietra, S. (ed.) Journal on Data Semantics X. LNCS, vol. 4900, pp. 174–211. Springer, Heidelberg (2008)
10. Schmidtke, H.R., Woo, W.: Towards ontology-based formal verification methods for context aware systems. In: Tokuda, H., Beigl, M., Friday, A., Brush, A.J.B., Tobe, Y. (eds.) Pervasive 2009. LNCS, vol. 5538, pp. 309–326. Springer, Heidelberg (2009)

Towards an Integrated Method for the Extension of MOF-Based Modeling Languages

Richard Braun[✉] and Werner Esswein

Chair of Wirtschaftsinformatik, esp. Systems Development,
Technische Universität Dresden, 01062 Dresden, Germany
{richard.braun,werner.esswein}@tu-dresden.de

Abstract. During the last years, various MOF-based modeling languages became de-facto standards in their field of application. Due to their common application and dissemination the need for extending these languages also increased in order to integrate domain-specific concepts or facilitate interoperability and tool support. However, only the minority of MOF-based modeling languages provides an extension mechanism and even those defining one, reveal some syntactical issues (e.g., BPMN). Also MOF itself does not provide an integrated and consistent extension mechanism. We therefore proclaim the application of the UML-based profile mechanism for extending the abstract syntax of MOF-based languages while keeping their original meta models unaffected. Further, the application of the Diagram Definition (DD) standard for extending the concrete syntax is outlined and both aspects are integrated. The research article proposes a generic extension method for MOF-based languages based on existing concepts and constructs from the MOF environment. In this context, the article also discusses the positions of the Profiles package and the Diagram Graphics (DG) package within the OMG meta hierarchy.

Keywords: Meta meta modeling · Meta model extensions · Profiles · Extension methods · Meta object facility · Abstract syntax

1 Introduction and Motivation

The Meta Object Facility (MOF) is a common meta modeling language and a range of business-oriented conceptual modeling languages are defined by MOF-based meta models (e.g., BPMN [1]). Some MOF-based modeling languages became de-facto standards in their particular field of application and this dissemination caused the need for language extensions or dialects [2–4]. However, only the minority of those languages provides a dedicated extension mechanism [2] and even those languages defining one, reveal some shortcomings or inaccuracies [5,6]. For instance, BPMN suffers from abstraction conflicts, as extension classes are defined within the meta model layer but have to be instantiated for realizing an extension definition. In addition, BPMN struggles with the concrete specification of those elements that are extended and there are no capabilities

© Springer International Publishing Switzerland 2015
L. Bellatreche and Y. Manolopoulos (Eds.): MEDI 2015, LNCS 9344, pp. 103–115, 2015.
DOI: 10.1007/978-3-319-23781-7_9

for specifying the concrete syntax of extensions [2]. The case of BPMN is symbolic in regard of the extensibility of MOF-based languages and even MOF itself does not provide a consistent extension mechanism. The missing level of standardization in terms of extensibility impairs interoperability, extension reusing as well as the integration of different extensions. Instead, extensions are designed in an ad hoc manner (cf. [7]). This research article therefore aims to outline a generic method for integrated extensibility of MOF-based modeling languages, which considers both abstract and concrete syntax. In contrast to the other approaches, we explicitly consider the concrete syntax, as graphical model representation is extremely important in business-oriented modeling[1]. The intended method should considerably reuse existing constructs from the MOF environment. Therefore the extension capabilities of MOF are examined with respect to a set of requirements, which are derived inductively by an analysis of BPMN's shortcomings according to extensibility [5]. Based on this analysis, the well-known profile mechanism from UML and the Diagram Definition (DD) standard from OMG are selected as appropriate means for extension design.

The remainder of this paper is as follows. Section 2 presents some fundamentals on language extensibility and related research work. Section 3 proposes the requirements set and discusses its fulfillment by several extension alternatives in the context of MOF. Section 4 justifies the meta meta modeling role of profiles and the Diagram Graphics (DG) package. Afterwards, the proposed extension method is outlined in Sect. 5 and the article ends with a brief conclusion and a consideration of further research topics in Sect. 6.

2   Fundamentals and Related Work

2.1   Fundamentals

This research articles primarily addresses MOF-based modeling languages. MOF is located on the top of the common four layer architecture from OMG which is the base for the definition of meta data specifications and conceptual modeling languages [8]. Single layers of the architecture are referred as M3, M2, M1 and M0. M3 is the meta meta model layer where MOF is located on. This layer aims to provide generic concepts for the definition of meta models on layer M2. Consequently, meta models are instances of meta meta models aiming to define particular data formats or modeling languages like UML or BPMN. Instances of M2 are referred as models. Models are located on layer M1 and represent considered real world problems. Instances of M1 are understood as objects, representing the most concrete concepts within the entire architecture. MOF enables the definition of conceptual modeling languages which constitute as semi-formal modeling languages in the context of business-oriented modeling. These languages combine aspects of formal languages and natural languages. The *syntax* of semi-formal modeling languages is defined formally within a meta model and can be divided into *abstract syntax* and *concrete syntax* [9]. The first

---

[1] Also, this aspect demarcates our work from rather formally driven DSL approaches.

one defines the modeling grammar by specifying elements, properties, rules and constraints. The latter covers the graphical representation in the form of icons, views or diagrams. *Semantics* of syntactical elements are usually described in natural language [10]. An *extension* can be understood as enhancing the expressiveness of a conceptual modeling language by introducing new types, properties or by specifying existing elements in order to represent purpose-specific concepts. In the narrower sense, an extension must comply with the extension mechanism of a modeling language in order to ensure conformity to the original meta model core. Generally, an extension is neither useful nor functional on its own (referring to [11]). The extended modeling language is also denoted as *host language* [3].

2.2   Related Work

Generally, there are only very few research articles explicitly addressing generic extension mechanisms in the MOF context or its methodical consequences. BRAUN (2015) presents the state of the art of extending enterprise modeling languages and detects a remarkable lack of precise extension mechanisms [2]. ATKINSON ET AL. (2013) present extension design principles and introduce a multi-level modeling approach for extending the concrete syntax and view definitions [3]. Besides, there are several works addressing extensibility of single languages: BRAUN & ESSWEIN (2014) examine BPMN extensions and the authors found that only few extensions are compliant to the meta model [6]. BRAUN (2015) conducts an in-depth analysis of the BPMN extension mechanism and reveals several problematic aspects [5]. KOPP ET AL. (2011) present an extensive analysis of BPEL extensions [11] and PARDILLO (2010) analyzes UML profiles [12]. Both works mainly focus on statistical insights. There are also some research works on particular techniques, which can be leveraged in the context of extensibility: For instance, multi-level modeling [13], meta model weaving [14] and even meta model reducing [15]. However, none of the stated articles considers extensibility already on the meta meta model layer in order to provide generic extensibility. Our approach aims to tackle this issue.

3   Requirements and MOF Extension Capabilities

3.1   Requirements

A recent study of BRAUN (2015) reveals syntactical inaccuracies of the BPMN extension mechanism and an other analysis of business-oriented MOF-based modeling languages demonstrates the general lack of extension mechanisms at all [2]. We inductively generalize the problem notices stated in [5] and create a set of requirements in accordance to related research work (cf. Sect. 2.2). Table 1 presents the requirements. Within this article, only syntactical aspects are considered.

The MOF environment provides some promising syntactical constructs for language extensions which are examined below. General meta model alterations (e.g., [7]) are not considered in detail as they do not represent actual extension

Table 1. Requirements for integrated extensibility of MOF-defined modeling languages with special focus on the syntax.

Req.	Title	Description
R1	Additive extension	The mechanism should enable additive extensions of the language core, ensuring its validity and a low coupling between host language and extension [3]
R2	Abstraction levels	The mechanism needs to correspond to the four-layered OMG architecture in order to avoid abstraction problems and ensure clear type instance relations between concepts of adjacent levels
R3	Element specification	It is required to exactly specify the extended original element
R4	Interdependencies between extension types	The extension mechanism should enable the design of complex extensions in the sense of specifying interdependencies between extension concepts by different relation types (e.g., aggregations and generalizations)
R5	Type vs. Attribute	The mechanism should explicitly distinguish type-wise and property-wise extensions
R6	Concrete syntax	Meta model concepts for specifying the concrete syntax of extensions are required
R7	Separation of concern	It should be possible, to explicitly organize the set of extension elements and their corresponding core elements coherently (cf. [3])
R8	Extension integration	The mechanism should support the application of multiple extensions in order to facilitate their integration and reuse

mechanisms. Although ad hoc modifications benefit from their accuracy of fit between specific requirements and the designed modeling language, they lack in terms of model exchangeability, tool support and standardization.

3.2 MOF's Capabilities for Extension Definitions

Tag-Based Extensions: EMOF provides a simple extension capability for associating a collection of name-value pairs with MOF model elements. Therefore, the *Tag* element is defined within EMOF's *Extension* package. A *Tag* refers to one or more *Elements* and owns a specific *name*. Each *Tag* has a string-typed *value* property in order to realize name-value pair extensibility of EMOF-based elements [8, p. 23]. This minimal kind of extension is rather useful for simple annotating information to meta model elements (e.g., author information), but it is not useful for expressive extensions as the name-value pairs are not made for further instantiation in order to enhance the vocabulary of the language and provide new elements on M1.

Profiles: Profiles provide a worthwhile medium for tailoring existing meta models towards specific platforms, domains or business objects [8, p. 14]. Profiles constitute as a lightweight extension mechanism, extending meta models with so-called stereotypes as well as properties or constrains [16, p. 193]. The mechanism allows the implementation of more restrictive conditions on meta models by specifying original types without overwriting original elements [16, p. 175]. Profiles are defined within the UML Infrastructure [16, p. 174].

Diagram Definition (DD): DD aims to provide a foundation for modeling and interchanging graphical notations [17, p. 1]. DD distinguishes two kinds of graphical information: Graphics under the control of a user and user-independent graphical definitions. Graphics under the control of a user are related to node positions and line routing points. These information need to be interchanged between tools as they refer to particular models on M1. In contrast, those graphics the user does not have necessarily control about, represent the concrete syntax of the language itself on M2. In the light of this differentiation, DD provides three packages: *Diagram Common (DC)*, *Diagram Interchange (DI)* and *Diagram Graphics (DG)*. DC provides primitive classes for diagram definitions [17, p. 7]. DI enables interchange of graphical information users have control over and the DG package actually specifies the concrete syntax.

3.3 Requirements Fulfillment

Table 2 presents the respective degree of requirements fulfillment of the discussed extension alternatives. The basic meta model alteration approach has its strengths in the apposite implementation of domain-specific constructs due to the high level of modeling freedom (cf. R3–R5), but lacks in fulfilling the required additive kind of the mechanism (R1). Also, this approach is located on meta model layer M2 which does not correspond to an accurate separation of abstraction layers. As meta model alterations are usually implemented in an ad hoc manner, it is further assumed that there is no specification of the concrete syntax (R6). Separation of concern could be achieved by simple packaging. The tag extension approach satisfies requirements R1–R3, but reveals major weaknesses according the definition of complex contents. Hence, the application of this approach would require the definition of further semantical rules on M2. Consequently, the tag extension approach should not be used as meta model extension mechanism. The profile mechanism satisfies nearly all requirements, but requirement R2 needs further investigation as the localization of the *Profiles* package within the four-layer architecture is ambiguous (cf. Sect. 4). The DD standard takes a special position as it covers only concrete syntax aspects and is less an extension mechanism at all. Consequently, DD lacks in specifying the conceptual content of an extension (cf. R3, R4, R5). On the other hand, it could enable additive extensions of the concrete syntax and ensures separation of abstract layers (R1, R2). Of course, the great benefit of DD lies in defining the concrete syntax of a MOF-based meta model (R6).

Based on the consideration of the single alternatives, our extension method builds on an integration of the profile mechanism (for the abstract syntax) and the DD specification (for the concrete syntax). However, there is uncertainty, whether profiles can be defined on M3 as it is actually part of the UML Infrastructure. This issue is therefore discussed in the following Section.

Table 2. Requirements fulfillment by the introduced extension alternatives.

Req.	M2		M3	
	Meta model	Tags	Profiles	DD
R1	o	+	+	+
R2	–	+	+ (cf. Sect. 4!)	+
R3	+	+	+	–
R4	+	–	+	–
R5	+	–	+	–
R6	–	–	o	+
R7	o	o	+	–
R8	o	+	+	–

4   Meta Meta Layer or Meta Layer?

4.1   Profiles

The *Profile* package is owned by the UML Infrastructure [16] and acts both as meta meta model and meta model within the MOF environment. On M3, the Infrastructure is merged and imported by the MOF for reusing fundamental concepts. On M2, the UML Infrastructure serves as vital part of the UML specification [16, p. 16]. The UML Infrastructure consists of three main packages: *Core*, *Profiles* and *Primitive Types*, whereby the first two packages are assigned to the Infrastructure Library package. The *Profiles* package contains all relevant concepts and constructs for profile definition. It becomes obvious, that the Infrastructure provides generic and reusable meta meta model concepts, as it "defines a reusable metalanguage kernel [Core package] and a meta model extension mechanism [Profiles]" [16, p. 27], which are merged and imported by MOF [8]. Moreover, the profile mechanism is even explicitly intended to be a tool for extending and adapting meta models for different purposes [16, p. 12]. We therefore assume, that the *Profile* package is located on M3 as the Infrastructure act as meta meta model. However, it remains a syntactical issue, as the current MOF specification does not provide a merge relation between the *Profile* package and EMOF [8]. This is actually required for the definition of profiles, since meta models are always instances of MOF itself. Nevertheless, we assume the application of the profile containing Infrastructure on meta meta layer M3 as there are numerous textual indications on that within the respective specifications. Locating the Infrastructure on M3 enables the adaptation of the profile mechanism for meta models of all MOF-based languages.

4.2   Diagram Definition (DD)

Examining integrated extensibility of MOF-based modeling languages requires a deeper analysis of MOF's general capabilities in (a) defining the concrete syntax and (b) integrating abstract and concrete syntax. While most modeling languages prefer a minimal definition of the concrete syntax in simple tables, the DD specification provides more sophisticated constructs [17]. With regard to the DD architecture presented in [17, p. 5], we criticize some abstraction issues: Basically, the DG package of DD should be located on the M3 layer as DG defines generic classes for concrete syntax specification which should be instantiated from M3 to M2. Furthermore, abstract and concrete syntax are per se on the same level of abstraction from a language-theoretic point of view. Hence we propose a relocation of the DG package to M3 and a particular instantiation of a meta-model-specific DG package on M2. This language-specific package (e.g., BPMN DG) determines the concrete graphical configuration of single elements by instantiating the generic DG package from M3. Actually, DD proclaims this definition for layer M1 (cf. [17, p. 5]), which violates the separation of types (meta models) and instances (models). The concrete syntax must be defined on M2 by specifying required graphical elements and their configuration. The instantiation of meta models for the concrete syntax leads to particular graphics on M1.

We assume, that the DG package is located on M3 and a language-specific instance of DG has to be defined on M2 in order to specify the concrete syntax. This relocation leads to a revision of the instantiation relation to MOF [17, p. 5]. According to the abstract syntax and MOF, DG should be also defined in a self-reflexive kind. This seems to be reasonable as DG provides generic and fundamental concepts for defining meta models - namely the concrete syntax. Besides, the mapping specification between abstract and concrete syntax has to be taken into account. We therefore proclaim a separate approach in Sect. 5.

5   Construction of the Extension Method

The generic extension method is presented in detail below and the main steps of the proposed method are depicted in Fig. 1. The abstract syntax is considered by introducing *Extension Profiles* (cf. Sect. 5.1). The *Extension Diagram Graphics* definition is represented by adapting the DG package from DD (cf. Sect. 5.2). Both syntax parts need to be integrated within a *Profile DG Mapping* by applying the MOF's Query View Transformation (QVT) [18]. Finally, the serialized interchange of the designed profiles needs to be addressed.

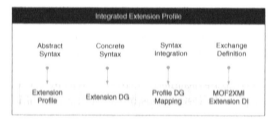

Fig. 1. Steps of the profile-based extension method and their particular outcome.

Figure 2 depicts the integration of relevant standards from the MOF environment, namely MOF itself, the UML Infrastructure and DD. MOF and the Infrastructure are applied for defining the abstract syntax by adapting profile concepts. The DD standard is adapted for the definition of the concrete syntax of extension elements. With regard to the previous Section, the Infrastructure and DD are both located on M3 and the instantiation of an extension DG is therefore required. Additionally, the integration of abstract and concrete syntax is outlined by the mapping package, which should work as connector between both language parts. Therefore, QVT has to be applied in order to map graphical elements to corresponding concepts. With respect to the space of this paper, only the first two stages of the proposed method are discussed in detail.

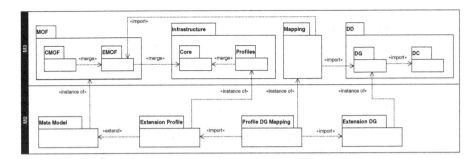

Fig. 2. Proposed profile extension architecture representing the major packages on M3 and M2 as well as their customized relations.

5.1   Abstract Syntax - Extension Profiles

Stereotypes and Tag Definitions for Meta Class Extension: A stereotype is the pivotal concept for extending original meta classes of modeling languages. Basically, extending an original meta class with stereotypes and tag definitions always refers to any kind of property-wise extension, since new properties in form of tag definitions are applied to an original meta class. Hence, the application of a stereotype always leads to a specification of the original meta class in the sense of a stereotyped meta class with a different signature.

From a semantical point of view we differentiate three types of extensions: (1) property-wise extension in a broader sense, (2) property-wise extension in a narrower sense and (3) de facto type definitions. The first case refers to the integration of additional properties, rather independent from original properties. This might be useful for the annotation of properties which are needed for model operations. Therefore, a stereotype with a meaningful name has be created and its tag definitions have to be assigned to that stereotype (cf. Fig. 3a).

The second case refers to restrictions of the valid range of meta class properties. In order to avoid contradictions due to complete redefinitions, it is recommended to only specify property ranges. For instance, if a meta class C has a property p with a range $r1$, a valid extension would constitute as the assignment

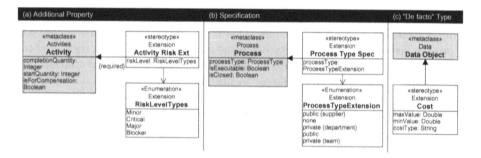

Fig. 3. Different purposes for extending meta classes and their implementation. The examples cover different extensions of BPMN meta classes.

of a stereotype S, having a tag definition t with the same identifier like p and a range $r2$. This can be interpreted as specification (or logical subset) of $r1$. Hence, this property-wise extension in a narrower sense can be seen as specification in accordance to the type limits of the original class. Technically, properties for this specification are constructed and applied like in the first case (cf. Fig. 3b).

The third case addresses purposes where it is required to define a new type. Such type-wise extensions are actually not possible within profile extensions as each defined stereotype strictly refers to a particular meta class and depends on it. This condition implies a semantical likeness between a meta class and the concept that should be integrated. Defining a new type would require the extension of a fairly generic meta class such as UML classes are. However, the most MOF-based modeling languages are not that generic. Defining a new type therefore depends on the existence of *sufficient generic meta class* in the host language. However, such meta classes should not have other sub classes, which would cause class overloading and missing specificity. While this issue is not discussed very well in literature so far (as profiles are solely used within UML), we see basically three alternatives for handling this issue:

1. The meta model provides a sufficient generic meta class which can be specialized. Technically, the new type is introduced in the same way as presented for the second case. The only difference consists in the fact, that the meta class is rather underspecified (cf. Fig. 3c).
2. A rather generic meta class, which is the super class of other meta classes, is extended. In order to avoid overloading of sub classes, OCL statements may restrict such applications.
3. If there is no appropriate meta class that can be leveraged, then the definition of new types by stereotypes should be avoided. Instead, it might be useful to reference external models [14].

Stereotypes within the meta model are depicted as normal class-like rectangles with a *stereotype* keyword on top. In contrast, original meta model classes from the host language are labeled with a *metaclass* keyword.

Constraints for Additional Restrictions: It is often necessary to define more complex restrictions on meta models. This is especially relevant in the context of profiles, as additive extensibility has some immanent limitations regarding to specificity as it allows no meta model alterations in the form of redefinitions or the introduction of new super classes to original classes. Constraint languages like OCL can remedy on that by determining formal statements on particular model values and ranges. Constraints are depicted either within a tag definition or within a separate box, owning a dotted line to the respective meta model element.

Profiles for Extension Packaging: Profiles are used as container for encapsulating related extension concepts. Hence, profiles act as logical and organizational unit within our approach. A particular meta model can apply a profile by instantiating the *Profile Application* class from the *Profile* package. A profile may also consist of several sub profiles, which allow a combination of multiple, purpose-specific extensions [16, p. 187]. It might be also useful to represent relations between a profile and the extended meta classes or affected packages from the meta model in order to provide an overview of existing dependencies by applying *metaclassReferences* and *metamodelReferences* [16]. A profile is graphically presented in the same way like a package. The only difference is the *profile* keyword above the profile name.

5.2 Concrete Syntax - Extension Diagram Graphics

The concrete syntax of an extension is defined by instantiating the DG package. Obviously, it is not possible to determine which classes have to be exactly used, as the graphical appearance of each stereotype-based concept relies to particular requirements and design preferences. However, we can provide an orientation about those classes which are defined in the DG package [17]. First of all, there is some kind of container classes, which can be used for grouping graphical elements. *Groups* refer to logical grouping, without visual manifestation, while *Canvas* represent a set of elements having a visual manifestation (e.g., a background color). Furthermore, there is an array of rather concrete classes for the specification of graphical elements and attributes, for instance: *Rectangles*, *Text*, *Images*, *Polygones* or *Circles* [17]. These classes are used for the actual definition of the concrete syntax and rely on classes of the DC package (e.g., *Bounds*, *Dimensions* or *LineTo*).

Figure 4 represents the concrete syntax of the *Cost* stereotype from Fig. 3. The defined graphic is conceptualized by an instance of the *Group* class in order to encapsulate all relevant graphical elements without a separate visual manifestation. We propose to denote the group in accordance to the related meta class. If there are multiple graphics for one meta class, then the group names should be appropriately differentiated. The *Cost Rectangle* class defines the visual borders of the entire graphic by defining maximal bounds. The border is specified within the *Cost Rectangle Style* class. The icon and its dimensions are defined by the *Cost Icon* class. Further, the graphic owns two text labels: *Cost Name*

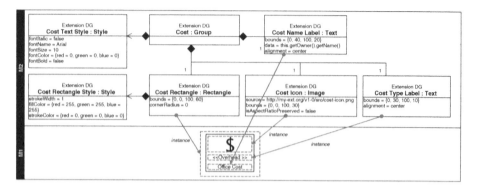

Fig. 4. Example for instantiating classes from the DG package in order to define the concrete syntax of the previously introduced *Cost* extension class.

Label and *Cost Type Label*. The first one represents the name of a particular cost instance and the latter explicates the particular cost type. In contrast to the original DG specification [17, p. 47], we use the *data* attribute of the *Text* class for referencing the property of the abstract syntax element which is depicted. The *Cost Name Label* simply renders the name of the extended element (*this.getOwner().getName()*). The *Cost Type Label* renders the attribute *costType* (cf. Fig. 3). The appearance of all textual elements is specified by the *Cost Text Style* class.

6   Conclusion and Further Research

This article tackles the issue of extending MOF-based modeling languages in a generic, integrated way and provides several contributions: We provide an extension method by adapting the profile mechanism and the DG package from DD. Hence, we aim to foster the exploitation and integration of existing standards within the MOF environment. We therefore conducted an in-depth analysis of the profiles package and the DG package in regard of their actual role within the meta hierarchy of OMG. We argue that both packages should be located on the topmost meta meta model layer as they provide fundamental concepts for meta model definitions. Some researchers may criticize the relevance of such fine-grained issues as MOF is a very common and prestigious standard, but we argue that the steady verification and revision of OMG-based standards is extremely important and also a central task for the research community at all.

Nevertheless, there are different topics for further research. For instance, the issue of defining new, delimitable types with profiles requires further investigation. Within UML, this problem does actually not exist as UML is a generic modeling language and stereotypes of classes are per se some kind of new types (cf. [19]). Other MOF-based languages like KDM or BPMN are rather domain-specific but provide also rather generic concepts within their particular domains. This issue might be solved by coupling profile-based extension with alternative extension techniques like model weaving in order to reuse external models and define new types in this way.

With respect to the outlined extension method, detailed definitions of QVT models within the mapping package are necessary. Results on that as well as a prototypical implementation of our approach within the Eclipse Modeling Framework will be published separately. Besides, it is necessary to consider serialization and interchange of the proposed extension method. Therefore, MOF2XMI transformations and the DI specification from DD should be applied. Finally, further research on methodical support for extension building is generally required (e.g., in terms of selecting appropriate classes for extension).

Acknowledgement. This research was funded by the German Research Foundation (DFG) within the research project *SFB Transregio 96*.

References

1. OMG: business process model and notation (BPMN) - version 2.0. Object Management Group (OMG) (2011)
2. Braun, R.: Towards the state of the art of extending enterprise modeling languages. In: MODELSWARD (2015)
3. Atkinson, C., Gerbig, R., Fritzsche, M.: Modeling language extension in the enterprise systems domain. In: Proceedings of the 17th IEEE EDOC, pp. 49–58 (2013)
4. Bjeković, M., Proper, H.A., Sottet, J.-S.: Enterprise modelling languages. In: Shishkov, B. (ed.) BMSD 2013. LNBIP, vol. 173, pp. 1–23. Springer, Heidelberg (2014)
5. Braun, R.: Behind the scenes of the bpmn extension mechanism - principles, problems and options for improvement. In: MODELSWARD (2015)
6. Braun, R., Esswein, W.: Classification of domain-specific BPMN extensions. Lect. Notes Bus. Inf. Process. **147**, 42–57 (2014)
7. Esswein, W., Weller, J.: Method modifications in a configuration management environment. In: Proceedings of the ECIS, 2002–2013 (2007)
8. OMG: meta object facility (MOF) core specification, version 2.4.2 (2014)
9. Wand, Y., Weber, R.: Research commentary: information systems and conceptual modeling - a research agenda. Inf. Syst. Res. **13**(4), 363–376 (2002)
10. Pfeiffer, D., Gehlert, A.: A framework for comparing conceptual models. In: Proceedings of the EMISA Workshop, pp. 108–122 (2005)
11. Kopp, O., Görlach, K., Karastoyanova, D., Leymann, F., Reiter, M., Schumm, D., Sonntag, M., Strauch, S., Unger, T., Wieland, M., et al.: A classification of BPEL extensions. J. Syst. Integr. **2**(4), 3–28 (2011)
12. Pardillo, J.: A systematic review on the definition of UML profiles. In: Petriu, D.C., Rouquette, N., Haugen, Ø. (eds.) MODELS 2010, Part I. LNCS, vol. 6394, pp. 407–422. Springer, Heidelberg (2010)
13. Atkinson, C., Gutheil, M., Kennel, B.: A flexible infrastructure for multilevel language engineering. IEEE Trans. Softw. Eng. **35**(6), 742–755 (2009)
14. Del Fabro, M.D., Valduriez, P.: Towards the efficient development of model transformations using model weaving and matching transformations. Softw. Syst. Model. **8**(3), 305–324 (2009)

15. Fondement, F., Muller, P.-A., Thiry, L., Wittmann, B., Forestier, G.: Big meta-models are evil. In: Moreira, A., Schätz, B., Gray, J., Vallecillo, A., Clarke, P. (eds.) MODELS 2013. LNCS, vol. 8107, pp. 138–153. Springer, Heidelberg (2013)
16. OMG: unified modeling language, infrastructure, version 2.4.1. OMG (2011)
17. OMG: diagram definition (DD), version 1.0 (2012)
18. OMG: meta object facility (MOF) 2.0 Query/View/Transformation (QVT), version 1.2 (2015)
19. Selic, B.: A systematic approach to domain-specific language design using UML. In: 10th IEEE International Symposium on Object and Component-Oriented Real-Time Distributed Computing, pp. 2–9 (2007)

Context Modeling and Model Transformation

Extending Semantic Databases to Handle Context
An Ontology Modeling Approach

Okba Barkat[✉]

LIAS/ISAE-ENSMA, Futuroscope, Poitiers, France
okba.barkat@ensma.fr

Abstract. The capturing of the semantics is a key challenge in Data Engineering. Indeed, it is a very complicated task and it involves various dimensions like Data Quality and Context. In this paper, we focus on the notion of Context in Data Engineering and on handling it at the level of database systems. First, we propose a formal and generic Model to represent Context, then, we propose a complete extension of an existing Semantic Database called *OntoDB*. This is realized by the extension of its ontology Meta-Model in order to support semantic definition of Context and the extension of *OntoQL* exploitation language in order to support context-aware querying. An implementation of the proposed extensions is described.

Keywords: Context modelling · Ontology model · Semantic database · Context-aware querying

1 Introduction

In information systems area, ontologies [6] have been introduced as knowledge models that describe the explicit semantics of a given domain. However, the capturing of the semantics is a very complicated task that involves various dimensions like Data Quality and Context.

Importance of context representation has been underlined by several researchers, Chen [3] suggested that Entity Relationship approach has to be extended to integrate data quality and context aspects. Pierra [7] claimed that the main difference between ontologies and conceptual models is the context-sensitivity and identified requirements for making ontologies less contextual.

The aim of the work presented in this paper is to focus on the notion of Context in Data Engineering domain and to propose a complete extension of Semantic Databases (SDBs) to handle Context and allow context-aware querying.

The paper is organized as follows: Sect. 2 presents the related work. Section 3 presents the background needed in this paper. Section 4 introduces our Context Model and its connexion with ontological concepts and presents in details the extension of the SDB *OntoDB* to handle Context. Section 5 presents a case study from the medical domain validating our proposal. Section 6 concludes the paper by summarizing the main results and suggesting future work.

© Springer International Publishing Switzerland 2015
L. Bellatreche and Y. Manolopoulos (Eds.): MEDI 2015, LNCS 9344, pp. 119–127, 2015.
DOI: 10.1007/978-3-319-23781-7_10

2   Related Work

Many approaches for representing Context and incorporating it in database (DB) systems have been proposed [2,10,11,13–15]. Table 1 summaries theses works and compare them according to six criteria: (1) C1: *Domain*: This criterion indicates the domain (DB or DW) in which the considered approach is presented. (2) C2: *Context Model*: this criterion indicates if the approach provides a generic Model of Context. (3) C3: *Modeling Level*: this criterion indicates if the Context is defined at the conceptual level. C4: *Storage of Context Model*: this criterion indicates if the approach allows physical storage of the proposed model. C5: *Semantic explicitation*: this criterion indicates if the approach gives solution to make explicit the semantic of data manipulated. C6: *Dedicated Exploitation Technique*: this criterion indicates if the approach offers dedicated techniques to exploit the proposed Model. The study of the table shows that our approach is more complete and overcomes other works' limitations.

Table 1. Related work comparison

Ref.	Description	C1	C2	C3	C4	C5	C6
[10]	A relational DB system that supports context and preference-aware query processing	DB					
[15]	Annotation of preferences with contextual information	DB		x			
[2]	Context-aware views over relational DBs	DB	x	x			x
[11]	A contextual cube model text OLAP	DW		x			x
[13,14]	Context-aware generalization fore cube measures	DW		x	x		x
Our app-roach	Extending Semantic Databases to handle Context	SDB	x	x	x	x	x

3   Background

3.1   OntoDB: A Semantic Database

SDBs are databases that contain data, ontologies and links between these data and the ontological elements that define their meaning [4,12].

OntoDB [5] is a SDB whose architecture consists of four parts: (1) the data part, (2) the ontology part and (3) the meta-schema part that represent respectively the abstraction levels: data instances, models and meta-model, and (4) the meta-base part that contains the system catalog of the database. *OntoDB* supports, when needed, the evolution and the extension of the used ontology model (Fig. 1).

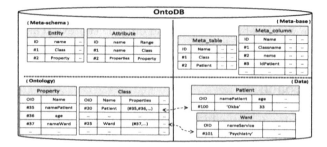

Fig. 1. OntoDB architecture

3.2 OntoQL Exploitation Language

OntoQL [8] is an exploitation language implemented on *OntoDB*. It exploits the power offered by the four quarts architecture of *OntoDB* and allows complete manipulation of ontological models and concepts. Indeed, *OntoQL* allows to define, manipulate and query the ontology model, its instances and its meta-model. It is defined from three components: (1) a Data Definition Language DDL (using CREATE and ALTER clauses), (2) a Data Manipulation Language DML (using INSERT INTO, UPDATE and DELETE clauses) and (3) a Data Query Language DQL (using SELECT clause). It is based on a core ontology language compatible with different ontology languages and can be extended with the *OntoQL* language itself (Table 2).

Table 2. Examples of *OntoQL* statements

Level	Statements
Meta model	CREATE ENTITY #Context(#oid int,...);
Model	CREATE CLASS Patient(name string, age int,...);
Instances	INSERT INTO Patient(name, age) VALUES ('Okba',33);

3.3 The Notion of Context

The Context has been studied in various fields of computer science and many interpretations of its notion have been emerged. The widely accepted definition for context is the one given by Dey and Abowd [1]: *"Any information that can be used to characterise the situation of an entity. An entity is a person, place, or object that is considered relevant to the interaction between a user and an application, including the user and application themselves"*.

Our conception of the Context follows database community's research works [7,9,13] which describe the context as a dependency relationship between contextualized and contextualizing attributes. The former is the attribute whose value depends on context and the latter, also called context parameters, are the parameters whose values impact on the value of the contextualized attribute. For example, the weight of a person depend on time context. The time here is a context parameter and the weight is a contextualized attribute.

4   Our Approach

Our approach, aiming to extend SDBs to handle Context, consists in a generic solution for any SDB that allow manipulating ontology model. More specifically, our proposal is based on four steps that we discuss in the next subsections:

4.1   Context Modelling

In order to define our Context Model, and based on our conception of context presented above, we classify Context into four main categories:

- **Mathematical Function Context:** we talk about Mathematical Function Context when the relationship between contextualized and contextualizing attributes is a mathematical function. For example, the calculation of the *Average Length of Stay (ALOS)* of patients in a hospital depends on Context. Indeed, depending on the *hospital ward*, the mathematical calculation formula of the *ALOS* change: for a long stay ward such as *'Psychiatry'*, we use the following formula: *"Average Length Of Stay = Total Inpatient Days Of Care/Total Admissions"*, for short stay *wards*, this formula is used: *"Average Length Of Stay = Total Discharge Days/Total Discharge"*.
- **Functional Dependency Context:** the context information is represented by a functional-dependency-like relationship[1] between the contextualized parameters and their context parameters. For example, the *category of the blood pressure* depends on some context parameters, indeed it is functionally dependent of the *age* of the patient, his *smoking status* and the measure of the *blood pressure* itself.
- **Unit of Measurement Context:** the context information is represented by associating quantitative attributes with their correspondent units or currencies. For example, the value of the property *price* depends on the currency context.
- **Spatio-Temporal Context:** the context information is represented by attaching the considered attribute to its eventual spatial or temporal context. For example, the price of medical procedures depends on temporal context (eg. the validity time of tariffs).

Once the classification is done, we define our Context Model presented in Fig. 2. The root entity of our Model is CONTEXT. Its sub-entities represent the different context categories introduced above. CONTEXT entity is associated with a CONTEXT_URI entity which characterizes each context with the following set of attributes: a *code*: used to give a unique identifier, a *name*: used to describe

---

[1] http://en.wikipedia.org/wiki/Functional_dependency.

the context with a linguistic term and a *classification*: used to associate a category to each context. In order to strengthen the formal and consensual aspects, our model communicates with other ontologies to define external parameters and elements. For example, time and units of measure used in our model are defined respectively by Time Ontology[2] (TO) and Ontology of Units of Measure[3] (OM).

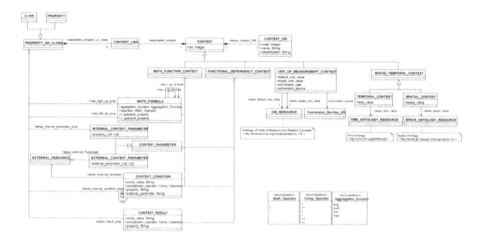

Fig. 2. UML representation of our context model

4.2   Extension of OntoDB with Context

OntoDB allows storing both ontological and Context models in the same repository. Thanks to *OntoQL* language, the manipulation of the different components of these models is possible. Hence, the extension of *OntoDB* to handle Context consists of defining a set of *OntoQL* CREATE clauses that extend the Ontology Model by creating the different elements of the proposed Context Model. For example, the creation of the Context_URI entity is done with the following clause: (Notice that the use of the symbol (#) means that the creation is done at the entity meta-model level.)

> CREATE Entity #Context_URI (#code int,#name string,#classification string);

4.3   Linking Ontology and Context

Once our Model is defined, a link with Ontology Model has to be define. It's the role of CONTEXT_LINK entity which attach any ontological concept represented by Property_or_Class entity to its correspondent context. The following *OntoQL* statement creates CONTEXT_LINK entity:

> CREATE ENTITY #Context_Link(
> #property_or_class REF (#Property_or_Class),#context REF(#Context));

---

[2] http://www.w3.org/2006/time#.
[3] http://www.wurvoc.org/vocabularies/om-1.8/.

4.4   Extension of OntoQL to Handle Context-Aware Querying

In order to incorporate Context in *OntoQL* queries, we developed a context interpreter on the top of the *OntoQL* engine by the introduction of a sub-clause *USING CONTEXT* to the *OntoQL* SELECT clause. The syntax of the new SELECT clause is as follows:

SELECT'selection' FROM'tableReference' Using Context'contextIdentifier'

Note that Context _URI whose role is to characterize the context is used as a context identifier. Beside the new syntax, an interpretation function is associated with each context category defined by our model. When the USING CONTEXT is interpreted, the query is automatically rewritten to a classical select query that take into account the specificities of the considered context. A detailed example is done in the next section.

5   Case Study

In order to validate our approach, we present a simplified case study from the medical domain. Let us consider a DB recording several observations about medical activities and patients. Our DB allows the storage of information about sojourns effectuated in a hospital (eg., Average Length Of Stay, Beds Utilization Rate) and different measures concerning patients (eg., Temperature, Blood Pressure, Heart Rate). We consider the ontology presented in Fig. 3 to define the medical domain concepts.

5.1   Ontology Creation and Instantiation

We use *OntoQL* language to create our ontology and instantiate it. For example, the following *OntoQL* statements create Measure and Patient classes.

CREATE #CLASS Patient (PROPERTIES(idPatient int, namePatient STRING, age INT, ageCategory Enum ('Infant','Adult','MiddleAged'), smoker boolean));

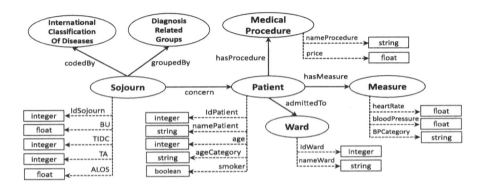

Fig. 3. Medical domain concepts

CREATE #CLASS Measure (PROPERTIES(heartRate int, bloodPressure int, BPCategory Enum
('low','Normal','High')));

Figure 4 shows the instantiation part of Measure and Patient classes. Note
that, for readability, the names are used in the figures instead of the identifiers.

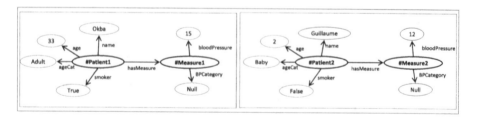

Fig. 4. Ontology instantiation example

5.2   Context Defining and Querying

In this section, in order to explain the practical usefulness of our proposal, we
give a detailed example of a real problem and explain how our approach can be
used to overcome it.

Lets take the example of the *category of the blood pressure* (High, Normal,
Low) which depends on the *age* of the patient, his *smoking status* and the measure of the *blood pressure* itself. Without considering these contextual information, our database is incapable to respond for example to a doctor who want to
know "which patient have a High Blood Pressure?". To fix this problem, such
contextual information have to be persisted into the database. Figure 5 shows
how our approach allows to do this through the instantiation of our Context
Model and linking it to the correspondent ontological concept.

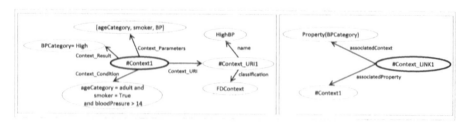

Fig. 5. Functional dependency context instantiation example

Once contextual information are defined, one can use the new clause *Using
Context* to formulate an *OntoQL* query that corresponds perfectly to the need of
the doctor: Select Patient.name, Measure.blood_pressure From Patient, Measure Using_context
High_Pressure;. When the *Using Context* clause is used in the case of a Functional
Dependency Context, the interpreter considers the conditions defined for this
context and rewrites the query by putting them in the *where* clause. Indeed, the

previous query is automatically rewritten as follows: "Select Patient.name, Measure.bloodPressure From Patient, Measure where (Measure.bloodPressure > 14) and (Patient.smoker = True) and (Patient.ageCategory = 'Adult')". Taking the ontology instantiation example presented in Fig. 4, the previous query returns the patient 'Okba' which is the accurate result.

6 Conclusion

In this paper, we have focused in the notion of Context in Data Engineering domain. We have proposed a formal and generic Model to represent it and have described how a Semantic database can be extended to handle context modelling and querying. The proposal has been validated through a comprehensive case study from the medical domain. We are currently working on the refinement of the proposed model and the implementation of new operators at the DDL and DML components levels of OntoQL language.

References

1. Abowd, G.D., Dey, A.K., Brown, P.J., Davies, N., Smith, M., Steggles, P.: Towards a better understanding of context and context-awareness. In: Gellersen, H.-W. (ed.) HUC 1999. LNCS, vol. 1707, pp. 304–307. Springer, Heidelberg (1999)
2. Bolchini, C., Quintarelli, E., Tanca, L.: Carve: context-aware automatic view definition over relational databases. Inf. Syst. **38**(1), 45–67 (2013)
3. Chen, B.-S., Chang, C.-H., Lee, H.-C.: The entity-relationship approach. In: Information Technology in Action: Trends and Perspectives, pp. 13–36. Prentice Hall (1993)
4. Dehainsala, H.: Explicitation de la smantique dans les bases de donnes: Base de donnes base ontologique et le modle OntoDB. Ph.D. thesis, Universit de Poitiers (2007)
5. Dehainsala, H., Pierra, G., Bellatreche, L.: OntoDB: an ontology-based database for data intensive applications. In: Kotagiri, R., Radha Krishna, P., Mohania, M., Nantajeewarawat, E. (eds.) DASFAA 2007. LNCS, vol. 4443, pp. 497–508. Springer, Heidelberg (2007)
6. Gruber, T.R.: Toward principles for the design of ontologies used for knowledge sharing? Int. J. Hum.-Comput. Stud. **43**(5), 907–928 (1995)
7. Guy, P.: Context representation in domain ontologies and its use for semantic integration of data. J. Data Semant. (JODS) **4900**, 174–211 (2008)
8. Jean, S.: OntoQL, un langage d'exploitation des bases de donnes base ontologique. Ph.D. thesis, Universit de Poitiers (2007)
9. Khouri, S., El Saraj, L., Bellatreche, L., Espinasse, B., Berkani, N., Rodier, S., Libourel, T.: CiDHouse: contextual semantic data warehouses. In: Decker, H., Lhotská, L., Link, S., Basl, J., Tjoa, A.M. (eds.) DEXA 2013, Part II. LNCS, vol. 8056, pp. 458–465. Springer, Heidelberg (2013)
10. Levandoski, J.J., Mokbel, M.F., Khalefa, M.E.: CareDB: A context and preference-aware location-based database system. Proceed. VLDB Endow. **3**(2), 1529–1532 (2010)

11. Oukid, L., Asfari, O., Bentayeb, F., Benblidia, N., Boussaid, O.: CXT-cube: contextual text cube model and aggregation operator for text OLAP. In: Proceedings of the Sixteenth International Workshop on Data warehousing and OLAP, pp. 27–32. ACM (2013)

12. Pierra, G., Hondjack, D., Ameur, Y.A., Bellatreche, L.: Bases de donnes base ontologique. principe et mise en oeuvre. Ingnierie des systemes d'information **10**(2), 91–115 (2005)

13. Pitarch, Y., Favre, C., Laurent, A., Poncelet, P.: Context-aware generalization for cube measures. In: Proceedings of the ACM 13th International Workshop on Data Warehousing and OLAP, pp. 99–104. ACM (2010)

14. Pitarch, Y., Favre, C., Laurent, A., Poncelet, P.: Enhancing flexibility and expressivity of contextual hierarchies. In: 2012 IEEE International Conference on Fuzzy Systems (FUZZ-IEEE), pp. 1–8. IEEE (2012)

15. Pitoura, E., Stefanidis, K., Vassiliadis, P.: Contextual database preferences. IEEE Data Eng. Bull. **34**(2), 19–26 (2011)

Knowledge-Based Entity Resolution with Contextual Information Defined over a Monoid

Klaus-Dieter Schewe[1,3]($\boxtimes$), Qing Wang[2], and Mariam Rady[3]

[1] Software Competence Center Hagenberg, Hagenberg, Austria
kd.schewe@scch.at
[2] The Australian National University, Canberra, Australia
qing.wang@anu.edu.au
[3] Johannes-Kepler-Universität Linz, Linz, Austria
{m.rady,kd.schewe}@cdcc.faw.jku.at

Abstract. Entity resolution (aka record linkage) addresses the problem to decide whether two entity representations in a database or stream correspond to the same real-world object. Knowledge-based entity resolution is grounded in *knowledge patterns*, which combine rules defined by Horn clauses with conditions prescribing when the rule is applicable, and conditions specifying when the application of the rule is not permitted. So far, these positive and negative conditions are expressed as bindings of the variables appearing in the Horn clause. In this paper the condition part of a knowledge pattern is generalised to a *context*, which is still defined by a positive and a negative part, but for both equations involving operators are permitted. The paper concentrates on conditions over a monoid for the constraints in a context. With this generalisation standard properties of knowledge patterns such as minimality, containment and optimality are investigated, which altogether minimise redundancy and thus optimise the inference of equivalences between entities.

1 Introduction

Entity resolution (aka record linkage) addresses the problem to decide whether two entity representations in a database or stream correspond to the same real-world object. It is widely accepted that entity resolution is one of the major impediments affecting data quality in information systems and stream data analysis. The difficulty of this problem has been widely acknowledged by research communities and industry practitioners [2,5,6]. State-of-the-art approaches to entity resolution favor similarity-based methods [3]. Numerous classification techniques have been developed under a variety of perspectives such as probabilistic [6,9], cost-based [14], ruled-based [4], active learning [1,10,13], and collective classifications [2,5].

A common rationale behind similarity-based methods is that, the more similar two entities are, the more likely they refer to the same real-world object. However, entities that look similar may refer to different objects, and entities

L. Bellatreche and Y. Manolopoulos (Eds.): MEDI 2015, LNCS 9344, pp. 128–135, 2015.
DOI: 10.1007/978-3-319-23781-7_11

that look different may refer to the same objects. Thus, similarity-based methods are far from perfect. Such problems become more evident when the information about entities is inadequate. For instance, if for two entities it is only known that they have the same name, deciding whether they refer to the same real-world object is impossible.

Knowledge-based entity resolution has been developed by the authors as an alternative approach to conquer such problems. The key idea is to use explicit knowledge about identification, which can be expressed by rules [11] together with a *context* comprising conditions that restrict, when the rule can be applied as well as exceptions, when the rule cannot be applied. Thus, the idea of knowledge-based entity resolution has been concretised by the introduction of *knowledge patterns* (ℓ, r) that combine a Horn clause ℓ with a context relation r ranging over all the attributes that correspond to the variables in ℓ. Each row in r is either positively or negatively marked, so each instantiation of ℓ using the bindings in a row of r defines a (positive or negative) query. The semantics of a set of knowledge patterns is then defined by an inflationary fixed-point [12].

The complexity of such a fixed-point computation depends heavily on the number of patterns and the number of queries defined by each of them. Therefore, the theoretical investigation of knowledge patterns for entity resolution emphasised redundancy among different patterns and within single patterns [12]. We have redundancy between patterns, if one pattern P_2 *contains* another one P_1, i.e. $P_1 \subseteq P_2$ iff on any database instance I we always obtain $P_1(I) \subseteq P_2(I)$. For a single pattern (ℓ, r) we are seeking that the number of rows in r is *minimal*, and for patterns with the same rule it is desirable to *optimize* the total number of rows in the context relations. Containment, minimality and optimisation were thus the focus of the research in [12].

The objective of this paper is to generalise the notion of context in knowledge patterns. We observe that each row in a context relation just defines a set of bindings, so we will now investigate contexts, where each (positive or negative) binding is generalised to permit more complex terms. However, we will first consider only terms involving a single operator defined by a monoid. This already captures equations involving string concatenation with unknowns. Then the applicability of an instantiated rule requires to ensure the satisfiability of a set of such constraints.

2   Knowledge Patterns with Context Relations

Let $S = \{R_1, \ldots, R_n\}$ be a relational database schema, where each R_i is associated with a set $\{A_1^i, \ldots, A_{n_i}^i\} \subseteq A$ of attributes, and each attribute $A \in A$ is associated with a countable domain $dom(A) \in \{D_i \mid i \in I\}$. Let one of the domains, say D_0, be a countable set of identifiers. Let $\mathcal{E} = \{E_1, \ldots, E_k\}$ be a set of binary relation symbols, disjoint from S, such that each E_i defines an equivalence relation over D_0.

A *knowledge pattern* P is a triple (ℓ, r^+, r^-) with a Horn clause ℓ of the form $E_i(x, y) \leftarrow \varphi(x_1, \ldots, x_m, x, y)$ with $E_i \in \mathcal{E}$, in which φ is a conjunction of atoms over $\mathcal{S} \cup \mathcal{E}$, and relations r^+ and r^- over attributes that are in 1-1 correspondence to the variables $x_1, \ldots, x_m$ in φ with the modification that the value $\lambda \notin \bigcup_{i \in I} D_i$ may appear as value for any attribute. The relations r^+ are r^- are called the positive and negative context relation of P, respectively.

Each tuple t in r^+ and r^-, respectively, defines an instantiation of the rule ℓ: for $t(A_i) = v_i \neq \lambda$ replace the variable x_i corresponding to the attribute A_i by v; for $t(A_i) = \lambda$ do not replace x_i. Denote this instantiation by $\varphi_t(\bar{x}_1, \ldots, \bar{x}_m, x, y)$, so $\bar{x}_i = v_i$ or $\bar{x}_i = x_i$. Then for a database instance I over $\mathcal{S} \cup \mathcal{E}$ define $P_t(I) = \{E_i(x, y) \mid \exists \boldsymbol{x}.\varphi_t(\bar{x}_1, \ldots, \bar{x}_m, x, y)\}$, where $\boldsymbol{x}$ refers to the sequence of variables x_i in φ_t. Using this we can associate an immediate consequence operator with a knowledge pattern P, which maps I to another instance $P(I)$ defined by $P(I)(R_i) = I(R_i)$ and $P(I)(E_i) = \bigcup_{t \in r^+} P_t(I) - \bigcup_{t \in r^-} P_t(I)$.

This can be extended to an immediate consequence operator for a finite set $\mathcal{P}$ of knowledge patterns. For each equivalence relation schema $E_i \in \mathcal{E}$ let $\mathcal{P}(I)(E_i) = \bigcup_{P \in \mathcal{P}} P(I)(E_i)$. In this way, starting from a database instance I_0 over $\mathcal{S}$, i.e. $I_0(E_i) =$, we obtain an ascending sequence $I_0 \subseteq I_1 \subseteq I_2 \subseteq \ldots$ with $I_{i+1} = I_i \cup \mathcal{P}(I_i)$. On these grounds the semantics J of $\mathcal{P}$ is defined by the inflationary fixed-point of such a sequence.

For the construction of the (inflationary) fixed-point it is desirable to minimise the application of the immediate consequence operator. Thus, for a single knowledge pattern $P = (\ell, r^+, r^-)$ the number of tuples in r^+ and r^- should be minimal.

We define $v \preceq \lambda$ for every $v \in D_i \cup \{\lambda\}$. Then we say that t_1 *subsumes* t_2 (notation: $t_2 \sqsubseteq t_1$) iff they belong both to r^+ or r^-, respectively, and $t_2(A) \preceq t_1(A)$ holds for each attribute A. Furthermore, for $t_1 \in r^-$ and $t_2 \in r^+$ we say that t_1 *upward subsumes* t_2 (notation: $t_2 \sqsubseteq_\uparrow t_1$) iff $t_2(A) \preceq t_1(A)$ holds for each attribute A. Then define P to be *minimal* iff for $t_2 \not\sqsubseteq t_1$ and $t_2 \not\sqsubseteq_\uparrow t_1$ hold for any two context tuples t_1, t_2. The following result states that for a minimal knowledge pattern P none of the context tuples can be omitted without changing the result of the immediate consequence operator for at least one database instance. In [12] it has been proven that *if P is a minimal knowledge pattern, then (1) $P_{t_1} \not\sqsubseteq P_{t_2}$, (2) $P_{t'_1} \not\sqsubseteq P_{t'_2}$ and (3) $P_{t_1} \not\sqsubseteq P_{t'_1}$ holds for any different context tuples $t_1, t_2 \in r^+$ and $t'_1, t'_2 \in r^-$.*

If $P_1(I) \subseteq P_2(I)$ holds for every database instance I, we say that the knowledge pattern P_1 is *contained* in the knowledge pattern P_2 (notation: $P_1 \subseteq P_2$). Naturally, if this is the case, P_1 could be removed from a set $\mathcal{P}$ of knowledge patterns containing also P_2, as it would not contribute anything to the inflationary fixed-point. With the following result containment of knowledge patterns can be reduced to containment of conjunctive queries, and thus is decidable. In [12] it was shown that *for knowledge patterns $P_i = (\ell_i, r_i^+, r_i^-)$ ($i = 1, 2$) we have $P_1 \subseteq P_2$ iff (1) for each $t_1 \in r_1^+$ there exists a $t_2 \in r_2^+$ with $P_{t_1} \subseteq P_{t_2}$, and (2) for each $t_1 \in r_1^+$ and $t'_2 \in r_2^-$ there exists a $t'_1 \in r_1^-$ with $P_{t_1} \cap P_{t'_2} \subseteq P_{t_1} \cap P_{t'_1}$.*

Optimisation targets to reduce the number of tuples in context relations in cases, where neither a tuple can be simply removed to obtain minimality, nor two knowledge patterns contain each other. Thus, call $\mathcal{P}'$ a *positive optimisation* of a set $\mathcal{P}$ of knowledge patterns iff $\mathcal{P}$ and $\mathcal{P}'$ are equivalent, the total number of tuples in positive context relations $r_i'+$ of $\mathcal{P}'$ does not exceed the total number of tuples in positive context relations r_i^+ of $\mathcal{P}$, and there is is no other $\mathcal{P}''$ also satisfying these properties with a strictly lower number of tuples in positive context relations than $\mathcal{P}'$. Analogously, call $\mathcal{P}'$ a *negative optimisation* of a set $\mathcal{P}$ of knowledge patterns iff $\mathcal{P}$ and $\mathcal{P}'$ are equivalent, the total number of tuples in negative context relations $r_i'^-$ of $\mathcal{P}'$ does not exceed the total number of tuples in negative context relations r_i^- of $\mathcal{P}$, and there is is no other $\mathcal{P}''$ also satifying these properties with a strictly smaller number of tuples in negative context relations than $\mathcal{P}'$. An *optimisation* of $\mathcal{P}$ is a positive optimisation of $\mathcal{P}$ that cannot be further optimised positively nor negatively.

Concentrate on knowledge patterns $P = (\ell, r^+, r^-)$ with the same rule part ℓ. For $t_1 \in r^+$ and $t_2 \in r^-$ we say that t_1 *downward subsumes* t_2 (notation: $t_2 \sqsubseteq_\downarrow t_1$) iff $t_2(A) \preceq t_1(A)$ holds for each attribute A. Furthermore, define the *intersection* $t_1 \curlywedge t_2$ of two tuples by building the minimum on each attribute with respect to $\preceq$. If this is not possible, the intersection is not defined. Analogously, define the *union* $t_1 \curlyvee t_2$ of two tuples by building the supremum on each attribute with respect to $\preceq$. According to [12] an optimisation of P can be obtained be applying the following three steps:

Normalisation. For $r^+ = \{t_1, \ldots, t_n\}$ replace P by n knowledge patterns $\mathcal{P}_i = (\ell, \{t_i\}, r^-)$.

Elimination. For $t_1 \in r_1^-$ and $t_2 \in r_2^+$ with $t_1 \sqsubseteq_\downarrow t_2$ replace t_1 by $\{t_1 \curlywedge t_3 \mid t_3 \in r_2^-\}$, if $r_2^- \neq \emptyset$, or otherwise omit t_1.

Composition. Define two patterns P_1, P_2 to be *compatible* iff $r_1^- \curlywedge r_2^+ \sqsubseteq r_2^-$ and $r_1^+ \curlywedge r_2^- \sqsubseteq r_1^-$ hold. Furthermore, if $P_1, \ldots, P_n$ are pairwise compatible, then $t_1 \in r_i^-$ and $t_2 \in r_j^-$ are *mergeable* iff for all $t \in r_k^+$ there exists a $t^- \in r_k^-$ with $t \curlywedge (t_1 \curlyvee t_2) \sqsubseteq t^-$. Then decompose the set $\mathcal{P}$ of knowledge patterns into sets of pairwise compatible knowledge patterns and for each such subset build a single knowledge pattern taking the union of the positive context relations, and the union of negative context relations, such that mergeable tuples t_1, t_2 are replaced by $t_1 \curlyvee t_2$. Choose the decomposition and the mergeable tuples in such a way that the resulting negative context relation has a minimum number of elements, which according to [12] is an **NP**-complete optimisation problem.

3   Knowledge Patterns with Contexts

For the generalisation of the notion of context in knowledge patterns we keep the basic definitions from the previous section with the following extensions. For some domains D_i (other than D_0) assume that they carry the structure of a monoid, i.e. we have an associative operator $\circ$ and a unit element $e \in D_i$. A standard example are strings over some alphabet with concatenation and the empty string as unit.

With monoid structures we obtain a richer set of *terms*: (1) Each variable and each constant $v \in D_i$ is a term. (2) If D_i is a monoid, then $t_1 \circ t_2$ is a term, whenever t_1, t_2 are terms. A *constraint clause* over D_i is a conjunction of equations $t_1 = t_2$ with terms t_1, t_2 (over D_i)

A very important result of Makanin states that the solvability of such conjunctions of equations over a monoid is decidable [8]. Furthermore, based on Makanin's decision procedure, Jaffar developed an algorithm which, when an equation has a solution, generates all its solutions and halts if the set of solutions is finite [7].

A *contextual knowledge pattern* P is a triple (ℓ, C^+, C^-) with a Horn clause ℓ of the form $E_i(x, y) \leftarrow \varphi(x_1, \ldots, x_m, x, y)$ with $E_i \in \mathcal{R}$, in which φ is a conjunction of atoms over $\mathcal{S} \cup \mathcal{E}$, and sets of constraint clauses C^+ and C^-. The sets C^+ and C^- are called the positive and negative *context* of P, respectively.

Note that this definition subsumes the original definition of knowledge patterns as a special case. A tuple t in r^+ (or r^-, respectively) defines a conjunction of equations: for $t(A_i) = v_i$ with A_i corresponding to the variable x_i we obtain the equation $x_i = v$. Likewise, we can consider each database instance I over $\mathcal{S} \cup \mathcal{E}$ as a set of constraint clauses.

Let $I = \{d_1, \ldots, d_k\}$ be the set of constraint clauses defining the database instance I. If the body of the rule ℓ contains an atom $R(t_1, \ldots, t_n)$, then this also defines a constraint clause of the form $x_1 = t_1 \wedge \ldots \wedge x_n = t_n$. If for each such atom we choose an applicable constraint clause d_i, then (after some necessary renaming of variables) the constraint clause $d_1 \wedge \ldots \wedge d_n \wedge x_1 = t_1 \wedge \ldots \wedge x_n = t_n$ defines an instantiation of the atom, while the conjunction of these instantiations defines a rule application. Furthermore, a constraint clause $c_j \in C^+$ adds further constraints. Thus, each such combination of a constraint from C^+, the constraints contained implicitly in the rule body, and constraints from I associated with the various atoms of the rule body defines a new constraint clause. Using Makanin's algorithm we can decide the satisfiability of this constraint clause. If it is satisfiable, it defines a tuple (x, y) for the head predicate E_i. As the constraint clauses defined by I enforce a unique binding of the variables x, y in the head, Let Φ^+ define the set of all such pairs. Analogously, determine a set Φ^- in the same way using the rule body, the given database instance I, and the constraint clauses in C^-. Thus, as before we can define an immediate consequence operator for P with $P(I)(E_i) = \Phi^+ - \Phi^-$. This can be extended for a finite set $\mathcal{P}$ of knowledge patterns by defining $\mathcal{P}(I)(E_i) = \bigcup_{P \in \mathcal{P}} P(I)(E_i)$.

In this way, starting from a database instance I_0 over $\mathcal{S}$, i.e. $I_0(E_i) = \emptyset$, we obtain an ascending sequence $I_0 \subseteq I_1 \subseteq I_2 \subseteq \ldots$ with $I_{i+1} = I_i \cup \mathcal{P}(I_i)$, and the semantics J of $\mathcal{P}$ is defined by the inflationary fixed-point of such a sequence. For instance, let the database instance be

AID	NAME	AFFILIATION	EMAIL
1	Q. Wang	PBRF Office, University of Otago	...
2	Qing Wang	Dept. of Information Science, University of Otago	...
3	Qing Wang	RSCS, Australian National University	...
4	Q. Wang	CAU Kiel, Germany	...
5	Q. Wang	Dept. of Information Systems, Massey University	...

Use the rule $E_{auth}(x,y) \leftarrow \text{AUTHOR}(x, x_1, x_2, x_3) \wedge \text{AUTHOR}(y, y_1, y_2, y_3)$ and the constraint clause c of the form $x_1 = \text{Q}z\text{Wang} \wedge x_2 = z_1\text{U}z_2\text{Otago} \wedge y_1 = \text{Q}z'\text{Wang} \wedge y_2 = \text{Dep}z\text{Information Science, U}z_2\text{Otago}$. Instantiating the atoms in the rule ℓ with the i'th and j'th tuple in this table, respectively, leads to constraint clauses d_{ij}, e.g. $d_{12} \equiv x = 1 \wedge x_1 = \text{Q. Wang} \wedge x_2 = \text{PBRF Office, University of Otago} \wedge y = 2 \wedge y_1 = \text{Qing Wang} \wedge x_3 = \ldots \wedge y_3 = \ldots \wedge y_2 = \text{Dept. of Information Science, U.... Otago}$. For $i = 1, 2$ and $j = 2$ the constraint clauses $c \wedge d_{ij}$ are solvable, so we get the pair $(1,2)$ for E_{auth} (plus more by building the reflexive, transitive closure).

4   Reduction of Redundancy

Let us now address the problem to reduce redundancy in the generalised setting of contextual knowledge patterns. As before we analyse three different cases: (1) the minimisation of the constraint theories associated with a sigle contextual knowledge pattern, (2) containment among knowledge patterns, and (3) optimisation of knowledge patterns with the same rule.

We want to generalise the result on minimality for knowledge patterns to contextual knowledge patterns. Basically, the minimality condition guarantees that positively (or negatively, respectively) generated tuples for the head predicate of ℓ using $t \in r^+$ (or $t \in r^-$, respectively) cannot always be produced by other context tuples $t' \in r^+$ (or $t' \in r^-$, respectively). Furthermore, positively generated tuples for the head predicate of ℓ using $t \in r^+$ should not always be producable by a negative context tuple $t' \in r^-$.

For constraint clauses instead of context tuples this naturally generalises to implication or equivalently inclusion of the set of solutions. On the grounds of Makanin's and Jaffar's algorithms we know that this is decidable. Therefore, we define a contextual knowledge pattern $P = (\ell, C^+, C^-)$ to be *minimal* iff for all different $c_1, c_2 \in C^+$ and different $c_1', c_2' \in C^-$ we always have $c_1 \not\approx c_2$, $c_1' \not\approx c_2'$ and $c_1 \not\approx c_1'$. If $P_c(I)(E_i)$ denotes the set of tuples for E_i generated by using the constraint clause c with the database instance I, we say $P_c \subseteq P_{c'}$ iff $P_c(I)(E_i) \subseteq P_{c'}(I)(E_i)$ holds for all database instances I. Then it can be shown: *If P is a minimal contextual knowledge pattern, then (1) $P_{c_1} \not\subseteq P_{c_2}$, (2) $P_{c_1'} \not\subseteq P_{c_2'}$ and (3) $P_{c_1} \not\subseteq P_{c_1'}$ hold for any different constraint clauses $c_1, c_2 \in C^+$ and $c_1', c_2' \in C^-$.*

Concerning containment the definition for knowledge patterns generalises naturally to contextual knowledge patterns. We have $P_1 \subseteq P_2$ iff $P_1(I) \subseteq P_2(I)$ holds for all database instances I. With this a generalisation of the containment result from [12] can be shown: *For contextual knowledge patterns $P_i = (\ell_i, C_i^+, C_i^-)$ ($i = 1, 2$) we have $P_1 \subseteq P_2$ iff (1) for each $c_1 \in C_1^+$ there exists a $c_2 \in C_2^+$ with $P_{c_1} \subseteq P_{c_2}$, and (2) for each $c_1 \in C_1^+$ and $c_2' \in C_2^-$ there exists a $c_1' \in C_1^-$ with $P_{c_1} \cap P_{c_2'} \subseteq P_{c_1} \cap P_{c_1'}$.*

However, the crucial question is, whether these conditions (1) and (2) are still decidable. For this first note that for any constraint clauses c_1 and c_2 the conjunction $c_1 \wedge c_2$ is also a constraint clause, and we have $P_{c_1}(I) \cap P_{c_2}(I) = P_{c_1 \wedge c_2}(I)$. Thus, decidability boils down to the problem, whether $P_c \subseteq P_{c'}$ is decidable. As this is equivalent to showing $c \Rightarrow c'$ decidability is a consequence of the results of Makanin and Jaffar.

Let us finally look at the optimisation steps for knowledge patterns with the objective to generalise them to contextual knowledge patterns. Normalisation can be immediately generalised to the replacement of a contextual knowledge pattern $P = (\ell, C^+, C^-)$ by n contextual knowledge patterns $P_i = (\ell, \{c_i\}, C^-)$ $(i = 1, \ldots, n)$ for $C^+ = \{c_1, \ldots, c_n\}$. Obviouly, the inflationary fixed-point defined by P is the same as the one defined by $\{P_1, \ldots, P_n\}$ on any database instance I.

For elimination the generalisation to contextual knowledge patterns is likewise straightforward, as downward subsumption $t_1 \sqsubseteq_{\downarrow} t_2$ generalises to implication $c_2 \Rightarrow c_1$ for constraint clauses. Thus, the elimination step for contextual knowledge patterns $P_i = (\ell, C_i^+, C_i^-)$ $(i = 1, 2)$ amounts to take $c_1 \in C_1^-$ and $c_2 \in C_2^+$ with $c_2 \Rightarrow c_1$ and to replace c_1 by $\{c_1 \wedge c_3 \mid c_3 \in C_2^-\}$, provided $C_2^- \neq \emptyset$ or otherwise simply omit c_1. Then it can be shown that *if $\mathcal{P}' = \{P_1', \ldots, P_n'\}$ results from $\mathcal{P} = \{P\}$ after normalisation and follow-on elimination of negative constraint clauses, then $\mathcal{P}'$ produces the same inflationary fixed-point as $\mathcal{P}$ on any database instance.*

For composition, for sets C' and C of constraint clauses write $C' \Rightarrow C$ iff for each $c' \in C'$ there exists some $c \in C$ with $c' \Rightarrow c$. Then two contextual knowledge patterns $P_i = (\ell, C_i^+, C_i^-)$ $(i = 1, 2)$ are *compatible* iff $\{c_1 \wedge c_2 \mid c_1 \in C_1^-, c_2 \in C_2^+\} \Rightarrow C_2^-$ and $\{c_1 \wedge c_2 \mid c_1 \in C_1^+, c_2 \in C_2^-\} \Rightarrow C_1^-$ hold. This is a natural generalisation of the compatibility condition for ordinary knowledge patterns.

Similarly, we obtain a generalisation of mergeability. For this let $P_i = (\ell, C_i^+, C_i^-)$ $(i = 1, \ldots, n)$ be pairwise compatible. We say that $c_1 \in C_i^-$ and $c_2 \in C_j^-$ are *mergeable* iff $\{c \wedge (c_1 \vee c_2) \mid c \in C_k^+\} \Rightarrow C_k^-$ holds for all $k = 1, \ldots, n$. So, analogous to the ordinary knowledge patterns we obtain a graph of compatible contextual knowledge patterns, and graphs of mergeable constraint clauses, out of which we have to select constraint clauses in a way that an optimal model (with minimised number of constraint clauses) results. It can then be proven that *the optimisation from a given set $\mathcal{P}$ of contextual knowledge patterns is* **NP**-*complete*.

5   Conclusion

In this paper we generalised the knowledge patterns from [11] to *contextual knowledge patterns*. Instead of defining instantiations of a Horn clause by context tuples we used constraint clauses instead. These are defined as conjunctions of equations over algebraic structures. For a start we considered only free monoids for these structures, because decidability of the equational theory on these structure is known for a long time [8]. On these grounds we could generalise the inflationary fixed-point semantics and argue that the theoretical results concerning the reduction of redundancy in knowledge patterns can be easily generalised to the new, more complex situation.

However, we can make already a very important observation. All generalisations discussed in this paper amount to replacing the relationships and operations on tuples exploited in [12] by logical relationships on the equational theory of monoids. This should also be the case for other structures. This means that the questions whether an equational theory on some structure is decidable is decisive for the further generalisation of our theory to even more complex contexts. This will be explored in future research on knowledge-based entity resolution with contexts.

References

1. Arasu, A., Götz, M., Kaushik, R.: On active learning of record matching packages. Proceed. SIGMOD **2010**, 783–794 (2010)
2. Bhattacharya, I., Getoor, L.: Collective entity resolution in relational data. TKDD **1**(1), 5 (2007)
3. Christen, P.: Data Matching. Springer, Heidelberg (2012)
4. Cohen, W.W.: Data integration using similarity joins and a word-based information representation language. ACM TOIS **18**(3), 288–321 (2000)
5. Dong, X., Halevy, A., Madhavan, J.: Reference reconciliation in complex information spaces. Proceed. SIGMOD **2005**, 85–96 (2005)
6. Fellegi, I.P., Sunter, A.B.: A theory for record linkage. J. Am. Statist. Assoc. **64**(328), 1183–1210 (1969)
7. Jaffar, J.: Minimal and complete word unification. J. ACM **37**, 47–85 (1990)
8. Makanin, G.: The problem of solvability of equations in a free semigroup. Math. USSR Sb. **32**, 129–198 (1977)
9. Newcombe, H., Kennedy, J.: Record linkage: making maximum use of the discriminating power of identifying information. Commun. ACM **5**(11), 563–566 (1962)
10. Sarawagi, S., Bhamidipaty, A.: Interactive deduplication using active learning. In: KDD, pp. 269–278 (2002)
11. Schewe, K.D., Wang, Q.: Knowledge-aware identity services. Knowl. Inf. Syst. **36**(2), 335–357 (2013)
12. Schewe, K.D., Wang, Q.: A theoretical framework for knowledge-based entity resolution. Theor. Comput. Sci. **549**, 101–126 (2014)
13. Tejada, S., Knoblock, C.A., Minton, S.: Learning object identification rules for information integration. Inf. Syst. **26**(8), 607–633 (2001)
14. Verykios, V., Moustakides, G., Elfeky, M.: A bayesian decision model for cost optimal record matching. VLDB J. **12**(1), 28–40 (2003)

Data Mining

Discovering Low Overlapping Biclusters in Gene Expression Data Through Generic Association Rules

Amina Houari[1][(⊠)], Wassim Ayadi[2,3], and Sadok Ben Yahia[1]

[1] LIPAH, Faculty of Siences of Tunis, University of Tunis El Manar, Tunis, Tunisia
aminahouari.fst@gmail.com, sadok.benyahia@fst.rnu.tn
[2] LATICE, Higher School of Siences and Technologies of Tunis, University of Tunis, Tunis, Tunisia
[3] LERIA, University of Angres, Angers, France

Abstract. Biclustering is a thriving and of paramount task in many biomedical applications. Indeed, the biclusters aim, among-others, the discovery of unveiling principles of cellular organizations and functions, to cite but a few.

In this paper, we introduce a new algorithm called, **BiARM**, that aims to efficiently extract the most meaningful, low overlapping biclusters. The main originality of our algorithm stands in the fact that it relies on the extraction of generic association rules. The reduced set of association rules faithfully mimics relationships between sets of genes, proteins, or other cell members and gives important information for the analysis of diseases. The effectiveness of our method has been proved through extensive carried out experiments on real-life DNA microarray data.

Keywords: Biclustering · Association rules mining · Data mining · Bioinformatic · DNA microarray data

1 Introduction

Clustering gene expression data is an important task in bioinformatics. It allows researchers to gather information such as cancer occurrences, specific tumor subtypes and cancer survival rates. Biclustering is a particular clustering type that helps achieve this. Cheng and Church [12] were the first to apply *biclustering* to gene expression data. Afterwards, many other algorithms were proposed. Biclustering tasks aim to discover sub-matrices (biclusters) of genes and conditions such that the rows exhibit a correlated pattern over a subset of columns. Thus it is a highly combinatorial problem and known to be NP-Hard [12].

Several surveys of biclustering algorithms have been given. According to [17], existing biclustering algorithms can be grouped into two main classes: Systematic search algorithms and stochastic search ones. Algorithms adopting systematic search contain: The Divide-And-Conquer (DAC) based approach [32,35], the

© Springer International Publishing Switzerland 2015
L. Bellatreche and Y. Manolopoulos (Eds.): MEDI 2015, LNCS 9344, pp. 139–153, 2015.
DOI: 10.1007/978-3-319-23781-7_12

Greedy Iterative Search (GIS) based approach [7,11] and the Biclusters Enumeration (BE) based approach [5,34]. While those adopting stochastic search include: The Neighborhood Search (NS) based approach [6,14], the Evolutionary Computation (EC) based approach [15,16] and the Hybrid (H) based approach [18,27].

Despite their large number, the algorithms mentioned above have limitations. Thus, they do not guarantee that their extracted biclusters are optimal. It was for this reason that researchers introduced the new Formal Concept Analysis (FCA)-based approaches. In [29], for instance, the authors proposed a new approach, called FIST, for extracting bases of extended association rules and conceptual biclusters, using the frequent closed itemsets. Whereas, in [22], they used the scaling of numerical data and considered that formal concepts are the groups of genes whose expression values are in the same intervals for a sub-set of conditions. In [21], the authors refer to the algorithm given in [22], using Triadic Concept Analysis in order to extract biclusters with similar values. In [26], the authors proposed GenMiner algorithm, which allows to mine association rules from genomic data. While in [33], they proposed the Debi algorithm which is based on 0/1 discretization, then, generate association rules. In [10], the authors proposed an association rules-based biclustering algorithm that uses the Apriori algorithm. The authors in [28] provide a recent review of various biological applications of association rules mining.

These biclustering algorithms using formal concept analysis, however, have the tendency to either focus on one type of biclusters, extract overlapping ones or refrain from biological validation.

In this paper, we address the issue of extracting biclusters from gene expression data using ARM (Association Rules Mining). The key of our BiARM concerns the use of the $\mathcal{IGB}$ (Informative Generic Base) representation defined by [19] as a set of valid association rules. The $\mathcal{IGB}$ is a generic base of association rules, based on the Galois connection semantics. This generic base is informative and compact [19]. The $\mathcal{IGB}$'s generic rules represent implications between minimal premises and maximal conclusions (in terms of the number of items). Indeed, It was proven in the literature that this type of rules is the most general (i.e., conveying the maximum of information).

The remainder of the paper is organized as follows: Sect. 2 recalls the main definitions and notations that will be used throughout the remainder. Section 3 is dedicated to the description of our *BiARM* algorithm. The encouraging results of the application of our algorithm on real microarray datasets are shown in Sect. 4. Conclusion and perspectives are sketched in Sect. 5.

2   Basic Notions and Preliminaries

We give, in the following, the basic notions and definitions needed in this work;

Definition 1 (Biclustering and Biclusters).   *The biclustering problem focuses on the identification of the best biclusters of a given dataset.*

In Biclustering, microarray data is represented by a data matrix $M(I, J)$, where each cell represents the gene expression level of a gene under an experimental condition.

A bicluster is a subset of genes associated with a subset of conditions in which these genes are co-expressed. The bicluster associated with the matrix $M(I, J)$ is a couple (A, B), such that $A \subseteq I$ and $B \subseteq J$, and (A, B) is maximal (if there does not exist a bicluster (C, D) with $A \subseteq C$ or $B \subseteq D$).

Definition 2 (Formal Context). A formal context is a triple $\mathcal{K} = (G, M, \mathcal{R})$ where G is a set of objects, M is a set of attributes and the binary relation $\mathcal{R} \subseteq G \times M$ shows which objects have which attributes. A formal context can be represented by a cross- table (Table 1). For $A \subseteq G$, we define: $A' = \{m \in M \mid \forall\, g \in A, (g, m) \in \mathcal{R}\}$ and dually for $B \subseteq M$: $B' = \{g \in G \mid \forall\, m \in B, (g, m) \in \mathcal{R}\}$. Roughly speaking, A' is the set of all attributes common to the objects of A, while B' is the set of all objects that have all attributes in B.

Definition 3 (Itemsets). A non-empty finite set of $\mathcal{I} \subseteq M$ in $\mathcal{K}$ is called an itemset. An itemset containing k items is kalled $k - itemset$.

Definition 4 (Support). The support of an itemset $\mathcal{I}$, denoted $supp(\mathcal{I})$, is the frequency of occurrence of $\mathcal{I}$ in $\mathcal{K}$.

$$Supp(I) = \frac{|\{g \in G | I \subseteq g\}|}{|\{G\}|}. \tag{1}$$

Definition 5 (Frequent Itemsets). The itemset I is frequent if the support of I in $\mathcal{K}$ is at least equal to the user-defined threshold minsupp.

Definition 6 (Frequent Closed Itemsets). An itemset $I \subseteq \mathcal{I}$ is said to be closed if the application of the Galois closure operator ω to I gives I $(I = \omega(I))$, and is said to be frequent with respect to the minsupp threshold if $supp(I) \geq minsupp$ [19].

Definition 7 (Association Rules). Association rule derivation is achieved from a set F of frequent itemsets in an extraction context $\mathcal{K}$, for a minimal support minsupp. An association rule R is a relation between itemsets of the

Table 1. Example of a formal context.

	A	B	C	D	E
1	×		×	×	
2		×	×		×
3	×	×	×		×
4		×			×
5	×	×	×		×

form $R : X \implies (Y - X)$, *in which* X *and* Y *are frequent itemsets, and* $X \subset Y$. *The itemsets* X *and* $(Y - X)$ *are called, respectively, the premise and the conclusion of the rule* R *[19].*

Definition 8 (Confidence). *The Confidence of an association rule* $R : X \implies (Y - X)$ *is the ratio of the support of the itemset* $X \bigcup Y$ *to the support of the antecedent in the rule* R

$$Conf(R) = \frac{|supp(X \bigcup Y)|}{|supp(X)|} \tag{2}$$

The valid association rules are those having $Conf(R)$ *greater than or equal to the minimal threshold of confidence minconf. If* $Conf(R) = 1$ *then* R *is called an exact association rule, otherwise it is called an approximative association rule.*

Definition 9 (The Generic Base $\mathcal{IGB}$). *Let* $\mathcal{FCI}$ *be the set of frequent closed itemsets and* $\mathcal{G}_I$ *the set of minimal generators of a frequent closed itemset I.*

$\mathcal{IGB} = \{R : g_s \Rightarrow (I\text{-}g_s) \mid I \in \mathcal{FCI} \wedge I \neq \emptyset \wedge g_s \in \mathcal{G}_{I'}, I' \in \mathcal{FCI} \wedge I' \subseteq I \wedge confidence(R) \geq minconf \wedge \nexists g' / g' \subset g_s \wedge confidence(g' \Rightarrow I\text{-}g') \geq minconf\}$ *[19].*

Definition 10 (Jaccard Indice). *The Jaccard measure of two biclusters* B_1, B_2 *is defined as follows [20]:*

$$Jaccard(B_1, B_2) = \frac{|B_1 \bigcap B_2|}{|B_1 \bigcup B_2|} \tag{3}$$

So, for the genes $i \in |I_1 \bigcap I_2|$ *and the conditions* $j \in |J_1 \bigcap J_2|$, *we can redefine the Jaccard measure as follows:*

$$Jaccard(I_1, I_2) = \frac{|I_1 \bigcap I_2|}{|I_1 \bigcup I_2|} \tag{4}$$

and

$$Jaccard(J_1, J_2) = \frac{|J_1 \bigcap J_2|}{|J_1 \bigcup J_2|}. \tag{5}$$

3   The BiARM Algorithm

The *BiARM* biclustering algorithm is an ARM-based algorithm that identifies biclusters from gene expression data. *BiARM* operates in four main steps. The first one is the *discretization step* which consists in the binarization of the elements of the input data matrix. In this step, we start by discretizing the initial numerical data matrix into a -101 data matrix that represents the relation between all conditions for the gene set in the gene expression matrix, then we discretize the -101 data matrix into a binary one. The second step is the *mining step* where we extract the generic ARs that represent the bicluster's conditions.

The third step is the *closing step*; this one corresponds to the discovery of genes that support the conditions extracted in the mining step. Finally, we have the *filtering step* in which we compute the similarity measure. This latter is defined as the ratio between the conjunctive support of two biclusters and their disjunctive support where we consider only those having the Jaccard measure not exceeding a given threshold *minjaccard*. This is done in order to remove the biclusters that have high overlap.

The pseudo-code description of *BiARM* is shown in Algorithm 1.

Algorithm 1. BiARM

Data: A gene expression matrix $\mathcal{M}$, *minsupp*, *minconf* and *minjaccard*.
Result: The set of biclusters β.

1 **begin**
2     $\beta := \emptyset$;
3   /* **The first step** */
4   Discretize $\mathcal{M}$ using Eq. 6 to obtain $\mathcal{M}2$;
5   /* **The second step** */
6   Discretize $\mathcal{M}2$ using Eq. 7 to obtain $\mathcal{M}3$;
7   /* **The third step** */
8   Extract all generic ARs using *minsupp* and *minconf*;
9   Extract genes that support the frequent items (the supporting transactions)
        // obtained from line 8 ;
10   /* **The fourth step** */
11   **for** *each two biclusters* B_1, B_2 **do**
12   **if** *jaccard* $(B_1, B_2) < minjaccard$ **then**
13            $\beta = \beta \bigcup \{B_1 and B_2\}$
14   **else**
15            $\beta = \beta \bigcup \{B_1 or B_2\}$
16   **return** β;

Table 2. Example of gene expression matrix.

	c1	c2	c3	c4	c5	c6
g1	10	20	5	15	0	18
g2	20	30	15	25	26	25
g3	23	12	8	15	20	50
g4	30	40	25	35	35	15
g5	13	13	18	25	30	55
g6	20	20	15	8	12	23

Table 3. The -101 data matrix (M2)

	C1	C2	C3	C4	C5	C6	C7	C8	C9	C10	C11	C12	C13	C14	C15
g1	1	-1	1	-1	1	-1	-1	-1	-1	1	-1	1	-1	1	1
g2	1	-1	1	1	1	-1	-1	-1	-1	1	1	1	1	0	-1
g3	-1	-1	-1	-1	1	-1	1	1	1	1	1	1	1	1	1
g4	1	-1	1	1	-1	-1	-1	-1	-1	1	1	-1	0	-1	-1
g5	0	1	1	1	1	1	1	1	1	1	1	1	1	1	1
g6	0	-1	-1	-1	1	-1	-1	-1	1	-1	-1	1	1	1	1

3.1 Step 1: From Numerical Data to -101 Data Matrix

Our method, at first, applies a preprocessing step to transform the original data matrix M into a -101 data matrix M2. This step aims to highlight the trajectory patterns of genes. According to both [25,31], in microarray data analysis, we add genes into a bicluster (cluster) whenever their trajectory patterns of expression levels are similar across a set of conditions.

Interestingly enough our proposed discretization step keeps track of the profile shape[1] over conditions and preserves the similarity information of trajectory patterns of the expression levels.

Before applying the ARM algorithm, we must first discretize the initial data matrix (Line 4). The discretization process outputs the -101 data matrix. It consists in combining in pairs, for each gene, all the conditions between them. Indeed, the -101 data matrix gives an idea about the profile. Furthermore, one can have a global view of the profile of all conditions between them.

In our case, each column of -101 data matrix represents the meaning of the variation of genes between a pair of conditions of M. The -101 data matrix offers useful information for the identification of biclusters i.e., up (1), down (-1) and no change (0).

Formally the matrix M2 (-101 data matrix) is defined as follows:

$$M2 = \begin{cases} 1 & \text{if } M[i,l] < M[i,l2] \\ -1 & \text{if } M[i,l] > M[i,l2] \\ 0 & \text{if } M[i,l] = M[i,l2] \end{cases} \tag{6}$$

with:

$i \in [1 \dots n]; l \in [1 \dots m-1] ; l2 \in [i+1 \dots m];$

Let us consider the dataset given by Table 2. Using Eq. 6, we represent the -101 data matrix as shown in Table 3.

---

[1] Which may be either monotone increasing, monotone decreasing, up-down or down-up, etc.

Table 4. The binary data matrix (M3)

	C1	C2	C3	C4	C5	C6	C7	C8	C9	C10	C11	C12	C13	C14	C15
g1	0	0	0	1	0	0	0	0	1	0	1	0	1	0	0
g2	0	0	0	0	0	0	0	0	1	0	0	0	0	0	1
g3	0	0	1	1	0	0	1	1	0	0	0	0	0	0	0
g4	0	0	0	0	1	0	0	0	1	0	0	1	0	1	1
g5	1	1	0	0	0	1	1	1	0	0	0	0	0	0	0
g6	1	0	1	1	0	0	0	0	0	1	1	0	0	0	0

3.2   Step 2: From −101 Data to Binary Data Matrix

Let $M2$ be a -101 data matrix (Table 3), in order to build the binary data matrix (Line 6), we compute the average number of repetitions for each column in the matrix $M2$, e.g., for the column $C1$ we have:

1. Maxrepeat that stands for the Maximum number of occurrences by column is set equal to 3 and corresponds to the maxvalue 1.
2. Minrepeat that stands for Minimum number of occurrences by column is set equal to 1 and corresponds to the minvalue -1. In addition, mediamrepeat is 2 and corresponds to the value 0. So, the *average value* is 0.

Then, we define the binary matrix as follows:

$$M3 = \begin{cases} 1 & \text{if } \; x_1 = average\ value \\ 0 & \text{otherwise} \end{cases} \tag{7}$$

Using Eq. 7 we obtain the binary matrix sketched in Table 4. It is better to choose the mean value since the maximum will produce a huge number of overlapping biclusters, while the minimum value generates biologically none-valid biclusters.

3.3   Step 3: Extracting Biclusters

After preparing the binary data matrix, we move to extract Biclusters from the matrix M3 (Table 4). To perform this task we divide the problem into two sub-problems:

1. Finding all the generic ARs that represent bicluster's conditions (from the transactional representation).
2. Extracting the genes that support the conditions extracted in the previous step.

The problem of mining association rules was initially applied to market basket analysis. This problem consists in finding interesting associations among items and itemsets from transactional datasets. ARM was introduced for pattern mining and knowledge discovery. It has been studied by many authors who tried

Table 5. Transactional representation of the binary data set given in Table 4.

Transactions	Items
1	4 9 11 13
2	9 15
3	3 4 7 8
4	5 9 12 14 15
5	1 2 6 7 8
6	1 3 4 10 11

Table 6. *IGB* basis association rules extracted from Table 5 ($minsupp = 40\%$, $minconf = 80\%$).

Association rule	Support	Confidence
$R1 : 3 \Longrightarrow 4$	0.33	1
$R2 : 7 \Longrightarrow 8$	0.33	1
$R3 : 11 \Longrightarrow 4$	0.33	1
$R4 : 8 \Longrightarrow 7$	0.33	1
$R5 : 15 \Longrightarrow 9$	0.33	1

to improve the task. Thus, there exists a wide range of efficient methods and techniques to ascertain association rules from enormous data repositories. The majority of these studies concentrated on finding the best way to extract the most relevant ARs. They proposed several theoretical frameworks in order to minimize the search space, improve the effectiveness of the AR extraction from the dataset and reduce the number of the generated rules. In this work, we use the $\mathcal{IGB}$ representation of the set of valid ARs defined by [19]. Our choice of this base is justified by the theoretical framework presented in [19]. We extract the generic ARs from the transactional representation (Table 5) that represent the bicluster's conditions with respect to *minconf* and *minsupp* measures (Line 8) where we use confidence as the homogeneity criteria. In other words, we try to increase the confidence and decrease the value of the support. After extracting the $\mathcal{IGB}$ base, we move to extract the supporting transactions (genes) from each rule in this base (Line 9).

By using the previous example we obtain as a result the association rules presented in Table 6. Taking the example of the rule $R1$, the obtained biluster is $B1 =< (g3, g4), (C3, C4) >$.

3.4 Step 4: The Similarity Measure

The *BiARM* algorithm has already been able to identify overlapping biclusters. In order to compute the similarity between two biclusters $B1$ and $B2$, we use the Jaccard measure (Definition 10). This latter measures the overlapping between two Biclusters. This score is used to measure the overlap between two *BiARM-Biclusters* in terms of both genes and conditions.

In fact, for the filtering process (Lines 13 and 15), we consider only biclusters with a low overlap (if two biclusters have a high overlap, then they have the same biological signification).

The correlation measure achieves its minimum of 0 when the biclusters do not overlap at all and its maximum of 1 when they are identical.

4   Experimental Results

In this section we provide the experimental results of using our algorithm on two well-known real-life datasets. The evaluation of the biclustering algorithms and their comparison are based on two criteria: *Statistical criteria* and *Biological criteria*. We compare our algorithm with the state-of-the-art biclustering algorithms and the Trimax algorithm[2] [21] which use Formal Concept Analysis.

4.1   Description of the used datasets

In order to assess the performance of our proposed algorithm and analyze its results, we conduct a series of experimentations on the following real gene expression datasets.

Yeast Cell-Cycle Dataset: The yeast cell-cycle[3] is a very popular dataset in the gene expression data. In fact, it is one of the most known organisms and the functions of each gene are well known. We used the *Yeast cell-cycle dataset* available in [13], it contains 2884 genes and 17 conditions. In the experimentations we conduct on this base, the parameters of *BiARM minsupp*, *minconf*, *minjaccard* are experimentally set to 20 %, 80 % and 25 %. The running time of BiARM on this test was 99 sec.

Human B-cell Lymphoma Dataset: The Human B-cell Lymphoma dataset [1] contains 4026 genes and 96 conditions[4]. We experimentally set the *BiARM* parameters *minsupp*, *minconf* and *minjaccard* to 20 %, 90 % and 25 %, for our experiments on this dataset. The running time of BiARM on this test was 279 sec.

4.2   Statistical Relevance

To evaluate the statistical relevance of our algorithm, we use the *p-values* by applying the web tool FuncAssociate and the coverage criteria.

---

[2] Available at https://github.com/mehdi-kaytoue/trimax.
[3] Available at http://arep.med.harvard.edu/biclustering/.
[4] Available at http://arep.med.harvard.edu/biclustering/.

Table 7. Human B-cell Lymphoma Coverage for different algorithms.

Human B-cell Lymphoma			
Algorithms	Total coverage	Genes coverage	Conditions coverage
BiMine	8.93 %	26.15 %	100 %
BiMine+	21.19 %	46.26 %	100 %
BicFinder	44.24 %	55.89 %	100 %
MOPSOB	36.90 %	-	-
MOEA	20.96 %	-	-
SEBI	34.07 %	38.23 %	100 %
CC	36.81 %	91.58 %	100 %
Trimax	8.50 %	46.32 %	11.46 %
BiARM	**73.12 %**	**99.97 %**	**100 %**

Table 8. Significant GO terms (process, function, component) for two biclusters on yeast cell-cycle data extracted by *BiARM*.

	Bicluster1	Bicluster2
Biological process	cytoplasmic translation (15.0 %, 2.4 %, 8.39e-51)	single-organism process (55.6 %, 49.5 %, 9.74e-13)
	DNA repair (8.8 %, 3.4 %, 7.55e-08)	cell cycle process (11.6 %, 8.3 %, 1.17e-11)
	organic substance biosynthetic process (40.7 %, 29.4 %, 2.98e-07)	single-organism cellular process (49.7 %, 44.0 %, 5.88e-11)
Molecular function	structural constituent of ribosome (14.4 %, 3.1 %, 3.80e-35)	structural molecule activity (6.8 %, 4.8 %, 8.88e-07)
	structural molecule activity (16.5 %, 4.8 %, 2.25e-28)	structural constituent of cytoskeleton (0.8 %, 0.3 % 0.00984)
Cellular component	cytosolic ribosome (15.2 %, 2.4 %, 1.90e-51)	non-membrane-bounded organelle (22.9 %, 18.3 %, 5.34 e-12)
	cytosolic part (15.7 %, 3.2 %, 4.53e-41)	intracellular non-membrane-bounded organelle (22.9 %, 18.3 %, 5.34e-12)
	cytosolic small ribosomal su bunit (7.3 %, 0.9 %, 3.43e-30)	organelle (65.4 %, 60.4 %, 2.60e-09)

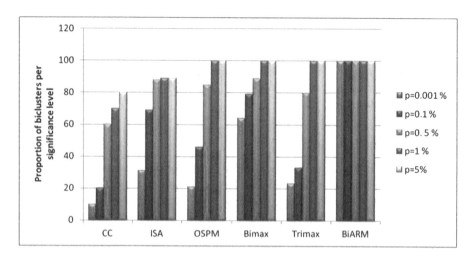

Fig. 1. Proportions of Biclusters significantly enriched by GO annotations (Yeast cell-cycle dataset)

Coverage: As in [4,23,24], we use the criterion of the coverage which is defined as the total number of cells in microarray data matrix covered by the obtained biclusters. We compare the results of our algorithm with Trimax [21] and those reported by [2], namely, CC [12], BiMine [3], BiMine+ [5], BicFinder [4], MOP-SOB [24], MOEA [27] and SEBI [16].

Table 7 presents the coverage of the obtained biclusters, we can show that most of the algorithms have relatively close results. For the Human B-cell Lymphoma dataset, the biclusters extracted by our algorithm cover 99.97 % of the genes, 100 % of the conditions and 73.12 % of the cells in the initial matrix. However, Trimax has low performance since it covers only 8.50 % of cells, 46.32 % of genes and 11.46 % of conditions. This implies that our algorithm can generate biclusters with high coverage of a data matrix due to the discretisation step where the combinations of all the paired conditions give useful information since a bicluster may be composed of a subset of non contiguous conditions.

P-Value: To assess the quality of the extracted biclusters, we use the web tool *FuncAssociate*[5] [9] in order to compute the adjusted significance scores for each bicluster (adjusted *p-value*[6]). Indeed, The best biclusters have an adjusted *p-value* less than 0.001 %. The results of our algorithm are compared with CC [12], ISA [8], OSPM [7] and Bimax [32], we report the results of the algorithms mentioned before from [2]. We also compare our algorithm with Trimax [21].

The obtained results of the Yeast Cell Cycle dataset for the different adjusted *p-values* (p = 5 %; 1 %; 0,5 %; 0,1 %; 0,001 %) for each algorithm over the

---

[5] Available at http://llama.mshri.on.ca/funcassociate/.
[6] The adjusted significance scores asses genes in each bicluster, which indicates how well they match with the different GO categories.

percentage of total biclusters are depicted in Fig. 1. The *BiARM* results show that 100 % of the extracted biclusters are statistically significant with the adjusted *p-value* $p < 0.001$ %. By contrast, Trimax achieves 100 % of statistically significant biclusters when $p < 1$ %. It is important to note that Bimax achieved its best results when $p < 0.1$ %, while CC, ISA and OSPM have a reasonable performance with $p < 0.5$ %.

4.3   Biological Relevance

The biological criteria allows to measure the quality of the resulting biclusters, by checking whether the genes of a bicluster have common biological characteristics.

To evaluate the quality of the extracted biclusters and identify their biological annotations, we use **GOTermFinder**[7] which is designed to search for the significant shared Gene Ontology (GO) terms of a group of genes. The ontologies are represented by direct acyclic graphs where GO terms represent nodes and the relationships between them represent edges. GO is organized according to 3 axis: *biological process, molecular function* and *cellular component*[8]. *GOTermFinder* can find the significant shared GO terms for genes within the same bicluster. We show in Table 8 the result of a random selected set of genes for the biological process, molecular function and cellular component, we report the most significant GO terms. The values within parentheses after each GO term in Table 8, such as (15.0 %, 2.4 %, 8.39e-51) in the first bicluster, indicate the cluster frequency, background frequency and the statistical significance, respectively. The cluster frequency shows that for the first bicluster, 15.0 % of genes belong to this process, while background frequency shows that this bicluster contains 2.4 % of the number of genes in the background set and the statistical significance is provided by a *p-value* of 8.39e-51 (highly significant).

The results on these real datasets show that our proposed algorithm can identify biclusters with a high biological relevance.

5   Conclusion

A new ARM-based biclustering method (**BiARM**) was proposed as a new biclustering algorithm for gene expression data. Our algorithm relies on the extraction of ARs from the dataset by discretizing this latter into a binary data matrix. The resulting biclusters were filtered with the help of the similarity measure in order to remove those with a high overlap.

The performance of the *BiARM* algorithm is assessed on two real DNA microarray datasets. These experimentations show that *BiARM* allows to extract high quality biclusters. These biclusters were evaluated with *Gene Ontology* (GO) annotations which checks the biological significance of biclusters. The obtained results confirm the *BiARM*'s ability to extract significant Biclusters.

---

[7] Available at http://db.yeastgenome.org/cgi-bin/GO/goTermFinder.

[8] http://geneontology.org/.

Other avenues of future work concern the application of *BiARM* on synthetic datasets where the original Jaccard measure is improved by using the match score to analyze our algorithm's ability to extract all implanted biclusters. Furthermore, we plan on using our method in other application domains such as text mining, target marketing and multimedia data processing. We also wish to extend our work to other correlations measures [30] through classifying them into classes of measures sharing the same properties. In addition to that we intend to confirm the efficiency of our algorithm by calculating its complexity.

References

1. Alizadeh, A.A., Eisen, M.B., Davis, R.E., Ma, C., Lossos, I.S., Rosenwald, A., Boldrick, J.C., Sabet, H., Tran, T., Yu, X., Powell, J.I., Yang, L., Marti, G.E., Moore, T., Hudson, J.J., Lu, L., Lewis, D.B., Tibshirani, R., Sherlock, G., Chan, W.C., Greiner, T.C., Weisenburger, D.D., Armitage, J.O., Warnke, R., Levy, R., Wilson, W., Grever, M.R., Byrd, J.C., Botstein, D., Brown, P.O., Staudt, L.M.: Distinct types of diffuse large b-cell lymphoma identified by gene expression profiling. Nature **403**(6769), 503–511 (2000)
2. Ayadi, W.: Algorithmes Systematiques et Stochastiques de Biregroupement pour l'Analyse des Donnees Biopuces. Ph.D. thesis, University of Angers, France (2011)
3. Ayadi, W., Elloumi, M., Hao, J.K.: A biclustering algorithm based on a bicluster enumeration tree: application to dna microarray data. BioData Min. **2**, 9 (2009)
4. Ayadi, W., Elloumi, M., Hao, J.K.: Bicfinder: a biclustering algorithm for microarray data analysis. Knowl. Inf. Syst. **30**(2), 341–358 (2012)
5. Ayadi, W., Elloumi, M., Hao, J.K.: Bimine+: An efficient algorithm for discovering relevant biclusters of dna microarray data. Knowl.-Based Syst. **35**, 224–234 (2012)
6. Ayadi, W., Elloumi, M., Hao, J.-K.: Iterated local search for biclustering of microarray data. In: Dijkstra, T.M.H., Tsivtsivadze, E., Marchiori, E., Heskes, T. (eds.) PRIB 2010. LNCS, vol. 6282, pp. 219–229. Springer, Heidelberg (2010)
7. Ben-Dor, A., Chor, B., Karp, R.M., Yakhini, Z.: Discovering local structure in gene expression data: The order-preserving submatrix problem. J. Comput. Biol. **10**(3/4), 373–384 (2003)
8. Bergmann, S., Ihmels, J., Barkai, N.: Defining transcription modules using large-scale gene expression data. Bioinformatics **20**(13), 1993–2003 (2004)
9. Berriz, G.F., King, O.D., Bryant, B., Sander, C., Roth, F.P.: Characterizing gene sets with funcassociate. Bioinformatics **19**, 2502–2504 (2003)
10. Boutsinas, B.: A new biclustering algorithm based on association rule mining. Int. J. Artif. Intell. Tools **22**(3) (2013). http://dx.doi.org/10.1142/S0218213013500176
11. Cheng, K.O., Law, N.F., Siu, W.C., Liew, A.W.C.: Identification of coherent patterns in gene expression data using an efficient biclustering algorithm and parallel coordinate visualization. BMC Bioinform. **210**(9), 1282–1283 (2008)
12. Cheng, Y., Church, G.M.: Biclustering of expression data. In: Proceedings of ISMB, UC San Diego, California, pp. 93–103 (2000)
13. Cheng, Y., Church, G.M.: Biclustering of expression data. Technical report, supplementary information (2006)
14. Das, S., Idicula, S.M.: Application of cardinality based grasp to the biclustering of gene expression data. Int. J. Comput. Appl. **1**, 44–53 (2010)

15. Divina, F., Aguilar-Ruiz, J.S.: A multi-objective approach to discover biclusters in microarray data. In: Genetic and Evolutionary Computation Conference, GECCO 2007, Proceedings, London, England, UK, July 7–11, 2007. pp. 385–392 (2007). http://doi.acm.org/10.1145/1276958.1277038

16. Divina, F., AguilarRuiz, J.S.: Biclustering of expression data with evolutionary computation. IEEE Trans. Knowl. Data Eng. **18**(5), 590–602 (2006)

17. Freitas, A., Ayadi, W., Elloumi, M., Oliveira, L.J., Hao, J.K.: Survey on biclustering of gene expression data. In: Biological Knowledge Discovery Handbook: Preprocessing, Mining, and Postprocessing of Biological Data. pp. 591–608 (2013)

18. Gallo, C.A., Carballido, J.A., Ponzoni, I.: Microarray biclustering: a novel memetic approach based on the PISA platform. In: Pizzuti, C., Ritchie, M.D., Giacobini, M. (eds.) EvoBIO 2009. LNCS, vol. 5483, pp. 44–55. Springer, Heidelberg (2009)

19. Gasmi, G., Yahia, S.B., Nguifo, E.M., Slimani, Y.: $\mathcal{IGB}$: a new informative generic base of association rules. In: Ho, T.-B., Cheung, D., Liu, H. (eds.) PAKDD 2005. LNCS (LNAI), vol. 3518, pp. 81–90. Springer, Heidelberg (2005). http://dx.doi.org/10.1007/11430919_11

20. Jaccard, P.: Etude comparative de la distribution florale dans une portion des alpes et du jura. Bulletin de la socit Vaudoise des Siences Naturelles **37**, 547–579 (1901)

21. Kaytoue, M., Kuznetsov, S.O., Macko, J., Napoli, A.: Biclustering meets triadic concept analysis. Ann. Math. Artif. Intell. **70**(1–2), 55–79 (2014). http://dx.doi.org/10.1007/s10472-013-9379-1

22. Kaytoue, M., Kuznetsov, S.O., Napoli, A.: Biclustering Numerical Data in Formal Concept Analysis. In: Jäschke, R. (ed.) ICFCA 2011. LNCS, vol. 6628, pp. 135–150. Springer, Heidelberg (2011)

23. Liu, J., Li, Z., Hu, X., Chen, Y.: Biclustering of microarray data with MOSPO based on crowding distance. BMC Bioinform. **10**(S-4) (2009). http://dx.doi.org/10.1186/1471-2105-10-S4-S9

24. Liu, J., Li, Z., Liu, F., Chen, Y.: Multi-objective particle swarm optimization biclustering of microarray data. In: 2008 IEEE International Conference on Bioinformatics and Biomedicine, BIBM 2008, 3–5 November 2008, Philadephia, Pennsylvania, USA, pp. 363–366 (2008). http://doi.ieeecomputersociety.org/10.1109/BIBM.2008.17

25. Luan, Y., Li, H.: Clustering of time-course gene expression data using a mixed-effects model with b-splines. Bioinformatics **19**(4), 474–482 (2003)

26. Martínez, R., Pasquier, N., Pasquier, C.: Genminer: mining non-redundant association rules from integrated gene expression data and annotations. Bioinformatics **24**(22), 2643–2644 (2008). http://dx.doi.org/10.1093/bioinformatics/btn490

27. Mitra, S., Banka, H.: Multi-objective evolutionary biclustering of gene expression data. Pattern Recogn. **39**, 2464–2477 (2006)

28. Mondal, K.C., Pasquier, N.: Galois closure based association rule mining from biological data. In: Elloumi, M., Zomaya, A.Y. (eds.) Biological Knowledge Discovery Handbook: Preprocessing, Mining, and Postprocessing of Biological Data, pp. 761–802. Wiley, USA (2014)

29. Mondal, K.C., Pasquier, N., Mukhopadhyay, A., Maulik, U., Bandhopadyay, S.: A new approach for association rule mining and bi-clustering using formal concept analysis. In: Perner, P. (ed.) MLDM 2012. LNCS, vol. 7376, pp. 86–101. Springer, Heidelberg (2012)

30. Omiecinski, E.R.: Alternative interest measures for mining associations in databases. IEEE Trans. Knowl. Data Eng. **15**, 57–69 (2003)

31. Peddada, S., Lobenhofer, E., Li, L., Afshari, C., Weinberg, C.: Gene selection and clustering for time-course and dose-response microarray experiments using order-restricted inference. Bioinformatics **19**, 834–841 (2003)
32. Prelic, A., Bleuler, S., Zimmermann, P., Wille, A., Buhlmann, P., Gruissem, W., Hennig, L., Thiele, L., Zitzler, E.: A systematic comparison and evaluation of biclustering methods for gene expression data. Bioinformatics **22**(9), 1122–1129 (2006)
33. Serin, A., Vingron, M.: Debi: discovering differentially expressed biclusters using a frequent itemset approach. Algorithms Mol. Biol. **6**, 18–29 (2011). http://dx.doi.org/10.1186/1748-7188-6-18
34. Tanay, A., Sharan, R., Shamir, R.: Discovering statistically significant biclusters in gene expression data. Bioinformatics **18**, S136–S144 (2002)
35. Teng, L., Chan, L.: Discovering biclusters by iteratively sorting with weighted correlation coefficient in gene expression data. J. Sig. Process. Syst. **50**, 267–280 (2008)

Data Engineering for Materials Identification, Damage Assessment and Restoration of Cultural Objects

Erion-Vasilis Pikoulis[1], Evangelos Sakkopoulos[1(✉)],
Emmanouil Viennas[1], Nick Achilleopoulos[1], Eleni Cheilakou[2],
Amani-Christiana Saint[2], Maria Koui[2], and Athanasios Tsakalidis[1]

[1] Graphics, Multimedia and GIS System Lab, Computer Engineering
and Informatics Department, University of Patras, 26504 Rio Patras, Greece
{pikoulis,sakkopul,biennas,achilleopoulos,
tsak}@ceid.upatras.gr
[2] Department of Materials Science and Engineering, NDT Lab,
School of Chemical Engineering, National Technical University of Athens,
Athens, Greece
{elenheil,markoue}@mail.ntua.gr, amani@central.ntua.gr

Abstract. Cultural objects and art works need ongoing conservation interventions in order to be available for the generations to come. The most object-friendly analysis approaches are based on non destructive techniques (NDTs) that allow both the materials characterization/evaluation as well as the decay detection and assessment of cultural artifacts.

Non destructive testing and evaluation includes the employment of several methods such as the well-established technique of Diffuse Reflectance Spectroscopy with Fiber Optics (FORS). FORS allows the reflectance spectral analysis of the pigments used in artifacts, which leads to their identification. Such techniques produce output with large volumes of data for each different pigment used in objects. In this work, we present a data management solution that contributes with (1) a library of known reference pigments/colors of archaeological objects along with (2) a proposed novel pattern matching technique that allows the automatic classification of any new pigment that is recovered from cultural objects using the FORS measurements. The proposed technique is based on a k-NN classifier. The experimental evaluation results of the proposed technique show that the data processing proposed is both effective and efficient. Feedback for the proposed approach is particularly encouraging as it allows automation and therefore radically decreased time for pigment/color matching and identification.

Keywords: Matching colors · Fiber optics diffuse reflectance spectroscopy · Data management · Non destructive techniques · NDT image analysis

1 Introduction

Cultural objects and art works need continuous conservation interventions in order to survive for the generations to come. The most object-friendly analysis approaches are based on non destructive techniques (NDTs) that allow the materials characterization as

© Springer International Publishing Switzerland 2015
L. Bellatreche and Y. Manolopoulos (Eds.): MEDI 2015, LNCS 9344, pp. 154–165, 2015.
DOI: 10.1007/978-3-319-23781-7_13

well as the decay detection and evaluation of conservation interventions on cultural works. Non-destructive methods are used for the examination of surfaces in situ [3], without sampling, thus without damaging the under investigation artifact. In archaeology, in situ refers to measurements performed on artifacts at their location (i.e. museum, archaeological site). Such an approach accords with strict regulations where sampling or micro-sampling, or even the transfer of the artifacts for laboratory analysis is prohibited, for the protection of their integrity.

NDT techniques such as FORS (Fig. A, Table 1) usually produce large amounts of data sets, typically consisting of images, spectral data and graphs. Therefore, it is imperative to work towards the data management in order to achieve a comprehensive analysis of the obtained data, aiming to define a specific data process which can be easily integrated in decision support systems finally. The aim is to rise as much as possible information on the materials identification and the decay patterns detection and characterization (i.e. type, extent) of the artifacts.

Table 1. VIS-Near IR Fiber Optics Diffuse Reflectance Spectroscopy (FORS) output description. **Fig. A.** Experimental set up: USB4000 Fiber Optic Reflectance Spectrometer (4) equipped with a reflection bifurcated probe (1), a tungsten-halogen light source (3) and a probe holder (2)

Method	in situ VIS – Near IR Fiber Optics Diffuse Reflectance Spectroscopy (FORS)
Output	
Diagrams/ Spectra	Diffuse reflectance spectra in the spectral range of 350 - 1000 nm (produced from Spec-trasuite Software)
x-axis	Wavelength (nm)
y- axis	Reflectance (%)
Spectrasuite data file (provid-ing values in notepad format)	Wavelength (λ) data vs Re-flectance (R) data (values in notepad format) which can be processed as needed (in excel, origin, etc environment) in order to produce the spectra in the range of 350 - 1000 nm

The generic characteristic of most of the non-destructive diagnostic methods is that they are recent technological applications and have not yet developed their full potential. In general, it is highly preferable to combine the employment of NDTs with advanced sophisticated methods to be used in laboratory on samples, when sampling is permitted, for the performance of a more detailed study regarding the identification of materials and damage assessment.

For this task, we have developed a new technique for the automatic classification of pigments, based on in situ VIS-Near IR Fiber Optics Diffuse Reflectance Spectroscopy (FORS) measurements, a technique that is further analysed in Sect. 2. The proposed data matching technique follows a pattern recognition approach and it is based on a kNN classifier, which constitutes the most popular representative of the family of deterministic methods [7, 8]. The goal of any automatic pattern recognition system is to estimate the correct label (class identifier) corresponding to a given feature vector or a template, based on the prior knowledge obtained through training [5, 6]. In our case, the goal is the automatic recognition of the pigment used on the object of interest, based on one (or more) FORS measurements obtained from it. The system uses prior knowledge that is provided in the form of a library data set of measurements, taken from known pigments identified by experts' analyses.

The proposed technique can be implemented either as a standalone system, or as part of a more comprehensive analysis/classification tool, in conjunction with other NDT techniques (i.e. portable XRF spectroscopy), and/or with the intervention of a human analyst. In any case, the obtained results are indeed very promising, thus encouraging the exploration of other similar approaches within the NDT framework.

The major tasks involved in the development process were (a) the selection of the system model (i.e. the k-NN classifier) out of a number of possible approaches, (b) the collection of the training and validation datasets, (c) the derivation of a suitable data-enhancement procedure, and (d) the selection of the system parameters through a series of validation experiments. The paper is organized as follows: Sect. 2 presents the FORS NDT method. Section 3 presents the novel algorithmic system. Section 4 presents validation experiments. Finally, Sect. 5 concludes the paper.

2 Image Processing Methods on the NDTs Methods and Output

In recent years, major effort has been made in order to develop techniques for the elaboration of data obtained by NDTs [2, 3]. These techniques are usually based on a set of basic tools developed for this purpose. These tools usually produce a low quality data set, typically a series of images, spectral data and graphs. Therefore, this action should include a comprehensive analysis of the obtained data, in collaboration with scientists working on the analysis of these data, aiming to define a specific data structure which can be easily integrated. The aim is to rise as much as possible information on the materials identification and the decay patterns detection and characterization (i.e. type, extent) of the artifacts.

The recognition procedures of specific regions or edges has been studied and improved as well. A great deal of effort will be devoted to study the various layers of NDTs processing procedures in order to exploit information which was not visible so far. Before proceeding to the presentation of new techniques, in order to exploit the information contained in spectral data and charts, we discuss shortly the experimental device and data output of FORS technique.

In situ VIS-Near IR Fiber Optics Diffuse Reflectance Spectroscopy (FORS) is used to identify pigments in pictorial layers of works of art by comparing the spectra collected in situ with suitable spectral databases of reference pigments. As mentioned above, measurements are non-invasive, even without any contact, and can be implemented in situ, without transferring the art works under investigation from the place where they are exposed. The experimental device, delivers a series of data (Table 1). The numerical processing of pigment identification is given below.

3   The Proposed System

3.1   Outline

The implementation of the proposed system can be divided into two major phases, namely the design phase, and the running phase. In the following subsections, we give a brief description of the steps involved during the design phase, as well as an outline of the proposed algorithm that will be executed during the running phase.

System Design. *Training & Validation data sets*: Collect a data set of FORS measurements, from known pigments (classes), from both real objects, as well as reference substances, according to the above presented guidelines.

- *Preprocessing.* Design a preprocessing procedure, tailored to the specific needs of the FORS measurements, with the goal of data enhancement.
- *Specification of system parameters*: Conduct a series of experiments using the validation data set, with the goal of maximizing system performance, with respect to the following degrees of freedom:
  - Pattern selection:
    - Case A: Every training sample is a pattern. In this case, each class is represented by the (whole) respective set of training instances.
    - Case B: Each class is represented by a single pattern. This single representative can be the average (or some other cendroid) of the training instances that belong to the same class.
  - Value of k.
  - Employed Distance Function.

Algorithm. *Input*: measurement array of unknown class (pigment).
  Preprocessing: apply the same procedure used for training data.

1. *Calculate distances* of input template form the patterns of the training data set.
2. *Sort* the resulting array of distance values.
3. *Count* the memberships of each class in the first k labels of the sorted distance array.
4. *Assign* the class with the highest membership to the input template.

3.2   Design Aspects

Training Data. As explained in the previous section, the proper selection of the training and validation data sets plays an important role in the design of a pattern recognition system, such as the kNN classifier presented here. On the one hand, the training data set comprises the knowledge of the system regarding the different classes it is required to recognize. On the other hand, the validation data set represents a sample of the future (unknown) measurements and can be used in order to estimate the system performance in real conditions.

With these goals in mind, we constructed our training data set from a series of pure reference pigments measurements, obtained in lab conditions. Each of the selected pigments represents the fundamental ingredient of its corresponding class, thus forming a basis of elements that is able to express the vast majority of the pigments encountered in real measurements. More specifically, the training data set consists of 10 reference measurements from each of the following classes (Table 2).

Table 2. Training data set, pigment library of ancient cultures

Class/ID	Pigment	Class/ID	Pigment
	(RED COLOR)		(GREEN COLOR)
1	Caput mortuum	9	Green Earth
2	Hematite	10	Malachite
3	Minium		(BROWN COLOR)
4	Red ochre		
5	Sienna Burnt	11	Umber Burnt
	(YELLOW COLOR)		(BLUE COLOR)
6	Sienna Raw	12	Azurite
7	Yellow Ochre	13	Egyptian Blue
8	Massicot	14	Ultramarine

Validation Data. The validation data set on the other hand, consists of measurements taken from real cultural objects and it is used in the final design stage for the evaluation of system performance and the selection of its parameters. An illustrative example of the measurement procedure, involving historic church wall paintings, is shown below. The results obtained from the FORS measurements on the red and green color impressions of the wall paintings presented in Fig. 1 (a and b) identified the presence of Cinnabar and Green Earth pigments, respectively. The respective FORS spectra acquired are demonstrated in Fig. 3a.

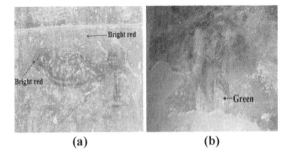

(a)   (b)

Fig. 1. Wall paintings decorating the Sanctuary of the Byzantine Theotokos Church at Meronas, Amari, Crete, representing: **(a)** the Melismos (*in Greek* Μελισμός), and **(b)** the presentation of the virgin (Color figure online).

Preprocessing. As it is readily apparent, the classification performance of kNN depends heavily on the separability of the class-representative measurements comprising the training data set. In cases where the discriminative (i.e. class-dependent) characteristics of the original measurements are obscured by irrelevant features (e.g. offset or amplitude), the introduction of preprocessing steps with the goal of eliminating the latter features and emphasizing the former ones, is unavoidable.

Since, as we are going to see, the FORS measurements comprising the training data set of the kNN pigment classifier fall into this category, a number of such data-enhancement steps are implemented in our system as well. The rationale behind these steps, as well as their enhancement effect, are best illustrated through a simple example involving three FORS measurements of red pigments from the given data set, with the first two corresponding to *hematite* (Fig. 2 *blue and red lines*), while the third one to *cinnabar* (Fig. 2 *black line*). The aforementioned measurements, which will be denoted as $x_1(\lambda_n), x_2(\lambda_n)$ and $x_3(\lambda_n)$, respectively, $n = 1, 2, \ldots, N$, with λ_n standing for wavelength (nm), are depicted following.

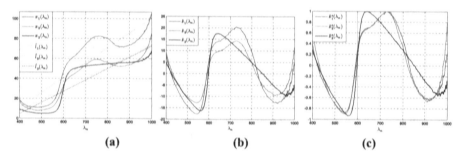

(a)   **(b)**   **(c)**

Fig. 2. **(a)** Original measurements (with their linear trends) **(b)** removal of linear trend **(c)** final outcome after normalization (Color figure online).

As it can be easily observed from above (Fig. 2a), $x_1(\lambda_n)$ and $x_2(\lambda_n)$ present common spectral characteristics (thus revealing their common identity), which are quite different from those of $x_3(\lambda_n)$. However, due to a number of factors that will be shortly analyzed, the true identity of the measurements is not reflected by their Euclidean distances, as the following table demonstrates.

Distance	$x_1(\lambda_n)$	$x_2(\lambda_n)$	$x_3(\lambda_n)$
$x_1(\lambda_n)$	–	9.7×10^5	11.9×10^5
$x_2(\lambda_n)$	9.7×10^5	–	0.76×10^5
$x_3(\lambda_n)$	11.9×10^5	0.76×10^5	–

To be more precise, according to the pairwise distances of the measurements, the nearest neighbor of $x_2(\lambda_n)$ is $x_3(\lambda_n)$ and not $x_1(\lambda_n)$, a fact that does not correspond to their true class memberships and could easily lead to misclassification errors in the final system. We must also stress here that this example does not represent an isolated case, but rather a common issue related to all measurements of the data set, as it will be demonstrated in the next section.

Linear Regression. A preprocessing approach that leads to an effective enhancement of the useful, class-dependent features of the measurements, is based on the observation that the initial measurements are distorted by different linear trends, as demonstrated in Fig. 2a. While these two features bare no useful information for the system (i.e. are not class dependent), they actually dominate the value of the Euclidean distance and account for the misleading measurement distances presented above. Thus, a preprocessing step able to neutralize their effect and yield a more representative version of the original measurements, must be introduced.

To this end, let us define the distortion model $\mathcal{M}$, as follows:

$$\mathcal{M} : x_i(\lambda_n) = c_i s_i(\lambda_n) + l(\lambda_n; a_i, b_i) + w_i(\lambda_n),$$

$$n = 1, 2, \ldots, N, i = 1, 2, \ldots, L,$$

where $s_i(\lambda_n)$ is the useful (i.e. informative) portion of the signal, $l(\lambda_n; a, b)$ is the unwanted linear trend, parameterized by the unknown parameters a_i, b_i, i.e.:

$$l(\lambda_n; a_i, b_i) = a_i \lambda_n + b_i,$$

and $w_i(\lambda_n)$ is some additive noise process. For our purposes, the effect of the additive noise will be considered as negligible (i.e. $w_i(\lambda_n) \approx 0$), since this is an issue that can be dealt with separately (e.g. by means of a denoising lowpass filter). The first goal of the preprocessing procedure is the estimation of the linear trend of the input measurement, i.e. of the unknown parameters a_i, b_i, in a least squares framework. By following this approach, the total estimation error $\varepsilon^2(a_i, b_i)$ is defined as the sum of the squared individual residuals, i.e.:

$$\varepsilon^2(a_i, b_i) = \sum_{n=1}^{N} r_i^2(\lambda_n; a_i, b_i),$$

where

$$r_i(\lambda_n; a_i, b_i) \equiv x_i(\lambda_n) - (a_i \lambda_n + b_i).$$

Then, the estimation of the unknown parameters a_i, b_i, is obtained by the solution of the following minimization problem:

$$\min_{a_i, b_i} \varepsilon^2(a_i, b_i),$$

which in our case leads to the following system of linear equations:

$$\begin{cases} \frac{\partial \varepsilon^2(a_i,b_i)}{\partial a} = 0 \\ \frac{\partial \varepsilon^2(a_i,b_i)}{\partial b_i} = 0. \end{cases}$$

After some mathematical manipulations, the optimal estimators of the unknown parameters can be obtained in a closed form solution, requiring only simple calculations over the input samples:

$$\hat{a}_i = \frac{N \sum_n [\lambda_n x_i(\lambda_n)] - \sum_n \lambda_n \sum_n x_i(\lambda_n)}{N \sum_n \lambda_n^2 - \left(\sum_n \lambda_n\right)^2}$$

$$\hat{b}_i = \frac{\sum_n \lambda_n^2 \sum_n x_i(\lambda_n) - \sum_n \lambda_n \sum_n [\lambda_n x_i(\lambda_n)]}{N \sum_n \lambda_n^2 - \left(\sum_n \lambda_n\right)^2}$$

Having obtained an estimation $\hat{l}_i(\lambda_n) = \hat{a}_i \lambda_n + \hat{b}_i$ of the linear trend of the measurement data, the desired useful signal $s_i(\lambda_n)$ can then be estimated by subtracting $\hat{l}_i(\lambda_n)$ from the original sequence $x_i(\lambda_n)$, i.e.:

$$\hat{s}_i(\lambda_n) = r_i(\lambda_n; \hat{a}_i, \hat{b}_i) = x_i(\lambda_n) - \hat{l}_i(\lambda_n).$$

The application of this preprocessing step to the measurements of the above mentioned example, namely $x_1(\lambda_n), x_2(\lambda_n)$ and $x_3(\lambda_n)$, results in the enhanced versions $\hat{s}_1(\lambda_n)$, $\hat{s}_2(\lambda_n)$ and $\hat{s}_3(\lambda_n)$, respectively, which are displayed in Fig. 1b.

As we can see, by removing the respective linear trends, the inherent class-dependent features of each measurement stand out and the new versions of the measurements can be more easily classified. Still, it is obvious that the amplitude difference, which is most observable between $\hat{s}_1(\lambda_n)$ and $\hat{s}_2(\lambda_n)$, introduces a false distance offset that does not correspond to the actual resemblance of the measurements. In order to eliminate this difference, we are going to introduce a simple normalizing step where we divide each of the above sequences by its maximal value. This yields the final versions of the measurements, denoted as $\hat{s}_1^o(\lambda_n)$, $\hat{s}_2^o(\lambda_n)$ and $\hat{s}_3^o(\lambda_n)$ that are depicted in Fig. 1c. (Note that in many cases, the maximum is taken in the middle of the λ_n interval, e.g. for $500 \leq \lambda_n \leq 900$ in order to avoid the extreme values that are sometimes present toward the ends of the interval. This is especially true for the measurements involving real objects, rather than the ones taken from pure pigments.

As we can see, the application of the presented preprocessing steps has had a very significant impact on the original measurements, with $\hat{s}_1^o(\lambda_n)$ and $\hat{s}_2^o(\lambda_n)$ being virtually identical, something that is verified by the pairwise Euclidean distances of the enhanced versions, shown in the Table 3 below.

As we can see, the distance between $\hat{s}_1^o(\lambda_n)$ and $\hat{s}_2^o(\lambda_n)$ is much less than the other two pairwise distances, something that is in total accordance with our expectations of two measurements taken from the same reference pigment in lab conditions. Figures 3 and 4 demonstrate the results of the proposed preprocessing step to a number instances from the available data set, both in reference, as well as real measurements.

Table 3. The pairwise Euclidean distances of the enhanced versions

Distance	$\hat{s}_1^o(\lambda_n)$	$\hat{s}_2^o(\lambda_n)$	$\hat{s}_3^o(\lambda_n)$
$\hat{s}_1^o(\lambda_n)$	–	31.5	178.6
$\hat{s}_2^o(\lambda_n)$	31.5	–	238.2
$\hat{s}_3^o(\lambda_n)$	178.6	238.2	–

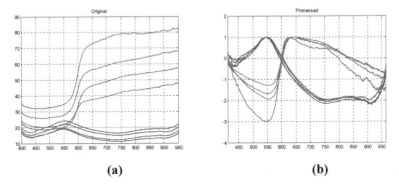

(a)   (b)

Fig. 3. A preprocessing example involving the real measurements of Cinnabar (red) and Green Earth (green), obtained from the objects that are displayed in Fig. 1. (a) Original, (b) processed (Color figure online).

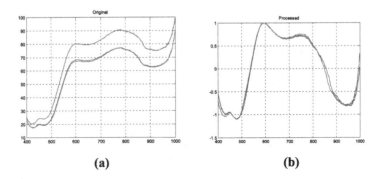

(a)   (b)

Fig. 4. A preprocessing example involving the reference measurements of Yellow Ochre. (a) Original, (b) processed. Μήπως εδώ θέλετε να πείτε Fig. 4 (Color figure online).

4   Validation Experiments

As already mentioned in previous section, the goal of the final system design stage is the evaluation of the validation performance of the system, for a set of different parameter values.

Based on these results, the values that yield the best overall performance are selected. By using the available validation data set (described in Sect. 4.2), we conducted a series of experiments, with the goal of examining the performance variations with regard to the following parameters:

(a) The number of patterns per class,
(b) The employed distance function, and
(c) The value of k.

In the first case, we examined the impact of selecting one pattern per class (i.e. the cendroid of the measurements), against considering each measurement as a pattern. In the second case, the performance achieved by the two distance functions that will be shortly defined, is examined. Finally, in the third experiment, we are concerned with the selection of the value of k. In each experiment, we fix the values of two parameters and evaluate the validation performance (i.e. the percentage of successful recognitions), for different values of the third one. The obtained results, as well the importance of each selection, are presented in the following subsections.

4.1 Number of Patterns Per Class

As already mentioned, two scenarios were examined:

1. ALL the instances of the training data set and conduct experiments with various values of k in order to select the most suitable. This implementation leads to the most comprehensive representation of the classes, and it is expected to yield the best classification results. On the other hand, it requires the calculation of N distance values, where N the number of training patterns, as well as a sorting scheme of the resulting $1 \times N$ array of distances, for the implementation of step 3 in the outline of k-NN presented in Sect. 3.3.
2. Construct a SINGLE representative for each class by using some "centroid" (e.g. the average or the median) of the patterns belonging to the same class. By definition, in this case k can only equal 1. Thus, the k-Nearest Neighbors rule degenerates simply to Nearest Neighbor. In other words, the unknown measurement is assigned to the class represented by the nearest centroid. Note that leads to a much lower cost implementation, since, on the one hand there is only one comparison per class and on the other, only the minimum of the distance array is required, which eliminates the need of a sorting algorithm.

The experimental results concerning the system at hand, regarding the number of patterns per class, are summarized in the following table. The parameter values, that led to the best results, are shown on the right hand side column of Table 4.

4.2 The Employed Distance Function

The examined distance functions were the Euclidean Distance and the Inverse Correlation Coefficient, as defined as follows:

Weighted Euclidean Distance:	*Inverse Correlation Coefficient:*
$d_w(\mathbf{x}, \mathbf{y}, \mathbf{m}) = \left(\sum_{i=1}^{d} m_i (x_i - y_i)^2 \right)^{\frac{1}{2}}$	$d_k(\mathbf{x}, \mathbf{y}) = \dfrac{\sqrt{\sum_{i=1}^{d} x_i^2 \sum_{i=1}^{d} y_i^2}}{\sum_{i=1}^{d} x_i y_i}$

Table 4. Number of patterns per class

Number of patterns per class (Distance: Euclidean, $k = 1, 4$, respectively)

Data set	One (mean)	All
Red Ochre (42 samples)	27 (64 %)	30 (71 %)
Red Cinnabar (5 samples)	4 (80 %)	4 (80 %)
Yellow Ochre (25 samples)	20 (80 %)	22 (88 %)
Green Earth (12 samples)	10 (83 %)	10 (83 %)
Total (84 samples)	**61 (73 %)**	**66 (79 %)**

The experimental regarding the selected distance function, are summarized in the following Table 5.

Table 5. Distance function

Distance function ($k = 4$, patterns: all)

Data set	Euclidean	Corr. Coeff.
Red Ochre (42 samples)	30 (71 %)	28 (64 %)
• Red Cinnabar (5 samples)	• 4 (80 %)	• 4 (80 %)
• Yellow Ochre (25 samples)	• 22 (88 %)	• 21(80 %)
• Green Earth (12 samples)	• 10 (83 %)	• 10 (83 %)
• Total (84 samples)	**• 66 (79 %)**	**• 63 (75 %)**

4.3   Selection of k

In cases where the data set presents itself with well-defined and well-separated classes, the particular selection of k is not overly important. Here, regardless of the selection of k, the k nearest neighbors of the unknown measurement, with high probability, will belong to the same (correct) class, and thus be the measurement will be correctly classified. This however is not the case in several cases where the distinction between classes is much more ambiguous. In these cases, the particular selection of k plays important role, and rigorous experimental exploration is necessary.

The experimental results concerning the system at hand, regarding the selected value of k, are summarized in the following Table 6.

Table 6. Different values of k

Value of k (distance: Euclidean, patterns: all)

Data set	$k = 4$	$k = 6$	$k = 8$	$k = 10$
Red Ochre (42 samples)	30 (71 %)	31 (74 %)	30 (71 %)	29 (69 %)
Red Cinnabar (5 samples)	4 (80 %)	5 (100 %)	5 (100 %)	4 (80 %)
Yellow Ochre (25 samples)	22 (88 %)	23 (92 %)	21 (84 %)	21 (84 %)
Green Earth (12 samples)	10 (83 %)	11 (91 %)	10 (83 %)	10 (83 %)
Total (84 samples)	**66 (79 %)**	**70 (83 %)**	**66 (79 %)**	**64 (76 %)**

5   Conclusions and Future Steps

In this work, we present a data management solution that contributes with (1) a library of known reference pigments/colors of archaeological objects along with (2) a proposed novel pattern matching technique that allows the automatic classification of any new pigment that is recovered from cultural objects using the FORS measurements. The proposed technique follows a pattern recognition approach and it is based on a kNN classifier. The experimental evaluation results of the proposed technique show that data management is both effective and efficient. The obtained results are indeed very promising, thus encouraging the exploration of other similar approaches within the NDT framework. Initial feedback for the proposed system is encouraging as it would allow automation and therefore radically decreased time for pigment/color identification and therefore it can contribute significantly towards the selection and employment of the most appropriate conservation-restoration procedures.

Future steps include the implementation of automatic classification for other NDT techniques such as in situ X-Ray Fluorescence Spectroscopy (XRF) that produce spectra with the characteristic X-ray emissions of chemical elements. Finally, the images, spectral data and charts obtained from the NDT techniques will be combined so as to make full use of NDTs data in a single window system.

Acknowledgements. Acknowledgements are attributed to the Doc-Culture research project entitled "Development of an Integrated Information Environment for assessment and documentation of conservation interventions to cultural works/objects with Non Destructive Techniques (NDTs)", which is coordinated by NTUA MIS:379472. The project is co-financed by the European Union (European Social Fund – ESF) and Greek national funds through the Operational Program "Education and Lifelong Learning" of the National Strategic Reference Framework (NSRF) Research Funding Program: THALES. Investing in knowledge society through the European Social Fund.

References

1. Potts, P.J.: A Handbook of Silicate Rock Analysis. Chapman and Hall, London (1987)
2. Rollinson, H.: Using Geochemical Data: Evaluation, Presentation, Interpretation. Wiley, Hoboken (1993)
3. WikiPedia Lemma "in situ". http://en.wikipedia.org/wiki/In_situ#Archaeology
4. Polikar, R.: Pattern Recognition", in Wiley Encyclopedia of Biomedical Engineering. Wiley, New York (2006)
5. Jain, A.K., Duin, R.P.W., Mao, J.: Statistical pattern recognition: a review. IEEE Trans. Pattern Anal. Mach. Intell. 22, 4–37 (2000)
6. Bishop, C.: Pattern Recognition and Machine Learning. Springer, Berlin (2006)
7. Duda, R., Hart, P., Stork, D.: Pattern Classification, 2nd edn. Wiley, New York (2000)

Improved Data Granularity Management Through a Generalized Model for Sensor Data and Data Mining Outputs in Telemonitoring Applications

Pierre Maret[1(✉)], Shin'ishi Warisawa[2], Fabrice Muhlenbach[1],
Guillaume Lopez[3], and Ichiro Yamada[2]

[1] CNRS, UMR 5516, Laboratoire Hubert Curien, Université de Lyon,
Saint-Étienne, France
pierre.maret@univ-st-etienne.fr
[2] Graduate School of Frontier Sciences, The University of Tokyo, Bunkyō, Japan
[3] Department of Integrated Information Technology, Aoyama Gakuin University,
Tokyo, Japan

Abstract. Telemonitoring systems are expected to accomplish two basic tasks: continuously collect data from data sources wherever they may be; and allow remote communication between stakeholders to access data. The implementation and maintenance of these systems requires specific attention of software engineers for data management because of the complexity of the management of various data sources and because of privacy-related issues of personal data. In this paper we propose a data model that is generic enough to describe and to support many kinds of telemonitoring applications, especially those combining sensor data with data mining techniques and outputs. We show that our data model is useful for a smooth management of data mining outputs and that it avoids the integration effort for dealing with different heterogeneous storage mechanisms. We show also that our data model eases the management of the granularity of data and that it facilitates software designers' tasks for the implementation of privacy protection mechanisms.

Keywords: Sensor data · Telemonitoring · Data model · Data mining · Data granularity · Privacy management

1 Introduction

Telemonitoring systems can be viewed as the conglomeration of various technologies and techniques which primary aim is to enable remote monitoring of an on-going process [11,19,23]. The *technology* aspect makes possible the collection of data related to this process, and data storage for subsequent access and analysis. Technologies are well distributed and embedded at all scales throughout everyday life, which offers for instance to monitored patients more freedom in mobility as well as restoring their independent living, and to researchers to follow

© Springer International Publishing Switzerland 2015
L. Bellatreche and Y. Manolopoulos (Eds.): MEDI 2015, LNCS 9344, pp. 166–177, 2015.
DOI: 10.1007/978-3-319-23781-7_14

any kind of events remotely. Moreover, technologies are developed to enable the communication among different parts of the system. Sophisticated sensors make the collection of various types of data and the prevalence of wireless devices and mobile technologies ensure that these data can be transmitted almost anywhere and at any time.

At their core, telemonitoring systems are expected to accomplish two basic tasks: continuously collect data from data sources wherever they may be; and remotely communicate with stakeholders, for instance patients, medical staff, and other stakeholders such as relatives or friends. Differences exist as to the target ailment or activity monitored. We cite a few of them in the domain of health-related telemonitoring. Some systems telemonitor patients suffering from cardiovascular and respiratory diseases [17, 20]. Others deal with less involved scenarios like a program for diet management and improvement of lifestyle. Lastly, dedicated systems are also implemented that telemonitor elderly patients [2, 7]. We can also distinguish existing telemonitoring systems as to how they handle and process the data they collect. It is worth noting that many telemonitoring systems only use, if they use at all, low level data processing techniques. Data sensed from a data source is (i) transmitted, and screened (ii) possibly stored in static and repositories, and (iii) sporadically accessed by the concerned individuals. There are efforts to apply higher level analytic to the stored data [18, 22, 24]. A solution has been proposed to integrate to the system newly created evolutions of data processing models [12].

Our belief is that systems that collect data and computes indicators (through processing models such as data mining) about the status and activities of the data sources should implement a generic data model adapted to combinations of data (including indicators). Also, these systems should store the newly calculated indicators. Indeed, indicators constitute different levels of information (from detailed to coarse-grained), which values can be used either to start automatic feedback programs or to compute other indicators. A concrete example of raw data are the *ECG signal* (Electrocardiogram) and the *accelerometer data*, and example of computed data are *instant heart rate, daily heart rate, health status.*

An essential feature is that data mining models can be conveniently created and updated whenever new information or new scenarios are available, and thus generate new indicators. The challenge is here to be generic enough to efficiently incorporate the entire process of creating, using, and updating models based on existing data and indicators, and to allow a uniform management of data without introducing different heterogeneous data management systems. Also telemonitoring systems' task is to communicate data and to take into account potential privacy issues. The approach most respectful of individual's privacy would probably be to enable them to decide themselves who is allowed to access their data. Additionally to privacy concerns, it is not meaningful allowing stakeholders to access data if they cannot understand it. Therefore, different granularities of data should be implemented according to the targeted users. We believe that privacy issue as well as granularity levels of information should be considered early in the design of a telemonitoring system, and that a generic and uniform model can ease and accelerate the software design, implementation and maintenance for the management of sensed and processed data.

In this paper, we propose a data model that is generic enough to describe telemonitoring applications' data and that eases the implementation of such applications. More generally, our approach targets the data architecture to ease the development of all types of applications dealing with the data collection, data analysis, data storage, and access delivery to sensitive information. We will first describe in Sect. 2 an illustrative scenario in the domain of health, then we will present in Sect. 3 our generic data model. Section 4 presents how our data model is useful as for the uniform management of different levels of information extracted using data mining models, and how it eases privacy management implementation. Sections 5 and 6 present respectively the discussion part and the conclusion.

2   An Illustrative Scenario

The illustrative scenario is situated in the field of e-health where we developed several applications. Michel is a man having metabolic syndrome disease. This disease is a combination of cardiac problems, diabetes, overweight and sleep disorders. Michel suffers from isolation, he lacks sportive activity, he eats unhealthy food, often, and he neglect taking drug prescriptions. Michel cannot be permanently accompanied by a care giver.

A telemonitoring application must be designed for both remote supervision and remote human support in order to quickly help him improve his lifestyle and health status. The supervision and the support can be given remotely by different types of actors: medical care givers (generalists, nurses, and psychologists), relatives and friends, other metabolic patients. Wearable sensors, communication means, and knowledge extraction processes are used to record, store and deliver to the actors timely and reliable health-related data concerning Michel. Data processing methods such as data mining are used to extract higher level information and identify regularities or abnormalities in the daily activities of Michel. However Michel is reluctant on letting the system broadcast all his personal data to each of his contacts (medical values, activities he has been doing, places he has visited, daily habits, etc.). He is also aware that some of his contacts may have difficulties in the interpretation of medical data and may infer wrong conclusions. He has created 3 groups of people in his contact list: care givers, family, and friends. He has assigned to each of these groups a data granularity level so that care givers have access to detailed medical information, family members access to some aggregated medical information (such as daily activity level), and friends have only access to his general profile.

Among different tasks, software engineers of the described software has to consider the storage of sensed and processed data, and they have to implement a privacy engine that filters the data delivered to stakeholders in combining their profile with the granularity of data. Our proposal aims to make these design and maintenance tasks easier in providing a generic data model.

3   A Generic Data Model for Telemonitoring Systems

The data model should be generic enough to cover data from diverse situations and for different uses. Data generated by sensors during a session appears in the form of files stored within a file system (FS). Depending on the objectives of the final application and on the processing needs, two types of approaches can be followed: self-supported and centralized. In the self-supported approach, data files are stored and processed directly on the wearable system [3]. In the centralized approach, files are transmitted (on the fly or after a temporary storage on the wearable device) to a server [4]. In both approaches the processing of data can be synchronous or asynchronous. It leads either to the creation of new files, or to the insertion of data into a data base (DB). Wearable devices generally do not host a DB Management System due to their inappropriate needs of resources.

The telemonitoring applications should consider 2 different types of records: simple file names with the access path in the file system (for data stored into files), and data records (for data stored into a data base). These 2 types of records (data files and data records) provide either directly from sensors or from data processing. A unification of these data sources and recording means is given in Fig. 1. Sensors (*i.e.* Raw Sensors, RS) produce Raw Sensor Data (RSD). Virtual Sensors (VS) can use as inputs RSD and (if any) Virtual Sensor Data (VSD). VS generate additional Virtual Sensor Data (VSD). VSD can then be obtained by means of combinations of any RSD and/or VSD. RSD and VSD can consist of data stored into files or into a DB. Finally, we use the term Generalized Sensor to abstract the two kinds of sensors (RS and VS). This modeling is convenient for describing in a unique form data records, whatever their means of production (sensor based or processed data).

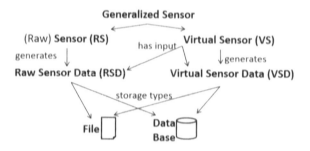

Fig. 1. Building a unified view for sensor data

The data model used for the design of a telemonitoring application should be generic enough in order to cover any kind of such applications. The model we propose (Fig. 2) is described in UML (Unified Modeling Language). In the figure, arrows indicate how to understand the names of relations, and important properties have been added after some relation's names. The model is based on the two abstract entities: *Generalized-Sensor* (from Fig. 1) and *Entity-or-Phenomenon* (EoP). The EoP entity represents things that can be sensed and that will provide values: a person, a connected object, or even phenomenons in the real or the digital world such as snow falls intensity or the estimated mood of friends on social networks. An EoP has properties that can be listed in the EoP Property table. EoPs can have an unlimited number of properties. They are modeled as values in the EoP Property table. At least we recommend the property *Composition* which is convenient for distinguishing simple and complex EoPs.

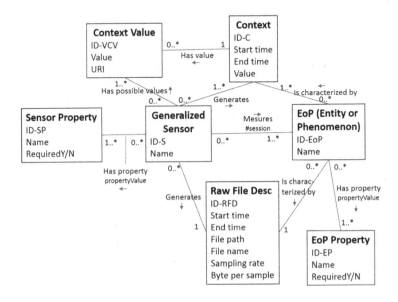

Fig. 2. Generic data model for telemonitoring applications

Similarly as for EoP, the Sensor Property table is used to describe properties of sensors. Properties can be easily added here. As a sensor produces either files or data into a data base we recommend to introduce the property *Storage type* with the property values = {file; data base}, and to describe this property as mandatory. Also, as a sensor (i.e. virtual sensor) can be based on combinations of other sensors, we introduce the *From* property which has to be repeated for each {SensorID} value composing this sensor.

Two entities are used to link sensors with the data they produce: *Raw file description* and *Context*. The *Raw file description* simply holds meta-data related to file generated by a sensor: file access path and name, start time stamp, end time stamp, sampling rate, bytes per sample. Some of these attributes may not be useful when files are auto-descriptive (self-sufficient). The *Context* entity holds data values generated by a sensor (i.e. generalized sensor). A context value $v(S, P)_{i,j}$ is the unique value delivered by the sensor S during the session P from time i to time j. The entity *Context Value* is used to introduce predefined values for contexts, as for example are $v(S) = $ {Normal, Abnormal} for blood pressure, $v(S') = $

{Standing, Sitting, Lying} for the person's position, etc. The field URI (Uniform Resource Identifier) is a string of characters that can be used to identify a context value through the web. This is a convenient way to make use of predefined context values from existing ontologies on the Web. The successive values delivered by a sensor S during session P and between time 0 and n will then be represented as $v(S,P)_{0,1}$, $v(S,P)_{1,2}$, $v(S,P)_{n-2,n-1}$, $v(S,P)_{n-1,n}$. Notice that the durations from time i to $i+1$ are not necessary identical for each i.

The next section will present the keys aspects of this model for telemonitoring applications, especially for the ease it produces for the management of data, the integration of data granularity and its compliance with data mining outputs and privacy control.

4   Usefulness of the Generic Data Model

We have previously written that the data model is generic enough to be used in many different telemonitoring applications. In this section, we emphasize the fact that this model is also suited for both integrating data mining processes and storing their results, and for dealing with privacy issues in the case of sensible personal data.

4.1   Integration of Data Mining Outputs

Numerous research papers have mentioned the crucial role of data mining in telemonitoring, especially when related to sensor based applications [10]. In a data mining project, there are typically six major steps [25]: (1) the problem understanding, (2) the data understanding, (3) the data preparation, (4) the modelling, (5) the evaluation, and (6) the deployment.

In our illustrative scenario (Michel who suffers from sleep disorders), our approach can be invaluable for helping him to restore a normal sleep. Data mining studies can be launched on top of our data model, combining different sensor data in order to extract higher level information: identification of characteristics, indicators of normal or abnormal situations, situation recognition, etc. The precise recognition of the sleep progress during the night and the identification of the different sleep stages (with rapid eye movement –REM– stages and non-rapid eye movement –NREM– stages, divided in 3 sub-stages NREM1 to NREM3) will allow the care givers to better understand the problem and then provide the treatment which will be the most appropriate for Michel.

In the proposed approach (summarized in Fig. 3 adapted from [12]), the process of introducing data mining models results in creating virtual sensors (for example a general "sleeping stage sensor" based on an accelerometer sensor and an eye movement detection sensor) and adding context values related to this newly created sensor. This new virtual sensor will facilitate the transitions between the 2nd (data understanding), 3rd (data preparation) and 4th (modelling) data mining steps: from raw data (signals generated from the sensors) to knowledge (the sleep stages identification with sequence mining techniques: NREM1, NREM2,

NREM3, REM). The execution of the data mining models produces then the insertion of context values (for example: stage value NREM3 from t_x to t_y).

Essential needs in data mining integration are the facts that (1) data generated from the models can be incorporated and readily accessible into the application and (2) processing models can be easily updated whenever new information is available.

For the former need, we stipulate that inputs of data mining models are either data from the raw files (entity Raw File Description) or from Context data, i.e. data from any generalized sensor and related to any Entity or Phenomenon (EoP). The data mining processes extract information from these inputs. Outputs of these processes are stored as instances of higher-level Context data. Thus the Context entity plays a central role in the data model and for the processing of data: any process combining different raw data and/or different context data generates additional context data. Thus, designers of software based on this data model has not to integrate 2 types of data storage in their project. Contrarily, the same data model can be used for sensed data and the processes data. This facilitates the design, the implementation and the maintenance of such systems.

As for the second need, there are thereby feedbacks from the 5th data mining step (the evaluation) to the 4th data mining step (the modeling) for improving the processing models (Fig. 3). We have proposed in [12] the so-called Knowledge Engineering (KE) component which is a convenient way for incorporating the creation, the use, and the evolution of data mining model in a single and coherent environment.

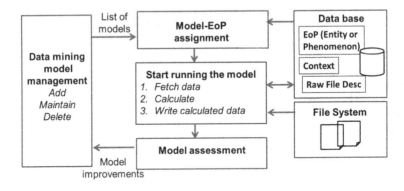

Fig. 3. Integrating data mining models into data sensing

4.2   Unified Data Granularity for a Simplified Privacy Management

Data granularity is an key concept in telemonitoring applications because it relates to the quantity and the interpretation of data delivered to users, and to the management of access control especially when it comes to personal data. These aspects must be considered very early in the design process. Our model fundamentally supports this aspect especially through the Context entity which can be used to characterize EoPs (Entity or Phenomenon) at different levels of granularity during the same time periods. For example, a person (EoP) can be initially "characterized" by raw files (ECG data, accelerometer data, temperature, sensed with high frequency) and by several inferred Contexts such as the Hourly medical status (with possible values: Fine, Medium, Bad), the Daily medical status (same possible values), the Current activity (with possible values Walking, Sitting, Running, Standing, etc.).

From a software design point of view since our data model unifies sensor data and processed data software engineers have only one single database to deal with, independently from the type of data and from the way data has been obtained. Consequently this significantly simplifies the design, implementation and maintenance processes. As a proof of concept, we have implemented on top of our data model and data access APIs the policy enforcement engine Protune [5]. We thus combine access policy principles with the various levels of granularity of data into rules. The policy enforcement engine interprets these rules and delivers access to the data to users. Our data modeling approach made this implementation much easier than if we would have to combine data records from different bases when expressing the rules and when interpreting them. The maintenance of the system is also much facilitated because evolutions of the data model uniformly impacts the system.

5   Discussion

Kortuem and Segall [14] have proposed the WearCom design methodology for rapid prototyping of wearable community systems. WearCom proposes a design language, a design process and a software platform [13], as well as 6 general principles that guide the design activity. This early contribution defines an epistemology of this domain (vocabulary, method, functions, etc.), however no data model nor application architecture is proposed for the design of such systems.

Numerous papers ([3, 4, 8, 9] to cite a few) propose application architectures for telemonitoring or sensor based applications. We observe that these descriptions generally start from the physical layer to progressively go through different higher-level layers such as data production layer, privacy layer, data aggregation or data mining layer, and application or user-oriented layer. We point out the fact that these layers are not associated to a generic data model and that this superposition of layers is not convenient for supporting the comprehensive interwoven processes of telemonitoring applications such as data mining processes and privacy issues management. Indeed, data production should not be limited to the sensor layer: data mining processes also generate data and knowledge. Thus, the application architecture as well as the data model supporting the application should be compatible with that and this would simplify the software design. Similarly, the management of data privacy requires a comprehensive approach of the data participating in the application. Debate and proposals on the topic *privacy* can be found in [15] (privacy by design), [16] (privacy by method), [21] (privacy by negotiation), [1] (user controlled privacy). Our proposal in this paper enables the privacy by design principles. Raw data as well as processed data is concerned by privacy issues. Thus, the data model we propose here makes convenient the development of a unified management of privacy for all levels of granularity of data. Descriptions of implementations of our approach in different applications can be found in [5, 6, 12]. An extract from the database and screenshot examples are given in Figs. 4, 5, and 6.

user_id	user_sensor_mapping_id	sensor_id	serial_no	sensor_type	sensor_name	storagetype
1000	1	9001	1	sensor	ECG	file
1000	2	9002	2	sensor	PPG	file
1000	3	9003	3	sensor	PAT	file
1000	4	9004	4	sensor	Continuous SBP	file
1000	5	9005	5	sensor	Heart Rate	file
1000	6	9006	6	context:bp	ABPM SBP	DB
1000	7	9007	7	context:heart	Mean Heart Rate	DB
1000	8	9008	8	sensor	Double Product	file
1000	9	9009	9	context:heart	AbHR	NULL
1000	10	9010	10	context:heart	devHR	NULL
1001	12	9001	1	sensor	ECG	file
1001	13	9002	2	sensor	PPG	file
1001	14	9003	3	sensor	PAT	file

Fig. 4. Extract of an implemented table mapping users and sensors (with sensor and context data types)

Fig. 5. Screenshot example of an application in telemonitoring

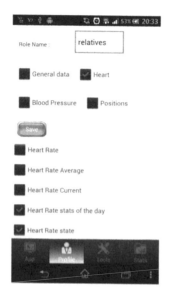

Fig. 6. Screenshot example for data granularity selection

6   Conclusion and Future Work

In this paper we have defined a data model which takes into account and articulates the fact that telemonitoring applications deal not only with raw data, but also very much with processed data *i.e.*, with combinations of raw and processed data, forming then an unlimited number of information levels. We have shown that our generic data model enables the management of these information levels and that it simplifies the software design, implementation and maintenance. Our approach is specifically convenient when telemonitoring applications requires the implementation of data mining processes and/or when they require the management of privacy related to personal data. Our model can be used for longitudinal as well as for cross-sectionals applications. Further research developments will lead us towards a generic application architecture. Following our data model, our aim is to use our experience in application development to propose a generic application architecture suited for many kinds of telemonitoring applications.

References

1. Abel, F., De Coi, J.L., Henze, N., Koesling, A.W., Krause, D., Olmedilla, D.: The RDF protune policy editor: enabling users to protect data in the semantic web. In: Cordeiro, J., Filipe, J. (eds.) WEBIST 2009. LNBIP, vol. 45, pp. 142–156. Springer, Heidelberg (2010)
2. Bakkes, S., Morsch, R., Kröse, B.: Telemonitoring for independently living elderly: inventory of needs and requirements. In: Maitland, J., Augusto, J.C., Caulfield, B. (eds.) Proceedings of the Pervasive Health 2011 Conference, pp. 152–159 (2011)

3. Campbell, A.T., Eisenman, S.B., Lane, N.D., Miluzzo, E., Peterson, R.A., Lu, H., Zheng, X., Musolesi, M., Fodor, K.A., Ahn, G.-S.: The rise of people-centric sensing. IEEE Internet Comput. **12**(4), 12–21 (2008)
4. Cuervo, E., Balasubramanian, A., Cho, D.-K., Wolman, A., Saroiu, S., Chandra, R., Bahl, P.: Maui: Making smartphones last longer with code offload. In: Proceedings of the 8th International Conference on Mobile Systems, Applications, and Services, MobiSys 2010(999), pp. 49–62, 999 (2010)
5. De Coi, J.L., Delaunay, G., Martins Albino, A., Muhlenbach, F., Maret, P., Lopez, G., Yamada, I.: The comprehensive health information system: a platform for privacy-aware and social health monitoring. In: Proceedings of IADIS e-Health 2012 (2012)
6. Djedou, Z.M., Muhlenbach, F., Maret, P., Lopez, G.: Can sequence mining improve your morning mood? toward a precise non-invasive smart clock. In: Proceedings of the 2014 International Workshop on Web Intelligence and Smart Sensing, IWWISS 2014, pp. 4:1–10. ACM, New York (2014)
7. Fouquet, Y., Franco, C., Demongeot, J., Villemazet, C., Vuillerme, N.: Telemonitoring of the elderly at home: Real-time pervasive follow-up of daily routine, automatic detection of outliers and drifts. In: Al-Qutayri, M.A. (ed.) Smart Home Systems, pp. 121–138. InTech (2010)
8. Guinard, D., Trifa, V.: Towards the web of things: Web mashups for embedded devices. In: Workshop on Mashups, Enterprise Mashups and Lightweight Composition on the Web (MEM 2009) in Proceedings of WWW (International World Wide Web Conferences), Madrid, Spain, Apr 2009
9. Guo, B., Zhang, D., Yu, Z., Liang, Y., Wang, Z., Zhou, X.: From the internet of things to embedded intelligence. World Wide Web **16**(4), 399–420 (2013)
10. Han, J., Kamber, M., Pei, J.: Data Mining: Concepts and Techniques, 3rd edn. Morgan Kaufmann Publishers Inc., San Francisco (2011)
11. Kim, Y., Yoo, S., Kim, D.: Ubiquitous healthcare: Technology and service. In: Ichalkaranje, N., Ichalkaranje, A., Jain, L. (eds.) Intelligent Paradigms for Assistive and Preventive Healthcare. SCI, vol. 19, pp. 1–35. Springer, Heidelberg (2006)
12. Kobayashi, V., Maret, P., Muhlenbach, F., Lhérisson, P.-R.: Integration and evolution of data mining models in ubiquitous health telemonitoring systems. In: Stojmenovic, I., Cheng, Z., Guo, S. (eds.) MOBIQUITOUS 2013. LNICST, vol. 131, pp. 705–709. Springer, Heidelberg (2014)
13. Kortuem, G.: Proem: a middleware platform for mobile peer-to-peer computing. ACM SIGMOBILE Mobile Comput. Commun. Rev. **6**(4), 62–64 (2003)
14. Kortuem, G., Segall, Z.: Wearable communities: augmenting social networks with wearable computers. IEEE Pervasive Comput. **2**(1), 71–78 (2003)
15. Langheinrich, M.: Privacy by design â principles of privacy-aware ubiquitous. In: Abowd, G.D., Brumitt, B., Shafer, S. (eds.) UbiComp 2001. LNCS, vol. 2201, pp. 273–291. Springer, Heidelberg (2001)
16. Lederer, S., Hong, J.I., Dey, A.K., Landay, J.A.: Personal privacy through understanding and action: Five pitfalls for designers. Personal Ubiquitous Comput. **8**(6), 440–454 (2004)
17. Lee, C.-H., Chen, J.C.-Y., Tseng, V.S.: A novel data mining mechanism considering bio-signal and environmental data with applications on asthma monitoring. Comput. Methods Programs Biomed. **101**(1), 44–61 (2011)
18. Lopez, G., Shuzo, M., Yamada, I.: New healthcare society supported by wearable sensors and information mapping-based services. Int. J. Netw. Virtual Organ. **9**(3), 233–247 (2011)

19. Mateo, R.M.A., Cervantes, L.F., Yang, H.-K., Lee, J.: Mobile agents using data mining for diagnosis support in ubiquitous healthcare. In: Nguyen, N.T., Grzech, A., Howlett, R.J., Jain, L.C. (eds.) KES-AMSTA 2007. LNCS (LNAI), vol. 4496, pp. 795–804. Springer, Heidelberg (2007)
20. Pecchia, L., Melillo, P., Bracale, M.: Remote health monitoring of heart failure with data mining via cart method on hrv features. IEEE Trans. Biomed. Eng. **58**(3), 800–804 (2011)
21. Raento, M., Oulasvirta, A.: Designing for privacy and self-presentation in social awareness. Personal Ubiquitous Comput. **12**(7), 527–542 (2008)
22. Scanaill, C.N., Carew, S., Barralon, P., Noury, N., Lyons, D., Lyons, G.M.: A review of approaches to mobility telemonitoring of the elderly in their living environment. Ann. Biomed. Eng. **34**(4), 547–563 (2006)
23. Sufi, F., Fang, Q., Mahmoud, S.S., Cosic, I.: A mobile phone based intelligent tele-monitoring platform. In: IEEE-EMBS International Summer School and Symposium on Medical Devices and Biosensors, pp. 101–104 (2006)
24. Viswanathan, M., Whangbo, T.K., Yang, Y.: Data mining in ubiquitous healthcare. In: Funatsu, K. (ed.) New Fundamental Technologies in Data Mining, pp. 193–200. InTech (2011)
25. Williams, G.: Data Mining with Rattle and R: The Art of Excavating Data for Knowledge Discovery. Use R!. Springer, New York (2011)

Query Processing

Security-Aware Elasticity for NoSQL Databases

Athanasios Naskos[1]([✉]), Anastasios Gounaris[1], Haralambos Mouratidis[2],
and Panagiotis Katsaros[1]

[1] Department of Informatics, Aristotle University of Thessaloniki,
Thessaloniki, Greece
{anaskos,gounaria,katsaros}@csd.auth.gr
[2] School of Computing, Engineering and Mathematics,
University of Brighton, Brighton, UK
H.Mouratidis@brighton.ac.uk

Abstract. We focus on horizontally scaling NoSQL databases in a cloud
environment, in order to meet performance requirements while respecting
security constraints. The performance requirements refer to strict latency
limits on the query response time. The security requirements are derived
from the need to address two specific kinds of threats that exist in cloud
databases, namely data leakage, mainly due to malicious activities of
actors hosted on the same physical machine, and data loss after one or
more node failures. We explain that usually there is a trade-off between
performance and security requirements and we derive a model checking
approach to drive runtime decisions that strike a user-defined balance
between them. We evaluate our proposal using real traces to prove the
effectiveness in configuring the trade-offs.

1 Introduction

Cloud computing is an evolving paradigm that has transformed the way organisations and individuals store, share and access their information. It introduces a
number of advantages and benefits by supporting a computational infrastructure
where availability of resources is dynamic, meaning that hardware and software
are provided on demand when users need them at a reasonable monetary cost.
On the other hand, the paradigm also creates challenges and introduces concerns
related to security. In fact, many organisations and individuals are still avoiding
cloud services mostly because they are not sure if the services provided, typically
by different providers, are suitable for their security requirements.

Security concerns related to *data leakage* and *data loss* are of particular
importance. Simply speaking, data leakage is the unauthorised transfer of data
from one user to another. Each user should have access to their own data and
not be able to access the data of others unless are authorised to do so. In the
cloud, the risk of data leakage is increased due to the storage of data in a multi-
tenant environment. A recent study [6] has shown that the risk of data leakage
is increased for a company when employees use cloud-based services. On the
other hand, data loss refers to a condition where data is destroyed and becomes

© Springer International Publishing Switzerland 2015
L. Bellatreche and Y. Manolopoulos (Eds.): MEDI 2015, LNCS 9344, pp. 181–197, 2015.
DOI: 10.1007/978-3-319-23781-7_15

unavailable. This could be the result of a malicious act (e.g. an attack to an organisation's data), due to human error or due to hardware/software/network failures. In a cloud environment - and in particular in a multi-tenant environment - the risk of data loss can be increased due to the multi-tenancy situation.

We deal with a particular feature of cloud databases, namely elasticity, in light of security concerns. Elasticity allows cloud users to modify the amount of resources used on-the-fly, so that they can always handle the external request load, even when load changes are unanticipated. It is manifested in three main forms, *horizontal scaling*, where virtual machines (VMs) are added or removed, *vertical scaling*, where the hardware configuration of the existing VMs is modified, and *migration*, where existing VMs are moved between physical hosting machines. More specifically, in this work, we extend our previous work [14] on performance-oriented horizontal scaling so that we can reach elasticity decisions that take into account both performance and security requirements. Performance requirements are expressed as a threshold regarding the maximum allowed response time to user requests, while security requirements are expressed through the probability of data leakage due to multi- tenancy and of data loss through hardware failure and/or due to multi-tenancy. Ideally, one would aim to attain zero violations of the performance threshold, no security incidents, while minimizing the monetary cost associated with the provision of cloud VMs.

Problem Challenges. The main challenge in the setting described above stems from the fact that the three requirements, that is bounded response times, minimal monetary cost and protection from failures and data leakage, are essentially intertwined and contradicting to a large extent, as explained below:

- NoSQL databases partition the data across several nodes and can benefit from the inherent feature of cloud infrastructures to dynamically provision resources. The combination of these two characteristics allow cloud databases to horizontally scale when the external load increases, so that more servers become available to respond to user requests. If horizontal scaling is performed carefully, for example, in a load balancing way that avoids over-reacting, the average response time can be maintained to a certain desired level regardless of any changes in the external load. More specifically, more VMs can be added (scale-out) when the load increases, but this comes at an increased monetary cost. Analogously, when the external load decreases, some servers can be released by the user on the grounds that over-provisioned servers incur unnecessary monetary cost. In private clouds, monetary costs are implicit (e.g., through increased energy consumption), whereas, in public clouds, a fee is actually paid.
- Online services may become unavailable due to failures of both the physical machines and the network, which can lead to data loss. The main mechanism to address this type of threat is through replication (or mirroring) that allows for data to be copied to several servers. The more the copies, the more resistant to failures the system becomes. However, this comes at the expense of higher response times when updating data, since eventually changes need to

be propagated to all copies. Moreover, the more VMs are employed, e.g., for performance reasons, the higher the probability a number of VMs equal to or greater than the replication factor to fail thus leading to data loss[1].

- Despite any efforts from cloud providers, there is always the danger that malicious cloud users hosted on the same physical machines as the databases get unauthorized access to data. Intuitively the more physical machines are used to host the database, the higher the danger, whereas, at the same time, public machines are more vulnerable.

To summarize, scaling out a database may improve the performance, but this may incur unnecessary monetary costs due to over-provisioning. Mirroring can be combined with scaling out and may cause performance problems but increases the robustness to failures. Scaling out may also exacerbate the data leakage and data loss threats. As such, keeping latency low through scaling-out is in contrast to monetary cost and avoiding the threat of data leakage and data loss.

Real-World Motivating Example. We take motivation for our work from a real-case scenario, the Greek National Gazette Infrastructure, involving the sharing and storage of large number of documents. The Greek National Gazette is responsible for publishing laws and legal decisions on the Government's newspaper in order for these laws and decisions to be active and applicable. Besides legal decisions there are also a number of decision categories originated from the private and public sector that by law must be send for publications to the Governments's newspaper. In such scenario, the dynamic provision of services with acceptable performance is very important as is the need to make sure that documents are not leaked before the official publication, and they are not lost after they are published.

Contributions. The contributions of this work are twofold. First, we present a Markov Decision Process (MDP) modeling approach to cloud elasticity, coupled with probabilistic model checking and accompanied by a security threat-aware decision mechanism; to this end, we build upon our performance-oriented proposal in [14]. The elasticity decision mechanism can account for user-defined trade-offs between performance and security requirements, while aiming to avoid over-provisioning in any case. Second, we present an evaluation that sheds light upon the impact of security requirements on the elasticity behavior. Our results show that our decision making proposal can effectively strike a configurable balance between the conflicting requirements mentioned above.

Structure. The remainder of this paper is structured as follows. In Sect. 2, we present the MDP models and the decision mechanisms developed. In Sect. 3, we evaluate our proposal for a wide range of security attack and failure probabilities using real cloud database traces. We discuss the related work in Sect. 4 and conclude in Sect. 5.

---

[1] The volume of lost data decreases with the number of VMs for the same replication factor.

2   Model-Based Security-Aware Elasticity

This section presents the probabilistic Markov Decision Process (MDP) model, which serves as the basis of our proposed security-aware elasticity decision making mechanism. We first introduce the basic modeling representation at a conceptual level and how it is used to drive performance-oriented elasticity (initially proposed in [14]); this approach is then extended and refined to cover both performance and security issues.

MDPs are specified by their states, actions, transition probabilities and rewards [17]. In our model, each state corresponds to a different cluster size, where the size equals to the number of active cloud virtual machines (VMs), vms_num, running a NoSQL database, such as HBase and Cassandra. The NoSQL database is typically both sharded and replicated; i.e., its tables are horizontally fragmented and each fragment is allocated to multiple VMs. For readability reasons, we denote a state as $s_{[vms\_num]}$. There are three types of possible actions on every state: (1) add for VM additions, (2) rem for removals, and (3) no_op for no operation. For every distinct number of VM additions or removals (ex. add_1, rem_2) there is a separate action, and the corresponding transitions between two states through the same action have aggregate probability 1.

Figure 1 (left) illustrates a simplified instance of the MDP model, where the states represent the number of active VMs. The edges represent the possible actions: (1) add_x (blue arrow), (2) rem_x (red arrow), and (3) no_op (black arrow); x is the number of new or removed VMs. In this example, the maximum number of VMs allowed to be added or removed in every step is 2, while the current number of active VMs is 3 (s_3 state). The action type is labelled

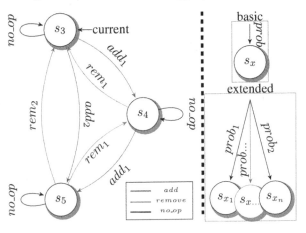

Fig. 1. MDP model overview (Color figure online).

on top of every transition ($[add_x/rem_x/no\_op]$). The MDP associates a reward value to each state and action taking into account the current external conditions. State and action rewards are calculated based on user-specified utility functions, as discussed later. The external conditions considered in this work are captured by the user external load λ, which is measured as the amount of submitted queries per time unit. When the model is verified at runtime, the reward at state $s_{[vms\_num]}$ essentially reflects the expected utility of the system when there are vms_num active VMs for the current value of external load.

The probabilistic nature of our model can easily capture the uncertainty of the environment that follows every elasticity decision; for example, for the same cluster size and external load, p% times in the past where no performance violations and (1-p)% there were ones. To mitigate uncertainty, Fig. 1 (right) illustrates an extension to the states of the model of Fig. 1 (left). Each model state for a specific cluster size is extended to n states, to better map the behavior of interest (i.e. performance, security). Each new smaller state corresponds to a different expected system behavior and is derived through clustering the log entries for the same external load and cluster size, resulting in deviations from expected behavior. The probability of transition to each possible state is commensurate to the probability of occurrence of the corresponding's state behavior.

2.1 Model-Based Elasticity for Performance

A common performance requirement is the latency lat of processing user requests, i.e. the time elapsed from query submission to answer, not to exceed a certain threshold x, regardless of the number of concurrent users. However, for the same number of VMs and the same amount of incoming load λ, the latency may vary significantly, due to factors that are both external to our model and hard to model; e.g., a time-consuming operating system process is initialized. To ameliorate this, as presented in Fig. 1 (right), there are more than one model states $(s_{x_1}, s_{x_{...}}, s_{x_n})$ for a single size x.

In [14], several elasticity policies are examined, and the most effective one was termed as $ADV+VC+PRE$, standing for $advanced+violation-cluster+prediction$. More specifically, the policy is termed as advanced because it computes the $cumulative$ reward after a pre-specified number of transitions in the model, called $steps$; this configurable parameter is set to 3, based on experimentation with different values [14]. The VC label indicates that one of the extended states in the model of Fig. 1 (right) covers those states that violate the response latency threshold, while the other extended states correspond to non-violating states with different behavior. PRE indicates that a prediction mechanism of future incoming load is utilized. Rewards are associated only to model states and are derived according to the following utility function: $u(vms) = \begin{cases} 0, & \text{if } lat > x \\ 1 + (1/vms), & \text{if } lat \leq x, \end{cases}$ where vms is the current number of VMs. As such, this utility function includes a user-specified constraint and manages to take into account both performance issues (through the lat threshold) and the monetary costs. The latter are implicitly considered by decreasing the utility in a way inversely proportional to the number of machines when there is no performance violation. Overall, this utility function penalizes both under-provisioning and over-provisioning. In this policy, one initial state in Fig. 1 (right) is mapped to more than one states to cover (i) the occasion of latency threshold violations and (ii) normal execution. The transition probability for each state is estimated according to log measurements of similar past conditions; the similarity is defined in terms of the external load. Finally, the model is equipped with a prediction module, which allows for predicting the evolution of the external load and thus computing the expected reward of each model state at each time step in the future more accurately. The probabilities and state rewards are instantiated every time elasticity actions are considered based on the current external load.

Then, a two-phase model verification procedure takes place to decide the optimal path considering the performance. To this end, the PRISM tool is used [10]. PRISM property specification language is PCTL probabilistic temporal logics. In the first phase, we ask for the maximum cumulative reward of the model, generating multiple optimal paths (sequences of states) that lead to the same optimal reward. Secondly, every first action of every optimal path is checked with another PCTL property to define its maximum probability of performance specific Service-Level Agreement (SLA) violation. The first action with the minimum maximum performance violation probability is the one selected from our decision mechanism:

$$Pmax =?[F(stop)\&(lat > x)\&(first\_action = [action]),$$

where [action] is every first action of every possible path which leads to the optimal cumulative reward and stop is a flag that indicates that the verification of a path should stop if the maximum number of steps is reached.

2.2 Model-Based Elasticity for Data Leakage

The performance-oriented model aims to avoid performance violations, while avoiding costly over-provisioning. In this section, we describe how our model is enhanced with capabilities to capture data leakages and consider them during elasticity decision making. The modifications refer to both the main model and the decision policy.

More specifically, we further extend the state transformation presented in Fig. 1 (right) introducing two-layer extensions. Hence, every s_{x_i} state is further transformed to $s_{x_{i_a}}$ and $s_{x_{i_{na}}}$ states, where $i \in [1, n]$, a stands for attack and na stands for no attack. The probability of these two new states is computed through the multiplication of the $prob_i$ probability and the probability of attack $prob_{i_a}$ or no attack $prob_{i_{na}}$, respectively, i.e., $prob_i = (prob_i \cdot prob_{i_a}) + (prob_i \cdot prob_{i_{na}})$, since the data leakage attacks and latency violations are considered to be independent events. We consider that there is an explicit mechanism to count and report the number of attacks leading to data leakages in a periodic manner, e.g. [15]. The data leakage probability information is used in our models to initialize the transition probabilities to states that represent safe or not safe states. A reasonable assumption is that the probability of attacks per VM is the same and equal to $prob_a$, and the attacks on different VMs are statistically independent; in that case, $prob_{i_a}$ becomes equal to $i \cdot prob_a$

In addition, we apply modifications to the above model verification procedure:

1. The utility function is extended to account for data leakages and performance trade-offs through a 3-parameter function. The exact formula employed is as follows:

$$u(vms) = \begin{cases} 0, & \text{if } attack = true \\ a, & \text{if } lat > x \\ b + (c/vms), & \text{if } lat \leq x \wedge attack = false. \end{cases}$$

where a, b and c are user defined values and $attack$ is a flag that indicates a data leakage. In Sect. 3 we show how setting the 3 parameters, can yield configurable trade-offs between the different objectives.

2. The second PCTL property (Sect. 2.1) is transformed to seek the first action with the minimum maximum probability of both performance specific SLA violation and data leakage:

$$Pmax =?[F(stop)\&(lat > x \| attack)\&(first\_action = [action]).$$

2.3   Model-Based Elasticity for Data Loss

As discussed in the introduction, data loss can be caused by malicious co-tenants and system failures. The attacks due to insecure multi-tenancy can be handled in exactly the same way as those leading to data leakage. For the data loss threat, the same 3-parameter utility function can be employed as well. However, the model transition probabilities to states corresponding to failures require a bit more attention and need to be aware of the degree of replication r. To suffer from data loss, at least r machines need to become unavailable at the same time. If the probability of failure of one machine is p_f, then the probability of r machines failing simultaneously is $\binom{n}{r}p_f^r$.

3   Evaluation

Experimental Setup. We have used logs from a real Cassandra infrastructure to conduct systematic experiments. The collected measurements are used firstly, to populate the initial logs, and secondly, to emulate a real situation. Through emulation, we have managed to fairly test each policy or configuration on an equal basis. The workload consists of asynchronous read requests (req), the volume of which evolves in a sinusoidal manner varying from 4000 to 16000 req/sec coupled with 2 plateau periods at 13000 req/sec for 1000 time units each. We collected measurements every 30 secs and, in our emulation, a time unit is equal to this measurement collection period. In each sine period, there are 360 measurements. We allow an elasticity action to take place every 10 time units, to emulate a system that may modify the VMs every 5 mins (or 10 mins is cases of add action, to allow the system to stabilize). As the emulated load is generated based on the logs, which also act as training set, we consider that the system is well trained, and as such, the MDP models are instantiated in an accurate manner. In every up-scale action, up to 3 VMs can be added, while during down-scaling, up to 2 VMs are allowed to be removed in a single step. The cluster sizes varies from 8 up to 18 VMs. Every experiment runs for 5 iterations. Further details are provided in [14].

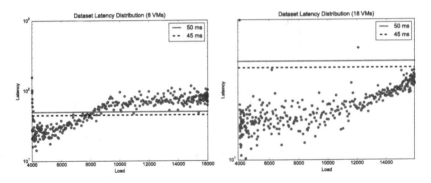

Fig. 2. Latencies for 8 (left) and 18 (right) VMs

Figure 2 presents the latency distribution in two characteristic states of the collected dataset, where the dotted line shows the latency threshold of 45 msecs and the solid line of 50 msecs in both figures. For the minimum cluster size and lowest amounts of load, there are few latency values that violate the thresholds (mostly caused by the cold cache of the system at the beginning of the measurement collection) and the system can handle load up to about 8000 req/sec. However, additional machines need to be added if the load further increases to avoid performance threshold violations. For the maximum number of active VMs (18), except from a few outlier measurements, the system can handle the full amount of the incoming load.

3.1   Experimental Results

Our experiments show the trade-offs between security attacks and latency violations for a series of utility function configurations and probabilities of attack incidents.

Data Leakage Results. The utility function presented in Sect. 2.1 tries to maintain the lowest number of active VMs, when there is no latency violation applies. In these cases, as the number of active VMs is placed in the denominator $(1 + (1/vms))$, over-provisioning is avoided, which additionally, alleviates the data leakage threat. The utility function presented in Sect. 2.2, aims to control the data leakage probability both more directly and in cases, where the performance threshold is exceeded, through deriving an acceptable tradeoff between the increase in the number of latency violations and the decrease in the number of data leakage attacks.

In the first set of experiments, the latency threshold in the utility function is set to either 45 msecs or 50 msecs. Initially, we set the probability of data leakage attack per VM per step to 0.1 %; later, we examine data leakage probabilities that differ by an order of magnitude. We examine four different parameter setups for the utility function presented in Sect. 2.2:

Table 1. Average number of active VMs (0.1 % attack probability)

	ADV+VC+PRE	DLeak-0	DLeak-1	DLeak-2	DLeak-3
45 msecs	12.5	8	12.3	11.7	12.4
50 msecs	12	8	11.8	11	11.9

- DLeak-0: $a = 100$, $b = 100$, $c = 1$
- DLeak-1: $a = 0.5$, $b = 1$, $c = 1$
- DLeak-2: $a = 100$, $b = 100$, $c = 160$
- DLeak-3: $a = 100$, $b = 1000$, $c = 1600$.

Intuitively, *DLeak-0* tries to avoid attacks at any performance cost. The other 3 policies place more importance on latency violations than *DLeak-0*. In Fig. 3, we present the adaptation of the number of VMs to the incoming load for each policy. The red dotted line represents the incoming load while the solid blue line represents the number of active VMs. Except few instabilities, due to imminent environment uncertainty infused in our emulations, all the policies/configurations can broadly follow the load variation.

Figure 4 (left) on the left presents the percentage of time steps where latency violations (left blue bar) and data leakages (right green bar) occur for the *ADV+VC+PRE* policy. In this experiment, the latency threshold is 45 msecs,

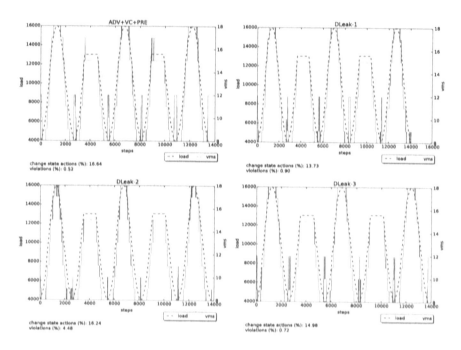

Fig. 3. Variation of the external load and the number of active VMs

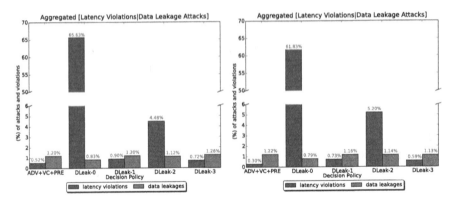

Fig. 4. Aggregated Latency Violations and Data Leakage Percentage for 45 msecs (left) and 50 msecs (right) latency thresholds and 0.1 % data leakage probability per VM (Color figure online).

and, for cluster size from 8 to 18 VMs, the attack probability ranges from 0.8 % (lower bound) to 1.8 % (upper bound)[2]. *ADV+VC+PRE* manages to yield a very low number of performance violations, at the expense of non-negligible secutiry attacks. The second pair of columns in the same figure presents the results for *DLeak-0*, where the system is actually penalized (zero reward) only for the attack situations, as the latency violation reward is very close to the no-attack no-violation case. As expected, the number of VMs is kept at the minimum possible number, i.e. 8 VMs; see Table 1. Overall, the attacks are reduced to their minimum, however the latency violations are reaching their highest percentage (65.63 %).

As we also observe in Fig. 4, the *DLeak-2* parameterisation achieves a reduction in the deviation from the lower bound of probability attacks of 20 % (from 0.4 % to 0.32 %) compared to the *ADV+VC+PRE* policy, at the expense of an increase in the latency violations, since the system is prohibited to scale in several cases to avoid data leakage attacks. *DLeak-1*, *DLeak-3* parameter setups increase the number of violations without being able to decrease the number of data leakages. As we observe in Table 1, *DLeak-2* keeps the number of active VMs lower than the *DLeak-1* and *DLeak-3* i.e. 11.7, which explains the decrease in the number of data leakages. This also is an indication that different parameter configurations can achieve different trade-offs but this needs to be performed carefully.

Figure 4 (right) presents an experiment where latency violation threshold becomes 50 msecs. The data leakages percentage is decreased in all the security enhanced policies, with *DLeak-3* achieving the optimal tradeoff. In *DLeak-3*,

---

[2] This implies that the database owner fully accepts the 0.8 % probability of attacks. However, all the numbers can be transferred to a setting, where the cloud is hybrid with 8 private VMs and up to 10 public VMs. If the attack probability is 0 % for the private ones, then all attack percentages become 0.8 % less.

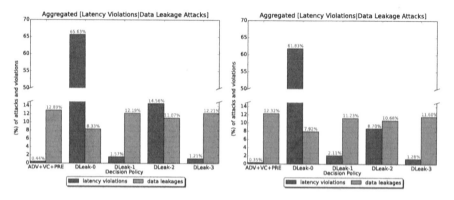

Fig. 5. Aggregated Latency Violations and Data Leakage Percentage for 45 msecs (left) and 50 msecs (right) latency thresholds and 1 % data leakage probability per VM

Table 2. Average number of active VMs (1 %)

	$ADV+VC+PRE$	$DLeak$-0	$DLeak$-1	$DLeak$-2	$DLeak$-3
45 msecs	12.4	8	12.2	10.9	12.2
50 msecs	12	8	11.4	10.8	11.6

the deviation of data leakages from their lower bound is reduced by 21 % while the latency violations are slightly increased. In the second line of Table 1, the average number of active VMs in the *DLeak-3*, is bigger than the one from *DLeak-2* achieving almost the same data leakages reduction albeit with a more significant increase in latency violations.

In Fig. 5 the data leakage probability because of multi-tenancy is changed to 1 %, hence the percentage of data leakage throughout the cluster ranges from 8 % to 18 % in a single step. As we observe, the data leakage percentage is reduced from 12.89 % to 11.70 % for the *DLeak-2* with an increase in the latency violations (i.e. 14.56 % from 0.44 % achieved by ADV+VC+PRE policy), reaching a significantly better trade-off than *DLeak-0*. The mean number of the active VMs in *DLeak-2* is reduced from 12.4 to 10.9, presented in Table 2. The parameter setups *DLeak-1* and *DLeak-3* achieve almost the same reduced percentage of data leakage attacks i.e. 12.2 %, while *DLeak-3* achieves lower latency violations number. When the latency violation threshold is changed to 50 msecs (see Fig. 5 (right)) the same trend applies, with the exception of an increase in the data leakage attacks of the *DLeak-3* compared to *DLeak-2* parameter setup. As it is expected the average number of active VMs is reduced in all the cases between the 45 msecs and the 50 msecs latency thresholds (presented in Table 2). Finally, *DLeak-2* achieves the most fair tradeoff between the data leakage attacks and the latency violations.

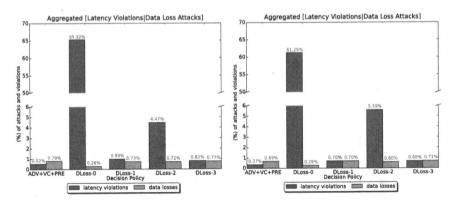

Fig. 6. Aggregated Latency Violations and Data Losses Percentage for 45 msecs (left) and 50 msecs (right) latency thresholds and $rep = 2$, $p_f = 1\%$

Table 3. Average number of active VMs ($r = 2$, $p_f = 1\%$)

	ADV+VC+PRE	DLoss-0	DLoss-1	DLoss-2	DLoss-3
45 msecs	12.4	8	12.3	11.7	12.4
50 msecs	12	8	11.8	11	11.9

Data Loss Results. In this set of experiments, we also try to achieve an acceptable tradeoff between the latency violations and the occurrences of data losses due to machine failures. The failure probability of one machine is set to $p_f = 1\%$, while we run experiments for two values of replication factor i.e. $r = 2$ and $r = 3$ and two values of latency threshold, 45 and 50 msecs. The utility function presented in Sect. 2.2 is utilized, and similar parameter setups are examined:

- *DLoss-0*: $a = 100$, $b = 100$, $c = 1$
- *DLoss-1*: $a = 0.5$, $b = 1$, $c = 1$
- *DLoss-2*: $a = 100$, $b = 100$, $c = 160$
- *DLoss-3*: $a = 100$, $b = 1000$, $c = 1600$.

Figure 6 presents the results for $p_f = 1\%$ and $r = 2$ for both 45 (left) and 50 (right) msecs latency thresholds. The data loss probability ranges from 0.28 % for 8 VMs, up to 1.5 % for 18 VMs. As we observe in the left figure, *DLoss-0* achieves the minimum possible percentage of data losses i.e. 0.28 %, with the cost of the highest observed latency violation percentage, i.e. 65.32 % as it maintains the minimum number of VMs (see Table 3). *DLoss-1* and *DLoss-2* obtain a good tradeoff reducing the data losses percentage up to 8.8 % in absolute numbers. *DLoss-3* is the less effective approach in this experiment. As we observe in Table 3, the amount of data loss incidents is correlated to the mean number of active VMs, as expected. Exactly the same trend is observed in the 50 msecs latency threshold experiments, shown in Fig. 6 (right). *DLoss-2* reduces the data losses by 13 %, while the latency violations are far less

Table 4. Average number of active VMs ($r = 3$, $p_f = 1\%$)

	$ADV+VC+PRE$	DLoss-0	DLoss-1	DLoss-2	DLoss-3
45 msecs	12.5	10.5	12.3	11.9	12.4
50 msecs	12	10.8	11.9	11	11.9

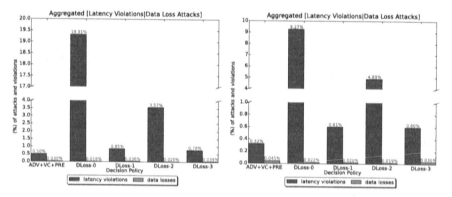

Fig. 7. Aggregated Latency Violations and Data Losses Percentage for 45 msecs (left) and 50 msecs (right) latency thresholds and $rep = 3$, $p_f = 1\%$

(i.e. 5.59 %) than the maximum possible. (i.e. 61.29 % see *DLoss-0* in the same figure). As previously noted the same trend applies for the mean active VMs number, presented in the second line of Table 3.

Next, we change the replication factor from $r = 2$ to $r = 3$ and repeat all the experiments. As the replication factor is increased, the data loss probability is reduced and ranges from 0.0056 % for 8 VMs, up to 0.0816 % for 18 VMs. Figure 7 presents the results. As we observe in this figure, the *DLoss-0* parameter setup behaves differently from all the previous experiments, as it achieves a tradeoff between the data losses and the latency violations, without keeping the amount of VMs to the lowest possible vale. As it is depicted in Table 4, the mean number of active VMs for the *DLoss-0* is 10.5, which explains the results of Fig. 7. The change in the behavior is explained by the reduction in the probability of the data loss incident. As the probability is too low, even the small difference (i.e. $1/VMs$) between the reward for the latency violation state (i.e. 100) and the reward for the no-attack no-violation state (i.e. $100 + 1/VMs$) makes the difference and guides the system to avoid latency violations. Taking into account the highest latency violation percentage, which is 65 %, *DLoss-0* is able to reduce both the data losses and the latency violations for both 45 and 50 msecs latency violation thresholds. *DLoss-3* in Fig. 7 (left) is not able to reduce the data losses as it utilizes almost the same mean number of VMs with the $ADV+VC+PRE$ policy. In Fig. 7 (right), where the latency threshold is set to 50 msecs, all the policies reduce the data losses, while the *Dloss-2* achieves the best tradeoff with mean number of VMs equal to 11 as depicted in Table 4.

Generic Lessons. A more thorough parameter analysis using also additional settings is left as future work. However, the lesson learnt from the above experiments is that the elasticity decision making approach along with the 3-parameter utility function in Sect. 2.2 provides a powerful tool for striking a balance between security and performance requirements. As a rule of thumb to be used by system administrators, we advocate setting the parameters a and b at the order of hundreds (2 orders of magnitude higher than the reward for the security incident) and the parameter c an order of magnitude higher than the maximum cluster size, in order to yield an effective approach in reaching a mid-way balance. Following this rule, our work can be applied in a real-world example, including the motivating one, given a desired threshold on performance and understanding of the maximum probability of occurrence of security-related events that can be tolerated. Our solution comes also with a clear interface with different cloud providers, various NoSQL databases and data leakage/loss reporting mechanisms [14] in order to provide a complete system, and, finally, it has very low running overhead.

4   Related Work

The literature is rich with research efforts that consider security issues within the context of cloud computing. Recent initiatives mainly from the industry and government organisations such as ENISA and Cloud Security Alliance, have sought to produce a number of guidelines and methods to help in the selection of cloud providers as well as addressing some specific security concerns of the cloud. Yet such guidelines appear often too cumbersome with no clear indications as to when a CSP may be considered as not being trustworthy. This makes the valuable information detailed within these documents hard to exploit.

Gong et al. [4] showed that using a side-channel attack, an attacker can instantiate new VMs of a target virtual machine so that the new VM can potentially monitor the cache hosted on the same physical machine. [7] identified four possible places where faults can occur in cloud computing: provider-inner, provider-across, provider user and user-across. Mulazzani et al. [13] showed that attackers can exploit data duplication techniques to access customer data by obtaining hash code of the stored file. Wenzel et al. [21] consider security and compliance analysis of outsourcing services in the cloud computing context.

There are also works that focus on the development of model-based approaches to security analysis in cloud environments. A goal-drivel approach is introduced to analyse security risks of cloud based system [8]. Goals, threats and risks are consider from three main components: data, service/application, and technical and organisational measure. We have also contributed to this line of research with the development of a model-based framework that enables elicitation, analysis of security and privacy requirements and selection of deployment models [9] and service providers [12] based on such requirements. These works provide important developments in analysing and modelling security in cloud computing but they do not take into account performance issues.

Our work is also related to proposals that deal with cloud elasticity to maintain specific performance characteristics. Tan et al. [19] combine cloud elasticity with anomaly prevention, which refers to the resource contention, software bugs or hardware failures. This proposal utilizes a prediction technique based on system metrics to vertically scale the resources of the VMs or to decide for VM migration, i.e. they consider different forms of elasticity, as is also the case in Shen et al. [18] and Gong et al. [5]. A work that indirectly solves MDP models utilizing reinforcement learning-based policies to guide elasticity appears in Tsoumakos et al. [20], which is extended in our previous performance-oriented work in [14]. Differently to our work which considers the same VM types, Hector et al. [3] and Qi et al. [22] deal with VM type heterogeneity issues. A significant number of proposals use rule-based techniques to guide the elasticity, e.g., Moore et al. [11] and Copil et al. [2]. In Copil et al. [2], a technique is proposed that addresses the implications of an elastic action across multiple dimensions, providing for example the cost implication of a horizontal scaling action. None of those techniques is accompanied by online probabilistic verification of elasticity properties. Finally, model checking and runtime quantitative verification for cloud solutions other than horizontal scaling has been proposed in Calinescu et al. [1] and Perez et al. [16]. The former, utilizes PRISM to guide service adaptation, while the latter presents a technique to predict the minimum cost of cloud deployments using PCTL over MDP models. In summary, to the best of our knowledge, our proposal is the first one that addresses the elasticity problem taking into account both performance and security issues.

5   Conclusions

This work presents a novel approach, to support elasticity decisions for cloud databases, which considers both performance and security requirements. Since, these requirements are contradicting, we have developed a probabilistic model checking solution that accounts for user-defined trade-offs between them. As demonstrated by the experiments, our proposal is capable of striking a configurable balance between security-related incidents and performance degradation.

We are working towards improving our approach towards the following directions. Additional utility functions can be investigated, along with further experimentation under different settings. Also, tackling data leakage and data loss concerns during elasticity solves only a part of the security problems in cloud databases. With a view to providing more holistic solutions, we aim to investigate model checking based techniques to help database owners decide the initial deployment of their systems on the cloud.

Acknowledgments. This research has been co-financed by the European Union (European Social Fund - ESF) and Greek national funds through the Operational Program "Education and Lifelong Learning of the National Strategic Reference Framework (NSRF) - Research Funding Program: Thales. Investing in knowledge society through the European Social Fund."

References

1. Calinescu, R., Grunske, L., Kwiatkowska, M., Mirandola, R., Tamburrelli, G.: Dynamic qos management and optimization in service-based systems. IEEE Trans. Softw. Eng. **37**(3), 387–409 (2011)
2. Copil, G., Moldovan, D., Truong, H.-L., Dustdar, S.: Multi-level elasticity control of cloud services. In: Basu, S., Pautasso, C., Zhang, L., Fu, X. (eds.) ICSOC 2013. LNCS, vol. 8274, pp. 429–436. Springer, Heidelberg (2013)
3. Fernandez, H., Pierre, G., Kielmann, T.: Autoscaling web applications in heterogeneous cloud infrastructures. In: IC2E (2014)
4. Gong, C., Liu, J., Zhang, Q., Chen, H., Gong, Z.: The characteristics of cloud computing. In: Proceedings of the 2010 39th International Conference on Parallel Processing Workshops, pp. 275–279. ICPPW (2010)
5. Gong, Z., Gu, X., Wilkes, J.: Press: Predictive elastic resource scaling for cloud systems. In: CNSM, pp. 9–16 (2010)
6. Grispos, G., Glisson, W.B., Storer, T.: Using smartphones as a proxy for forensic evidence contained in cloud storage services. CoRR abs/1303.4078 (2013)
7. Grobauer, B., Walloschek, T., Stocker, E.: Understanding cloud computing vulnerabilities. IEEE Secur. Priv. **9**(2), 50–57 (2011)
8. Islam, S., Mouratidis, H., Kalloniatis, C., Hudic, A., Zechner, L.: Model based process to support security and privacy requirements engineering. IJSSE **3**(3), 1–22 (2012)
9. Kalloniatis, C., Mouratidis, H., Islam, S.: Evaluating cloud deployment scenarios based on security and privacy requirements. Requir. Eng. **18**(4), 299–319 (2013)
10. Kwiatkowska, M., Norman, G., Parker, D.: Prism: probabilistic model checking for performance and reliability analysis. SIGMETRICS **36**(4), 40–45 (2009)
11. Moore, L., Bean, K., Ellahi, T.: A coordinated reactive and predictive approach to cloud elasticity. In: CLOUD COMPUTING, pp. 87–92 (2013)
12. Mouratidis, H., Islam, S., Kalloniatis, C., Gritzalis, S.: A framework to support selection of cloud providers based on security and privacy requirements. J. Syst. Softw. **86**(9), 2276–2293 (2013)
13. Mulazzani, M., Schrittwieser, S., Leithner, M., Huber, M., Weippl, E.: Dark clouds on the horizon: Using cloud storage as attack vector and online slack space. In: USENIX Security Symposium (2011)
14. Naskos, A., Stachtiari, E., Gounaris, A., Katsaros, P., Tsoumakos, D., Konstantinou, I., Sioutas, S.: Dependable horizontal scaling based on probabilistic model checking. In: CCGrid. IEEE (2015)
15. Papadimitriou, P., Garcia-Molina, H.: Data leakage detection. IEEE Trans. Knowl. Data Eng. **23**(1), 51–63 (2011)
16. Perez-Palacin, D., Calinescu, R., Merseguer, J.: Log2cloud: Log-based prediction of cost-performance trade-offs for cloud deployments. In: ACM SAC, pp. 397–404 (2013)
17. Puterman, M.L.: Markov Decision Processes: Discrete Stochastic Dynamic Programming. John Wiley and Sons Inc., New York (1994)
18. Shen, Z., Subbiah, S., Gu, X., Wilkes, J.: Cloudscale: Elastic resource scaling for multi-tenant cloud systems. In: SOCC, pp. 5:1–5:14 (2011)
19. Tan, Y., Nguyen, H., Shen, Z., Gu, X., Venkatramani, C., Rajan, D.: Prepare: Predictive performance anomaly prevention for virtualized cloud systems. In: ICDCS, pp. 285–294 (2012)

20. Tsoumakos, D., Konstantinou, I., Boumpouka, C., Sioutas, S., Koziris, N.: Automated, elastic resource provisioning for nosql clusters using tiramola. In: CCGrid, pp. 34–41 (2013)
21. Wenzel, S., Wessel, C., Humberg, T., Jürjens, J.: Securing processes for outsourcing into the cloud. In: 2nd International Conference on Cloud Computing and Services Science, April 2012
22. Zhang, Q., Zhani, M.F., Boutaba, R., Hellerstein, J.L.: Harmony: Dynamic heterogeneity-aware resource provisioning in the cloud. In: ICDCS, pp. 510–519 (2013)

Estimating Power Consumption of Batch Query Workloads

Amine Roukh[✉]

University of Mostaganem, Mostaganem, Algeria
roukh.amine@univ-mosta.dz

Abstract. Today we are noticing a significant increase in energy costs used by High-Performance Computing. However, increasing demand for information processing have led to cheaper, faster and larger data management systems. This demand requires employing more hardware and software to meet the service needs which in turn put further pressure on energy costs. In data-centric applications, DBMSs are one of the major energy consumers. So faced to this situation, integrating energy in the database design becomes an economic necessity. To satisfy this key requirement, the development of cost models estimating the energy consumption is one of the relevant issues. While a number of recent papers have explored this problem, the majority of the existing work considers prediction energy for a single standalone query. In this paper, we consider a more general problem of multiple concurrently running queries. This is useful for many database management's tasks, including admission control, query scheduling and execution control with energy efficiency as a first-class performance goal. We propose a methodology to define an energy-consumption cost model to estimate the cost of executing concurrent workload via statistical regression techniques. We first use the optimizer's cost model to estimate the I/O and CPU requirements for each query pipeline in the workload, then we fit statistical models to the observed energy at these query pipelines, finally we use the combination of these models to predict concurrent workload energy consumption. To evaluate the quality of our cost model, we conduct experiments using a real DBMS with a dataset of TPC-H and TPC-DS benchmarks. The obtained results show the quality of our cost model.

1 Introduction

The growth and creation of new data centers now days, in conjunction with the increase in electricity and cooling prices and a great concern for the environment, induce an emerging paradigm shift for data center administrators and managers. Previous issues faced by administrators such as manageability, scalability, efficiency and security in the data centers have now to add the energy efficiency concern in hardware and software systems they manage. Data centers consume an enormous amount of energy: estimates for 2010 indicate that they consume around 1.5 % of the total electricity used worldwide [9]. Electricity cost thus represents a significant burden for managers. The report issued by the US Environmental Protection Agency (E.P.A.) in August of 2007 estimated that

© Springer International Publishing Switzerland 2015
L. Bellatreche and Y. Manolopoulos (Eds.): MEDI 2015, LNCS 9344, pp. 198–212, 2015.
DOI: 10.1007/978-3-319-23781-7_16

the consumption of data center servers would be from 2005 to 2010 to roughly 100 billion kWh of energy at an annual cost of $7.4 billion [21]. Database Management Systems (DBMS) in large data centers are today one of the major challenges towards energy efficiency. Generally, database servers are a huge customer of computational resources in data centers, which turn DBMS to be a major energy consumer [16].

Traditionally, designing a database application mainly focuses on speeding up the query processing cost to satisfy the needs of end users (e.g., decision makers). This design ignores the energy dimension. Therefore, there is a need to develop DBMSs with energy efficiency as a first-class performance goal [20]. The *Claremont report* on database research [1] states the importance of "designing power-aware DBMSs that limit energy costs without sacrificing scalability". As a result, energy management has become an active research topic in the database research community. Current work in energy-aware DBMS has focused on energy-aware query optimization that considers both processing time and energy consumption [10,23]. Unlike other studies that deal with prediction energy for a single standalone query, this paper addresses a more general problem of multiple concurrently running queries. Since in real-world database servers, the queries are generally executed concurrently, estimating power consumption for concurrent queries is more important than estimating for standalone queries. This is useful for a number of database management tasks, such as admission control, query scheduling and execution control with energy efficiency as a first-class performance goal. Also, with the current tendency of database as a service (DaaS) this solution will be even more attractive, in a way that service level agreements (SLAs) violations and energy consumption are minimized.

In this paper, we propose *a methodology to define an energy-consumption cost model to estimate the cost of executing concurrent query workloads*. Specifically, we study the following problem: "Given a collection of queries $q_1, q_2, \cdots, q_n$, concurrently running by the database system, predict the energy that entire workload will consume."

Our methodology is based on a machine-learning approach. We first use the optimizer's cost model to estimate the I/O and CPU requirements for each query *pipeline* in the workload, we choose pipeline level modeling because, based on our experiments observation, we found that power consumption usually change when current running pipeline change, and not when running queries change (we will show this in the next sections), this is because most databases are usually implemented in an iterator model [6]. Then we fit statistical models based on multivariate regression technique to the observed energy at these query pipelines, in order to capture the energy behavior of queries under concurrency. Finally, we use the combination of these models to predict concurrent workload energy consumption. As stated in [7,23], we claim that estimating the energy consumption of query workload running by a DBMS is an essential part toward energy-aware computing system.

1.1   Effect of Concurrency on Power Consumption

We demonstrate the effect of varying multiprogramming levels (MPL) (i.e., the number of queries executing concurrently) on workload power consumption using

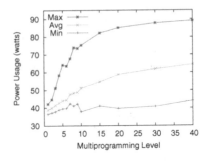

Fig. 1. Variation of workload power consumption with different multiprogramming levels (MPLs).

a real example based on the widely-used TPC-H decision-support benchmark[1,2]. In this example, we created workloads for each 22 query templates based on a given MPL, the workload contain the same query but with different instances, we executed the workloads and logged their power consumption. Then we calculated the minimum, maximum and average power at each MPL. Figure 1 shows the results. As expected, the power consumption increases as we increase the degree of concurrency, this is because the system becomes more loaded. In fact, the system reaches its maximum throughput at $MPL = 40$ and consume its maximum power (95 W) as provided by the hardware manufacturer. Moreover, we observe a large difference between the minimum, maximum, and average power consumption at the same MPL. Thus, modeling for a concurrency running queries is far more challenging than for standalone query. One of the main difficulties to define power cost models is the identification of parameters related to the used materials (e.g., size of buffer, page size of the disk, etc.), the workload (e.g., type of queries, the selectivity factors, sizes of intermediate results, etc.) and the execution strategies. The main technical contributions of this paper are: (i) we experimentally demonstrate that pipelines are a robust indicator to estimate power consumption for concurrent queries, (ii) we develop a multivariate regression model that predicts the power consumption for a given workload based on its I/O and CPU costs, (iii) we show experimental results obtained from a real benchmarks study that supports our claims and verifies the effectiveness of our predictive models. Our predictions are on the average within 6 % of the actual values, and 10.5 % as maximum. The remainder of this paper is organized as follows: Sect. 2 describes in details our power cost models and a motivating example for using the pipeline-based model in power estimation is presented. Section 3 highlights our theoretical and real experiments that we conduct to evaluate the quality of our cost model. Section 4 reviews the most important works on power consumption in the database context. Section 5 concludes the paper.

---

[1] http://www.tpc.org/tpch/.
[2] The datasets and the system setup we used in our experiments can be found in Sect. 3.

2   Methodology

We begin with an overview of our power consumption predictor of concurrency running queries. Figure 2 shows the overall workflow of our modeling process. As a first step, we generate different training query mixes samples, then we run a series of experiments using a client coordinator. Our client coordinator is a client-side program that creates client threads, each with a separate connection to the DBMS. Every thread then selects and runs a query from a given query mix. Once the desired query mix is running, we start measuring its power consumption using the power meter. We then get pipeline phases for the query mix. For each given pipeline, we calculate its plan costs using our DBMS, and its power consumption. The collected data from all experiments is used to train an *offline* statistical model that captures the power of the pipelines. The model is then used *online* to estimate the power of future workloads based on their pipelines cost. In the next sections, we detail each step of our modeling process.

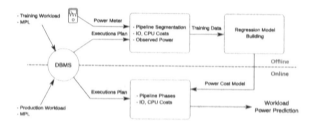

Fig. 2. Overview over power cost model

2.1   Pipeline Segmentation

In this section, we motivate the need for modeling power based on query pipelines. We start by showing an example of query *Q9* from the TPC-H benchmark. Figure 3a shows the active power consumption during the execution of the query, the query start at 10 s and finish at 143 s, we can see three different segments, we refer to these segments as *pipelines*, the pipelines are the concurrent execution of a contiguous sequence of operators, this is because most databases are usually implemented in an iterator model. The pipeline segmentation of the optimizer plan for query *Q9* is shown in Fig. 3b, there are 7 pipelines, and a partial order of the execution of these pipelines is enforced by their terminal *blocking* operators (e.g., PL6 cannot begin until PL5 is complete). Although the query has 7 different pipelines, only 4 pipelines are important in our discussion (the other finish very fast). The power-to-pipelines determination are done by the help of our DBMS Real-Time SQL Monitoring module, which gives us a real-time statistics at each step of the execution plan with the elapsed time, based on this, we segment the power log to their respective pipelines. If we compare the power changing points with the pipeline switching points in Fig. 3, we can see that *when a query switches from one pipeline to another, its power consumption*

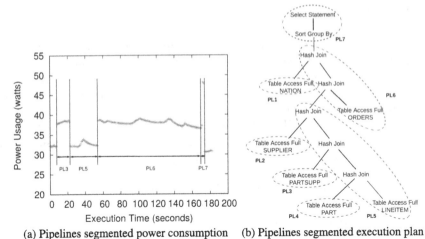

(a) Pipelines segmented power consumption   (b) Pipelines segmented execution plan

Fig. 3. Power consumption and execution plan of TPC-H benchmark query *Q9* with corresponding pipeline annotation.

also changes. During the execution of a pipeline, the power consumption usually tends to be approximately constant. To execute an SQL query by a DBMS, the query optimizer choose an *execution plan*. A plan is a tree composed of physical operators, such as scan, join or sort. Figure 3b presents an example of the execution plan returned by the query optimizer. A physical operator can be either *blocking* or *nonblocking*.

Definition 1. *An operator is blocking if it cannot produce any output tuple without reading as least one of its inputs (e.g., sort operator).*

Based on the notion of blocking/nonblocking operators, we decompose a plan in a set of pipelines delimited by blocking operators. Thus, a pipeline is [13]:

Definition 2. *A pipeline consists of a set of concurrently running operators.*

As in previous work [5,14], the pipelines are created in an inductive manner, starting from the leaf operators of the plan. Whenever we encounter a blocking operator, the current pipeline ends, and a new pipeline starts. As a result, the original execution plan can be viewed as a tree of pipelines, as showed in Fig. 3b. Further, based on our analysis, we found that the DBMS executes pipelines in a sequential order, so there is no pipeline concurrency.

2.2   Prediction Algorithm

Suppose that we have a workload of queries $q_1, q_2, \cdots, q_n$, after segmenting their execution plans into sets of pipelines, the workload of queries can be viewed as multiple phases of mixes of pipelines. This is illustrated in Fig. 4. In this example, we have a workload of 5 queries $q_1, \cdots, q_5$. After segmentation of their plans,

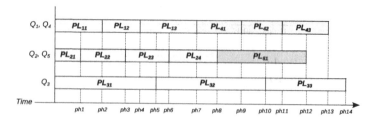

Fig. 4. Pipelines segmented queries workload

q_1 is represented as a sequence of 3 pipelines $P_{11}P_{12}P_{13}$, and so on for other queries. We use $PLij$ to denote the jth pipeline of the ith query, and use ph_k to denote the phase when a certain PL_{ij} finishes. As we see, we can identify a new mix of pipelines as soon as certain a pipeline finishes. In our example, at the end, we will have 14 mixes of pipelines, separated by the blue dashed lines that indicate the finish time for the pipelines. The execution of the workload is simulated as the execution of a sequence of pipeline mixes. The execution of each mix is called a pipeline phase. A phase change happens when a running pipeline finishes and another one starts. Our goal is to determine the execution of pipeline phases and the transitions among them, and to estimate how much power each phase will consume. The predicted workload power consumption is the total power consumed by all phases. This idea is presented in Algorithm 1. In this algorithm, we first generate the execution plan $Plan_i$ for each query q_i by calling the query optimizer, then we create the pipelines segmentation PL_i of each $Plan_i$. The first pipeline PL_{i1} in each PL_i is added to the current running mix $CurrentPLMix$. Then we continue phase by phase while the current mix is not empty. We determine the pipeline PL_{ij} with the shortest execution time t_{min}. Then we calculate the *cost of total work done* by each pipeline PL_{ik} in current mix, by multiplying each pipeline cost by $\frac{t_{min}}{t_{ik}}$, where t_{ik} is the execution time of the pipeline PL_{ik}. We call power prediction procedure to get the power of the current pipeline mix, and we remove P_{ij} from the mix. If PL_i contains more pipelines after P_{ij} finishes, we add the next one $P_{i(j+1)}$ into the current mix and we repeat this process until all queries in the workload are completed. The estimated power consumption of the workload is the sum of all its phase's power. We not that the prediction procedure will be called at the maximum as the total number of pipelines in the workload. The remaining task is to define the power prediction model for a mix of pipelines. We discuss our approach in next section.

2.3   Pipelines Phases Modeling

As discussed in the previous section, at each mix of pipelines we calculate the cost of total work done. In a traditional DBMS, query execution cost is treated as a linear combination of three components: CPU cost, I/O cost, and communication cost [23]. Inspired by this methodology, we propose to use these costs to model

Algorithm 1. Prediction Algorithm

Input: $W = \{q_1, \cdots, q_n\}$, a workload of n SQL queries
Output: P_w, predicted power consumption for the workload W
1: **foreach** query $i \in W$ **do**
2:     $Plan_i \leftarrow GetPlan(i)$;
3:     $PL_i \leftarrow GetPipelines(Plan_i)$;
4: **end for**
5: $CurrentPLMix \leftarrow \emptyset$;
6: **foreach** query $i \in W$ **do**
7:     $CurrentPLMix \leftarrow CurrentPLMix + PL_{i1}$;
8: **end for**
9:
10: **while** $CurrentPLMix \neq \emptyset$ **do**
11:     $PL_{ij} \leftarrow ShortestPipeline(CurrentPLMix)$;
12:     $t_{min} \leftarrow t_{ij}$;
13:     $Cost \leftarrow 0$;
14:     **foreach** $PL_{ik} \in CurrentMix$ **do**
15:         $Cost \leftarrow Cost + Cost_{ik} \times \frac{t_{min}}{t_{ik}}$;
16:     **end for**
17:     $P_w \leftarrow P_w + PredictPower(Cost)$;
18:     Remove PL_{ij} from $CurrentMix$;
19:     **if** $HasMorePipelines(PL_i)$ **then**
20:         $CurrentPLMix \leftarrow CurrentPLMix + PL_{i(j+1)}$;
21:     **end if**
22: **end while**
23:
24: **return** P_w;

---

pipelines mixes. Given a certain workload, the query optimizer is responsible for estimating CPU and I/O costs. Our strategy for pipeline modeling is to leverage the cost models that are built into the database systems for query optimization. To process tuples, each operator in a pipeline needs to perform CPU and/or I/O tasks. The cost of these tasks represents the "cost of the pipeline", which is the active power to be consumed in order to finish the tasks. In this paper, we focus on a single server setup and leave the study of distributed databases as future work. Thus, the communication cost can be ignored. More formally, for a given workload W of n pipeline phases $\{PL_1, PL_2, \ldots, PL_n\}$. The power cost model for overall workload is defined as follows:

$$Power(W) = \frac{\sum_{i=1}^{n} Power(PL_i) * Time(PL_i)}{Time(W)} \qquad (1)$$

$Time(PL_i)$ and $Time(W)$ represent respectively, the execution time of the pipeline phase i and the workload W. In our estimation, we pick these factors from the DBMS statistics module. However, to test the quality of our model, we will use the real execution time. Let a pipeline phase PL_i composed of n

algebraic operations $\{OP_1, OP_2, \ldots, OP_n\}$. The power cost $Power(PL_i)$ of the pipeline phase PL_i is the sum of CPU and I/O costs of all its operators:

$$Power(PL_i) = \beta_{cpu} \times \sum_{j=1}^{n_i} CPU\_COST_j + \beta_{io} \times \sum_{j=1}^{n_i} IO\_COST_j \qquad (2)$$

where β_{cpu} and β_{io} are the model parameter (i.e., unit power costs) for the pipelines. For a given query, the optimizer uses the query plan, cardinality estimates, and cost equations for the operators in the plan to generate counts for various types of I/O and CPU operations. It then converts these counts to time by using system-specific parameters such as CPU speed and I/O transfer speed. Therefore, in our model, we take I/O and CPU estimations before converting them to time. System parameters are calculated at the creation of the database, and cloud be highly unreliable. We calibrate these parameters to ensure resource estimation accuracy and optimal execution plan, as recommended by the DBMS vendor. The IO_COST is the predicted number of I/O it will require for DBMS to run the specified operator. The CPU_COST is the predicted number of CPU Cycle and buffer cache get it will require for DBMS to run the specified operator. By using I/O and CPU costs, we do not rely on SQL operators type or implementation. As a result, our model can handle complex queries like those of TPC-DS benchmark. Now, it remains to estimate the parameters β_{cpu} and β_{io} of the Eq. 2. This estimation will be described in the next section.

2.4   Estimation Parameters of IO and CPU Costs

Our methodology uses regression technique to compute these power cost parameters. We use multiple polynomial regression technique. This technique is suitable when there is a *nonlinear* relationship between the independents variables and the corresponding dependent variable (I/O, CPU costs and power). Based on our experiments, the order $m = 6$ gives us the best results (the residual sum of squares is the smallest). The power cost $Power(PL_i)$ of the pipeline phase PL_i is computed as:

$$\begin{aligned} Power(PL_i) &= \beta_0 + \beta_1(IO\_COST) + \beta_2(CPU\_COST) + \\ &\beta_3(IO\_COST^2) + \beta_4(CPU\_COST^2) + \beta_5(IO\_COST \times CPU\_COST) + \\ &\cdots + \\ &\beta_{26}(IO\_COST^6) + \beta_{27}(CPU\_COST^6) + \epsilon \end{aligned} \qquad (3)$$

where IO_COST, CPU_COST denote the pipelines I/O and CPU costs respectively, these costs are provided by the DBMS statistics module, and ϵ is a noise term that can account for measurement error. The β parameters are regression coefficients that will be estimated while learning the model from training data. Thus, the regression models are solved by estimating the model parameters β, and this is typically done by finding the least squares solution [15].

Training. As mentioned above, the β parameters are estimated while learning the model from training data. Here, we perform series of observations in which mixes of queries are well-chosen, and the power values consumed by the system are collected using measuring equipment while running these mixes at different multiprogramming levels. In the same time, for each training instance, we segment the query operators in a set of pipelines, and group them in a set of pipeline mixes in respect to their starting time, then calculate their costs. After collecting training queries power consumption, I/O and CPU costs. We apply the regression Eq. 3 to find our model parameters. Finally, after extracting the parameters, we can estimate the power of new queries without having to use measuring equipment, using our final cost model (Fig. 2).

3   Experimental Evaluation

In this section, we present experimental results showing the effectiveness of our proposed model. We first describe the experimental setup and datasets used, then evaluate the performance of our power estimator. ***The used Machine, Software and Hardware*** To measure power usage, we created a similar setup to previous studies [10,18,22]. Specifically, we use a "Watts UP? Pro ES" power meter which has a maximum resolution of one second. The device is directly connected between the power supply and the database workstation under test, to measure the workstation's overall power consumption (Fig. 5). The power values are logged and processed in a separate monitor machine. We used a Dell PowerEdge R210 II workstation having an Intel Xeon E3-1230 V2 3.30 GHz processor, 10 GB of DDR3 memory and a 2x500 GB hard drive. Our workstation machine is installed with the latest version of Oracle 11gR2 DBMS under Ubuntu Server 14.04 LTS with kernel 3.13, to minimize spurious influences, we disabled unnecessary background tasks, and we cleared system and Oracle cache on each query execution. ***Datasets and MPL*** In the experiments we use TPC-H and TPC-DS benchmarks datasets and queries. We varied the multiprogramming level (MPL), i.e., the number of queries that are concurrently running, we use MPL $\in \{2, \cdots, 10, 13, 15\}$. Finally, we run each experiment multiple times to ensure confidence in the observed values. ***Prediction Errors*** In the testing phase, given the predicted power cost offered by our model for n query mixes, we compare it with the actual observed system active power consumption. To quantify the model accuracy, we used the following *mean relative error* metric (MRE):

$$MRE = \frac{1}{n} \sum_{i=1}^{n} \frac{|observed_i - predicted_i|}{observed_i}. \tag{4}$$

3.1   Training Workloads

In the training phase, we created a workload with 12 TPC-H query templates. Specifically, the templates we used are TPC-H queries 1, 3, 4, 5, 9, 11, 14, 16,

Database Server

Power Meter   Monitor PC

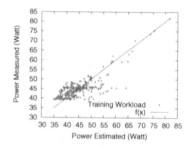

Fig. 5. The experiment Setup

Fig. 6. Training workload power consumption and regressions fit.

18, 19, 21, and 22, with scale factor 10, we refer to this set as *known* templates. For each MPL, we then generated mixes of TPC-H queries containing the same query template but with different instances using TPC-H tools. This result in 287 pipeline mixes composed from 132 query mixes. At each query mix execution, we collect statistics of pipelines and power usage. These collected data are used by the R language[3] software to find the best values of our model parameters. We do not consider large datasets in our study because they take a long time to finish, for instance, a simple mix of five queries generated from 100 GB TPC-H benchmark takes 3 h to complete its execution, this can translate in weeks of training and testing our model. Also, in this cases it is likely that a mix of queries could complete all of their executions in isolation faster than running its queries concurrently. The results of the training phase, against the fitted values from the polynomial model (Eq. 3) are plotted in Fig. 6. As we can see from the figure, the predicted and actual power consumption approximate the diagonal lines closely, denoting that our model can make reasonable power prediction. There is some variance between the predicted and the observed power for some mixes of queries. Much of this can attributed to the errors made by the DBMS query optimizer in estimating IO and CPU costs for these queries. Since our study treat the DBMS as "black box", we can't verify the model based on true costs which are obtained after the execution of the queries.

3.2   Testing Workloads

In the testing phase, we used various combination of datasets and workloads to check the overall model accuracy.

Known Templates. To evaluate our model, first, we created workloads based on TPC-H *known* templates. For each MPL, we generated 12 new mixes of queries, which result in 132 query mixes. However, generating mixes randomly may produce mixes of queries from the same templates repeatedly, hence, this technique doesn't cover the space of possible mixes well. Therefore, we used Latin

---

[3] http://www.r-project.org/.

Hypercube Sampling (LHS) [2]. LHS creates a hypercube with the same dimensionality as the number of query templates T. Each dimension is divided into n equal subranges. The subrange i represents the number of possible instances of the template i. LHS then selects n mixes from the space such that each subrange of each query template appears in exact one mix. Intuitively, LHS has better coverage of the space of mixes than random technique. We tested the prediction accuracy of our model over the generated mixes of known templates. Figure 7 shows the results of the experiments. As we can see from the figure, the average error over all MPLs is 6.3 % which is typically small considering the variety of concurrency level. Also, the maximum error is usually below 9 %. As a side note, we can see that the error is slightly larger when the MPL is small (MPL = 2, 3 or 4). We found that, when the MPL is high, the execution time of pipeline phases are large and our model can capture their power consumption, contrary to small MPLs, where some pipeline phases complete their execution quickly and our model can't estimate their power consumption accurately. This behavior is also observed in some of other experiments.

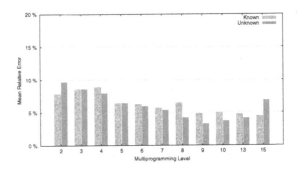

Fig. 7. Power estimation errors in TPC-H benchmark for known and unknown templates.

Unknown Templates. In order to test our cost model against *new* unseen templates from TPC-H benchmark, we created workloads based on the rest of queries not used in the training phase, using LHS technique. Specifically, for each MPL, we generated 10 new mixes of queries, which result in 110 query mixes. Results are shown in Fig. 7. It can be observed that the model predictions are within 10 % for the *unknown* templates, thus confirming their robustness.

Unknown Datasets. To verify the portability of the model, we experimentally tested it against TPC-DS benchmark, which is more complex than TPC-H benchmark due to its schema diversity, dataset distribution and decision support query workload. Motivated by [17], we selected 16 queries out of 99 queries template, wherein the queries are characterized by resource utilization pattern, such as CPU intensive queries or I/O intensive queries. The average length of pipelines is 7. Using LHS technique, we generated 16 mixes of queries for each

MPL, which result in 176 query mixes. Figure 8 shows the experiment results. It can be observed that the model predictions error is less than 10.5 %, which shows that pipeline modeling is a robust indicator for power prediction in the case of unknown dataset and queries.

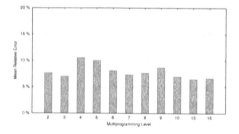
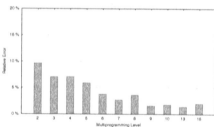

Fig. 8. Power estimation errors in TPC-DS benchmark.

Fig. 9. Power estimation errors in TPC-H benchmark for all templates.

Random Workloads. Lastly, we evaluate the accuracy of our model when predicting power consumption for all TPC-H query templates in more realistic way. In these experiments, to construct the query workload, we go through the given list of query templates and add one instance of each template. Going through the list again in a round-robin manner, we keep adding one instance of each query template to the workload until all the queries are added. Based on TPC-H 22 query, we used 4 instances for each query template, this result in a workload of 88 query. For each MPL M we run the first M mix of query, whenever a query finishes among the M queries running currently, a new query from the workload will be scheduled in its place based on First in, First out (FIFO) scheduling policy. This gives us long-running workloads, on average taking 2 h to finish. The results are shown in Fig. 9. As in previous experiment small MPLs give large errors compared to high MPLs. Our suggestion to deal with scenario, is to model the power for each group of MPL, for example, creating model for MPL $M1 \in \{2, \cdots, 5\}$, $M2 \in \{6, \cdots, 10\}$, $M3 \in \{11, \cdots, 15\}$ and so one. In future work, we may extend our framework with a similar grouping strategy. The experiment shows that the maximum estimation error is 9.6 %. Thus, our model can deal with realistic workloads. The above experimental results clearly state our model offers prediction errors comparable to the state-of-art in power prediction for known templates without concurrency [10,23]. Therefore, our framework offers a significant improvement over existing techniques as it can deliver comparable prediction accuracy on more complex scenarios (i.e., unknown templates and datasets) and queries executed in realistic concurrently level.

4   Related Work

By exploring the state-of-art, we identify the large panoply of research studies on power and energy-efficient resource management in computing systems. These works can be divided into two approaches: *Hardware-Driven Approaches ($\mathcal{HDA}$)* and *Software-Driven Approaches ($\mathcal{SDA}$)*.

$\mathcal{HDA}$: They use naive solutions like disabling electronic component during periods of inactivity and advanced ones such as dynamically changing the performance of component for better energy efficiency, such as Dynamic Voltage and Frequency Scaling technique used by today's CPU [4]. Lang *et al.* proposed a PVC (Processor Voltage/Frequency Control) mechanism to trade energy consumption for performance [12]. It aims at executing instructions at a lower processor voltage and frequency by leveraging the ability of modern processors. In another work, a co-engineering between Oracle and Intel in helps to decrease operating costs and effectively meet green computing goals with the Oracle Exadata Database Machine [8]. $\mathcal{SDA}$: At the software level, we identify works that consider (i) single query and (ii) concurrent queries, in single query case, the first work which incorporate energy in databases was early in 90's, the authors in [3] proposed to modify the database query optimizer to choose more energy efficient query plans to increase the effective battery life of mobile computers. The work in [12] proposed an Improved Query Energy-Efficiency (QED) by Introducing Explicit Delays mechanism, which uses query aggregation to leverage common components of queries in a workload. In [23], the authors discussed the opportunities for energy-based query optimization, and a power cost model is developed in the conjunction of PostgreSQL's cost model to predict single query power consumption. A static power profile for each basic database operation in query processing is defined and incorporated into the DBMS to calculate the power cost of a query. However, relying on SQL operators type or implementation limit the portability of the model, in our work, we use I/O and CPU costs provided by the DBMS to handle complex queries like those of TPC-DS benchmark. In the same direction, the work of [11] shows that processing a query as fast as possible does not always turn out to be the most energy-efficient way to operate a DBMS. Based on this observation, the authors proposed a framework for energy-aware database query processing. It augments query plans with an energy consumption prediction for some specific database operators like select, project and join. The proposed model is very simple and doesn't consider complex queries. The authors of [10] propose a deep research in modeling the peak power of database operations, where peak power is the maximum power consumed during query execution. Like us, a pipeline-based model of query execution plans was developed to identify the sources of peak power consumption for a single query and to recommend plans with low peak power. However, their approach needs to retrain the model for every new pipeline. [18] attempts to model energy and peak power of simple selection queries on single relations, therefore their study does not reflect complex benchmark schema and queries. In our previous work [19], we proposed cost model to predict the power consumption of single queries. Our model is based on pipeline segmenting of the query and predicting their power based on its I/O and CPU costs, using polynomial regression techniques. In the case of concurrent queries, the authors of [23] adapt their static model to dynamic workloads using a feedback control mechanism to periodically update model parameters using real-time energy measurements. Limits of this approach are the needs for using measurements equipment all the time, and retraining the model parameter frequently. In contrast, our solution requires just one-time training phase.

5   Conclusion

In this paper, we studied the problem of predicting power consumption for concurrent database workloads. Our approach builds a cost model based on empirical results obtained from a training workloads that were carefully created, than we used optimizer's cost model to estimate the I/O and CPU operations for each mix of pipelines, finally, the hardware parameters are obtained by multivariate polynomial regression algorithms. Furthermore, we performed tests on our framework with a real database, by running a set of workloads from TPC-H and TPC-DS benchmarks, and comparing their power cost with those predicted by the model. Our results show that the model, which only uses optimizer estimated costs as inputs, can predict workload power consumption with high accuracy. For future work, an interesting direction is to enhance classic workload management tasks such as admission control, query scheduling and execution control with energy efficiency dimension. All these ideas deserve future research effort.

References

1. Agrawal, R., Ailamaki, A., Bernstein, P.A., Brewer, E.A., Carey, M.J., Chaudhuri, S., et al.: The claremont report on database research. ACM SIGMOD Rec. **37**(3), 9–19 (2008)
2. Ahmad, M., Duan, S., et al.: Predicting completion times of batch query workloads using interaction-aware models and simulation. In: EDBT, pp. 449–460. ACM (2011)
3. Alonso, R., Ganguly, S.: Energy efficient query optimization. In: Matsushita Info Tech Lab, Citeseer (1992)
4. Beloglazov, A., Buyya, R., Lee, Y.C., et al.: A taxonomy and survey of energy-efficient data centers and cloud computing systems. Adv. Comput. **82**(2), 47–111 (2011)
5. Chaudhuri, S., Narasayya, V., Ramamurthy, R.: Estimating progress of execution for sql queries. In: SIGMOD, pp. 803–814. ACM (2004)
6. Garcia-Molina, H., Ullman, J.D., Widom, J.: Database System Implementation, vol. 654. Prentice Hall, Upper Saddle River (2000)
7. Harizopoulos, S., Shah, M., Meza, J., Ranganathan, P.: Energy efficiency: the new holy grail of data management systems research. arXiv preprint arXiv:0909.1784 (2009)
8. Intel, Oracle: Oracle exadata on intel® xeon® processors: Extreme performance for enterprise computing. White paper (2011)
9. Koomey, J.: Growth in data center electricity use 2005 to 2010. A report by Analytical Press, completed at the request of The New York Times (2011)
10. Kunjir, M., Birwa, P.K., et al.: Peak power plays in database engines. In: Proceedings of the 15th International Conference on Extending Database Technology, pp. 444–455. ACM (2012)

11. Lang, W., Kandhan, R., Patel, J.M.: Rethinking query processing for energy efficiency: slowing down to win the race. IEEE Data Eng. Bull. **34**(1), 12–23 (2011)
12. Lang, W., Patel, J.: Towards eco-friendly database management systems. arXiv preprint arXiv:0909.1767 (2009)
13. Li, J., Nehme, R., Naughton, J.: Gslpi: a cost-based query progress indicator. In: 2012 IEEE 28th International Conference on Data Engineering (ICDE), pp. 678–689. IEEE (2012)
14. Luo, G., Naughton, J.F., Ellmann, C.J., Watzke, M.W.: Toward a progress indicator for database queries. In: SIGMOD, pp. 791–802. ACM (2004)
15. McCullough, J.C., Agarwal, Y., Chandrashekar, J., et al.: Evaluating the effectiveness of model-based power characterization. In: USENIX Annual Technical Conference (2011)
16. Poess, M., Nambiar, R.O.: Energy cost, the key challenge of today's data centers: a power consumption analysis of tpc-c results. PVLDB **1**(2), 1229–1240 (2008)
17. Poess, M., Nambiar, R.O., Walrath, D.: Why you should run tpc-ds: a workload analysis. In: VLDB, pp. 1138–1149. VLDB Endowment (2007)
18. Rodriguez-Martinez, M., Valdivia, H., Seguel, J., Greer, M.: Estimating power/energy consumption in database servers. Procedia Comput. Sci. **6**, 112–117 (2011)
19. Roukh, A., Bellatreche, L.: Eco-processing of olap complex queries. In: Data Warehousing and Knowledge Discovery. Springer (2015, to appear)
20. Tu, Y.C., Wang, X., Zeng, B., Xu, Z.: A system for energy-efficient data management. ACM SIGMOD Rec. **43**(1), 21–26 (2014)
21. Wang, J., Feng, L., Xue, W., Song, Z.: A survey on energy-efficient data management. ACM SIGMOD Rec. **40**(2), 17–23 (2011)
22. Xu, Z., Tu, Y.C., Wang, X.: Exploring power-performance tradeoffs in database systems. In: ICDE, pp. 485–496 (2010)
23. Xu, Z., Tu, Y.C., Wang, X.: Dynamic energy estimation of query plans in database systems. In: ICDCS, pp. 83–92. IEEE (2013)

Scalable Trajectory Similarity Search Based on Locations in Spatial Networks

Eleftherios Tiakas and Dimitrios Rafailidis[✉]

Department of Informatics, Aristotle University of Thessaloniki,
54124 Thessaloniki, Greece
{tiakas,draf}@csd.auth.gr

Abstract. In this paper, we propose an efficient query processing algorithm that returns the trajectory results in a progressive manner. We limit the calculation of pairwise shortest path distances between the set of query locations and the spatial nodes, by highly reducing the preprocessing requirements. Also, we introduce a spatiotemporal similarity measure, based on which the temporal-to-spatial significance of the trajectory results can be easily modified and the query locations can be spatially prioritized according to users' preferences. In our experiments with a real-world road network, we show that the proposed method has approximately ten times less preprocessing requirements than the competitive methods and reduces the search time by two orders of magnitude at least.

Keywords: Spatial/Temporal databases · Indexing methods · Spatial networks

1 Introduction

In trajectory similarity search by locations methods [2–6], the query is considered as a small set of locations with or without an order specified, so as to find the k best connected trajectories and consequently to connect the designated locations geographically. In contrast to the conventional trajectory search, the methods of searching trajectories by locations focus on the connection provided by a trajectory to the specified query locations. The query is no longer a full trajectory or any subsequence, as it is considered in conventional trajectory similar search, but a few locations, making thus the query more flexible. This new query type has many novel applications, e.g. trip planning which demands to find trajectories that connect a few selected locations, those that are close to all the locations. For example, given a set of coordinates of locations, trajectory query by locations can help travelers in planning a trip to multiple places of interest in an unfamiliar city by providing similar routes traveled by other people for reference. In addition to location-based queries, personalized trajectory similarity search methods [3,4,6] have been introduced. Such methods combine the query trajectory with users' textual attributes [3,6] or consider a user-defined significance, by weighting each

© Springer International Publishing Switzerland 2015
L. Bellatreche and Y. Manolopoulos (Eds.): MEDI 2015, LNCS 9344, pp. 213–224, 2015.
DOI: 10.1007/978-3-319-23781-7_17

location in the query [4]. Given user's textual attributes or predefined weights for each sample point in the query trajectory, such methods retrieve the most similar trajectory, by also considering users' preferences.

Nevertheless, given the spatial network, searching trajectories by locations and personalized methods face several issues. **(I1):** The preprocessing cost is high either by building a complex spatial index [2,5] or by including a preliminary step to precompute the all-to-all pairwise node distances in the spatial network based on the Dijkstra's algorithm [3,4]. **(I2):** The aforementioned methods have high space requirements for preserving the spatial index or the all-to-all pairwise node distances over the trajectory similarity search, crucial for large-scale spatial networks. **(I3):** They assume that trajectories do not necessarily comply with the spatial networks constraints, by either ignoring the temporal information [5] or allowing trajectories to move in free Euclidean spaces [6].

In this paper we propose a scalable and progressive query processing algorithm for searching trajectories by locations in spatial networks. Our contribution is summarized as follows: **(C1):** The preprocessing step of our method has linear complexity, since the computation of all-to-all pairwise shortest path distances is avoided, by limiting the calculation of pairwise node distances from the small set of query locations to the nodes of the spatial graph. **(C2):** Our spatial index, an extended adjacent list representation, requires linear space, since it establishes connections directly to the original stored trajectory data on disk. The proposed extended adjacent list representation connects adjacent nodes with trajectories clusters, without the requirement of building any complex spatial index. **(C3):** Personalized searching trajectories by locations is supported by designing a spatiotemporal similarity measure which can be easily adapted to users' preferences, making the query more spatial or temporal-oriented. Additionally, weights can be set to spatially prioritize the locations.

The rest of the paper is organized as follows. Section 2 presents the fundamental concepts in trajectory similarity search in spatial networks. Section 3 details the proposed method. In Sect. 4 the experimental results are presented. Finally, in Sect. 5 the basic conclusions of our study are drawn.

2   Preliminaries

2.1   Spatial Networks and Trajectories

In this Section the fundamental concepts in trajectory similarity search in spatial networks are presented.

Spatial Networks: The spatial networks are represented as connected graphs. A spatial network $G(V, E)$ contains a set of vertices V and a set of weighted edges E. In their graph representation, the vertices and the edges indicate the road intersections and their connections, respectively. An edge (v_i, v_j) $\in E$ represents a road segment and the weight $w(v_i, v_j)$ is the travel distance from node v_i to node v_j. However, depending on the application, additional factors may be embedded into the edge weights; for example, travel time, availability, and other possible restrictions. For each pair of nodes $v_a, v_b \in V$, not necessary neighbors, their distance is the shortest path (network distance), calculated by the accumulated edge weight of the shortest path between v_a and v_b.

Trajectories: In a large number of applications the objects are allowed to move only on predefined paths of a spatial network rather than moving freely to the Euclidean space (2D or 3D). Therefore, trajectories are constrained into the paths of the network providing motion restrictions. Let T be the set of the trajectories. Each trajectory $T_i \in T$ is represented as a directed sequence/set $T_i = \{(v_{i1}, t_{v_{i1}}), (v_{i2}, t_{v_{i2}}), ..., (v_{ir_i}, t_{v_{ir_i}})\}$ of r_i time-labeled spatial points, which are nodes $v_{i1}, v_{i2}, ..., v_{ir_i} \in V$ with their corresponding timestamps $t_{v_{i1}}, t_{v_{i2}}, ..., t_{v_{ir_i}}$. We assume that the spatial points of the trajectories lay on the nodes of spatial network G. Otherwise, if the spatial points of the trajectories lie on the edges, then they can be aligned to the closest nodes using map-matching methods. Each trajectory T_i may have its own length r_i of spatial points, which is called description length. Therefore, we assume that trajectories are of arbitrary description lengths in T, which means that for two different trajectories T_i, T_j, with $i \neq j$, it may hold that $r_i \neq r_j$. Finally, the multiset[1] of the spatial points from all trajectories is denoted as R, and the multiset of all trajectory edges as RE. Both multisets R, RE represent the trajectory data, where: $|R| = \sum_{i=1}^{|T|} r_i$ and $|RE| = \sum_{i=1}^{|T|}(r_i - 1) = |R| - |T|$.

2.2   Problem Formulation

Let G be a spatial network and T a dataset of trajectories. Let Q be a set of query locations $q_1, q_2, ..., q_m$ which are the spatial points (nodes of the graph G), that the resulted trajectories have to pass close. Let $qt_2, qt_3, ..., qt_m$ be the corresponding inter-arrival times which are $m - 1$ tolerance time intervals, acceptable by users for travelling between the query locations, where $qt_i = \infty$ denotes the lack of time restriction for location q_i. Let $w_1 ... w_m$ be the users' predefined weights, expressing the personal preferences to the m query locations, where $0 < w_j < 1, j = 1, ..., m$ and $\sum_{j=1}^{m} w_j = 1$. Given a similarity function $sim(Q, T_i)$ between the set Q of query locations and a trajectory $T_i \in T$, the goal is: *to find the k most similar trajectories in T with the highest similarity score to Q.*

3   Proposed Method

3.1   Spatial Index - Preprocessing

In the preprocessing step, the spatial network $G(V, E)$ is stored using an adjacency list representation. The main idea is to extend the adjacency list by using trajectory clusters. Given a node v_i and the adjacency list representation of p adjacent nodes, then for each edge $(v_i, v_j) \in E$, with $j = 1, ..., p$, the respective

---

[1] Multiset is a generalization of the notion of set in which members are allowed to appear more than once.

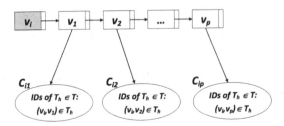

Fig. 1. The extended adjacency list index of node v_i, with p adjacent nodes and the respective p trajectory clusters.

cluster C_{ij} is generated. Each cluster C_{ij} consists of the trajectory Id's of the respective trajectories $T_h \in T$ that pass through edge (v_i, v_j). In case that an edge $(v_i, v_j) \in E$ is not included in any trajectory of the T set, the respective cluster C_{ij} remains empty. Each cluster C_{ij}, which is generated by the edge (v_i, v_j), is connected with the adjacent node v_j of node v_i. Figure 1 depicts the extended adjacency list index of node v_i, with p trajectory clusters, connected with the respective p adjacent nodes. Therefore, given $|V|$ nodes in the G graph the main index consists of $|V|$ extended adjacent lists with the adjacent nodes being connected with the respective trajectories clusters.

The set of the $|V|$ extended adjacent lists is generated in the preprocessing step and consists the main index of our method. The implementation has low complexity, since the set is built during the load of the network and the trajectory data. Algorithm 1 depicts the preprocessing procedure. Since the trajectory clusters are implemented as dynamic lists, an one-pass linear scan of the trajectories data is required. During the scan, the trajectory data are retrieved through a hash function $hash(\cdot)$ which takes as argument the trajectory Id and returns the address (pointer) of the stored trajectory on disk. Then, each edge of the trajectories is traversed and the corresponding trajectory Ids that contain the specific edge are dynamically inserted into the respective cluster C_{ij} of the index. In our implementation, we used the hash function $hash(\cdot)$ of modulo: $Id \bmod |T|$. Alternatively, many other hash functions could be used, without affecting the performance of our method.

Algorithm 1. Preprocessing

Input: spatial network G, set of trajectories T, hash function $hash(\cdot)$
Output: main indexer

---

01. **for each** trajectory $T_i \in T$
02.   allocate data of T_i through $hash(T_i.Id)$
03.   **for each** edge $(v_i, v_j) \in T_i$
04.   insert $T_i.Id$ in cluster C_{ij}
05.   **end-for**
06. **end-for**

The time complexity of the preprocessing algorithm is $O(|V| + |E| + |RE|)$, by performing a linear scan of the trajectory data. The space complexity of the index is $O(|V|+|E|+|RE|)$ for storing both the network data and the trajectory clusters. The proposed indexing scheme has many advantages. Linear space is required to store both network data and trajectory Ids. The proposed indexing scheme requires linear building time. Additionally, the trajectory clustering approach generates smaller clusters than the recent work of [4] does. The main difference is that we propose an edge-based clustering which distributes the trajectories to many small clusters, whereas Shang et al. in [4] propose a node-based clustering which produces significantly larger clusters. For each trajectory Id a hashing key can instantly be retrieved, by directly connecting to the trajectory data which are stored on disk.

3.2 Proposed Similarity/Distance Measures

In this Section, we present the proposed distance functions $Ds(\cdot)$ and $Dt(\cdot)$ in the spatial and temporal domains respectively, along with the final spatiotemporal similarity measure $sim(\cdot)$. The proposed measures express the similarity between a trajectory $T_i \in T$ and the user-defined query locations in set Q. Therefore, the proposed measures are functions in the $|Q| \times |T|$ space, instead of the $|T| \times |T|$ space, by significantly speeding up computations.

Spatial Distance Function $Ds(\cdot)$. The spatial similarity expresses how close is a trajectory to the query locations according to the restrictions of the spatial network. Due to these restrictions we consider the main spatial distance function $d(\cdot)$ between a trajectory node and a query location, where $d(\cdot)$ is calculated based on the network/shortest-path distance, with the rest of possible network restrictions being already embedded into the edge weights of the network.

Given a single query location $q_j \in Q$ and a trajectory $T_i \in T$ which contains the nodes $v_1, v_2, ..., v_r$, the spatial distance of the trajectory T_i from a query location q_j is defined as

$$ds(q_j, T_i) = \min_{h=1,...,r} d(q_j, v_h) \tag{1}$$

Therefore, the spatial distance from a query location q_j is the minimum spatial distance from the nodes of the trajectory T_i to the query location. Let $vmin_j$ be the corresponding node of the trajectory T_i with the minimum distance from the query point q_j. Then, the spatial proximity between a query location and a trajectory is equal to $ds(q_j, T_i) = d(q_j, vmin_j)$. In trajectory similarity search by locations, a specific node of the trajectory lies close to a query location. Therefore, for each query location $q_j, j = 1, ..., m$, the corresponding nodes $vmin_j$ are detected independently[2].

---

[2] Similar selection strategy of measure ds is followed by [2,5], however, the measure is termed as *matched pairs* based on Euclidean distances, ignoring the spatial constraints.

A desired characteristic of the spatial similarity of a trajectory to the query locations is to have at least j nodes as close to q_j as possible (pairwise similarities/distances). In order to consider that, we must aggregate the spatial distances of the trajectory from each query location q_j. Therefore, we define the spatial distance of the trajectory T_i from the whole query set Q as follows:

$$Ds(Q, T_i) = \frac{1}{m} \sum_{j=1}^{m} ds(q_j, T_i) \tag{2}$$

The spatial distance of a trajectory T_i to the set Q of query locations is computed as the average distance function $ds(\cdot)$ from each query location. Additionally, in case that a user-specific spatial-priority in the spatial locations q_j must be included, the following weighted average distance is used:

$$Ds(Q, T_i) = w_1 \cdot ds(q_1, T_i) + \dots + w_m \cdot ds(q_m, T_i) \tag{3}$$

where $w_j, j = 1, ..., m$, are users' predefined weights, with $0 < w_j < 1, j = 1, ..., m$ and $\sum_{j=1}^{m} w_j = 1$. A value of w_j close to 1 (or 0) means that the distance from the query location q_j contributes more (or less) to the total distance, affecting the spatial closeness or farness of q_j to T_i.

Temporal Distance Function $Dt(\cdot)$. An important characteristic of our proposed methodology is that the time information of all the resulted k trajectories are not necessarily required, which means that the time-stamps of all the trajectory nodes are not essential to the calculations of the temporal distance function. This happens because the corresponding inter-arrival times $qt_2, qt_3, ..., qt_m$, tolerance time intervals, which are acceptable by users for traveling between the locations, exclusively define the time restrictions in the temporal domain. In this Section, we present the temporal distance function $Dt(Q, T_i)$ between the set Q of query locations and a trajectory T_i.

In the calculations of the $Ds(\cdot)$ spatial distance function, the corresponding nodes $vmin_j, j = 1, ..., m$, that express the spatial proximity of T_i from Q are retrieved, for each query location q_j. Let $t_{vmin_j}, j = 1, ..., m$, be the corresponding times instances of the nodes $vmin_j$ of the trajectory T_i. We calculate the corresponding inter-arrival times $dt_2, dt_3, ..., dt_m$ between the resulted nodes $vmin_j$, which can be computed instantly by summing the inter-arrival times of the intermediate nodes, through the trajectory path. For each location $j \in 2, 3, ..., m$, there are the following cases for the inter-arrival times qt_j and dt_j, **Case 1:** $(dt_j = qt_j)$: The query tolerance time interval qt_j is equal to the actual time interval dt_j from the trajectory. Since the time intervals are identical the temporal distance must be zero. **Case 2:** $(dt_j > qt_j)$: The query tolerance time interval qt_j is less than the actual time interval dt_j from the trajectory. In this case a temporal distance between the trajectory and the query locations must be considered, since the trajectory requires more time for the travel. The temporal distance is: $|qt_j - dt_j|$. **Case 3:** $(dt_j < qt_j)$: The query tolerance time interval qt_j is greater than the actual time interval dt_j from the trajectory. Therefore, the trajectory requires less time than the query restrictions and we must not consider any temporal distance between the trajectory and the query locations, i.e. the temporal distance must be zero. In order to have a unified formula we set $dt_j = qt_j$ and the temporal distance is preserved zero, as in the case of $(dt_j = qt_j)$. Considering the aforementioned three cases, the temporal distance function $Dt(Q, T_i)$ between the trajectory T_i and the query set Q is calculated as follows:

$$Dt(Q, T_i) = \frac{1}{m-1} \sum_{j=2}^{m} \frac{|qt_j - dt_j|}{\max\{qt_j, dt_j\}}. \tag{4}$$

Spatiotemporal Similarity Measure $sim(\cdot)$. The proposed spatiotemporal similarity measure $sim(\cdot)$ is a linear weighted aggregation of the spatial $Ds(\cdot)$ and temporal $D_t(\cdot)$ distance functions,

$$sim(Q, T) = 1 - dist(Q, T)$$

$$dist(Q, T) = a \cdot Ds(Q, T) + (1 - a) \cdot Dt(Q, T) \tag{5}$$

where $a \in [0, 1]$ is a weighting parameter, which expresses the temporal to spatial preference. Values of a close to 0 and 1 denote user's preference to temporal and spatial domains, respectively. The final distance and similarity measures $(dist(\cdot)$ and $sim(\cdot))$ are real numbers in the interval $[0, 1]$. Also, parameter a of Eq. (5) can be used to define the importance of temporal to spatial similarity. In case of $a = 1$ the spatial similarity solely contributes to the final similarity score of $sim(\cdot)$ or distance of $dist(\cdot)$. On the contrary, in case of $a = 0$ the temporal similarity exclusively contributes to the final score. Therefore, a user can select the desired value of the a parameter, depending on the application.

3.3 Query Processing by Locations

A preliminary step to the query processing algorithm is required, where the computation of the pairwise shortest path distances between the query locations and the nodes of the graph is performed. In the preliminary step, the calculations of the shortest-path distances are limited to the $m \times |V|$ pairwise distances between the user-selected query locations $q_1, q_2, ..., q_m$ and the nodes of the spatial network G. This comes in contrast to previous works [3, 4] where the computation of all-to-all pairwise node distances ($|V| \times |V|$) is performed. The distances are calculated based on the Dijkstra algorithm in $O(m * (\log |V| + |E|))$ time, equipped with a Fibonacci Heap structure. The shortest-path distances are stored in memory, requiring $O(m * |V|)$ space.

The main strategy of the proposed algorithm consists of the following steps: *(a) from each query location, perform a Dijkstra expansion step incrementally, following a round-robin strategy; (b) collect the trajectory Ids that are included in the trajectory clusters of the visited edges; (c) compute the spatiotemporal similarities based on Eq. (5) and generate the top-k results progressively. The* pseudo-code of the proposed query processing by locations method is presented in Algorithm 2.

The five main steps of the proposed algorithm are the following, **(S1):** From each query location, in a round-robin manner (initially $v_j = q_j$), each neighbor node v_i of v_j is retrieved in the Dijkstra expansion step (lines 5–13). Each query location q_j uses a Fibonacci Heap HQ_j, in which the corresponding shortest-path distances from the Dijkstra expansion are updated. Then, the candidate trajectories T_h are collected from the corresponding edge cluster C_{ij} of the extended adjacency list index (line 14). **(S2):** The spatiotemporal distances $dist$ between the collected candidate trajectories T_h and the query location set Q are calculated (Eq. (5)). In order to avoid recalculations in any step of the algorithm, a bit-set B with $|T|$ bits in memory is used where the corresponding bit of each calculated trajectory distance is enabled on-the-fly (lines 15–20). Therefore, during the query processing, the distances are calculated only once for each trajectory. The currently top-k calculated trajectory distances and their corresponding trajectory Ids are preserved and updated in a priority heap H (ordered by $dist$) on-the-fly (line 19). Heap H has a limited size of k items, since only the most similar k results are required. **(S3):** Then, a threshold L is updated (initially set to 0), according to the average sum of the network distances between the query locations and the set of $vmin_j$ nodes: $L = \frac{a}{m} \sum_{j=1}^{m} d(q_j, vmin_j)$, where $vmin_j$ is the closest node to query location q_j in the current Dijkstra expansion level, i.e. $vmin_j$ has the shortest path distance to q_j among all the detected nodes in the current round from q_j. The threshold L is a lower bound of the final distance function $dist$, and it is used for generating the results. In each round, L is increased, (when the expansion level is changed), by comparing the current $Lcurr$ value with the previously calculated one. In particular, if the currently computed $Lcurr$ value is greater than the previous L value of the last round, then the $Lcurr$ value of the current round is updated accordingly (lines 24, 25). Since the temporal distances Dt are aggregated with the spatial distances Ds in the final distance function $dist(\cdot)$, L is a lower bound for both spatial and spatiotemporal distances. Moreover, in case that w_j weights are used (Eq. (3)), then threshold L is calculated as: $L = a \cdot \sum_{j=1}^{m} w_j \cdot d(q_j, vmin_j)$. **(S4):** After the end of each round, the trajectories in the current top-k list in heap H are examined based on condition that they have a distance $dist$ lower than L. If the condition is satisfied for a subset of trajectories in H, then these trajectories are instantly added to the top results list (lines 26–28). The trajectory insertion proceeds progressively until L reaches a value greater than the distance of the k-th element in H or in the extreme case that the spatiotemporal distances of all trajectories in T have been calculated (stopping condition, line 29). **(S5):** In case that not all top-k results have been retrieved, the algorithm proceeds to the next expansion round, where the algorithm repeats the loop in lines 5–30.

The total time complexity of the proposed query processing algorithm is $O(m * (|V| \log |V| + |E|) + |RE|)$. An $m * (|V| \log |V| + |E|)$ cost is required for the Dijkstra expansion from the m query locations. The candidate trajectories are collected from the clusters C_{ij} of the extended adjacency list index;

Algorithm 2. Progressive Query Processing Algorithm

Input: the spatial network G, the set of trajectories T, the set of the query locations Q, the number of results k

Output: top-k trajectories (progressively)

```
01.  L = 0, Lcurr = 0, top = 1
02.  initialize vQⱼ = qⱼ, ∀j = 1, ..., m
03.  initialize distQⱼ[vQⱼ] = 0, ∀j = 1, ..., m
04.  HQⱼ.insert(vQⱼ, 0), ∀j = 1, ..., m
05.  while HQⱼ.size > 0, ∀j = 1, ..., m
06.     for j = 1 to m
07.        vQⱼ = HQⱼ.extractMin(), vminⱼ = vQⱼ
08.        for each neighbor uQⱼ of vQⱼ in the adjacency list
09.           if distQⱼ[uQⱼ] > distQⱼ[vQⱼ] + w(vQⱼ, uQⱼ) then
10.              distQⱼ[uQⱼ] = distQⱼ[vQⱼ] + w(vQⱼ, uQⱼ)
11.              if uQⱼ ∈ HQⱼ then HQⱼ.decreaseKey(uQⱼ, distQⱼ[uQⱼ])
12.           end-if
13.           if uQⱼ ∉ HQⱼ then HQⱼ.insert(uQⱼ, distQⱼ[uQⱼ])
14.              for each trajectory (Tₕ.Id) in cluster C₍ᵥQⱼ,ᵤQⱼ₎ from edge (vQⱼ, uQⱼ)
15.                 if B[h] = false then
16.                    retrieve data of trajectory Tₕ through hash(Tₕ.Id)
17.                    compute dst = dist(Q, Tₕ)
18.                    B[h] = true
19.                    H.insert(Tₕ.Id, dst)
20.                 end-if
21.              end-for
22.           end-for
23.        end-for
24.        Lcurr = \frac{a}{m} Σⱼ₌₁ᵐ d(qⱼ, vminⱼ)
25.        if Lcurr > L then L = Lcurr
26.        for i = top to k
27.           if H[i].dst < L then top++, return trajectory H[i].Id
28.        end-for
29.        if L > H[k].dst or B.count = |T| then stop
30.  end-while
```

nevertheless, the total amount of trajectory Ids that exist into the clusters is $|RE|$, since RE contains all the trajectory edges of the dataset, i.e. $\sum_{i,j} |C_{ij}| = |RE|$. The existence of the bit-set B avoids recalculations when trajectories are discovered from different locations explaining the additional $|RE|$ cost in the total complexity.

4   Experimental Evaluation

4.1   Settings

In our experiments we used the North America Road Network[3] (**NA**), which contains 175,813 nodes and 179,179 edges. We compared the proposed method against the following personalized methods for searching trajectories by locations: (a) "Two-phase PTM", (b) "PTM without heuristic" and (c) "Balanced", on the common evaluation data set of the North America Road Network, recently presented in [4]. "Two-phase PTM" is the personalized matching method of

---

[3] Real Datasets for Spatial Databases: http://www.cs.utah.edu/~lifeifei/Spatial Dataset.htm

Shang et al. [4]. "PTM without heuristic" and "Balanced" methods are two naive approaches, also used in [4] for comparison. The following evaluation metrics were used: (a) the required CPU-time for the main query processing algorithm and (b) the number of visited trajectories during the trajectory similarity search. Following the evaluation protocol of [4], the number of visited trajectories represents the required accesses to trajectory data that are stored on disk. The number of visited trajectories reflects to the real disk I/O cost at a certain degree, since the systems may have hidden buffers and cash-memories, making thus difficult to measure the real I/O cost more accurately.

To generate the trajectories in the North America Road Network we used the Brinkhoff's generator [1], which defines the velocity in the trajectory parts of each moving object/vehicle and categorizes the vehicles in classes according to these velocities. For each generated trajectory data set, the average vehicle velocity is computed and then, for each query the tolerance time intervals qt_i are set equal to the fraction of the network distances between the query locations q_i and the average velocity. Moreover, since the query locations are randomly selected, we set equal w_i weights to $1/m$. Following the personalized trajectory matching method of "Two-Phase PTM", the weight w of each sample point in a query trajectory was randomly generated (integers in [1, 5]), to evaluate the performance of the proposed method. Nevertheless, in our experiments we observed that the performance of the proposed method is preserved either considering equal or randomly generated and different weights in the query locations. Therefore, in the experimental results equal weights are considered.

In order to perform fair comparison against the personalized trajectory matching methods of [4], "Two-phase PTM", "PTM without heuristic" and "Balanced", on the common evaluation data set of North America Road Network, we regenerated the trajectories in the data set by setting the same parameters to the Brinkhoff's generator with the work of [4]. We varied the description lengths r between 20–100 spatial points, which were mapped to the nodes of the spatial graph. For the number of selected trajectories $|T|$ we performed the same variation of: 10 K, 15 K, 20 K, 25 K, 30 K. We set $k = 1$, similar to the examined algorithms in [4], where the case of the most similar trajectory (top-1) is considered. Additionally, we set the default value of $m = 60$. Finally we set $a = 0.5$, equal to the default λ value for the spatiotemporal similarity measure of [4], which also expresses the temporal-to-spatial significance. The resulted values of the common evaluation metrics of CPU-Time and number of visited trajectories, are averaged by 50 queries with random selected query locations.

All experiments have been conducted on a machine with Quad Core 3 GHz CPU, 2 TB SATA3 Hard Disk, running Windows 7 64 bit.

4.2   Results

In Table 1, the preprocessing requirements of the examined methods are depicted. The proposed method has lower preprocessing requirements than the competitive methods. This happens because the preprocessing time of the proposed method is to build the spatial index (18.687 s) and to compute the $m \times |V|$

Table 1. Preprocessing cost.

	Preproc. Time (sec)	Mem. Space (MB)
Proposed method	24.014	100.8
Balanced	380.8	1516.9
PTM without heuristic	380.8	996.3
Two-phase PTM	380.8	996.3

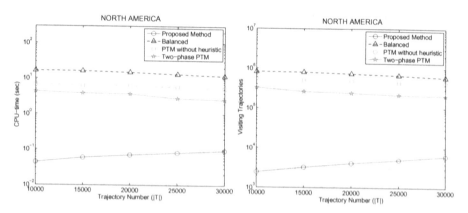

Fig. 2. Methods comparison in terms of CPU-time (sec) and number of visiting trajectories.

shortest path distances from the $m = 60$ query locations (5.327 s), whereas the competitive methods require to compute the $|V| \times |V|$ all-to-all shortest path distances (380.8 s), also mentioned in [4]. Additionally, the proposed method requires 80.5 MB to preserve the precalculated distances in the memory, added by 20.3 MB for the spatial index space. The competitive methods require a memory space of 630.6 MB to maintain the all-to-all pairwise distances, added by the required space during the query processing for (a) preserving the extra labels in the trajectories to determine if they are touched in the spatial or the temporal domain (partial or full match) from each query location; and (b) using the priorities to select the candidates and perform the appropriate scheduling, resulting in an additional space of 886.3, 365.7 and 365.7 MB for the "Balanced", "PTM without heuristic" and "Two-phase PTM" methods, respectively. Therefore, the proposed method has approximately 10 times less preprocessing requirements than the competitive methods.

In the experimental results of Fig. 2, the proposed method outperforms all the competitive methods in terms of CPU-Time and number of visiting trajectories. In the query processing algorithm of the most competitive method of "Two-phase PTM", for each query location the respective most similar trajectory is visited by searching in the spatial and temporal domains separately. Therefore, by incrementally retrieving the candidate most similar trajectories for all query locations the algorithm terminates when the Lower Bound (LB) exceeds the Upper Bound (UB) [4]. In doing so, "Two-phase PTM" may perform multiple visits for the same trajectories, by significantly increasing the CPU-time and the number of accesses to the trajectories. Moreover, our proposed method performs an edge-based clustering which distributes the trajectories to many small clusters, whereas the "Two-phase PTM" method performs a node-based clustering which produces larger clusters. The different searching strategies can explain the high performance of the proposed method, which achieves a speed up factor of 100 against the most completive method of "Two-phase PTM".

5 Conclusions

In this paper, we presented a scalable query processing by locations algorithm, by also taking into account the spatial importance of the query locations based on the users' preferences. In our experiments, we showed that the proposed method significantly outperformed competitive personalized trajectory similarity search methods, where the proposed method has approximately ten times less preprocessing requirements and reduces the query runtime by two orders of magnitude at least. An interesting research direction is to extend the proposed method to an approximate algorithm based on probabilistic bounds, in order to perform similarity search in spatial networks for uncertain trajectories [7].

References

1. Brinkhoff, T.: A framework for generating network-based moving objects. Geoinformatica 6(2), 153–180 (2002)
2. Chen, Z., Shen, H.T., Zhou, X., Zheng, Y., Xie, X.: Searching trajectories by locations: an efficiency study. In: Proceedings of the ACM SIGMOD International Conference on Management of Data, pp. 255–266 (2010)
3. Shang, S., Ding, R., Yuan, B., Xie, K., Zheng, K., Kalnis, P.: User oriented trajectory search for trip recommendation. In: Proceedings of the 15th International Conference on Extending Database Technology, pp. 156–167 (2012)
4. Shang, S., Ding, R., Zheng, K., Jensen, C.S., Kalnis, P., Zhou, X.: Personalized trajectory matching in spatial networks. VLDB J. 23(3), 449–468 (2014)
5. Tang, L.-A., Zheng, Y., Xie, X., Yuan, J., Yu, X., Han, J.: Retrieving k-nearest neighboring trajectories by a set of point locations. In: Pfoser, D., Tao, Y., Mouratidis, K., Nascimento, M.A., Mokbel, M., Shekhar, S., Huang, Y. (eds.) SSTD 2011. LNCS, vol. 6849, pp. 223–241. Springer, Heidelberg (2011)
6. Wang, H., Liu, K.: User Oriented Trajectory Similarity Search. In: Proceedings of the ACM SIGKDD International Workshop on Urban, Computing, pp. 103–110 (2012)
7. Zheng, K., Trajcevski, G., Zhou, X., Scheuermann, P.: Probabilistic range queries for uncertain trajectories on road networks. In: Proceedings of the 14th International Conference on Extending Database Technology, pp. 283–294 (2011)

Modeling Activities and Inference

Object π-Calculus and Document Workflows

Bartosz Zieliński[✉], Ścibor Sobieski, Piotr Kruszyński, Maciej Sysak,
and Paweł Maślanka

Department of Computer Science, Faculty of Physics and Applied Informatics,
University of Łódź, ul. Pomorska nr 149/153, 90-236 Łódź, Poland
bzielinski@uni.lodz.pl

Abstract. There are two basic approaches to business process modeling. One based on Petri nets, the other, newer, but with growing popu-
larity, based on process algebras such as π-calculus. We have created a
new variant of π-calculus which we call Object π-calculus. It has high
level object oriented features such as method calls, mixins and additional
process combinators. The calculus is of general interest, but it is particularly geared towards applications in business process modeling, especially
document workflow modeling. Accordingly, we provide a proof-of-concept
specification of a paper submission system in our dialect of π-calculus.

1 Introduction

There are two basic approaches to business process modeling. One based on
Petri nets (see e.g., [1]), the other based on process algebras such as CCS or
π-calculus (see e.g., [18–20, 25], for a critique of this approach see [2]). The algebraic approach was used successfully in many applications, such as modeling of
educational workflows [11], formalizing web service choreographies [7], analysis
of security protocols [23], and coordination between components in concurrent
systems [13]. More relevantly, process algebras can be used to specify workflows
[20], and CCS process algebra is the theoretical basis of S-BPM ONE [9].

One of the advantages of algebraic methods in business process modeling is
the natural potential for compositionality and reuse of components. In contrast,
diagrammatic languages, such as those based on Petri nets, while user friendly,
in their basic form do not scale well and poorly support reuse. This is not
true, though, when more advanced versions of Petri net based formalisms are
concerned, such as Recursive ECATNets [4] extending the algebraic term nets
(see e.g. [6]) with recursion [12] or YAWL [26]. Transitions in the algebraic term
nets can perform computations through rewriting on algebraic terms passed as
tokens. Both Recursive Petri nets and YAWL permit modeling dynamic structure
and structuring specifications through, respectively, spawning paralell threads
and composite tasks. Unfortunately, these additional features vastly increase
complexity of diagrammatic languages while they are (more) naturally supported
by algebraic formalisms. For instance, recursion, process spawning and dynamic
communication structure via exchange of communication links is built into the

© Springer International Publishing Switzerland 2015
L. Bellatreche and Y. Manolopoulos (Eds.): MEDI 2015, LNCS 9344, pp. 227–238, 2015.
DOI: 10.1007/978-3-319-23781-7_18

plain π-calculus. Complex types and term rewriting may be more natural in the context of process algebras. Moreover, the π-calculus itself is Turing complete and algebraic terms and computations can be emulated through π-processes.

The capabilities of π-calculus can be boosted by the introduction of high level features permitting advanced combination of components with less code. Such extensions do not necessarily increase the expressivity of calculus — for instance, sending multiple values through channels in polyadic π-calculus [14] can be easily emulated in pure π-calculus using auxilliary channels — but they increase the ease of use and reduce the amount of coding when writing a specification.

In this paper we introduce a new variant of π-calculus which we call Object-π calculus. Among its novel capabilities are high level object oriented features such as method calls, mixins and additional process combinators. The calculus is of general interest, but it is particularly geared towards applications in business process (especially document workflow) modeling. Accordingly, we provide a proof-of-concept specification of a paper submission system in Object-π calculus. In addition, we present a small collection of reusable components which may be useful for the specification of document workflow systems.

Note that intimate connections between π-calculus and object oriented programming (see e.g. [27,28]), as well as actor model (see e.g. [21]), are well known. However, previously π-calculus was used to define semantics of objects or actors, whereas here we extend π-calculus itself with object oriented features.

2   Preliminaries

A good introduction to process algebras and structured specifications can be found in [5,8]. Here we try to make the paper self-contained.

2.1   Labeled Transition Systems

Processes interacting with their environment can be modeled as LTS'es: A *labeled transition system* (LTS) $(S, \Lambda, \to)$ consists of a set of states S, a set of labels Λ and a relation $\to \subseteq S \times \Lambda \times S$. We write $x \xrightarrow{a} y$ iff $(x, a, y) \in \to$. Labels correspond to interactions with the environment or other processes. Elements of S represent internal states of the system. Alternatively, each $x \in S$ represents a proces understood as all possible future interactions of the system, assuming it started in the state x. Thus, it is customary to call the elements of S processes and to read a statement $x \xrightarrow{a} y$ as "process x after an a-interaction becomes process y". An LTS can be presented graphically as a labeled graph (cf. Fig. 1).

Example 1. The LTS presented in Fig. 1 specifies a flawed vending machine for hot beverages. Assume we start at p_1. The user inserts a 1\$ coin and then (the state is now p_2) either she can choose tea or coffee or the system can perform an internal transition (happening without any external interaction) back to the initial state p_1. Internal transitions are denoted by the label τ. The choice of coffee causes transition to p_4. Then picking the coffee returs the system to p_1. If the user chooses tea then the machine non-deterministically transitions either to p_3 (where the user can pick tea) or to p_5, where no further interaction is possible.

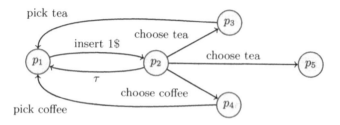

Fig. 1. An example of an LTS

The current state of the system is invisible to the user. Thus, there may be many different LTS'es interacting in the same way with the external world. This leads to various notions of behavioural equivalence (see e.g., [5]) between LTS'es.

2.2 π-Calculus

A process algebra most relevant for this paper is π-calculus [15] and its variants, especially polyadic π-calculus [14]. A good introduction to π-calculus can be found in [16]. Here we recall only basic facts about π-calculus and our (rather informal and brief) presentation is based largely on [16].

Names can occur both free and bound in terms. For a term t we denote by Free(t) and Bound(t) the sets of free and bound names in t, respectively. We denote by P, Q, R, etc., arbitrary processes, by $\mathcal{P}$, $\mathcal{Q}$, $\mathcal{R}$, etc. arbitrary logical expressions, by a, b, c, etc., arbitrary names, and by $v, v_1, \ldots, v_n$, etc. arbitrary values. The process terms in π-calculus have one of the following forms:

- **0** — an empty process which does nothing.
- $a!v.P$ — an output prefix. It sends (synchronously) value v through channel a and afterwards behaves as P. Channel names are allowed as values (in pure π-calculus nothing else is a value, we use elements of arbitrary types).
- $a?x.P$ — an input prefix. It receives some value v through channel a and afterwards behaves like $P[v/x]$, where $P[v/x]$ denotes P with all free occurrences of x replaced by v (with some additional renaming of bound names to avoid capture). Note that x in $a?x.P$ is not free but bound.
- $\tau.P$ — a silent prefix. After internal action τ it behaves as P.
- $P + Q$ — a sum of processes. It behaves as either P or Q.
- $P \mid Q$ — a parallel composition of processes.
- $[\mathcal{Q}]P$ — a guard. If a condition $\mathcal{Q}$ is satisfied then it behaves as P, otherwise it behaves as **0**.
- $\nu x.P$ — restriction. It behaves as P but x is guaranteed to be a fresh value. Note that ν binds x.
- $A(v_1, \ldots, v_n)$ — an identifier. It must have some definition of the form $A(x_1, \ldots, x_n) := P$. In this case $A(v_1, \ldots, v_n)$ evolves as $P[v_1/x_1, \ldots, v_n/x_n]$. Definitions can be recursive.

In polyadic π-calculus input and output prefixes can send and receive tuples of values (also empty ones), and channels can have signatures restricting the types of values sent through them (see the next section).

Syntactically different terms may denote the same process. Following [16] we use the structural congruence "$\equiv$" facilitating "obvious" identifications:

Definition 1. *The structural congruence is the smallest congruence $\equiv$ which:*

- *includes α-equivalence, i.e., $\nu x.P \equiv \nu y.P[y/x]$ and $a?x.P \equiv a?y.P[y/x]$,*
- *makes "—" and "+" associative and commutative with $\mathbf{0}$ as the common unit element, i.e., $P \mid Q \equiv Q \mid P$, $P + (Q + R) \equiv (P + Q) + R$, $P \mid \mathbf{0} \equiv P$, etc.,*
- *if $A(x_1, \ldots, x_n) := P$ then $A(v_1, \ldots, v_n) \equiv P[v_1/x_1, \ldots, v_n/x_n]$,*
- *satisfies the rules for scope extension:*

$$\nu x.\mathbf{0} \equiv \mathbf{0}, \quad \nu x.(\nu y.P) \equiv \nu y.(\nu x.P),$$
$$\nu x.([\mathcal{Q}]P) \equiv [\mathcal{Q}](\nu x.P) \text{ if } x \notin \text{Free}(\mathcal{Q}),$$
$$\nu x.(P + Q) \equiv P + \nu x.Q \text{ if } x \notin \text{Free}(P),$$
$$\nu x.(P \mid Q) \equiv P \mid \nu x.Q \text{ if } x \notin \text{Free}(P).$$

Process terms can be given a precise meaning using operational semantics which assignes a labeled transition system to a process algebra. More precisely, an LTS is defined using rules. Each rule has the form

$$\frac{t_1 \xrightarrow{\alpha_1} s_1 \quad t_2 \xrightarrow{\alpha_2} s_2 \quad \cdots \quad t_n \xrightarrow{\alpha_n} s_n}{t \xrightarrow{\beta} s},$$

where $t_1, \ldots, t_n$, $s_1, \ldots, s_n$, t and s are process terms, $\alpha_1, \ldots, \alpha_n$ and β are action terms. An LTS $\mathcal{L}$ satisfies the rule if for all ground substitutions σ of metavariables such that all $\sigma(t_i) \xrightarrow{\sigma(\alpha_i)} \sigma(s_i)$, $i \in \{1, \ldots, n\}$, are transitions in $\mathcal{L}$, also $\sigma(t) \xrightarrow{\sigma(\beta)} \sigma(s)$ is a transition in $\mathcal{L}$. One can prove that for a given set of rules there exists the unique smallest LTS in which all the rules are satisfied. Such an LTS is said to be defined by the set of rules. Some rule formats permit negative assumptions of the form "there is no α-transition from t". In the presence of negative assumptions an LTS defined by the rules might not exist or be non-unique (see e.g. [10]). Negative assumptions are not used in Object-π.

An operational semantics for π-calculus (with late name binding) is given in Fig. 2. There are four types of actions: an internal action τ, value send $a!v$, value receive $a?x$ and bound value send $a!\nu x$, the latter sends a fresh, private value through a. Note that this implies that, in the case of value receive $a?x$, the name x is, in a sense, bound to the received value "after" the transition takes place — hence late name binding mentioned above. This influences the notion of behavioural equivalence. Note also, that the rules complementary to Sum, Com and Par, e.g., $\mathsf{Sum}' \frac{Q_1 \xrightarrow{\alpha} Q_2}{P + Q_1 \xrightarrow{\alpha} Q_2}$ follow immediately from Cong and the fact that the commutes of sums and paralell compositions are congruent to the originals.

$$\text{Sum}\frac{P_1 \xrightarrow{\alpha} P_2}{P_1 + Q \xrightarrow{\alpha} P_2}, \quad \text{Par}\frac{P_1 \xrightarrow{\alpha} P_2}{P_1 \mid Q \xrightarrow{\alpha} P_2 \mid Q}, \quad \text{Prefix}\frac{}{\alpha.P \xrightarrow{\alpha} P},$$

$$\text{Pred}\frac{P_1 \xrightarrow{\alpha} P_2}{[Q]P_1 \xrightarrow{\alpha} P_2}\text{if } Q, \quad \text{Com}\frac{P_1 \xrightarrow{c?x} P_2 \quad Q_1 \xrightarrow{c!v} Q_2}{P_1 \mid Q_1 \xrightarrow{\tau} (P_2[v/x]) \mid Q_2},$$

$$\text{Res}\frac{P_1 \xrightarrow{\alpha} P_2}{\nu x.P_1 \xrightarrow{\alpha} \nu x.P_2}\text{if } \alpha \neq x!v, x?y, \quad \text{Open}\frac{P_1 \xrightarrow{a!x} P_2}{\nu x.P_1 \xrightarrow{a!\nu x} P_2}\text{if } a \neq x,$$

$$\text{Cong}\frac{P_1 \xrightarrow{\alpha} P_2}{Q_1 \xrightarrow{\alpha} Q_2}\text{if } P_1 \equiv Q_1 \text{ and } P_2 \equiv Q_2.$$

Fig. 2. Transition rules for π-calculus. Here α is an arbitrary transition.

3   Object Oriented π-Calculus

In this section we present Object-π — a novel variant and extension of π-calculus with an object oriented flavour. It is a variant, because we limit and change the ways in which communication channels are used. It is also an extension because we add new process combining operators to the algebra.

3.1   Channels and Objects

In Object-π we use exclusively two-part channel names in a way which resembles a call to an object's method. In our approach, the channel's name consists of an object (agent) reference and a method name, and of these two only references can be passed as values or restricted using the ν operator. An object reference gives the agent a unique identity throughout transitions and allows other processes to address this particular unique agent (cf. [21]). All method names have signatures which describe what tuples of values can be sent through the reference/method channel — we can send and receive multiple values like in polyadic calculus. All references belong to the single type Ref. As the behaviour of the agent changes with each transition, we do not introduce static types for references. However, methods may be scoped with respect to mixins: agents are dynamically composed of mixins, each of which defines standard behaviour parametrized by the reference of process in which the mixin occurs, and each method name must be unique within the mixin. Thus mixins may partially play the role of classes.

If r is a reference and m is a method name then $r\langle m \rangle$ is a channel name. Sending or receiving values on this channel is intended to be interpreted as executing action m on object referenced by r. To make this interpretation valid we must ensure that one of the participants in a communication facilitated through channel $r\langle m \rangle$ should always be the process (agent) associated with r. Method names allow to describe interactions of standarized component templates, while references serve to distinguish between different instances of those components. In order to ensure a conflictless usage of mixins we permit prefixing of a method name with a mixin name (they should be separated by a slash).

We write $v : T$ if the value v has type T. We assume that all the names are typed. Name binding operations type their arguments (see below). Each method m has a signature: we write $m : \langle T_1, T_2, \ldots, T_n \rangle$ if m has n arguments such that the i'th argument has type T_i, for $i \in \{1, \ldots, n\}$.

Suppose that r is a reference and m is a method name such that $m : \langle T_1, T_2, \ldots, T_n \rangle$. As $r\langle m \rangle$ is treated as a channel in polyadic π-calculus we have two possible kinds of transitions associated with $r\langle m \rangle$:

- $r\langle m \rangle!(v_1, \ldots, v_n)$ which sends values $v_1, \ldots, v_n$, such that v_i is of type T_i, $i \in \{1, \ldots, n\}$. We allow values to be references, but not whole channel names, i.e., we can send a reference r but not $r\langle m \rangle$. The transition can also have the form $r\langle m \rangle!(v_1, \ldots, v_{i-1}, \nu x, v_{i+1}, \ldots, v_n)$ which sends (among other values) a fresh value x (which may be a fresh reference or the result of unspecified internal computations).
- $r\langle m \rangle?(x_1, \ldots, x_n)$, which receives values then substituted for $x_1, \ldots, x_n$.

Accordingly, instead of prefixes presented in the preliminaries we have input and output prefixes of the form $r\langle m \rangle!(v_1, \ldots, v_n)$ and $r\langle m \rangle?(x_1, \ldots, x_n)$, respectively, and a congruence rule

$$r\langle m \rangle?(x_1, \ldots, x_n).P \equiv r\langle m \rangle?(y_1, \ldots, y_n).P[y_1/x_1, \ldots, y_n/x_n]. \tag{1}$$

We also require that now the restrictions are typed, e.g., $\nu x : T$. We impose some obvious typechecking requirements. If $m : \langle T_1, T_2, \ldots, T_n \rangle$ then in order for terms $r\langle m \rangle!(v_1, \ldots, v_n).P$ and $r\langle m \rangle?(x_1, \ldots, x_k).Q$ to be well-formed we must have $n = k$, $v_i : T_i$ for all $i \in \{1, \ldots, n\}$, and Q remains type-correct when, for all $i \in \{1, \ldots, n\}$, x_i is assigned type T_i.

The Com and Open transition rules (see Fig. 2) get replaced by

$$\text{Com}_O \frac{P_1 \xrightarrow{r\langle m \rangle?(x_1, \ldots, x_n)} P_2 \quad Q_1 \xrightarrow{r\langle m \rangle!(v_1, \ldots, v_n)} Q_2}{P_1 \mid Q_1 \xrightarrow{\tau} (P_2[v_1/x_1, \ldots, v_n/x_n]) \mid Q_2},$$

$$\text{Open} \frac{P_1 \xrightarrow{r\langle m \rangle!(v_1, \ldots, v_n)} P_2}{\nu x : T.P_1 \xrightarrow{r\langle m \rangle!(w_1, \ldots, w_n)} P_2} \text{if } r \neq x, \quad \text{where } w_i = \begin{cases} \nu v_i & \text{if } v_i = x \\ v_i & \text{if } v_i \neq x. \end{cases}$$

The restriction operator ν can hide references but not subsets of the methods associated with a given reference. For that we need a separate operator: Let M be a set of method names, let r be an object reference, and let P be any process. $\mathbf{Hide}_M^r(P)$ behaves like P except external interactions through channels $r\langle m \rangle$, $m \in M$ are disabled, i.e., its operational semantics is defined through the rule

$$\text{Hide} \frac{P_1 \xrightarrow{\alpha} P_2}{\mathbf{Hide}_M^r(P_1) \xrightarrow{\alpha} \mathbf{Hide}_M^r(P_2)} \text{if channel}(\alpha) \neq r\langle m \rangle, \; m \in M,$$

where for any transition label α we denote by channel(α) the channel used for communication, i.e., channel$(r\langle m \rangle!v) = r\langle m \rangle$, etc.

Because our calculus is typed we require that the definitions of identifiers should declare the types of parameter names, e.g., they should have the form

$$A(x_1 : T_1, \ldots, x_n : T_n) := P.$$

3.2   Mixins

Mixins allow us to compose behaviour of agents from smaller, more easily manageable parts. Mixins are basically just π-processes, but parametrized with respect to parent agent reference. The same mixin may be "mixed into" different agents. In the mixin's definition the special name self is used to reference the parent — it is bound to parent's reference after mixin's mix into the parent. The self name cannot be bound by input prefix or by restriction operator ν. To make the notation simpler, self can be omitted from input/output prefixes and transition labels in the mixin definition, so that we can write, e.g., $\langle m \rangle ! v$ instead of self$\langle m \rangle ! v$. To avoid the conflicts between method names in different named mixins we use two-part method names: All methods owned by the mixin R must have names of the form R/m, where m is the local part of the method name. We allow to use $/m$ instead of R/m in the definition of R mixin.

Named mixins are defined as identifiers, i.e., a mixin R with parameters $x_1 : T_1, \ldots, x_n : T_n$, is defined by expression of the form $R(x_1 : T_1, \ldots, x_n : T_n) := P$.

Mixins can be combined with one another using usual process combinators yielding (unnamed) mixins. A mixin is distinguished from the usual π-process by the presence of self references. In order for a mixin to become a regular process, a mixin needs to be associated with some object reference. Let P be a mixin and let r be an object reference. Then $r \triangleright P$ is a process which behaves like $P[r/\text{self}]$.

In what follows we will need an additional process/mixin combinator: a semi-parallel composition $Q \ll P$ of Q and P. It will be crucial for defining inheritance of mixins. The following transition rules provide it with operational semantics:

$$\text{Inherit} \frac{P_1 \stackrel{\alpha}{\longrightarrow} P_2}{Q \ll P_1 \stackrel{\alpha}{\longrightarrow} Q \ll P_2}, \quad \text{Own} \frac{Q_1 \stackrel{\alpha}{\longrightarrow} Q_2}{Q_1 \ll P \stackrel{\alpha}{\longrightarrow} Q_2}.$$

The semiparallel composition does not permit internal communication between components. We say that the process $Q \ll P$ inherits the behaviour from P and extends it with Q. We might also say that $Q \mid P$ inherits behaviour from both P and Q, however, in $Q \mid P$ both processes are independent, whereas in $Q \ll P$ process Q, in some sense, "governs" $Q \ll P$ — it can make $Q \ll P$ transition into something which is not a composition with P.

Note that, with the above interpretation, the multiple inheritance can be easily emulated using combination of "$\ll$" and "$\mid$" operators, e.g., we will say that the process $Q \ll P_1 \mid \cdots \mid P_n$ multiply inherits behaviour from processes $P_1, \ldots, P_n$ (note that we assigned to "$\mid$" a higher precedence than to "$\ll$").

This process combinator becomes very useful when combined with identifiers and recursion. Let P be a process/mixin. Then the term $A(x_1, \ldots, x_m) \ll P$ is called an identifier with inheritance. It should be given a definition (which may be recursive) of the form

$$A(x_1, \ldots, x_m) \ll P := Q, \tag{2}$$

where Q is some mixin term such that its free names contain the union of $\{x_1, \ldots, x_m\}$ and all the free names in P. Let $\{y_1, \ldots, y_n\}$ be the free names of P distinct from those in $\{x_1, \ldots, x_m\}$. Then the semantics of definition from Eq. (2) is given by the following congruence:

$$A(z_1 : T_1, \ldots, z_m : T_m) \ll (P[(z,r)/(x,y)])$$
$$\equiv (Q[(z,r)/(x,y)]) \ll (P[(z,r)/(x,y)]), \tag{3}$$

where $[(z,r)/(x,y)] := [z_1/x_1, \ldots, z_m/x_m, r_1/y_1, \ldots, r_n/y_n]$.

4   Algebra of Document Workflow

In this section we will demonstrate applications of Object-π in describing document workflows. First, we will introduce some reusable mixins which are useful for describing parts of such workflows, and then we present, as an example, an algebraic specification in Object-π calculus of (a fragment of) a paper submission subsystem of a typical conference management system.

4.1   Mixins for a Document Workflow

Document Content Mixin. Let $\mathbb{D}$ be the type of documents. A document contains both its content and all the metadata. For simplicity we will not consider any operations on document beyond checking of correctness through the predicate $\mathcal{C}$ defined elsewhere. We define the named mixin cont as follows (methods have signatures cont/get : $\langle \mathbb{D} \rangle$, cont/set : $\langle \mathbb{D} \rangle$, cont/isOk : $\langle \mathsf{Bool} \rangle$):

$$\mathrm{cont}(d : \mathbb{D}) := \langle /\mathrm{get} \rangle! d.\mathrm{cont}(d) + \langle /\mathrm{set} \rangle? x.\mathrm{cont}(x)$$
$$+ [\mathcal{C}(d)]\langle /\mathrm{isOK} \rangle! \mathsf{true}.\mathrm{cont}(d) + [\neg \mathcal{C}(d)]\langle /\mathrm{isOK} \rangle! \mathsf{false}.\mathrm{cont}(d).$$

Multiple Approval Mixin. Let FRef denote the type of finite sets of references. Frequently, in different document workflows, we encounter the situation where some document has to be approved by multiple people in any order. The named mixin appr assists in the task (here the method signatures are appr/appr$\langle \mathsf{Ref} \rangle$, appr/dis-appr$\langle \mathsf{Ref} \rangle$):

$$\mathrm{appr}(r : \mathsf{FRef}, p : \mathsf{FRef}, n : \mathsf{FRef})$$
$$:= \langle /\mathrm{appr} \rangle? x. ([x \in r]\mathrm{appr}(r \setminus \{x\}, p \cup \{x\}, n) + [x \notin r]\mathrm{appr}(r, p, n))$$
$$+ \langle /\mathrm{dis\text{-}appr} \rangle? x. ([x \in r]\mathrm{appr}(r \setminus \{x\}, p, n \cup \{x\}) + [x \notin r]\mathrm{appr}(r, p, n)).$$

The interpretation is that r is the set of references to approvers which are still required to approve the document, and p and n are sets of references to approvers which, respectively, approved and dissaproved the document.

Approver Mixin. Mixin rappr assists in describing the behaviour of the approving person equipped with a set sd of documents to approve:

$$\mathrm{rappr}(\mathrm{sd}:\mathsf{FRef}):=\sum_{d\in\mathrm{sd}}d\langle\mathrm{cont/get}\rangle?x.(\tau.d\langle\mathrm{appr/appr}\rangle!\mathrm{self}.\mathrm{rappr}(\mathrm{sd}\setminus\{d\})$$

$$+\,\tau.d\langle\mathrm{appr/dis\text{-}appr}\rangle!\mathrm{self}.\mathrm{rappr}(\mathrm{sd}\setminus\{d\})).$$

Note that this mixin does not own any methods, it uses methods from cont and appr mixins. It also assumes that both cont and appr are mixed into the same object. Note also the use of internal transition τ to describe (non-deterministic) decision of the approving person to approve or reject the document.

4.2   Example: Paper Submission System

We will describe a very simplified version of such a system. There are five kinds of agents: Author, Reviewer, Editor, System and Document. We assume that there is only one instance of Editor and of System and that these have publicly known references, say, $\mathfrak{E}$ and $\mathfrak{S}$. To simplify, we assume also that all the referees are registered with the system and are known to the editor. We will also omit some of the details, especially about the workings of Author and Editor.

The submission process starts with the author receiving, through the execution of system/init : $\langle\mathsf{Ref}\rangle$ on System, the reference i to the new document stub:

$$\mathrm{system}(s:\mathsf{FRef},\ldots):=\nu i:\mathsf{Ref}.\langle/\mathrm{init}\rangle!i.\big((i\triangleright\mathrm{init\text{-}doc})\mid\mathrm{system}(s\cup\{i\},\ldots)\big)$$

$$+\,\text{some other behaviour}\ldots$$

The system stores the references to submitted stubs in the s parameter and it also creates the initial document stub $i\triangleright\mathrm{init\text{-}doc}$. The init-doc mixin facilitates the initial submit of the paper through the method init-doc/submit : $\langle\mathsf{Ref},\mathbb{D}\rangle$:

$$\mathrm{init\text{-}doc}:=\langle/\mathrm{submit}\rangle?(a,d).(\mathrm{doc}(a)\lll\mathrm{cont}(d))+\text{other behaviour}\ldots$$

It is worthwhile to see how one models the behaviour of the Author during the initial part of paper submission:

$$\mathrm{author}(\ldots):=\tau.\mathfrak{S}\langle\mathrm{system/init}\rangle?x.\nu d:\mathbb{D}.x\langle\mathrm{init\text{-}doc/submit}\rangle(\mathrm{self},d).\mathrm{author'}(\ldots)$$

$$+\,\text{some other behaviour}\ldots$$

The document submitted by the author is a new one, but we do not specify the computational (or rather thought) process which led to its creation: instead, we simply use the ν operator to create the new value.

After the first submission of content d and the author's reference a for future contact, the init-doc mixin evolves into $\mathrm{doc}(a)\lll\mathrm{cont}(d)$. It is defined as

$$\mathrm{doc}(a)\lll\mathrm{cont}(d)$$

$$:=\ \langle/\mathrm{start\text{-}rev}\rangle?r.\Big(\mathrm{docr}(a)\lll\big(\mathbf{Hide}^{\mathrm{self}}_{\{\mathrm{cont/set}\}}(\mathrm{cont}(d))\mid\mathrm{appr}(r,\emptyset,\emptyset)\big)\Big)$$

$$+\,\text{some other behaviour like retracting, etc.}\ldots$$

In accordance with the definition of "$\ll$", the mixin $\mathrm{doc}(a) \ll \mathrm{cont}(d)$ behaves as $\mathrm{cont}(d)$ (i.e., it allows the author to replace the manuscript or its metadata and query the correctness of submission) until the editor starts the review process on the document using the method doc/start-rev : $\langle\mathsf{FRef}\rangle$, sending additionally the set of references to reviewers assigned to the paper. After that, it transitions into $\mathrm{docr}(a) \ll \left(\mathbf{Hide}^{\mathsf{self}}_{\{\mathrm{cont/set}\}}(\mathrm{cont}(d)) \mid \mathrm{appr}(r, \emptyset, \emptyset)\right)$. Because this mixin inherits from $\mathbf{Hide}^{\mathsf{self}}_{\{\mathrm{cont/set}\}}(\mathrm{cont}(d))$ it still allows for reading the contents d of the paper (e.g., by the author or some reviewer, as in the definition of approver mixin) but not for modifying it. Similarly, the inherited behaviour of the appr multiple approval mixin allows to gather the positive and negative reviews of the paper. The own behaviour of docr mixin is defined as follows:

$$\mathrm{docr}(a) \ll \left(\mathbf{Hide}^{\mathsf{self}}_{\{\mathrm{cont/set}\}}(\mathrm{cont}(d)) \mid \mathrm{appr}(r, p, n)\right)$$
$$:= \quad [r = \emptyset]\langle/\mathrm{finalize}\rangle!(d, p, n).\Big($$
$$\langle/\mathrm{accept}\rangle?.(\langle/\mathrm{accepted}\rangle! \mid \{\text{Further processing} \ldots\})$$
$$+ \langle/\mathrm{reject}\rangle?.(\langle/\mathrm{rejected}\rangle! \mid \{\mathfrak{S}\langle\mathrm{rejected}\rangle!(\mathsf{self})).\Big)$$

When all the reviewers finished their work ($r = \emptyset$) the process can accept call to the method docr/finalize : $\langle\mathbb{D}, \mathsf{FRef}, \mathsf{FRef}\rangle$ by the Editor, who receives, through this call, the paper's contents as well as the information about positive (p) and negative (n) reviews. Based on this information she can make the final decision about the paper's fate, which is then communicated through the asynchronous call to one of the methods docr/accepted, docr/rejected : $\langle\rangle$, intended to be received by the paper's author. In addition, the accepted paper is further processed, and the rejected one sends the appropriate information to the System (identified by the reference $\mathfrak{S}$), and finishes execution.

5   Conclusion

We have presented a new variant of typed polyadic π-calculus which we call Object-π calculus. Its features like methods, which in our opinion are an elegant way to assign types to channels, or mixins, which allow to build more reusable code, are of general interest, but they were geared towards specification of document workflows. We have also presented some reusable mixins useful in the specification of such workflows.

Our work so far is a proof of concept, but in a future work we intend to create a complete document workflow specification system based on Object-π calculus. We would also like to examine the properties of Object-π algebra, in particular the notions of bisimilarity for this process algebra.

Note that some of our extensions can be considered to be a notational variants of the usual typed polyadic π-calculus [17]. For instance, instead of defining a mixin identifier $R(\ldots)$ with a special self reference inside, and then instantiating it as in $r \triangleright R(\ldots)$ with the reference r, we could have defined instead a plain identifier $R(\mathsf{self}, \ldots)$, and then instantiate it as in $R(r, \ldots)$. On the other hand, doing so for combinations of identifiers (like in $R_1(r, \ldots) | R_2(r, \ldots)$ vs $r \triangleright (R_1(\ldots) | R_2(\ldots))$) is error prone and does not emphasize the role of r. We did not found, however, a simple way to implement methods and "$\ll$" operator in the usual polyadic π-calculus [14].

Finally, the ability to express and reason about timing constraints is crucial for some applications. There are many variants of both Petri net (see e.g. [3,22]) and process algebra (see e.g. [24]) based formalisms which permit modeling such constraints. In our future work we plan to extend Object-π calculus with timing constraints, perhaps along the lines of [24].

Acknowledgements. I would like to thank the anonymous reviewers for their suggestions.

References

1. Van der Aalst, W.M.: The application of Petri nets to workflow management. J. Circ. Syst. Comput. **8**(01), 21–66 (1998)
2. Van der Aalst, W.M.: Pi calculus versus Petri nets: Let us eat humble pie rather than further inflate the pi hype. BPTrends **3**(5), 1–11 (2005)
3. Barkaoui, K., Boucheneb, H., Hicheur, A.: Modelling and analysis of time-constrained flexible workflows with time recursive ECATNets. In: Bruni, R., Wolf, K. (eds.) WS-FM 2008. LNCS, vol. 5387, pp. 19–36. Springer, Heidelberg (2009)
4. Barkaoui, K., Hicheur, A.: Towards analysis of flexible and collaborative workflow using recursive ECATNets. In: ter Hofstede, A.H.M., Benatallah, B., Paik, H.-Y. (eds.) BPM Workshops 2007. LNCS, vol. 4928, pp. 232–244. Springer, Heidelberg (2008)
5. Bergstra, J.A., Ponse, A., Smolka, S.A.: Handbook of Process Algebra. Elsevier, Amsterdam (2001)
6. Bettaz, M., Maouche, M.: How to specify non determinism and true concurrency with algebraic term nets. In: Bidoit, M., Choppy, C. (eds.) Abstract Data Types 1991 and COMPASS 1991. LNCS, vol. 655, pp. 164–180. Springer, Heidelberg (1993)
7. Brogi, A., Canal, C., Pimentel, E., Vallecillo, A.: Formalizing web service choreographies. Electron. Notes Theor. Comput. Sci. **105**, 73–94 (2004)
8. De Nicola, R.: A gentle introduction to process algebras. Notes **7** (2014). https://goo.gl/ZkLOK1
9. Fleischmann, A.: What Is S-BPM? In: Buchwald, H., Fleischmann, A., Seese, D., Stary, C. (eds.) S-BPM ONE 2009. CCIS, vol. 85, pp. 85–106. Springer, Heidelberg (2010)
10. van Glabbeek, R.J.: The meaning of negative premises in transition system specifications II. In: Meyer auf der Heide, F., Monien, B. (eds.) ICALP 1996. LNCS, vol. 1099. Springer, Heidelberg (1996)
11. Goel, A., Choppella, V.: Algebraic modelling of educational workflows. In: 2012 IEEE Fourth International Conference on Technology for Education (T4E), pp. 153–156. IEEE (2012)

12. Haddad, S., Poitrenaud, D.: Modelling and analyzing systems with recursive Petri nets. In: Boel, R., Stremersch, G. (eds.) Discrete Event Systems, pp. 449–458. Springer, USA (2000)

13. Kleine, M.: CSP as a coordination language. In: De Meuter, W., Roman, G.-C. (eds.) COORDINATION 2011. LNCS, vol. 6721, pp. 65–79. Springer, Heidelberg (2011)

14. Milner, R.: The Polyadic π-Calculus: A Tutorial. Springer, Heidelberg (1993)

15. Milner, R.: Communicating and Mobile Systems: The Pi Calculus. Cambridge University Press, Cambridge (1999)

16. Parrow, J.: An introduction to the π-calculus. In: Bergstra, J.A., Ponse, A., Smolka, S.A. (eds.) Handbook of Process Algebra, pp. 479–543. Elsevier, Amsterdam (2001)

17. Pierce, B., Sangiorgi, D.: Typing and subtyping for mobile processes. In: Proceedings of Eighth Annual IEEE Symposium on Logic in Computer Science, 1993, LICS 1993, pp. 376–385. IEEE (1993)

18. Puhlmann, F.: Why do we actually need the pi-calculus for business process management? BIS **85**, 77–89 (2006)

19. Puhlmann, F., Weske, M.: Using the π-calculus for formalizing workflow patterns. In: van der Aalst, W.M.P., Benatallah, B., Casati, F., Curbera, F. (eds.) BPM 2005. LNCS, vol. 3649, pp. 153–168. Springer, Heidelberg (2005)

20. Puhlmann, F., Weske, M.: A look around the corner: the pi-calculus. In: Jensen, K., van der Aalst, W.M.P. (eds.) Transactions on Petri Nets and Other Models of Concurrency II. LNCS, vol. 5460, pp. 64–78. Springer, Heidelberg (2009)

21. Raja, N., Shyamasundar, R.: Actors as a coordinating model of computation. In: Bjorner, D., Broy, M., Pottosin, I.V. (eds.) PSI 1996. LNCS, vol. 1181, pp. 191–202. Springer, Heidelberg (1996)

22. Ramchandani, C.: Analysis of asynchronous concurrent systems by timed Petri nets (1974)

23. Ryan, M.D., Smyth, B.: Applied pi calculus (2011)

24. Saeedloei, N., Gupta, G.: An extension of π-calculus with real-time and its realization in logic programming. In: Symposium on Logic-Based Program Synthesis and Transformation (LOPSTR 2012), p. 153 (2012)

25. Smith, H., Fingar, P.: Workflow is just a pi process. BPTrends, pp. 1–36, November 2003

26. Van Der Aalst, W.M., Ter Hofstede, A.H.: Yawl: yet another workflow language. Inf. Syst. **30**(4), 245–275 (2005)

27. Walker, D.: π-calculus semantics of object-oriented programming languages. In: Theoretical Aspects of Computer Software. pp. 532–547. Springer (1991)

28. Walker, D.: Objects in the π-calculus. Inf. Comput. **116**(2), 253–271 (1995)

Automatic Generation of ETL Physical Systems from BPMN Conceptual Models

Orlando Belo[1](✉), Claudia Gomes[1], Bruno Oliveira[1],
Ricardo Marques[2], and Vasco Santos[1]

[1] ALGORITMI R&D Centre, Department of Informatics,
School of Engineering, University of Minho,
Campus de Gualtar, 4710-057 Braga, Portugal
obelo@di.uminho.pt
[2] WeDo Technologies, Centro Empresarial de Braga,
Ferreiros, 4705-319 Braga, Portugal

Abstract. ETL conceptual modeling is a very important activity in any data warehousing system project implementation. Owning a high-level system representation allowing for a clear identification of the main parts of a data warehousing system is clearly a great advantage, especially in early stages of design and development. However, the effort to model conceptually an ETL system rarely is properly rewarded. Translating ETL conceptual models directly into something that saves work and time on the concrete implementation of the system process it would be, in fact, a great help. In this paper we present and discuss a hybrid approach to this problem, combining the simplicity of interpretation and power of expression of BPMN on ETL systems conceptualization with the use of ETL patterns to produce automatically an ETL skeleton, a first prototype system, which has the ability to be executed in a commercial ETL tool like Kettle.

Keywords: Data warehousing systems · ETL conceptual modeling · BPMN specification models · Domain-Specific languages · ETL skeletons · Kettle

1 Introduction

In many software engineering areas we can find products that cover quite well the entire cycle of production of an ETL (*Extract-Transform-Load*) system [5, 17], where the generation of small physical systems (prototypes) it is possible from a well-defined conceptual or logical model. However, the difficulties to achieve that stage of development often begins with the ability of a conceptual model to represent effectively the tasks, workflows, or other entities that are involved with the representation of the system. After reviewing a wide range of modeling options, we choose *Business Process Modeling Notation* (BPMN) [18] as the election formalism to support ETL conceptual modeling. In large part, this was due to the influence of the work of Akkaoui and Zimànyi [1]. We believe that modeling an ETL conceptual model using BPMN is quite effective, since it simplifies the implementation of the entire ETL system as well as increases construction quality, reduces implementation errors, and consequently decreases the costs of the entire project. BPMN also provides the necessary bridges to translate conceptual models to more detailed ones using *Business Process Execution Language* (BPEL) or BPMN 2.0.

© Springer International Publishing Switzerland 2015
L. Bellatreche and Y. Manolopoulos (Eds.): MEDI 2015, LNCS 9344, pp. 239–247, 2015.
DOI: 10.1007/978-3-319-23781-7_19

Besides this, using the extension mechanism of BPMN 2.0 meta-model, it is also possible to represent specific concepts related to the planning and implementation of ETL processes, and extending them to pre-defined elements of BPMN notation [9].

Such feature, has led some authors to explore a new strand in the conceptual specification of ETL systems: the definition of ETL patterns [7]. This is not a new reference in the area [6]. Although, these authors based their proposal on the software engineering field, presenting this concept as a generalization of tasks that are frequently implemented in ETL systems – e.g. *change data capture* (CDC), *surrogate key pipelining* (SKP), or *slowly changing dimensions* (SCD) - formalized them as meta-models using a new extension of BPMN. This extension allowed hosting the definition of ETL patterns and their later incorporation into conceptual models. In fact, this approach dramatically reduced the number of elements in a conceptual model, making it simpler and more readable, as well as makes transparent implementation and specification details to final users. This also minimizes potential ambiguities and increases the efficiency of the implementation of an ETL system. Using techniques like these, we find that the development of an ETL system will be more agile and less demanding in terms of the detail used on task and control descriptions.

But, at this time we still have only a non-functional model, which is far from a physical implementation that could be used to show the viability and usefulness of the system in the application context for which it was developed. In fact, the distance between a conceptual model and a physical one is still big at this time. Having that, we cannot use the work we have done so far in the implementation of the model itself, at least directly. In this sense, and continuing following our objectives, we shortcut a little bit the conventional process of developing an ETL system. We started to do some semantic enrichment work of the BPMN models based on ETL standards, in order to export (translate) them to something that could be executed in some computational platform. To do this, we developed a *domain specific language* (DSL) for the specification of the behavior of ETL patterns. With this language it is possible to specify how each of these patterns will act, individually or collectively. The descriptions of the patterns produced with the language are then incorporated in the correspondent BPMN element that is present in the conceptual model. Then, we export the model and process it in accordance with the functional and operational requirements of a given commercial ETL tool.

In this paper we present and discuss the referred process. Thus, after a brief exposure of some related work (Sect. 2), we present and discuss briefly a demonstration scenario using some of the most ETL common patterns that we can find in a conventional ETL process specification using BPMN (Sect. 3). Next, we present and demonstrate how to generate and import an ETL skeleton in order to be used inside a conventional ETL systems development tool (Sect. 4). Finally, in Sect. 5, we present some brief conclusions and point out some lines of working for a near future.

2   Related Work

The most accepted proposals for *data warehousing systems* (DWS) modeling and development based their ETL components in some *ad-hoc* approaches with no formalization or standard notation. In consequence, several authors proposed specific modeling approaches based in a clear separation of the different stages of design: conceptual, logical and physical. In [15] Vassiliadis et al. presented a novel approach for the conceptual design of an ETL process, using meta-models in conjunction with diagrammatic symbols that once applied facilitate user interpretation of the sources involved in the process as well as the necessary attribute mappings and transformations. Trujillo and Luján-Mora [14] used an extension to the *Unified Modeling Language* (UML) to incorporate typical mechanisms associated with ETL processes. This new specification approach tried to minimize the learning gap required by the previous proposal of Vassiliadis et al. by using a standard well-known notation. In a logical perspective of an ETL system, any workflow that needs to populate appropriately a data warehouse should be modeled after a well-established and correct conceptual modeling phase. Only after all the sources and attribute transformations are identified we can elaborate the sequence of operations needed. With this in mind, in [11, 16] and reference [12] was proposed a new graphical notation to represent data flows and transformations in an ETL system. The development of this approach led to the study of optimization processes and algorithms that could be applied to ETL workflows [13]. More recently, Akkaoui and Zimànyi presented a mixed approach where BPMN was used to model conceptual/logical models of ETL systems [1]. In this work the authors propose also the use of the BPEL as the language to execute the models developed using BPMN. Although, BPMN is a standard notation. Its successful application in ETL system modeling is conditioned to the fact that ETL patterns should be developed for wide acceptance and use. Later, Akkaoui et al. [2, 3] provided a BPMN-based meta-model for an independent ETL modeling approach. They explored and discussed the bridges to a model-to-text translation, providing its execution in some ETL commercial tools. More recently, Oliveira and Belo [7, 8] proposed ETL patterns using BPMN has a step forward to the generalization of common ETL tasks in the conceptual modeling phase, demonstrating the utility of their modeling approach through the use of some well-known DWS process patterns.

3   Pattern-Based ETL Systems Conceptualization

Conceptual models provide a way to simplify ETL system development, offering a more clear perception of the entire process, which is very useful on preliminary development stages. We believe that coupling the BPMN richness representation with the use of specific patterns to build ETL packages will facilitate process design and implementation. Basically we are proposing a set of pre-configured components to simplify ETL representation and implementation. Since we are working with composite constructs, target users will design models based on a pallet of more abstract concepts that were previous created to implement repetitive and error-prone tasks. In real-world ETL scenarios, repetitive clusters of tasks are frequently used for different ETL development stages. We can categorize them in specific clusters that share the same purpose. Generally, we organized ETL patterns in three classes: gathers, transformers and loaders. Independently from their application, each pattern is composed by a set of input and output interfaces that are used to communicate with their internal architecture. Depending on the process requirements, a task can receive in-memory data sets or the correspondent connection parameters to use data already stored in some kind of repository. Similarly, the data output can be directed to an intermediate stored area, or can be used on the fly as an input of other subsequent ETL patterns. Based on a set of connection parameters, the gathers patterns are responsible for data extraction according to some specific policies, i.e. can be used for initial, incremental or differential data extraction. After data extraction, transformers patterns are used to convert extracted data accordingly the requirements of the target schema repository. Typically, several conforming and cleaning procedures are used to handle several schemas anomalies, such as inconsistent data about a same subject, incompatible data formats, duplicate records, currency conversions, generation of surrogate keys or aggregation tasks, just to name a few. When all data is processed (conformed and integrated), the loaders patterns should load records into the data warehouse respecting all the integrity constraints and history maintenance policies implemented.

Considering a set of ETL patterns pre identified, we propose a multi-layer approach to represent them using BPMN. The BPMN pools are used to represent several layers of abstraction. Each one of them is composed by several lanes, which have the ability to receive the activities that should be applied for each group of similar records (from the same subject). For each lane, we can represent the patterns and clusters of patterns that are used for data integration using BPMN sub-processes. Each sub-level represents the decomposition of a parent sub-process, which provides a way to get different views. The use of patterns allows for a clear separation between the coordination layer of the process and the data transformation layer. This component-based approach provides the necessary consistency to enable the translation of conceptual models to their correspondent physical representations – physical models. Patterns are designed with the possibility to make them executable in existing ETL engines.

In order to demonstrate the feasibility of our approach, let us consider the data mart conceptual structure presented in Fig. 1 using the DFM notation [4]. This schema represents a simplified view over a fictional mobile company, storing data related to some phone calls established between different customers in a specific date and location. The dimensions "Customer", "Source Call Location", "Date" and "Time" are used to represent, respectively, the customer data (the caller and called customer), the location where the caller started the call, and the date and time when the call happened. A degenerate dimension - "Type" - was also used to identify the type of the call (national or international). To represent the caller and the called customer, a shared hierarchy was defined in the dimension "Customer". The fact table "Calls" integrates two additive measures "Duration" (in minutes) and "Cost" (in Euro), characterizing each call made by a customer – the decision-support grain.

Using only ETL patterns we designed and built a BPMN specification model representing the populating process referred before, which basically transports the data gathered on a CSV file to a repository where the data mart is located (Fig. 2). All activities presented on the BPMN model were configured with a multi-instance parallel marker, which means that each activity can be performed several times with different data sets in parallel. The number of instances can be configured at the process level or at the activity level. The # character was use in the activities to mark ETL patterns, in order to distinguish them from conventional BPMN sub-processes.

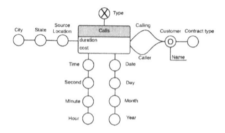

Fig. 1. A star-schema for phone calls detailed records

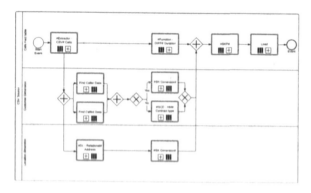

Fig. 2. The BPMN model for the populating process using patterns

The populating process starts extracting data using a gather pattern configured to gather data from the referred CSV file. Next, output data are separate to fulfill the needs of each lane responsible for populating each table dimension. At the "Customer" layer, two composite tasks were integrated to find the name and the contract type of the caller and of the called customer. The "Find caller data" and the "Find Called data sub processes" encapsulate two data lookup patterns, which use the identification of the customer, perform data lookups in specific dictionary tables to find the customer's name, and contract type values. These tasks are managed by two parallel gateways that separate the initials flows promoting their execution in parallel mode. After their execution, both flows are synchronized. Next, an exclusive gateway is used to identify new or existing records. In the case of a new record, a new surrogate key will be generated and the correspondent-mapping table updated. For the existing records, a SCD pattern, with history maintenance, is used to preserve the history of the customer's contract type.

The "Location" dimension is composed by a data lookup pattern to guarantee the referential integrity of the address associated with the caller initial location, using the mobile cell id is used to identify the address. We also used a surrogate key generator pattern to generate new surrogate keys for the new records. Finally, to populate the fact table we used a function pattern to calculate the difference in seconds between the start and end call date. The measure "Cost" is updated using a simple correspondence procedure that is presented in the "Load" sub process. When all the transformation tasks were done, a SKP pattern is triggered to populate the fact table with all the surrogate keys already defined. The dimensions "Date" and "Time" were not included in the description of this process because we considered that they are populate periodically by special-oriented processes. Due to space limitations, the logic of the BPMN process "Load" was hidden. However, this composite task is responsible to populate the several dimensions of the data mart as well as the fact table "Calls", guaranteeing all relational integrity constraints previously established in the star-schema.

Based on the description of all ETL patterns, as well on their basic characteristics and instantiation details, we developed a DSL. With this language each pattern can be configured and extended using a specific syntax especially oriented to describe ETL tasks. The formalization of the internal behavior of a pattern provides a way to instantiate abstract constructors using (semi) automatic methods to enable its posterior execution in an ETL commercial tool, with a minimal configuration effort. A small excerpt of a configuration of a gather is presented in Fig. 3. This still is the first complete definition of the DSL and was used in the early stages of research and development of new ETL patterns conceptual models using BPMN 2.0. The DSL was the way we find to describe more formally and precisely the behavior of any ETL pattern, and thus reinforcing ETL conceptual models with behavioral information (a kind of information quite hard to represent in BPMN), which provides the basis to establish the necessary bridges for achieving a corresponding physical model in an automatic way.

```
use Gather on sources{
BEGIN data=C:/Users/ASUS/Desktop/CDR_example_done.csv,type=CSV input END
}
and target{
BEGIN name=teste, server=localhost, database=test, table=cdr{
  fields{id, type, caller_id, called_id, caller_number, called_number, time_start, time_end}
}, technology=MySQL, access=Native, user=root, password=Saphira23, type=relational
END
}
options{parallel operation=source, number of threads=10, number of rows in batch=10}
```

Fig. 3. A small excerpt of the configuration of a gather pattern

4   Automatic Generation of ETL Physical Systems

The transformation process of a conceptual model relies on a converter (a program written in JAVA) to take the BPMN models, parse them and construct the final product, which will be imported later to an ETL development tool such as Kettle [10]. After some research work done analyzing the export formats of some BPMN tools (and on what would be more easily integrated in an ETL tool) it was decided that the export and import format for conceptual models would be XML. Consequently, the first step in the conversion of the model is to export it to XML, including all patterns' behavior specifications. Then, the conversion process starts by parsing all BPMN files exported extracting all the relevant information from them. To make the parsing of the files, we needed to study the structure of the XML exported by the BPMN tool. Looking closely, some key entities (XML tags representing BPMN components) were identified for the conversion process and for the future physical system, namely: (1) activity, which is a BPMN component that represents a normal task in a BPMN model; it contains a name, a unique identifier and a description, with the former holding the information about the semantic behavior of the pattern (in the case of the general BPMN model); and (2) transition, which is a BPMN component that represents a connection between two tasks in the BPMN model; it contains a unique identifier and two fields: *from* and *to*, whose values are, respectively, the identifiers of the source and destiny tasks of a connection. The result of the parsing process integrates two structures: (1) a map, whose key is the identification of the activity, and a value that is a class embodying all the details about the XML node activity; and (2) a graph, which contains information about all the existing connections in the BPMN model, whose vertex are a JAVA class as well. Lastly, if the BPMN component to be parsed has a child node "Description" of the XML node "Activity", with specific details about the behavior of a pattern, it is created a class "TaskBehavior" with all the elements that were parsed and recognized.

Having all the necessary information extracted in the previous stage, it is necessary to build the XML file that will be imported by the ETL tool. This process is divided in two phases: (1) verification of all the patterns present in the BPMN conceptual model and converting each of the identified patterns into a single XML; and (2) afterwards, the general XML Kettle schema that will be imported is generated; this schema has an almost direct correspondence to the BPMN conceptual design. In the first phase, it was created a class to represent a something close to a Kettle component named "Transformation". Also, a class "Transition" was created to represent, as faithfully as possible, the connections that exist between two or more components in Kettle. Since there are so many different patterns having its own behavior, it is necessary to create a class for each different pattern, implementing its own version of two distinct methods: (1) *buildTransformations()*, which creates a list of "Transformation" based on the BPMN tasks parsed in the previous stage; and (2) *buildTransitions()*, which builds a list of Transition based on the connections parsed from the BPMN XML specification.

In the first phase of the identification of the patterns is the class "Creator". This class looks up the name of a task (or a pattern) and, if it contains a set of predefined keywords, then it will make a call to the correct class that represents that pattern. For example, suppose that the class "Creator" is currently analyzing a task named "CDC Calls". Hence, this class will make a call to the class "ChangeDataCapture" in order to build the connections and components in Kettle for this pattern in particular. In a second phase, the creator is also responsible for building the set of transformations and transitions represented in the BPMN model, which will be converted then into XML to be imported later by Kettle. Lastly, the generation of the XML tags is accomplished through a class "XMLConstructor". For each transformation created by the specific pattern classes and also by the class "Creator" is read by this class and builds its XML accordingly. For example, if the transformation being read at the moment is of type "Table Input", then it will build the XML of the "Table Input" component from Kettle. Moreover, this class will also complete the generation of each XML component with the details about the semantic behavior of the pattern – the details contained in the "TaskBehavior" class – so that the final XML schema will be the most accurate and complete as possible. At this point the conversion process is over. It only remains to import the XML file that was generated to the Kettle's environment. The XML file it will be easy to identify since it has the same name has the BPMN model diagram. Next, the user should verify that Kettle recognize and treat appropriately the file imported and that all components have the specifications that match the formal description of the patterns in the BPMN model – in Figs. 4 and 5. we can see two ETL packages that were generated by the tool for the treatment of calls records and to support the execution of a lookup pattern, respectively.

Fig. 4. The package for calls records treatment

Fig. 5. The lookup pattern implementation

5 Conclusions and Future Work

Using BPMN and a set of ETL patterns (and their respective behavior description), we designed and implemented a specific ETL development process that enhances the importance of building an ETL conceptual model. This contribution is reflected not only in the design phase, discussion or study of the many aspects of the ETL system, but also later in the implementation phase, since it is possible to use a lot of the material applied in the conceptual specification as a catalyst for a possible physical imple-mentation. We use the term ETL skeletons to designate the ETL systems we generated from a conceptual model specification in BPMN. At this stage, they still are a primary approach of the translation process that in a near future we want to improve. Therefore, at short-term we intend to investigate how we can enrich the current conceptual models, in order to allow the generation of more effective physical models that will be beyond a simple ETL package skeleton.

Acknowledgment. This work was developed under the project RAID B2K - RAID Enterprise Platform/NUP: FCOMP-01-0202-FEDER-038584, a project financed by the Incentive System for Research and Technological Development from the Thematic Operational Program Com-petitiveness Factors.

References

1. El Akkaoui, Z., Zimanyi, E.: Defining ETL worfklows using BPMN and BPEL. In: DOLAP 2009 Proceedings of the ACM Twelfth International Workshop on Data warehousing and OLAP, pp. 41–48 (2009)

2. El Akkaoui, Z., Zimànyi, E., Mazón, J.-N., Trujillo, J.: A model-driven framework for ETL process development. In: Proceedings of the ACM 14th International Workshop on Data Warehousing and OLAP, DOLAP 2011, pp. 45–52 (2011)
3. El Akkaoui, Z., Zimányi, E., Mazón, J.-N., Trujillo, J.: A BPMN-based design and maintenance framework for ETL processes. Int. J. Data Warehouse. Min. 9, 46–72 (2013)
4. Golfarelli, M.: The DFM: a conceptual model for data warehouse. In: Wang, J. (ed.) Encyclopedia of Data Warehousing and Mining, 2nd edn, pp. 638–645. IGI Global, Hershey (2008)
5. Kimball, R., Caserta, J.: The Data Warehouse ETL Toolkit: Practical Techniques for Extracting, Cleaning, Conforming, and Delivering Data. Wiley, New York (2004)
6. Köppen, V., Brüggemann, B., Berendt, B.: Designing data integration: the ETL pattern approach. Eur. J. Inform. Prof. **XII**(3), 49–55 (2011)
7. Oliveira, B., Belo, O.: BPMN patterns for ETL conceptual modelling and validation. In: Proceedings of the 20th International Symposium on Methodologies for Intelligent Systems (ISMIS 2012), Macau, 4–7 December 2012
8. Oliveira, B., Belo, O.: ETL standard processes modelling - a novel BPMN approach. In: Proceedings of 5th International Conference on Enterprise Information Systems (ICEIS 2013), Angers, France, 4–7 July 2013
9. OMG: Documents Associated With Business Process Model and Notation (BPMN) Version 2.0 (2011)
10. Pentaho: Pentaho data integration. http://www.pentaho.com/product/data-integration. Accessed 16 March 2015
11. Simitsis, A.: Mapping conceptual to logical models for ETL processes. In: Proceedings of the 8th ACM international workshop on Data warehousing and OLAP, Bremen, Germany, pp. 67–76 (2005)
12. Simitsis, A., Vassiliadis, P., Sellis, T.: Logical optimization of ETL workflows. In: Proceedings of the 4th Hellenic Data Management Symposium, Athens, Greece, pp. 55–65 (2005)
13. Simitsis, A., Vassiliadis, P., Sellis, T.: State-space optimization of ETL workflows. IEEE Trans. Knowl. Data Eng. 17, 1404–1419 (2005)
14. Trujillo, J., Luján-Mora, S.: A UML based approach for modeling ETL processes in data warehouses. In: Song, I.-Y., Liddle, S.W., Ling, T.-W., Scheuermann, P. (eds.) ER 2003. LNCS, vol. 2813, pp. 307–320. Springer, Heidelberg (2003)
15. Vassiliadis, P., Simitsis, A., Skiadopoulos, S.: Modeling ETL activities as graphs. In: Proceedings of the 4th International Workshop on Design and Management of Data Warehouses 2002, DMDW'2002, Toronto, Canada, pp. 52–61 (2002)
16. Vassiliadis, P., Simitsis, A., Skiadopoulos, S.: On the logical modeling of ETL processes. In: Pidduck, A.B., Mylopoulos, J., Woo, C.C., Ozsu, M.T. (eds.) CAiSE 2002. LNCS, vol. 2348, pp. 782–786. Springer, Heidelberg (2002)
17. Vassiliadis, P.: A survey of extract–transform–load technology. Int. J. Data Warehouse. Min. 5(3), 1–27 (2009)
18. Wohed, P., van der Aalst, W.M.P., Dumas, M., ter Hofstede, A.H.M., Russell, N.: On the suitability of BPMN for business process modelling. In: Dustdar, S., Fiadeiro, J.L., Sheth, A. P. (eds.) BPM 2006. LNCS, vol. 4102, pp. 161–176. Springer, Heidelberg (2006)

Bayesian Model Selection for Diagnostics

Gregory Provan$^{(\boxtimes)}$

Computer Science Department, University College Cork, Cork, Ireland
g.provan@cs.ucc.ie

Abstract. Model-Based Diagnosis (MBD) addresses the task of isolating the most likely fault given a set of system measurements. The model used for diagnostics is critical to this isolation task, yet little work exists for specifying which type of model is best suited to MBD. We apply Bayesian model selection to identify the model that optimizes a diagnostics task, according to key fault-isolation metrics. We illustrate our approach using a tank benchmark system, demonstrating the trade-offs possible by using different models for this benchmark.

Keywords: Bayesian model selection · Diagnostics

1 Introduction

Model-Based Diagnostics (MBD) addresses on the task of accurately isolating faults within a range of real-world systems. There has been significant progress in developing algorithms for systems of increasing complexity. However, there has not been comparable progress in scaling-up to real-world models, as multiple-fault diagnostics algorithms are currently limited by the size and complexity of the models to which they can be applied. In addition, there is still a great need for defining metrics to measure diagnostics accuracy, and to measure the computational complexity of inference and of the models' contribution to inference complexity.

Model fidelity is a crucial issue in diagnostics [15]: models that are too simple can be inaccurate, yet highly detailed and complex models are expensive to create, have many parameters that require significant amounts of data to estimate, and are computationally intensive to perform inference on.

We are interested in analyzing how model properties (such as model accuracy and complexity) influence MBD performance, as measured by metrics such as MBD inference accuracy and computational complexity. For example, does increasing model complexity, measured by properties such as type of equations (e.g., linear vs. non-linear dynamics) always lead to higher MBD inference accuracy? Work in machine learning [6] on a bias/variance trade-off indicates that highly complex models may be less accurate than simpler ones. We aim to study the relation of model properties and MBD properties.

Bayesian model selection (BMS) [9] is a statistical approach for selecting a model ϕ from a collection Φ of potential models, such that the chosen model optimizes a metric μ. There has been an increasing use of BMS approaches within the

© Springer International Publishing Switzerland 2015
L. Bellatreche and Y. Manolopoulos (Eds.): MEDI 2015, LNCS 9344, pp. 248–256, 2015.
DOI: 10.1007/978-3-319-23781-7_20

physical sciences to evaluate the adequacy of models for simulation (e.g., [8,16]). We adopt and extend the BMS framework for analyzing MBD models. Several differences between simulation and MBD exist, so it is not possible to apply BMS approaches directly to MBD. MBD differs from simulation in the following key ways. First, MBD addresses a more complex task than simulation, in that it estimates the most likely system state given data, rather than simulating the trajectory of a system given initial conditions; roughly speaking, MBD requires model inversion, whereas simulation requires just forward inference. Second, an MBD model ϕ is more complex than simulation models, as ϕ describes not just the single behaviour of a simulation model, but multiple additional behaviours, one for each possible failure behaviour. Third, the computational complexity of state estimation is significantly higher than that of simulation, with the MBD model playing an even more central role than a simulation model in posing limitations to inference capability. Fourth, whereas the metrics for simulation accuracy are well understood (e.g., an error measure between simulation and real data), metrics for MBD performance are more complex and are much less well understood.

To date, there has been no prior work in using Bayesian model selection (BMS) approaches for evaluating MBD models. This article provides the first BMS evaluation framework for MBD. We extend the simulation-focused BMS framework to a more complex MBD-focused framework. Our contributions are as follows:

1. We formulate the MBD task as estimating the most likely system state given data.
2. We specify an MBD model, and its inherent source of inference complexity.
3. We describe MBD performance metrics, and how they extend the classical BMD framework.
4. We demonstrate our extended framework on a dynamical systems benchmark.

2   Modeling and Inference for Simulation and Diagnostics

This section formalises the notion of tasks and models within the process of simulation and of diagnostics inference.

2.1   Simulation Task

Assume that we have a system S defined in terms of variables denoting state, $\tilde{X}$, measurement $\tilde{Y}$, and control inputs, U. We assume that a *behaviour* of S describes the state of S over time. This behaviour is described by $\mathcal{E}$, a set of equations.

We further assume that we have a discrete vector of measurements, $\tilde{Y} = \{\tilde{y}_1, ..., \tilde{y}_n\}$ observed at times $t = \{1, ..., n\}$ that summarizes the response of the system S to control variables $U = \{u_1, ..., u_n\}$. Let $Y_\phi = \{y_1, ..., y_n\}$ denote the corresponding predictions from a dynamic (e.g., non-linear) model, ϕ, with parameter values θ: this can be represented by $\boldsymbol{Y}_\phi = \phi(x_0, \theta, \xi, \tilde{\boldsymbol{U}})$, where x_0 signifies the initial state of the system at t_0.

The *simulation task* is to generate a prediction $\boldsymbol{Y}_\phi$ that minimises s residual vector, $\mathcal{R}(\tilde{\boldsymbol{Y}}, \boldsymbol{Y}_\phi)$, which is an error measure between the predictions and measurements. An example of a residual vector is the mean-squared-error (MSE).

2.2 Diagnosis Task

Diagnosis involves a system $\mathcal{S}_\mathcal{D}$ that can describe multiple possible behaviours: one behaviour corresponds to a nominal mode of operation of $\mathcal{S}$, ξ_N, and other behaviours correspond to a faulty mode, ξ_F, where $\varXi$ is the set of possible modes of $\mathcal{S}$. A diagnosis model thus has a set $\mathcal{E}$ of equations, such that there is a subset $E_\xi \subseteq \mathcal{E}$ for each mode $\xi \in \varXi$.

We have, as before, measurements $\tilde{\boldsymbol{Y}}$ and predictions $\boldsymbol{Y}_\phi$. We assume that we have a prior probability distribution $P(\varXi)$ over the modes $\varXi$ of the system. This distribution denotes the likelihood of the failure modes of the system.

We assume a fixed diagnosis task $\mathcal{T}$ throughout this article, e.g., computing the most likely diagnosis, or a deterministic multiple-fault diagnosis.

The classical definition of diagnosis is as a state estimation task, whose objective is to identify the system mode corresponding to the state that minimises the residual vector, $\xi^* = \mathrm{argmin}_{\xi \in \varXi} \mathcal{R}(\tilde{\boldsymbol{Y}}, \boldsymbol{Y}_\phi)$ Since this is a minimisation task, we typically need to run multiple simulations over the space of parameters and modes to compute ξ^*. We can abstract this process as performing model-inversion, i.e., computing some $\xi^* = \phi^{-1}(x_0, \theta, \xi, \tilde{\boldsymbol{U}})$ that minimises $\mathcal{R}(\tilde{\boldsymbol{Y}}, \boldsymbol{Y}_\phi)$.

During this diagnostics inference task, a model ϕ can play two roles: (a) simulating a behaviour to estimate $\mathcal{R}(\tilde{\boldsymbol{Y}}, \boldsymbol{Y}_\phi)$; (b) enabling the computation of $\xi^* = \phi^{-1}(x_0, \theta, \xi, \tilde{\boldsymbol{U}})$. It is clear that diagnostics inference requires a model that has good fidelity and is also computationally efficient for performing these two roles.

We generalise that notion to incorporate inference efficiency as well as accuracy. We can define an inference complexity measure as $\mathcal{C}(\tilde{\boldsymbol{Y}}, \phi)$. We can then define our diagnosis task as jointly minimising a function g that incorporates the accuracy (based on the residual function) and the inference complexity:

$$\xi^* = \underset{\xi \in \varXi}{\mathrm{argmin}}\ g\left(\mathcal{R}(\tilde{\boldsymbol{Y}}, \boldsymbol{Y}_\phi), \mathcal{C}(\tilde{\boldsymbol{Y}}, \phi)\right). \tag{1}$$

Here g specifies a loss or penalty function that induces a non-negative real-valued penalty based on the lack of accuracy and computational cost.

In forward simulation, a model ϕ, with parameters θ, can generate multiple observations $\tilde{\boldsymbol{Y}} = \{\tilde{y}_1, ..., \tilde{y}_n\}$. The diagnostics task involves performing the inverse operation on these observations. Our objective thus involves optimising the state estimation task over a future set of observations, $\tilde{\boldsymbol{Y}} = \{\tilde{\boldsymbol{Y}}_1, ..., \tilde{\boldsymbol{Y}}_n\}$. Our model ϕ and inference algorithm $\mathcal{A}$ have different performance based on $\tilde{\boldsymbol{Y}}_i, i = 1, ..., n$: for example, [5] shows that both inference-accuracy and -time vary based on the fault cardinality. As a consequence, to compute ξ^* we want to optimise the *mean* performance over future observations. This notion of *mean* performance optimisation has been characterised using the Bayesian model selection approach, which we examine in the following section.

3   Running Example: Three-Tank Benchmark

In this paper, we use the three-tank system shown in Fig. 1 to illustrate our approach. The three tanks are denoted as T_1, T_2, and T_3. Each tank has the same area $A_1 = A_2 = A_3$. For $i = 1, 2, 3$, tank T_i has height h_i, a pressure sensor p_i, and a valve V_i, $i = 1, 2, 3$ that controls the flow of liquid out of T_i. We assume that gravity $g = 10$ and the liquid has density $\rho = 1$.

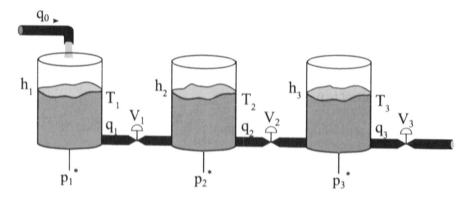

Fig. 1. Diagram of the three-tank system.

Tank T_1 gets filled from a pipe, with measured flow q_0. Using Torricelli's law, the model can be described by the following non-linear equations:

$$\frac{dh_1}{dt} = \frac{1}{A_1}\left[-\kappa_1\sqrt{h_1 - h_2} + q_0\right], \tag{2}$$

$$\frac{dh_2}{dt} = \frac{1}{A_2}\left[\kappa_1\sqrt{h_1 - h_2} - \kappa_2\sqrt{h_2 - h_3}\right], \tag{3}$$

$$\frac{dh_3}{dt} = \frac{1}{A_3}\left[\kappa_2\sqrt{h_2 - h_3} - \kappa_3\sqrt{h_3}\right]. \tag{4}$$

In Eq. 2, the coefficient κ_1 denotes a parameter that captures the product of the cross-sectional area of the tank A_1, the area of the drainage hole, a gravity-based constant ($\sqrt{2g}$), and the friction/contraction factor of the hole. κ_2 and κ_3 can be defined analogously.

Finally, the pressure at the bottom of each tank is obtained from the height: $p_i = g\,h_i$, where i is the tank index ($i \in \{1, 2, 3\}$).

We use the parameters κ_i, $i = 1, 2, 3$ to "diagnose" our system in term of changes in κ_i, $i = 1, 2, 3$. Consider a physical valve R_1 between T_1 and T_2

that constraints the flow between the two tanks. We can say that the valve changes proportionally the cross-sectional drainage area of q_1 and hence κ_1. The diagnostic task will be to compute the true value of κ_1, given p_1, and from κ_1 we can compute the actual position of the valve R_1.

Note that this model has a total of 6 parameters, i.e., $\boldsymbol{\theta} = \{\{A_1, A_2, A_3\}, \{\kappa_1, \kappa_2, \kappa_3\}\}$.

Fault Model. In this article we focus on valve faults, where a valve can have a blockage or a leak. We model this class of faults by including in Eqs. 2 to 4 an additive parameter β, which is applied to the parameter κ, i.e., as $\kappa_i(1+\beta_i)$, $i = 1, 2, 3$, where $-1 \leq \beta_i \leq \frac{1}{\kappa_i} - 1$, $i = 1, 2, 3$. $\beta > 0$ corresponds to a leak, such that $\beta \in (0, 1/\kappa - 1]$; $\beta < 0$ corresponds to a blockage, such that $\beta \in [-1, 0)$. The fault equations allow faults for any combination of the valves $\{V_1, V_2, V_3\}$, resulting in system modes $\varXi = \{\xi_N, \xi_1, \xi_2, \xi_3, \xi_{12}, \xi_{13}, \xi_{23}, \xi_{123}\}$, where ξ_N is the nominal mode, and ξ. is the mode where · denotes the combination of valves (taken from a combination of $\{1, 2, 3\}$) which are faulty. This fault model has 9 parameters.

4   Model Selection Process

This section first summarizes the BMS approach, and then outlines the MBD metrics that we adopt.

4.1   Bayesian Model Complexity

Bayesian model complexity measures whether the increased "complexity" of a model with more parameters is justified by the data. The Bayesian approach chooses a model ϕ from a set $\varPhi$ of competing models such that the value of a Bayesian criterion is maximized (or prediction uncertainty in choosing a model structure is minimized).

Statistical model selection trades off bias (distance between the average estimate and truth) and variance (spread of the estimates around the truth). The idea is that by adding parameters to a model we obtain improvement in fit, but at the expense of making parameter estimates "worse"' because we have less data (i.e., information) per parameter. In addition, the computations typically require more time. So the key question is how to identify how complex a model works best for a given problem.

Several metrics for evaluating model "quality" have been proposed. These include the Deviance Information Criterion (DIC), Akaike Information Criterion (AIC) and Bayesian Information Criterion (BIC).

DIC [14] measures the number of model parameters that the data can constrain: $DIC = \overline{D} + p_D$, where $\overline{D}$ is a measure of fit (expected deviance), and p_D is a complexity measure, the *effective* number of parameters. AIC [1,2] balances the accuracy, $\mathcal{L}$, with a penalty $(2k)$ for the number of parameters: $AIC = \mathcal{L}(\hat{\boldsymbol{\theta}}) + 2k$, where $\hat{\boldsymbol{\theta}}$ is the Maximum Likelihood Estimate (MLE) of $\boldsymbol{\theta}$ and k is the number of parameters. BIC [12] is similar to AIC, but uses a log-based parameter penalty $k log n$: $BIC = -2\mathcal{L}(\hat{\theta}) + k log n$, where k is the number of *estimable* parameters, and n is the sample size (number of observations).

4.2 Diagnostics Model Metrics

As mentioned earlier, we need to extend BMS to incorporate metrics that better estimate diagnostics performance properties. In other words, we replace the accuracy metric (e.g., $\mathcal{L}$ in AIC) with a diagnostics metric. This section describes the metrics that can be applied to estimate properties of a diagnosis model. We describe two types of metrics, dealing with accuracy (fidelity) and complexity.

Model Accuracy. Simulation accuracy concerns the ability of a model to mimic a real system, i.e., to use a model to simulate behaviours that distinguish nominal and faulty behaviours sufficiently well that appropriate fault isolation algorithms can identify the correct type of fault when it occurs. As such, a diagnostics model needs to be able to simulate behaviours for multiple modes with "appropriate" fidelity. In contrast, diagnosis inference accuracy concerns being able to isolate the true fault given an observation and the simulation output of a model.

Model Complexity. At present, there is no commonly-accepted definition of model complexity, whether the model is used purely for simulation, diagnostics or control. Several complexity definitions have been proposed, based on issues like (a) number of variables [8], (b) model structure [11], (c) number of free parameters [10], (d) number of parameters that the data can constrain [14], (e) a notion of model weight [4], or (f) *type* and *order* of equations for a nonlinear dynamical model [3], where type corresponds to non-linear, linear, etc.; e.g., order for a non-linear model is such that a k-th order system has k-th derivates in $\mathcal{E}$. In this article, we specify model complexity in terms of number k of parameters. In future work we plan to examine a wider range of specifications.

5 Experimental Analysis

This section compares three tank benchmark models according to various model-selection measures. We adopt as our "correct" model the non-linear model. We will examine the fidelity and complexity trade-offs of two simpler models over a selection of failure scenarios.

The diagnostic task computes the most-likely failure mode assignment for valve faults, where a valve can be OK, blocked or leaking. In particular, we estimate the true value of κ_1 given p_1.

5.1 Alternative Models

This section describes the two alternative models that we compare to the non-linear model, a linear and a qualitative model.

Linear Model. We compare the non-linear model with a linearised version. We can perform this linearised process in a variety of ways [13].

We linearise the non-linear 3-tank model by replacing the non-linear sub-function $\sqrt{h_i - h_j}$ with the linear sub-function $\eta_{ij}(h_i - h_j)$, where η_{ij} is a parameter (to be estimated) governing the flow between tanks i and j. The linear model has 4 parameters, η_{12}, η_{12}, η_{23}, η_3. The fault model has 7 parameters, adding to the parameters of the linear model an additive fault parameter β_i associated with each κ_i, $i = 1, 2, 3$.

Qualitative Model. We replace the non-linear sub-function $\sqrt{h_i - h_j}$ with a qualitative sub-function $M^+(h_i - h_j)$, where M^+ is the set of reasonable functions f such that $f' > 0$ on the interior of its domain [7].

5.2 Empirical Comparison

This section summarizes our experiments. We have compared the performance of the three models on 10 scenarios, 5 nominal and 5 fault scenarios. The nominal scenarios differ by the starting state x_0.

We used the non-linear model to generate data for the comparison, and used this data for the linear and qualitative models to diagnose faults. We used the AIC and BIC metrics to compare the non-linear model against the linear and qualitative models using pairwise comparisons. The AIC and BIC metrics comprise two aspects: one aspect for model accuracy, and a second aspect for penalizing model parameters. We extend the accuracy aspect (which typically measures simulation accuracy) by using a weighted sum of two diagnostics metrics, as described below.

Diagnostics "Accuracy" Metrics. We use a weighted sum of the following two metrics, denoted γ_1 and γ_2.

γ_1: To compute a measure of diagnostics error (or loss), we use the difference between the true fault (which is known for each simulation) and the computed fault. We denote the true fault existing at time t using the pair (ω, t); the computed fault at time t is denoted using the pair $(\hat{\omega}, \hat{t})$. Hence, we define a measure of diagnostics error over a time window $[0, T]$ using

$$\gamma_1^D = \sum_{t=0}^{T} \sum_{\xi \in \Xi} |P(\hat{\omega}) - \omega|, \tag{5}$$

where $P(\hat{\omega})$ is the probability computed for diagnosis ω and Ξ is the set of failure modes for the model.

γ_2: Our second metric covers the fault latency, i.e., how quickly the model identifies the true fault (ω, t):

$$\gamma_2 = t - \hat{t}. \tag{6}$$

Table 1 summarises our results. The AIC and BIC values are such that the lower the value, the better is the model. The data show that, as model fidelity decreases, the error γ_1 increases significantly and the inference times γ_2 decrease modestly. From the results, we see that AIC metric identifies the non-linear model as best, while the BIC metric indicates the qualitative model as the best. The metric-dependence of the results is significant: BIC typically will choose the simplest model, which AIC will choose the most accurate. Further work is needed to examine this metric-dependence of the results, and to better align the metrics to particular diagnostics applications.

Table 1. Data for 3-tank model, using Non-linear, Mixed, Linear and Qualitative representations, given a fault (valve V_1 at 50 %) after 25 s

	γ_1	γ_2	AIC	BIC
Non-Linear	0.97	23.7	29.45	43.7
Linear	77.43	10.57	35.76	37.55
Qualitative	304.41	9.74	43.01	29.13

6 Conclusions

This article has presented a BMS framework for evaluating the competing properties of diagnostics models. We have extended the classical BMS approach to incorporate MBD metrics; we focused on two MBD metrics, namely diagnostics accuracy (γ_1) and computational complexity (γ_2).

Using the proposed Bayesian metrics for MBD model evaluation, we conducted some preliminary experiments to illustrate how these metrics may be applied. Our data indicate that the model selected as "best" is highly metric-dependent. This work thus constitutes a *start* to a full analysis of model performance. We plan to extend this work by performing a more formal analysis of modeling and model evaluation, since there is no framework in existence for this task. Further, the experiments are only preliminary, and are meant to demonstrate how a framework can be applied to model comparison and evaluation.

Significant work remains to be done, on a range of fronts. In particular, a thorough empirical investigation is needs on diagnostics modeling. Second, the real-world utility of our proposed framework needs to be determined.

Acknowledgement. This work was supported by SFI grant 12/RC/2289.

References

1. Akaike, H.: A new look at the statistical model identification. IEEE Trans. Autom. Control **19**(6), 716–723 (1974)
2. Akaike, H.: Likelihood of a model and information criteria. J. Econometrics **16**(1), 3–14 (1981)
3. Antoulas, A.C., Sorensen, D.C., Gugercin, S.: A survey of model reduction methods for large-scale systems. Contemp. Math. **280**, 193–220 (2001)

4. Du, J.: The "weight" of models and complexity. Complexity (2014)
5. Feldman, A., Provan, G.M., van Gemund, A.J.: Computing observation vectors for max-fault min-cardinality diagnoses. In: AAAI, pp. 919–924 (2008)
6. Hastie, T., Tibshirani, R., Friedman, J.: The elements of statistical learning (2009)
7. Kuipers, B., Åström, K.: The composition and validation of heterogeneous control laws. Automatica 30(2), 233–249 (1994)
8. Kunz, M., Trotta, R., Parkinson, D.R.: Measuring the effective complexity of cosmological models. Phys. Rev. D 74(2), 023503 (2006)
9. Laud, P.W.: Bayesian model selection. In: Handbook of Survival Analysis, p. 285 (2013)
10. Pande, S., Arkesteijn, L., Savenije, H., Bastidas, L.: Hydrological model parameter dimensionality is a weak measure of prediction uncertainty. Nat. Hazards Earth Syst. Sci. Discusions 11, 2014 (2014)
11. Provan, G.M., Wang, J.: Automated benchmark model generators for model-based diagnostic inference. In: IJCAI, pp. 513–518 (2007)
12. Schwarz, G.: Estimating the dimension of a model. Ann. Statist. 6, 461–466 (1978)
13. Spanos, P.D.: Linearization techniques for non-linear dynamical systems. Ph.D. thesis, California Institute of Technology (1977)
14. Spiegelhalter, D.J., Best, N.G., Carlin, B.P., Van Der Linde, A.: Bayesian measures of model complexity and fit. J. Roy. Stat. Soc.: Ser. B (Statistical Methodology) 64(4), 583–639 (2002)
15. Struss, P.: What's in sd? towards a theory of modeling for diagnosis. In: Harmscher, W., Console, L., de Kleer, J. (eds.) Readings in Model-Based Diagnosis, pp. 419–449. Morgan-Kaufmann Publishers, San Mateo (1992)
16. Vrugt, J.A., Sadegh, M.: Toward diagnostic model calibration and evaluation: Approximate bayesian computation. Water Resour. Res. 49(7), 4335–4345 (2013)

Prediction and Recommendation

Predicting Student Performance in Distance Higher Education Using Semi-supervised Techniques

Georgios Kostopoulos[(⊠)], Sotiris Kotsiantis, and Panagiotis Pintelas

Educational Software Development Laboratory (ESDLab),
Department of Mathematics, University of Patras, Patras, Greece
kostg@sch.gr, {sotos,pintelas}@math.upatras.gr

Abstract. Students' performance prediction in distance higher education has been widely researched over the past decades. Machine learning techniques and especially supervised learning have been used in numerous studies to identify in time students that are possible to fail in final exams. The identification of in case failure as soon as possible, could lead the academic staff to develop learning strategies aiming to improve students' overall performance. In this paper, we investigate the effectiveness of semi-supervised techniques in predicting students' performance in distance higher education. Several experiments take place in our research comparing to the accuracy measures of familiar semi-supervised algorithms. As far as, we are aware various researches deal with students' performance prediction in distance learning by using machine learning techniques and especially supervised methods, but none of them investigate the effectiveness of semi-supervised algorithms. Our results confirm the advantage of semi-supervised methods and especially the satisfactory performance of Tri-Training algorithm.

Keywords: Distance higher education · Performance prediction · Semi-supervised learning · Tri-training · C4.5 decision tree

1 Introduction

Nowadays, online and distance learning offer innovative educational curricula of a similar quality as conventional universities do. Students have the potential to attend flexible courses in accordance with their personal needs studying at their place and at any time in a digital and interactive environment. Unfortunately, many students attending distance courses have often family obligations and job commitments which make difficult to complete their studies successfully.

So, it is important for tutors to identify low performance students in good time during the academic season. The early identification of possible low performers could lead the academic staff to develop learning strategies (seminars, extra learning material, exercises, training tests, recurrence of basic concepts, mentoring programs, etc.) aiming to improve students' performance and increase retention rates [9, 19].

In this paper we examine the effectiveness of semi-supervised methods in predicting students' success and academic performance in distance higher education.

L. Bellatreche and Y. Manolopoulos (Eds.): MEDI 2015, LNCS 9344, pp. 259–270, 2015.
DOI: 10.1007/978-3-319-23781-7_21

In more detail, we measure the accuracy of semi-supervised learning (SSL) techniques in students' performance prediction. Our experiments show that the Tri-Training algorithm [25] is the best performer of all SSL algorithms that are included in KEEL (an open source software environment for data mining). Furthermore, in all steps of the experiments, Tri-Training prevails when compared to a widely known supervised learning algorithm, such as C4.5 Decision Tree [14].

Section 2 presents a survey of machine learning techniques that have been used for predicting students' success and performance in higher education over the past few years pointing the lack of studies of semi-supervised methods. In Sect. 3 there is a shortly report of the SSL algorithms that are used in our study, while Sect. 4 provides a description of the data set and the principle study questions. In Sect. 5 we present the experiments that take place and the accuracy measure results of the SSL algorithms that are used in comparison to a well known supervised algorithm. The paper concludes by considering the challenges and novelties related to the usage of semi-supervised methods in educational data mining.

2 Review of Data Mining Applications for Performance Prediction

Students' performance prediction is estimated as one the most commonly and, at the same time, very difficult studied problem in educational data mining. The difficulty lies in the numerous factors affecting students' academic performance such as demographic, family, social, and many other [17]. Various researches deal with students' performance prediction in distance learning by using machine learning techniques. These researches examine the effectiveness of several supervised techniques such as classification and regression for predicting students' performance. Moreover, they study the impact of the attributes influencing students' academic progress.

Kotsiantis et al. [8] study the accuracy of six common machine learning algorithms for predicting students' performance in a distance higher education course of the Hellenic Open University. These algorithms are Naive Bayes (NB), C4.5 Decision Tree, Back Propagation (BP), Sequential Minimal Optimization (SMO), 3-NN classification algorithm and Logistic Regression. Their study shows that NB algorithm is the most accurate for predicting students' performance. It scores 62.95 % accuracy using only the demographic data and reaches 82.14 % before the final exams as new attributes are added on gradually [8].

Kovacic [9] explores the impact of social, demographic and academic variables in the performance of students in the "Information Systems" course at the Open Polytechnic of New Zealand. He uses three classification tree models, namely CHAID, exhaustive CHAID and CART in order to identify the variables that influence students' performance and calculate the probability of success for a new student. Ethnicity, course program and course block are the most influential factors that impact students outcome in his research. In addition, CART tree is giving better results than the others recording an overall accuracy measure of 60.5 % [9].

Mashiloane and Mchunu [10] study the performance of three well known classification algorithms, namely J48 Decision Tree, Naïve Bayes and Decision Table, for predicting first year students' failure in the School of Computer Science at the University of Witwatersrand. Student data from recent years were used for the training phase identifying J48 classifier algorithm as the best performer. In the testing phase, 92 % of the instances were predicted correctly, indicating that decision trees can be a powerful tool in predicting very precisely first year students' performance from the middle of the academic year [10].

Kabakchieva [7] investigates the effectiveness of several classification algorithms to classify the students of three universities into five output classes, taking into account of the pre-university characteristics. These classifiers are C4.5 Decision Tree, Naive Bayes and BayesNet, OneR and JRip rule learners and a Nearest Neighbor algorithm (IBk) from WEKA Explorer. The results show that C4.5 is the best classifier, while the Bayes classifiers are less accurate than the others. Additionally, she concludes that the prediction rates of all algorithms are not very significant [7].

Romero et al. [17] examine the use of several data mining techniques for predicting students' final performance from participation in on-line discussion forums. Taking into account of their active involvement and daily usage in a Moodle forum they try to predict whether a student is going to pass or fail the course in the final exams. Instead of traditional classification algorithms, they propose a classification via clustering method to improve the prediction of first-year students' performance. In accordance with this method, clustering algorithms generate two clusters for predicting the two outcome classes (pass or fail). The algorithms that are used are EM (Expectation Maximization), Hierarchical Cluster, sIB (sequential Information Bottleneck), SimpleKMeans, Xmeans and FarthestFirst and are provided by Weka. The results show that EM is the best performer, while at the same time attributes related to the subjects of the course give better results than the whole data set [17].

Huang and Fang [6] investigate the effectiveness of four mathematical models in predicting student academic performance in an engineering dynamics course. These models are multiple linear regression, multilayer perception network, radial basis function network and support vector machine. Experiments based on 323 undergraduate students reveal that there is no outstanding difference in prediction accuracy measure of the four models, with a rate between 89.6 and 90.1 % [6].

It is clear that several machine learning techniques (classification, regression, decision trees, clustering, etc.) have been used for predicting students' performance and progress in distance higher education. As far as, we are aware none of them investigate the effectiveness of semi-supervised methods in students' academic performance. Since SSL is at the core of machine learning recently, we explore if the usage of SSL algorithms could be useful for predicting students' performance in distance higher education.

3   Semi-supervised Techniques

Machine learning has already been the focus of attention in the field of computer science and information technology. Data analysis is more essential now than ever due to the increasing amounts of data which we are being overwhelmed with on a daily basis. There are mainly three basic and commonly used types of machine learning: supervised, unsupervised and semi-supervised learning.

In supervised learning the training data set consists only of labeled data. During the learning process, a function f is trained with the goal to predict the labels on future unseen data. Classification or pattern recognition and regression are the two primarily supervised problems depending on the nature of the function f, particularly classification for discrete function and regression for continuous [12].

Unsupervised learning tries to find interesting and regular patterns on unlabeled data without human intervention. The training set consists of unlabeled data and there is no teacher to provide help to recognize these patterns. Clustering, novelty detection and dimensionality reduction are some common supervised methods [23].

Today, there is a multitude of large amounts of data, especially data stored in universities databases and are often related to students academic progress. Unfortunately, extracting and labeling educational data is difficult as it requires a lot of time, many experts and it is too expensive. SSL exploits that lack of labeled data by using unlabeled data. It is a mixture of supervised and unsupervised learning processes which seeks to achieve better results with fewer labeled examples [23]. In SSL the training data set consists of both labeled and unlabeled data. So, students' data of the previous years may be used from tutors as the training set, while a new group of students could be used as the testing set for the prediction of their performance.

Co-Training [2], Self-Training [21], Democratic Co-Training [24], Tri-Training [25], Tri-Training with Editing [4], RASCO [20] and Rel-RASCO [22] are very familiar semi-supervised techniques that have been used effectively in many scientific fields with stunning results.

Co-Training algorithm works under the condition that each instance of the data set can be described using two distinct and sufficient for learning views. Two learning algorithms are trained, one per view, and the highest confident predictions of each algorithm are used to augment the training sample of the other in an iterative process until all unlabeled instances are labeled [2]. The classification accuracy of Co-Training depends on the existence of two views of each example and the cooperation of the two learning algorithms during the Co-Training procedure.

Self-Training is an iterative procedure of self-labeling unlabeled data. According to Cardie and Ng (2003) "*self-training is a single-view weakly supervised algorithm*" [3]. Labeled data set is augmented gradually using a classifier trained on its own most confident predictions. The classifier can be a k-Nearest Neighbor (kNN) algorithm, a C4.5 decision tree algorithm, a Naive Bayes (NB) algorithm or a very complicated one. The procedure is being repeated for several times until all the examples are labeled [11]. Self-Training is a very simple method that does not require partitioning the features of instances into two distinct subsets. However, mistakes on the early stages of labeling may generate inaccurately labeled data [23].

Democratic Co-Training algorithm uses different learning algorithms to train a set of classifiers. These classifiers predict the labels on unlabeled data. Unlabeled data are added gradually to the training set of the classifiers that are not in compliance with the predicted labels and the process is repeated until all are labeled [24].

Tri-Training algorithm is an extension of Co-Training algorithm that uses three classifiers to label unlabeled examples. Each classifier labels an unlabeled example under the agreement of the other two and the process is repeated until all examples are finally being labeled. Its simplicity and efficiency is notable since it does not require two distinct subsets of views as the Co-Training algorithm. Experiments show that Tri-Training outperforms Self-Training and Co-Training [25].

De-Tri-Training is a combination of Tri-Training algorithm and Nearest Neighbor Rule based data editing technique. The algorithm is seeking to improve Tri-Training by eliminating incorrect classifications and detecting noisy data. Using data editing techniques to identify and reduce incorrectly labeled data Tri-Training with Editing intends to improve the quality of Tri-Training labeling procedure [4].

RASCO (Random Subspace for Co-training) algorithm is an extension of the Co-Training algorithm to multiple views (subspaces) of the feature space. Different classifiers are trained in random subspaces by using co-learning, under the assumption that they are usually sensitive to different features. In this way, the classifiers complement each other finding different patterns in the data set [20]. For example, there are 35 4-dimension subspaces of a 7-dimension feature space, which means that 35 classifiers are trained leading to better results than Co-Training.

Rel-RASCO algorithm is a mixture of RASCO and semi-supervised ensemble learning. Random subspaces are being selected so as the features in each subspace are closely being related as possible. This is done by using feature probabilities proportional to relevance scores. In comparison with RASCO, it seems to achieve the same accuracy with fewer classifiers [22].

4   Study Questions and Data Description

The main question of this study is the possibility to predict students' performance in distance higher education with a satisfactory accuracy using semi-supervised techniques. The outcome attribute "Final" is whether the student is going to pass or fail the course in the final exams. Our mainly study sub-questions are three.

1. Which SSL algorithm produces more accurate predictions?
2. How SSL algorithms perform in comparison to familiar supervised techniques?
3. How early can we predict students' performance during the academic season?

For the purpose of our study, we used a data set of 344 students attending the twelve course module "Computer Science" of the Hellenic Open University (HOU). Each module, such as "Introduction to Informatics" requires the submission of four written assignments, four optional face to face sessions and the final examination. Students may participate in the final examination if they have successfully completed their written assignments and their success requires a grade greater than or equal to five (on a scale of one to ten) in the final examination. Each instance in the data set is characterized by the values of 16 attributes (Table 1).

The first seven attributes are related with student's demographic data and general information such as gender, age, domestic, children, working time, computer knowledge and occupation, and are also being referred as time-invariant attributes. It should be noted that they form the core of several studies in student retention and performance prediction in universities and distance higher learning. Moreover, many studies have shown that such attributes have a material impact in students' success in distance higher education [13]. The next eight time-variant attributes refer to the students'

Table 1. Description of the attributes

Attribute	Type	Values	Description
Gender	Nominal (binary)	Male, female	Student's gender
Age	Integer	[24, 32]	Student's age
Domestic	Nominal (binary)	Single, married	Student's domestic
Children	Integer	[0, 4]	Number of children
Work	Integer	[0, 3]	Working time
ComputKnowledge	Nominal (binary)	Yes, no	Computer knowledge
ComputerJob	Integer	[0, 2]	Job relation to computers usage
OCSi, i = 1, 2, 3, 4	Integer	[0, 1]	Absence/presence in the i-th optional contact session
TESTi, i = 1, 2, 3, 4	Real	[−1, 10]	Grade of the i-th written assignment
Final	Nominal (binary)	Pass, fail	Final estimation

performance on the four written assignments (TEST1, TEST2, TEST3, TEST4) and their presence or absence in the four optional contact sessions with academic staff (OCS1, OCS2, OCS3, OCS4). These attributes are being added gradually during the academic year and are the influential attributes in students' performance prediction as explained in detail in the next session. Grades in written assignments range from −1 to 10 (−1 corresponds to no submission of the written assignment). Presence or absence in contact sessions corresponds to values 1 and 0 respectively.

5 Experiments Sequence and Results

For the purpose of our study the data set has been partitioned into ten subsets of equal size, using the 10-fold cross validation procedure provided by KEEL. After splitting the data set, each one of the training sets is divided randomly into two parts of 10 % labeled data and 90 % of unlabeled data. Our experiments were conducted in two distinct parts of five consecutive steps each one.

The scope of our study is to evaluate the performance of SSL algorithms that are being included in KEEL, namely Self-Training, Democratic, De-Tri-Training, Tri-Training, Co-Training, RASCO and Rel-RASCO in comparison to a well known supervised algorithm, such as C4.5 Decision Tree. So, we measure the accuracy of the above algorithms in each step of the experiments. Accuracy is the percentage of correctly predicted instances and is being defined as follows:

$$ACCURACY = \frac{TP + TN}{n} 100\%$$

- *TP*: a student that pass classified as pass,
- *TN*: a student that fail classified as fail
- *n*: number of instances (students).

The 1st step includes all time-invariant attributes related to student's demographic data and the output attribute. In the 2nd step, attributes OCS1 and TEST1 are being added to the previous attributes. The 3rd step includes the attributes of the previous step and the attributes OCS2 and TEST2 of the second optional contact session and written assignment. In the 4th step the attributes OCS3, TEST3 are being added and the last 5th step includes all the attributes of the data set.

The accuracy performance of the SSL algorithms in the first part of the experiments is detailed in Table 2 for all the steps of our experiments. As Table 2 shows, Co-Training (NN), Rel-RASCO (NN), Rel-RASCO (NB), Co-Training (C4.5) and Tri-Training (NN) algorithms appear to be superior in the first step based only on demographic data with an accuracy measure around 58 %. In the final step the Democratic algorithm accuracy exceeds 81 %, while Rel-RASCO (NB) algorithm

Table 2. The accuracy (%) of SSL algorithms

	1st step	2nd step	3rd step	4th step	5th step	Overall
Self-Training (C4.5)	55.52	60.80	69.76	79.39	76.18	68.33
Self-Training (NN)	57.24	58.70	63.36	69.46	71.55	64.06
Self-Training (NB)	47.69	51.76	66.60	75.60	77.67	63.86
Self-Training (SMO)	53.81	58.43	69.17	73.82	78.24	66.69
De-Tri-Training (C4.5)	54.06	58.72	66.04	73.59	77.65	66.01
De-Tri-Training (NN)	56.06	54.92	68.03	75.07	77.96	66.40
De-Tri-Training (NB)	57.26	59.35	73.55	73.87	77.40	68.28
De-Tri-Training (SMO)	57.23	57.51	69.50	73.89	79.97	67.62
Tri-Training (C4.5)	57.24	61.66	70.34	77.06	79.68	69.19
Tri-Training (NN)	57.53	56.63	66.57	70.89	72.41	64.08
Tri-Training (NB)	53.76	59.05	73.27	78.55	72.41	67.41
Tri-Training (SMO)	56.95	56.10	68.05	72.11	75.62	65.77
Co-Training (C4.5)	57.55	57.61	69.46	73.55	79.09	67.45
Co-Training (NN)	58.11	59.89	68.03	72.98	73.27	66.46
Co-Training (NB)	54.35	53.50	72.10	77.66	79.70	67.46
Co-Training (SMO)	52.29	58.14	66.52	73.82	74.43	65.04
Rel-RASCO (C4.5)	57.27	58.41	70.03	71.54	73.84	66.22
Rel-RASCO (NN)	57.86	57.00	60.79	66.33	65.99	61.59
Rel-RASCO (NB)	57.57	55.55	75.60	74.50	80.61	68.77
Rel-RASCO (SMO)	55.21	62.25	63.69	69.22	66.89	63.45
RASCO (C4.5)	56.98	56.67	67.16	70.07	68.68	63.91
RASCO (NN)	56.98	59.00	63.10	64.60	63.70	61.48
RASCO (NB)	52.00	59.31	69.82	78.26	79.42	67.76
RASCO (SMO)	54.73	58.14	65.95	70.62	74.20	64.73
Democratic	57.27	55.48	69.48	77.66	81.18	68.21

reaches 80.61 %. Moreover, there is a marked increase of accuracy measure for all algorithms in the 3rd step by adding OCS2 and TEST2 attributes.

The best overall average performance in our 5-step experiments for the particular data set is obtained by Tri-Training algorithm with a C4.5 Decision Tree base classifier (69.19 %), as also confirmed by the Friedman test results [5] that are being presented in Table 3.

Table 3. Average ranking of SSL algorithms (Friedman)

Tri-Training (C4.5)	5.5
Rel-RASCO (NB)	7.2
De-Tri-Training (NB)	7.6
Self-Training (C4.5)	8.2
Democratic	8.8
RASCO (NB)	9.2
De-Tri-Training (SMO)	9.8
Co-Training (C4.5)	10.4
Co-Training (NN)	10.7
Tri-Training (NB)	10.7
Co-Training (NB)	11.1
Rel-RASCO (C4.5)	11.9
Self-Training (SMO)	12.9
De-Tri-Training (NN)	13.7
De-Tri-Training (C4.5)	14.8
Tri-Training (SMO)	15.6
Tri-Training (NN)	16.1
Co-Training (SMO)	16.6
Self-Training (NB)	16.8
Self-Training (NN)	17.1
Rel-RASCO (SMO)	17.0
RASCO (SMO)	17.7
RASCO (C4.5)	17.9
Rel-RASCO (NN)	18.4
RASCO (NN)	18.9

So, we chose Tri-Training algorithm to compare with a supervised algorithm that is being included also in KEEL, in particular the C4.5 Decision Tree algorithm. Classification trees are a common and simple way to figurate the instances structure of a data set and consist of nodes and edges. Each node corresponds to an attribute and each branch is being labeled with its relevant values [15]. The root of the tree is a node that has no incoming edges, while nodes with no outgoing edges are called leafs. Instances are classified into a predefined set of classes in accordance to the values of their attributes from the root of the tree down to a leaf. A widely used algorithm that produces a decision tree is C4.5 algorithm introduced by Quinlan [14, 16]. The attribute that best splits data set into subsets is the root of the tree and a quantitative measure of such an attribute is "information gain" [18]. Then, the splitting procedure is being repeated in the same way until the data set is finally separated into subsets of the same class [1].

During the second part of our experiments we compare the accuracy and specificity measures of the algorithms. Specificity is the percentage of student that failed and classified correctly and is being defined as follows:

$$\text{SPECIFICITY} = \frac{TN}{TN + FP} 100\%$$

- *TN*: a student that fail classified as fail
- *FP*: a student that fail classified as pass
- *TN + FP*: number of students that fail in true.

The results of our new 5-steps experiments are reflected in Table 4 (accuracy %) and Table 5 (specificity %).

Table 4. Accuracy (%) results

	1st step	2nd step	3rd step	4th step	5th step
C4.5	55.77	56.14	66.52	76.76	78.5
Tri-Training (C4.5)	57.24	61.66	70.34	77.06	79.68

Table 5. Specificity (%) results

	1st step	2nd step	3rd step	4th step	5th step
C4.5	82.01	62.43	77.78	77.78	73.54
Tri-Training (C4.5)	77.78	75.13	80.95	78.84	79.37

The results indicate that a good predictive accuracy can be achieved with Tri-Training algorithm in comparison to a well known supervised learning algorithm, such as C4.5 Decision Tree. C4.5 reaches 55.77 % accuracy in the 1st step, while Tri-Training reaches 57.24 %. In the final step, C4.5 reaches 78.50 % accuracy, while Tri-training reaches 79.68 %. With regard to the specificity, Tri-Training algorithm scores 79.37 % in the final step, while C4.5 Decision Tree scores 73.37 %.

In the matter of attributes impact in algorithms accuracy OCS2, TEST2, OCS3 and TEST3 are the influential attributes in student performance prediction as it reflected in Table 4 (3rd and 4th step respectively). In addition, the prediction of Tri-Training algorithm in correctly classifying students that fail is outstanding, as specificity ranges from 75.13 to 80.95 %.

For the purpose of our study we developed a web-based tool that can predict the performance of an individual student according to the values of the above mentioned attributes using SSL techniques (Fig. 1). The first column refers to demographic and job information, while the second one refers to student's performance in written assignments and optional contact sessions.

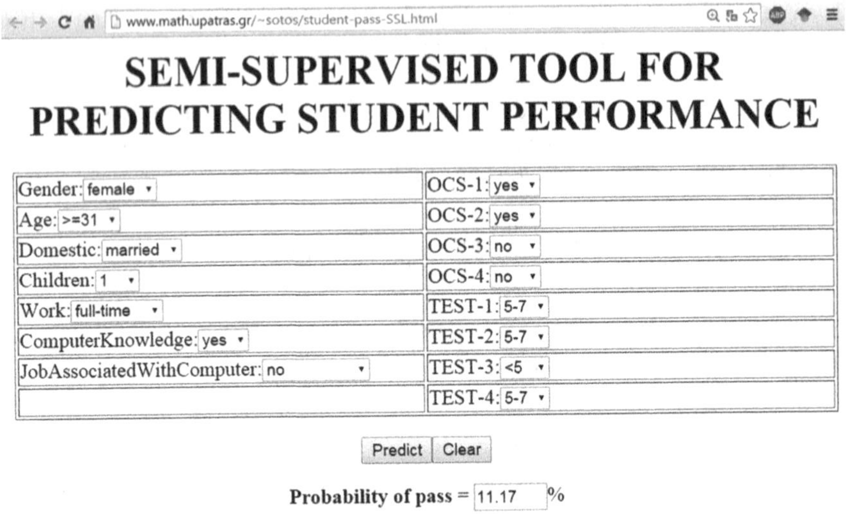

SEMI-SUPERVISED TOOL FOR PREDICTING STUDENT PERFORMANCE

Gender: female ▾	OCS-1: yes ▾
Age: >=31 ▾	OCS-2: yes ▾
Domestic: married ▾	OCS-3: no ▾
Children: 1 ▾	OCS-4: no ▾
Work: full-time ▾	TEST-1: 5-7 ▾
ComputerKnowledge: yes ▾	TEST-2: 5-7 ▾
JobAssociatedWithComputer: no ▾	TEST-3: <5 ▾
	TEST-4: 5-7 ▾

Predict   Clear

Probability of pass = 11.17 %

Fig. 1. Screenshot of the web-based tool

6   Conclusions

In this study we explore the performance of various SSL algorithms to predict students' success in distance higher education. Identifying low performance students as soon as possible could lead the academic staff to develop learning strategies in accordance with students' personal needs and specificities. The main question of this study is the possibility to predict students' performance (pass or fail) in distance higher education with a satisfactory accuracy using semi-supervised techniques.

In our experiments we have concentrated on semi-supervised methods comparing and evaluating the accuracy measures in an educational data set provided by the HOU. Our main sub-questions are three. Which SSL algorithm produces more accurate predictions? How SSL algorithms perform in comparison to familiar supervised techniques? How early can we predict students' performance during the academic year?

According to the accuracy results, it can be clearly observed that several SSL algorithms score a predictive accuracy around 58 % in the first step based on time-invariant attributes. In the final step Democratic algorithm exceeds 81 %, while De-Tri-Training (SMO), Tri-Training (C4.5), Co-Training (C4.5), Co-Training (NB), Rel-RASCO (NB) and RASCO (NB) algorithms reach almost 80 % accuracy. In the case of accuracy overall performance, Tri-Training multi-classifier algorithm with a C4.5 base classifier performs better than the rest of SSL algorithms. Its overall accuracy is 69.19 % ranging from 57.24 % at the start of the academic year and is increased continuously as new curriculum data are added reaching 79.68 % at the end of the academic year. Moreover, it is clearly observed that Tri-Training performs much better than C4.5 Decision Tree. It is also worth noting that C4.5 specificity measure is constantly decreasing and rates between 82.01 at the 1st step and 62.43 % in the 2nd step, while Tri-Training specificity measure ranges from 75.13 to 80.95 %. In the matter of attributes impact in algorithms accuracy OCS2, TEST2, OCS3 and TEST3 are the influential attributes in students' performance prediction. Especially, OCS2 and TEST2 trigger a substantial increase in accuracy measure (from 61.66 to 70.34 % for Tri-Training) underlying their impact. So, tutors may predict possible failure of students before the middle of the academic year providing extra support to low performers.

This study is an initial step of SSL algorithms implementation for predicting students' performance in distance higher education. The experimental results are quite encouraging, compared with a well known supervised method. We consider that further experiments are needed to predict with a great precision, not only the performance but also the grades of students in the final exams by examining the attributes and other criteria that significantly influence the performance and the quality of the prediction. Furthermore, we must carefully compare supervised methods with semi-supervised not only from the point of view of the accuracy of the results, but also from the point of view of the cost of data labeling. SSL is the appropriate tool for this, since it uses much less labeled data.

References

1. Adhatrao, K., Gaykar, A., Dhawan, A., Jha, R., Honrao, V.: Predicting students' performance using ID3 and C4.5 classification algorithms. Int. J. Data Min. Knowl. Manage. Process 3(5), 39–52 (2013)
2. Blum, A., Mitchell, T.: Combining labeled and unlabeled data with co-training. In: 11th Annual Conference on Computational Learning Theory, pp. 92–100. ACM (1998)
3. Cardie, C., Ng, V.: Weakly supervised natural language learning without redundant views. In: Proceedings of the 2003 Conference of the North American Chapter of the Association for Computational Linguistics on Human Language Technology, vol. 1, pp. 94–101. Association for Computational Linguistics (2003)
4. Deng, C., Guo, M.-Z.: Tri-training and data editing based semi-supervised clustering algorithm. In: Gelbukh, A., Reyes-Garcia, C.A. (eds.) MICAI 2006. LNCS (LNAI), vol. 4293, pp. 641–651. Springer, Heidelberg (2006)
5. García, S., Fernández, A., Luengo, J., Herrera, F.: Advanced nonparametric tests for multiple comparisons in the design of experiments in computational intelligence and data mining: experimental analysis of power. Inf. Sci. 180(10), 2044–2064 (2010)
6. Huang, S., Fang, N.: Predicting student academic performance in an engineering dynamics course: a comparison of four types of predictive mathematical models. Comput. Educ. 61, 133–145 (2013)
7. Kabakchieva, D.: Predicting student performance by using data mining methods for classification. Cybern. Inf. Technol. 13(1), 61–72 (2013)
8. Kotsiantis, S., Pierrakeas, C., Pintelas, P.: Predicting students' performance in distance learning using machine learning. Appl. Artif. Intell. 18(5), 411–426 (2004)
9. Kovacic, Z.: Early prediction of student success: mining students' enrolment data. In: Proceedings of Informing Science and IT Education Conference (InSITE), pp. 647–665 (2010)
10. Mashiloane, L., Mchunu, M.: Mining for marks: a comparison of classification algorithms when predicting academic performance to identify "students at risk". In: Prasath, R., Kathirvalavakumar, T. (eds.) MIKE 2013. LNCS, vol. 8284, pp. 541–552. Springer, Heidelberg (2013)

11. Mihalcea, R.: Co-training and self-training for word sense disambiguation. In: Proceedings of the Conference on Computational Natural Language Learning (2004)
12. Murphy, K.P.: Machine Learning: A Probabilistic Perspective. MIT Press, Cambridge (2012)
13. Navarro, P., Shoemaker, J.: Performance and perceptions of distance learners in cyberspace. Am. J. Distance Educ. **14**(2), 15–35 (2000)
14. Quinlan, J.R.: C4.5: Programs for Machine Learning. Elsevier, Amsterdam (1993)
15. Rokach, L.: Data Mining with Decision Trees: Theory and Applications. World scientific, Singapore (2007)
16. Rokach, L., Maimon, O.: Data Mining with Decision Trees: Theory and Applications. World scientific, Singapore (2015)
17. Romero, C., López, M.I., Luna, J.M., Ventura, S.: Predicting students' final performance from participation in on-line discussion forums. Comput. Educ. **68**, 458–472 (2013)
18. Ruggieri, S.: Efficient C4.5 classification algorithm. IEEE Trans. Knowl. Data Eng. **14**(2), 438–444 (2002)
19. Simpson, O.: Predicting student success in open and distance learning. Open Learn. **21**(2), 125–138 (2006)
20. Wang, J., Luo, S.W., Zeng, X.H.: A random subspace method for co-training. In: IEEE International Joint Conference on Neural Networks, pp. 195–200. IEEE (2008)
21. Yarowsky, D.: Unsupervised word sense disambiguation rivaling supervised methods. In: Proceedings of the 33rd Annual Meeting on Association for Computational Linguistics, pp. 189–196. Association for Computational Linguistics (1995)
22. Yaslan, Y., Cataltepe, Z.: Co-training with relevant random subspaces. Neurocomputing **73** (10), 1652–1661 (2010)
23. Zhu, X., Goldberg, A.B.: Introduction to semi-supervised learning. Synth. Lect. Artif. Intell. Mach. Learn. **3**(1), 1–130 (2009)
24. Zhou, Y., Goldman, S.: Democratic co-learning. In: ICTAI 2004, pp. 594–602. IEEE (2004)
25. Zhou, Z.H., Li, M.: Tri-training: exploiting unlabeled data using three classifiers. IEEE Trans. Knowl. Data Eng. **17**(11), 1529–1541 (2005)

Recommending Friends and Locations over a Heterogeneous Spatio-Temporal Graph

Pavlos Kefalas[✉] and Panagiotis Symeonidis

Department of Informatics, Aristotle University of Thessaloniki,
54124 Thessaloniki, Greece
{kefalasp,symeon}@csd.auth.gr
http://delab.csd.auth.gr

Abstract. Recommender systems in location-based social networks (LBSNs), such as Facebook Places and Foursquare, have focused on recommending friends or locations to registered users by combining information derived from *explicit* (i.e. friendship network) and *implicit* (i.e. user-item rating network, user-location network, etc.) subnetworks. However, previous's work models were static, failing to capture adequately user preferences as they change over time. In this paper, we provide a novel recommendation method by incorporating the time dimension into our model through an auxiliary artificial node (i.e. session). In particular, we construct a hybrid tripartite (i.e., user, location, session) graph, which incorporates 7 different unipartite and bipartite graphs. Then, we run on it the well known Random Walk with Restart (RWR) algorithm, which randomly propagate through the network structure which has 7 differently weighted edge types (i.e., user-location, user-session, user-user, etc.) among its entities. We evaluate experimentally how RWR improve the procession of the recommendations during different time-windows against one state-of-the-art algorithm over the GeoSocialRec and the Foursquare datasets.

Keywords: Algorithms · Link prediction · Location recommendation · Social networks

1 Introduction

Users utilize location-based social networks (LBSNs) to share their location with their friends, by incorporating in their posts the longitude and latitude information of their location. In LBSNs, users *explicitly* build a friendship network by adding each other as friends. In addition, users form *implicit* sub-networks through their daily interactions, like commenting on same posts or rating similarly same products/services in places they have co-visited.

Previous works have focused on recommending friends or locations [5,11] to users by combining information derived from multi-modal and heterogeneous explicit and implicit networks. In particular, there has been extensive research in this area, which mainly focuses on information derived from users' interaction

© Springer International Publishing Switzerland 2015
L. Bellatreche and Y. Manolopoulos (Eds.): MEDI 2015, LNCS 9344, pp. 271–284, 2015.
DOI: 10.1007/978-3-319-23781-7_22

with locations over user-location bipartite network ties. However, such models are static, failing to capture adequately users' preferences as they change over time. That is, time is an important factor in LBNSs, which affects the accuracy of recommendations. For example, users periodically perform daily activities in specific locations (e.g. home, work, etc.).

To incorporate the time dimension into their model, Xiang et al. [12] proposed the construction of tripartite graphs (i.e., users, locations, sessions) known as *Session-based Temporal Graph (STG)*. But, STG graph do not incorporate edges among nodes of the same set, i.e. failing to exploit information from all three unipartite networks (user-user, location-location and session-session). For instance, STG do not have links among user nodes. But, intuitively friends tend to visit similar locations at close time points, which means that friendship links could leverage the accuracy of location recommendations. A second problem of STG stems from their own structure. That is, STG do not connect directly users either with locations or sessions, which results to lower recommendation accuracy when data (i.e., session/location nodes) are sparse.

In this paper, we provide recommendations based on a Heterogeneous Spatio-Temporal graph (HST graph) by incorporating time dimension into our model. To build this HST graph, we create a new type of an artificial node, denoted as session node, which is associated with the co-location of two or more users in a location at a specific time period. Our HST graph incorporates 7 different unipartite or bipartite graphs, which makes it more informative in comparison to STG. Moreover, we follow a star-schema structure, where users are directly connected with locations and sessions. This structure can be more resistant in cases of sparsity (e.g. when there are not enough session nodes as a result of the fact that users check-into locations at different time periods).

Based on our HST graph that incorporates user, location and session nodes, we run the well known Random Walk with Restart algorithm (RWR) to provide spatio-temporal recommendations. RWR has properties, which can adequately capture the notion of user-user similarity or the user-location relevance in our HST graph. That is, social drivers which influence the ties formation in communities like homophily, social influence, common friendship, etc. are incorporated by nature in RWR algorithm, as it will be shown later.

The contributions of this paper are summarized as follows: (*i*) We propose the construction of HST graph, which is a tripartite graph that consists of 3-disjoint sets of nodes (i.e. sessions, users, locations), and incorporates edges among nodes of the same set, including also three unipartite graphs (*ii*) We use the Random Walk with Restart algorithm (RWR) on this new graph to examine how spatial and temporal features can leverage the recommendations according to proximity and time distance. (*iii*) We have compared our method with one state-of-the-art algorithm over two real world datasets.

The rest of this paper is organized as follows. Section 2 summarizes the related work, whereas Sect. 3 describes the construction of our HST graph, its edge weighting and our proposed algorithm. Experimental results are given in Sect. 4. Finally, Sect. 5 concludes this paper.

2 Related Work

Time is a crucial factor in LBSNs, since it could leverage the accuracy of friend, location and activity recommendations. Recently, Yuan et al. [14] exploited spatio-temporal characteristics of POIs by using a unified framework consisting of spatial and temporal dimensions.

Gao et al. [2] proposed the *Location Recommendation with Temporal effects* (LRT) algorithm. They argue that time dimension is crucial in recommendation and introduce a framework to make time-aware recommendations. In the same direction, a time-aware method was proposed by Marinho et al. [6] to improve location recommendations in LBSNs. Ho et al. [4] extract spatio-temporal information for future events from news articles. Furthermore, Raymond et al. [8] proposed a method to provide location recommendations for users that use buses. Their method is based on users' location histories and spatio-temporal correlations among the locations. By combining collaborative filtering algorithms with link propagation, they are able to predict origins, destinations and arrival times of buses.

The creation of artificial session nodes has been originally proposed by Xiang et al. [12], who designed a framework that models users' long-term and short-term preferences over time. Their model is based on a Session-based Temporal Graph (STG), which incorporates user, location and session information. In addition, Xiang et al. [12] proposed a novel recommendation algorithm named Injected Preference Fusion (IPF) and extended the personalized Random Walk for temporal recommendation.

Assume that, there are 2 users, 4 locations and 3 session nodes. User U1 has visited locations L1, L2 and L3, whereas user U2 has visited locations L3 and L4. Notice also that locations L1 and L2 are linked to Session 1 node. This means, both locations (L1 and L2) were co-visited by U1 at the same period T1 (e.g. during the morning of Thursday 19 September 2013). Based on the aforementioned graph, the user-location bipartite graph denotes the long term preferences of a user, whereas the location-session bipartite graph denotes the short term preferences of a user.

Our work is inspired by the work of Xiang et al. [12]. However, our HST graph has two main differences in comparison with STG. Firstly, in our case we create session nodes that connect users and not locations. That is, user nodes are the heart of a star schema graph and, thus, they are connected with direct links with both location and session nodes. The second difference is the graph structure per se. It is not only a 3-partite graph that consists of 3-disjoint sets of nodes (i.e. sessions, users, locations). In contrast, it incorporates also edges among nodes of the same set, i.e. three unipartite graphs, which makes it even richer in information.

3 Background and Preliminaries

In this section, we introduce the most important notations with the necessary definitions and a motivating example depicted in Fig. 1. Also, we provide an

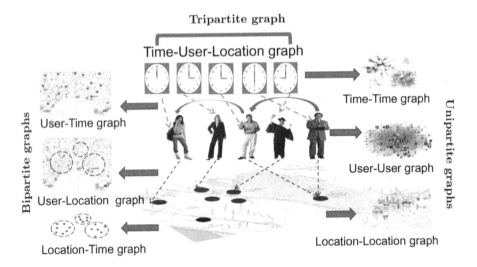

Fig. 1. Latent relations among time, users, locations dimensions of an LBSN and the generated k-partite graphs

analytical description of the basic entities that interact in a LBSN, i.e. users, locations, and time dimension and discuss the information types that can be extracted from the connections among them. Figure 1 shows the relations among the aforementioned entities. As shown in Fig. 1, we have 3 layers (one layer for each entity) and 5 users who have visited some places. For each visit we keep the time of the user's check-in. As also shown in Fig. 1, there are 7 graphs of different participating entities (i.e. three unipartite, three bipartite and one tripartite). On the right side of Fig. 1, we can see the 3 generated unipartite graphs (Time-Time graph, User-User graph, and Location-Location graph). On the left side of Fig. 1, we observe 3 bipartite graphs (User-Time graph, User-Location graph, and Location-Time graph). Finally, on top of Fig. 1, we can see the tripartite graph (Time-User-Location graph).

It is necessary to emphasize that the above graph is not a k-partite graph, since there can exist also edges among nodes of the same set (e.g. an edge between a user and another user, i.e. friendship). We denote this special case of a graph henceforth, as hybrid k-partite graph because it is a k-partite graph that consists of k-disjoint sets of nodes (i.e. time, users, locations), incorporating edges among nodes of the same set as well.

As depicted in Fig. 1, our data are in the form of $\langle time, user, location \rangle$ triplets, which are usually modeled by a tripartite graph or a tensor. However, if we had to use a tripartite graph or a tensor for capturing the time dimension as well, then we should create a new node for each different timestamp. This would create a huge tensor or a temporal graph with an enormous number of time nodes creating severe noise in the model.

Based on the above considerations, we choose to create a new type of an artificial node, denoted as session node, which is associated with the co-location of two or more users in a location at a specific time period. This co-location of two or more users reflects their interest for a place at a specific time. For example, two users can visit a music band at a bar every Thursday night. Thus, the possibility of having both common music interests is very high. That is, two users who visit a location at a common time period have a higher possibility to become friends than those users who visit a location but not on the same timestamp.

To create a new session node, in the same direction as [12], we transform the ⟨user, location, time⟩ into ⟨user, location⟩ and ⟨user, session⟩ by dividing the time into discrete intervals (bins). Then, we associate each bin with corresponding users who visited a place at the same time slot. Notice that a session node combines a number of users, with a location at a specific time interval. The length of a session can last from one hour, to six hours, or even one day etc. Based on the ⟨user, location⟩ and ⟨user, session⟩ we create our temporal graph, i.e. HST graph.

3.1 Session Node Extraction

Users may visit locations all day long. The huge amount of these check-ins, prevent us from understanding their trends and their likes, without before pre-processing the time dimension of this information. To have an abstract and thorough understanding of the users' behavior, we create artificial session nodes based on SQL statements. For our running example, let's assume that we create a table, which holds information about users, locations, and the time of their check-ins.

We extract the artificial session nodes, by using an SQL statement as shown in SQL Statement 1. This SQL statement finds co-locations between two or more users during the same time period, i.e. a session. In our running example, we set the time window for a co-location of two or more users equal to 6 hours. It is obvious that we can also use other lengths of a session's time window (i.e. we can split time into bins of an hour, a day, a month or a year, depending on the desired session for extraction).

Sql Statement 1. SQL query for session nodes extraction

```
SELECT A.userID, B.userID, A.Locationid
FROM ultime as A,ultime as B
WHERE A.LocationID = B.LocationID AND A.userID <> B.userID AND
(DATEDIFF(HOUR, A.tmp, B.tmp) / 24=0) AND (DATEDIFF(HOUR, A.tmp,
B.tmp) \% 24 between 0 and 6)
```

3.2 Constructing the Heterogeneous Spatio-Temporal Graph

We define a hybrid 3-partite graph as $\mathcal{G}(\mathcal{S}, \mathcal{U}, \mathcal{L}, \mathcal{E}^{(\mathcal{US})}, \mathcal{E}^{(\mathcal{SU})}, \mathcal{E}^{(\mathcal{UL})}, \mathcal{E}^{(\mathcal{LU})}, \mathcal{E}^{(\mathcal{SS})}, \mathcal{E}^{(\mathcal{UU})}, \mathcal{E}^{(\mathcal{LL})})$, which consists of 3-disjoint sets of nodes ($\mathcal{S}$ for session, $\mathcal{U}$ for user,

$\mathcal{L}$ for location). $\mathcal{G}$ is called "hybrid" because it has also edges among nodes of the same set. Similarly, there are edges among sessions and edges among locations. $\mathcal{E}^{(\mathcal{US})}$ represents the edges between nodes in $\mathcal{U}$ and $\mathcal{S}$. Vice versa, $\mathcal{E}^{(\mathcal{SU})}$ represents edges between nodes in $\mathcal{S}$ and $\mathcal{U}$. $\mathcal{E}^{(\mathcal{UL})}$ represents edges between nodes in $\mathcal{U}$ and L, whereas on the other hand $\mathcal{E}^{(\mathcal{LU})}$ represents edges between the nodes in $\mathcal{L}$ and U. $\mathcal{E}^{(\mathcal{SS})}$ represents the edge set linking the nodes in $\mathcal{S}$. $\mathcal{E}^{(\mathcal{UU})}$ represents the edge set linking the nodes in $\mathcal{U}$. Finally, $\mathcal{E}^{(\mathcal{LL})}$ represents the edge set linking the nodes in $\mathcal{L}$. For clarity, in Table 1 we provide a list of all used symbols notations and descriptions. We assume that graph $\mathcal{G}$ is directed and weighted. We also assume that graph $\mathcal{G}$ may have multiple edges connecting two nodes s and u.

3.3   Edge Weighting

In this section, we define the weights between nodes in our HST graph. By incorporating the artificial session nodes into our HST graph, we have the following 7 types of edges, which have to be weighted differently: (a) an edge from a session

Table 1. Symbols notations and descriptions

Symbol	Description
S	Set of sessions, $S = \{s_1, s_2, ..., s_n\}$
S_u	Set of sessions a user participated
S_l	Set of sessions a location shown
s, s'	Some sessions
U	Set of users, $U = \{u_1, u_2, ..., u_n\}$
U_u	Set of users who are friends with user u
U_s	Set of users who participated in a session s
U_l	Set of users who visited a location l
u, u'	Some users
L	Set of locations, $L = \{l_1, l_2, ..., l_n\}$
L_u	Set of locations visited by a user u
l, l'	Some locations
$d_{l,l'}$	Distance between locations l and l'
$\mathcal{E}^{(\mathcal{US})}$	Set of edges linking nodes of U to nodes of S
$\mathcal{E}^{(\mathcal{SU})}$	Set of edges linking nodes of S to nodes of U
$\mathcal{E}^{(\mathcal{UL})}$	Set of edges linking nodes of U to nodes of L
$\mathcal{E}^{(\mathcal{LU})}$	Set of edges linking nodes of L to nodes of U
$\mathcal{E}^{(\mathcal{SS})}$	Set of edges linking the nodes of S
$\mathcal{E}^{(\mathcal{UU})}$	Set of edges linking the nodes of U
$\mathcal{E}^{(\mathcal{LL})}$	Set of edges linking the nodes of L

node s to a user node u, (b) an edge from a user u to a session s, (c) an edge from a user u to a location l, (d) an edge from location l to a user u, (e) an edge from a user u to another user u', (f) an edge from a location l to another location l', and (g) an edge from a session s to another session s'.

In the following, we define the edge weights for the 7 different edge types, starting from the edges of the bipartite graphs (session-user and user-location). Firstly, we set the weight $w(s, u)$ of the edge from a session node s to a user node u as:

$$w(s, u) = \frac{1}{|U_s|}, \tag{1}$$

where ($|U_s|$) is the number of users who participated in a session s. Notice that we weight differently an edge that starts from a user u and ends to a session s. Specifically, $w(u, s)$ is:

$$w(u, s) = \frac{1}{|S_u|}, \tag{2}$$

where $|S_u|$ is the number of sessions in which a user u has participated. That is, the probability of a user to join a session is equally divided on all sessions he has participated.

Next, we define the edge weight $w(u, l)$ of the edge from a user node u to a location node l as:

$$w(u, l) = \frac{n_{u,l}}{\sum_{\forall l \in L} n_{u,l}}, \tag{3}$$

where $n_{u,l}$ is the number of times a user u visited a location l and $\sum_{\forall l \in L} n_{u,l}$ is the total number of check-ins in all locations by user u. For define the edge weight $w(l, u)$, that starts from location l and ends at a user u as:

$$w(l, u) = \frac{n_{l,u}}{\sum_{\forall u \in U} n_{l,u}}, \tag{4}$$

where the $n_{l,u}$ is the number of times a location l is visited by a user u and $\sum_{\forall u \in U} n_{l,u}$ is the total number of check-ins of all users in location l.

We proceed with the edge weighting of the unipartite graphs (user-user, location-location, session-session). First, the edge weight $w(u, u')$ between two user nodes u and u' is defined as the fraction of 1 to the number of users (U_u), who are friends with a user u:

$$w(u, u') = \frac{1}{|U_u|}, \tag{5}$$

The edge weight between two location nodes l and l' is defined as:

$$w(l, l') = \left(1 - \frac{(geodist_{l,l'})}{\sum_{\forall l, l' \in L} (geodist_{l,l'})}\right), \tag{6}$$

In this case, we set as link weight the geographical distance between two location nodes l and l'. To obtain all weights, we calculate the distance between all pairs of locations.

Finally, for the edge weighting between two session nodes s and s', we take under consideration both the location and the time dimensions of each session nodes after normalizing both dimensions, by using the following equation:

$$w(s, s') = \left(1 - \frac{(geodist_{s,s'})}{\sum\limits_{\forall s,s' \in S} (geodist_{s,s'})} \right) + \left(1 - \frac{(timediff_{s,s'})}{\sum\limits_{\forall s,s' \in S} (timediff_{s,s'})} \right), \quad (7)$$

where $geodist_{s,s'}$ and $timediff_{s,s'}$ are the geographical distance and the time difference between two session nodes s and s', respectively.

3.4   Construction of the Transition Probability Matrix

Random walk processes on graphs have been extensively used in social network analysis [7,13]. To apply a random walk on a heterogeneous spatio-temporal graph, we have to construct a transition probability P matrix to configure and set all transition probabilities among the nodes of our HST graph. To represent all possible transitions on the HST graph, the size of the P matrix should be $(|\mathcal{S}| + |\mathcal{U}| + |\mathcal{L}|) \times (|\mathcal{S}| + |\mathcal{U}| + |\mathcal{L}|)$. By combining Eqs. 1–7, we compute the transition probability matrix P which comprises of several sub-matrices that correspond to our HST graph, as follows:

$$\mathbf{P} = \begin{bmatrix} \mathcal{SS} & \mathcal{SU} & 0 \\ \mathcal{US} & \mathcal{UU} & \mathcal{UL} \\ 0 & \mathcal{LU} & \mathcal{LL} \end{bmatrix} \quad (8)$$

where $\mathcal{SS}$ is a $|\mathcal{S}| \times |\mathcal{S}|$ sub-matrix representing the transition probability between session nodes to session nodes, as defined in Eq. 7. $\mathcal{UU}$ is a $|\mathcal{U}| \times |\mathcal{U}|$ sub-matrix, which is not symmetric because transition probabilities between two user nodes are defined based on the number of neighbors of each user node (see Eq. 5). $\mathcal{LL}$ is a $|\mathcal{L}| \times |\mathcal{L}|$ sub-matrix representing the transition probability from location nodes to location nodes, as defined in Eq. 6. $\mathcal{US}$ sub-matrix holds the transition probabilities from user nodes to session nodes, whereas $\mathcal{SU}$ sub-matrix holds the transition probabilities from session nodes to user nodes. Similarly, $\mathcal{UL}$ sub-matrix holds the transition probabilities from user nodes to location nodes, whereas $\mathcal{LU}$ sub-matrix holds the transition probabilities from location nodes to user nodes.

3.5   Normalization

In Sect. 3.3, we described the edge weighting among nodes of our HST graph in both unipartite and bipartite sub-networks. We aimed to assign weights on edges in the interval [0,1]. All these weights will be inserted in a probability transition matrix P, and then we will run our method for capturing the notion of similarity between the nodes of the HST graph. However, in several cases the distribution of the weight values in the interval [0,1] between the 7 edge types (i.e. session-user, user-user, etc.) differs significantly. For example, consider the case that the most weights in $\mathcal{E}^{(\mathcal{US})}$ are normally distributed between 0 and 0.1, whereas most similarity values of $\mathcal{E}^{(\mathcal{LL})}$ are normally distributed between 0.9 and 1. That is, the weighting values of $\mathcal{E}^{(\mathcal{US})}$ will always be dominated by those of $\mathcal{E}^{(\mathcal{LL})}$.

To avoid this problem, we present a normalization step for the construction of the final transition probability P matrix: (a) We compute the mean similarity value m_P of the matrix P. (b) We compute the standard deviation value s_P of the matrix P. (c) For each (i, j) cell of the P matrix, where $i \neq j$, we apply the transformation:

$$P(i, j) = \frac{P(i, j) - m_P}{s_P} \qquad (9)$$

(d) Finally, we scale and translate the derived values back in the interval [0,1]:

$$P(i, j) = \frac{P(i, j) - min_P}{max_P - min_P} \qquad (10)$$

where min_P, max_P are the minimum and maximum values of matrix P after the transformation by Eq. 9, respectively. Please notice, that by adding the probabilities of propagation through the nodes of a each column, we gain the maximum probability. Thus, after normalization step, each column of our transition probability matrix P cast up to 1.

3.6 Random Walk on the Normalized Transition Probability Matrix

Random walk with restart (RWR) algorithm [10] is a variation of the well-known PageRank algorithm. RWR has properties, which can adequately capture the notion of user-user similarity or the user-location relevance for a specific user u of our HST graph. The main advantage of RWR over PageRank is its teleporting characteristic, which obliges the random walker to re-start his walk from the initial node u. As expected, RWR assigns more importance/similarity to the nearby nodes of u. Thus, if two users are close to each other, the probability of becoming friends is larger. Moreover, RWR can capture the notion of similarity among users who share a large number of common friends. For the user-location graph, if two users visit the same locations, then the overall probability for connecting them (via a location node) increases. The same holds for two users via a session node.

RWR considers one random walker starting from an initial user node u and randomly choosing among the available edges with a probability α. In addition, each time the random walker may return back to the initial node with a probability $1 - \alpha$. Therefore, the random walk process can be represented as:

$$S^{(UU)}(t + 1) = \alpha \times P \times S^{(UU)}(t) + (1 - \alpha) \times I \qquad (11)$$

where $S^{(UU)}(t)$ and $S^{(UU)}(t+1)$ are the state probability matrices at time t and $t+1$, respectively. $S^{(UU)}$ is a matrix that represents the link relevance from all HST graph nodes to the target user u. Parameter a is the prior probability that the random walker will leave its current state. Moreover, I is the identity and P the transition-probability matrix.

4 Experimental Evaluation

In this section, we compare experimentally RWR [10] with a fast version of the classic Katz algorithm, denoted as Fast-Katz [1] The parameters used to evaluate the performance of this algorithm are identical to those reported in the original paper. However, for datasets that were not used in these papers, we tuned the parameters so as to get the best results possible.

4.1 Data Sets

We performed our experiments using two real-world datasets, i.e., Foursquare[1] and GeoSocialRec[2]. Foursquare [3] dataset contains 18,107 users 2,073,740 check-ins, 847,081 locations and 231,148 social ties among users. This dataset is collected between March 2010 and January 2011. Please notice that we did not use the dataset of our main competitor [15] because it does not incorporate the friendship network. GeoSocialRec [9] dataset concerns 149 users who have 595 social ties among them (i.e. friendship network). Also, they have performed 853 check-ins to 438 locations. This dataset is collected between August 2011 and January 2012.

Detailed information about both networks is illustrated in Table 2. In particular, information about friendship networks can be seen in Table 2(a), where we present the type of each network (i.e. directed or undirected), the number of users, the number of links among users, the nodes' Average Degree (ADG) and the Local Clustering Coefficient (LLC). As expected, the sparsity of the user-user matrix is very big, i.e., 97.31 % and 99.92 % for the GeoSocialRec and the Foursquare datasets, respectively.

Furthermore, Table 2(b) contains information about the bipartite user-location network. In this table, we present the number of users, the number of locations, and the number of check-ins. Moreover, parameter AVG_u denotes the average number of check-ins per user, whereas parameter AVG_l denotes the average number of check-ins per location. Please notice that the average number of check-ins per user is 11.08 and 101.00 for the GeoSocialRec and the Foursquare dataset, respectively. This is a huge difference in terms of density between the two datasets. It is inevitable that the accuracy of recommendations for the GeoSocialRec data set will be low for both algorithms.

In Fig. 2 we show statistics on the GeoSocialRec and the Foursquare datasets. Notice that both x-axis and y-axis are in the log scale. As shown, the datasets

---

[1] http://www.public.asu.edu/~hgao16/dataset.html.

[2] http://delab.csd.auth.gr/~symeon/GeoSocialRec_Dataset.rar.

Table 2. Datasets specifications

(a) Friendship Network

Dataset	Type	Users	Edges	ADG	LCC
GeoSocialRec	undirected	149	595	6.3013	0.0342
Foursquare	undirected	18107	231148	10.5800	0.1841

(b) User-Location Network

Dataset	User	Location	Check-ins	AVG_u	AVG_l
GeoSocialRec	149	438	853	11.08	2.08
Foursquare	18107	847081	2073740	101	48.16

(c) User-Location-Session Network

Dataset	Users	POIs	Session nodes				
			3 Hour	6 Hour	9 Hour	12 Hour	24 Hours
GeoSocialRec	149	438	16	27	35	35	47
Foursquare	18107	847081	36606	78402	89079	90012	93204

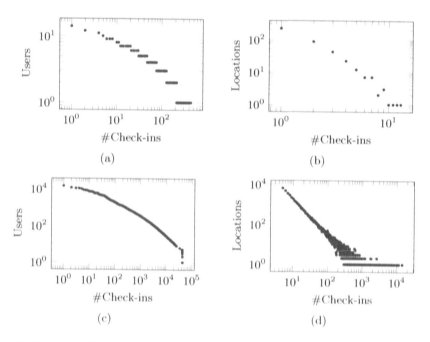

(a)

(b)

(c)

(d)

Fig. 2. Power law distribution diagrams for GeoSocialRec [(a) and (b)] and foursquare [(c) and (d)] datasets

follow a power law distribution for both the number of users' check-ins (Figs. 2(a) and (c)) and the number of visits to a particular location (Figs. 2(b) and (d)). As shown in Figs. 2(a) and (c), there is a small number of users who have checked-in to many locations (short head) and many users that have only checked-in a small number of locations (long tail). Similarly, as shown in Figs. 2(b) and (d), few locations have many visits, whereas many locations have a small number of visits. Notice that, it is very difficult for all algorithms to recommend accurately locations, which have not been visited from many users (i.e., recommendation in the long tail of the distribution).

In addition, as shown in Table 2(c) we have created artificial session nodes to study the effect of the length of a session slot. We have created session nodes based on 3 hours, 6 hours, 9 hours, 12 hours and 24 hours. Please notice that the average session per user (when session is set to 3 Hours) is 0.10 and 2.02 for the GeoSocialRec and the Foursquare dataset, respectively. This means that it is very difficult to find co-locations among users in the first dataset, which will affect the recommendation accuracy of all algorithms, as will be shown experimentally later.

4.2   Comparison with Other Methods

In this section, we compare the well known RWR algorithm with other one state-of-the art comparison partner i.e. Fast-Katz, in terms of precision and recall. As the number N of the recommended users/locations varies starting from the top-1 to top-N, we examine the precision and recall scores. Achieving high recall scores while precision follows with the minimum decline indicates the robustness of the examined algorithm.

For the friend recommendation task, in Figs. 3(a) and (c), we visualise the precision versus recall curve for the GeoSocialRec and Foursquare datasets, respectively. As N increases, precision falls, while recall increases as expected for both algorithms. RWR attains the best results achieving the highest precision, against Fast-Katz algorithm. The reason is that RWR exploits effectively information from all sub-networks (i.e., friendship, user-location, etc.) in contrast to Fast katz algorithm which exploits the relations of the nodes with the target node in depth of 4 hops. Please notice, that hidden relation may exist in greater depth than 4 hops. Thus, it is obvious why our approach gains higher values of precision versus recall in contrast to our competitor. Also, notice that while experimenting with GeoSocialRec dataset, the precision and the recall values are low. Thats is because there are only few relations among the nodes of constructed HST graph which tackles the performance of both algorithms.

For location recommendations, we get similar results as shown in Figs. 3(b) and (d), for the GeoSocialRec and Foursquare datasets, respectively. Notice, that RWR outperforms again the other algorithm. The reason is that RWR exploits information from more sub-networks than Fast-Katz. Thus, RWR has more options to walk through the network structure using different paths and edge types. Moreover, RWR is more robust as we increase the number of top-N recommended locations because it achieves high recall scores while precision score drops smoothly. Please notice, that Fast Katz traverse globally the network, missing to capture adequately the local characteristics of the HST graph. Also, Fast Katz defines a measure that directly sums over all paths between any pair of nodes in the graph, exponentially damped by length to count short paths

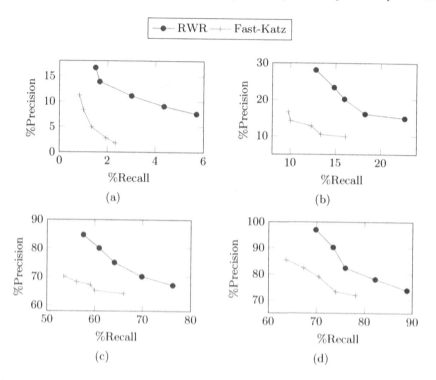

Fig. 3. Comparing RWR against Fast-Katz performance in term of precision and recall at top-N recommended [(a) users and (b) locations] on GeoSocialRec dataset, [(c) users and (d) locations] on foursquare dataset.

more heavily. This way Fast Katz misses the relations existing in greater depth in contrast to our approach which takes them into account.

5 Conclusions

Since recommender systems incorporate information from *explicit* and *implicit* sub-networks to provide recommendation we argue that time is an important factor. Thus, we introduce the creation of an artificial node which captures the time dimension into our model. Moreover, we construct a novel hybrid k-partite graph which holds information from all participating networks. Then, we evaluate to what extent the well RWR algorithm improves its recommendation agains Fast-Katz algorithm in terms of precision and recall.

References

1. Foster, K.C., Muth, S.Q., Potterat, J.J., Rothenberg, R.B.: A faster katz status score algorithm. Comput. Math. Organ. Theory **7**(4), 275–285 (2001)

2. Gao, H., Tang, J., Hu, X., Liu, H.: Exploring temporal effects for location recommendation on location-based social networks. In: Proceedings of the 7th ACM Conference on Recommender Systems (RecSys), pp. 93–100 (2013)
3. Gao, H., Tang, J., Liu, H.: Exploring social-historical ties on location-based social networks. In: Proceedings of the 6th International Conference on Weblogs and Social Media (ICWSM), pp. 114–121 (2012)
4. Ho, S.-S., Lieberman, M., Wang, P., Samet, H.: Mining future spatiotemporal events and their sentiment from online news articles for location-aware recommendation system. In: Proceedings of the 1st ACM SIGSPATIAL International Workshop on Mobile Geographic Information Systems (MobiGIS), pp. 25–32 (2012)
5. Lu, Z., Savas, B., Tang, W., Dhillon, I.S.: Supervised link prediction using multiple sources. In: Proceedings of the 10th IEEE International Conference on Data Mining (ICDM), pp. 923–928 (2010)
6. Marinho, L.B., Nunes, I., Sandholm, T., Nóbrega, C., Araújo, J.A., Pires, C.E.S.: Improving location recommendations with temporal pattern extraction. In: Proceedings of the 18th Brazilian Symposium on Multimedia and the Web (WebMedia), pp. 293–296 (2012)
7. Noulas, A., Scellato, S., Lathia, N., Mascolo, C.: A random walk around the city: New venue recommendation in location-based social networks. In: Proceedings of the International Conference on Privacy, Security, Risk and Trust (PASSAT), and International Conference on Social Computing (SocialCom), pp. 144–153 (2012)
8. Raymond, R., Sugiura, T., Tsubouchi, K.: Location recommendation based on location history and spatio-temporal correlations for an on-demand bus system. In: Proceedings of the 19th ACM International Conference on Advances in Geographic Information Systems (SIGSPATIAL), pp. 377–380 (2011)
9. Sattari, M., Toroslu, I., Karagoz, P., Symeonidis, P., Manolopoulos, Y.: Extended feature combination model for recommendations in location-based mobile services. Knowl. Inf. Syst. 44, 1–33 (2014)
10. Tong, H., Faloutsos, C., Pan, J.: Fast random walk with restart and its applications. In: Proceedings of the 6th International Conference on Data Mining (ICDM), pp. 613–622 (2006)
11. Vasuki, V., Natarajan, N., Lu, Z., Savas, B., Dhillon, I.: Scalable affiliation recommendation using auxiliary networks. ACM Trans. Intell. Syst. Technol. (TIST) 3(1), 3:1–3:20 (2011)
12. Xiang, L., Yuan, Q., Zhao, S., Chen, L., Zhang, X., Yang, Q., Sun, J.: Temporal recommendation on graphs via long- and short-term preference fusion. In: Proceedings of the 16th ACM International Conference on Knowledge Discovery and Data Mining (KDD), pp. 723–732 (2010)
13. Yin, Z., Gupta, M., Weninger, T., Han, J.: A unified framework for link recommendation using random walks. In: Proceedings of the IEEE International Conference on Advances in Social Networks Analysis and Mining (ASONAM), pp. 152–159 (2010)
14. Yuan, Q., Cong, G., Ma, Z., Sun, A., Thalmann, N.M.: Time-aware point-of-interest recommendation. In: Proceedings of the 36th ACM International Conference on Research and Development in Information Retrieval (SIGIR), pp. 363–372 (2013)
15. Yuan, Q., Cong, G. Sun, A.: Graph-based point-of-interest recommendation with geographical and temporal influences. In: Proceedings of the 23rd ACM International Conference on Conference on Information and Knowledge Management (CIKM), pp. 659–668 (2014)

Knowledge Discovery from Geo-Located Tweets for Supporting Advanced Big Data Analytics: A Real-Life Experience

Alfredo Cuzzocrea[1]([⊠]), Giuseppe Psaila[2], and Maurizio Toccu[2]

[1] DIA Department, University of and ICAR-CNR, Trieste, Italy
alfredo.cuzzocrea@dia.units.it
[2] Department of Engineering, University of Bergamo, Bergamo, Italy
{psaila,maurizio.toccu}@unibg.it

Abstract. Tourists are an important asset for the economy of the regions they visit. The answer to the question "where do tourists actually go?" could be really useful for public administrators and local governments. In particular, they need to understand what tourists actually visit, where they actually spend nights, and so on and so forth.

In this paper, we introduce an original approach that exploits geo-located messages posted by *Twitter* users through their smartphones when they travel. Tools developed within the *FollowMe* suite track movements of *Twitter* users that post tweets in an airport and reconstruct their trips within an observed area. To illustrate the potentiality of our method, we present a simple case study in which trips are traced on the map (through KML layers shown in *Google Earth*) based on different analysis dimensions.

1 Introduction

Modern smartphones are enabling the concept of *Mobile Social Computing*, i.e. the capability of exploiting computation services to deal with social information (*Social Computing*) enhanced with capabilities of mobile devices (e.g., [1]). In particular GPS localization, provided by most of mobile devices, gives an important contribution: (with respect to social networks) people can post geo-localized messages and pictures, giving this way much more indirect information than non-localized posts (e.g., [7,10]). Among all social networks, *Twitter* (as well as other social networks that adopt the same approach) is particularly attractive for the purpose of searching interesting messages: in fact, every user can see messages by other users without limitations. Nevertheless, observe that geo-localized posts represent a kind of voluntary contribution, because users voluntarily install the (*Twitter*) app and voluntarily post messages (tweets).

These posts' knowledge, hardly acquirable with traditional survey methods, can be very useful for public administrations that like to understand how tourists travel on the region they govern, especially when the region is served by an International Airport. One typical hard question to answer is:
Where do tourists actually go?

© Springer International Publishing Switzerland 2015
L. Bellatreche and Y. Manolopoulos (Eds.): MEDI 2015, LNCS 9344, pp. 285–294, 2015.
DOI: 10.1007/978-3-319-23781-7_23

The intuition is that *Mobile Social Computing* can help to understand where travelers actually go, what they actually visit, where they actually spend nights: in fact, by gathering the geo-localized tweets they post during their travel, it should be possible to reconstruct their trips (e.g., [8,9,11,12]). This aspect plays a critical role, especially when dealing with *Big Data Analytics* (e.g., [2–6]).

The *FollowMe* project originated from these considerations. The aim is to develop techniques and build a suite of tools (the so-called *FollowMe* suite) that query social networks to discover posts sent by travelers and trace them during their trip. At the moment, we developed tools working with *Twitter* and tweets; in the next stages of the project we will consider other social networks. In this paper, we present: the approach we followed, the way reconstructed trips can be analyzed, the *FollowMe* suite from a technical point of view and a case study built with the initial data sets we collected.

The paper is organized as follows. Section 2 deals with problem definition and analysis dimensions. Section 3 reports about architecture of *FollowMe* suite. Section 4 reports the case study. Finally, Sect. 5 draws our conclusions and future work.

2   Problem Definition and Analysis Dimensions

The aim of the project is to build techniques and tools that permit to study the movements of tourists visiting a given region. The choice of *Twitter* is motivated by the fact that messages are short and visible to every user, without limitations.

2.1   Problem Definition

A key point was to find a way to identify traveling users: in fact, it is not feasible to detect them simply asking *Twitter* API to retrieve geo-located post in a given area: who is actually traveling? who resides in the area?

The answer can be found by observing the typical behavior of travelers, depicted in Fig. 1.

While they are waiting for boarding, travelers have time to post tweets, notifying friends that their trip is beginning. After the flight, they transit through the arrival airport (represented by the cue ball reached by the dashed arrow), but here they do not post tweets; in particular, this happens in small airports for passengers with hand-baggage only. Instead, they usually post tweets when they are visiting some wonderful place/tourist attraction or in the hotel (represented by the other cue balls). This gives us the solution to the above mentioned problem. It is necessary to find travelers that (potentially) reached the region of interest by retrieving tweets posted in the departing airport connected with airports close to the region of interest.

Tweet Gathering. The *Gathering Problem* can then be stated as follows.

Problem 1. Given one or more regions of interest R, identify the airports A_R that serve R. Then, identify the airports A_O which flight having destination in A_R originate from.

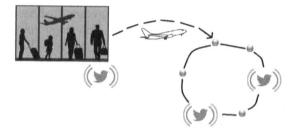

Fig. 1. Movements and tracking of passengers by *Twitter*.

Every day d, collect the set $H(d, A_O)$ of *hang tweets*, i.e., geo-loacetd tweets posted in the area of an airport in A_O; the union H of the daily gathered tweets is $H = \bigcup_d H(d, A_O)$.

Them for each user u having a tweet $h \in H$, gather all geo-located tweets posted by user u (i.e., his/her *timeline*) in the next 8 days after $h.date$, i.e., the date of the hang tweet h, denoted as $T(u, t.date)$. The set of overall collected timelines is $T = \bigcup_{u,d} T(u, d)$.   □

Trip Querying. Once hang tweets and timelines are collected (Problem 1), it is necessary to extract trips from T, as far as they touch the region of interest. This is the *Trip Querying* problem and is stated as follows.

Problem 2. Consider the set $T = \bigcup_{u,d} T(u, d)$ of gathered timelines. Given a region of interest $\overline{R}$, a query q is the pair $q = (T, \overline{R})$.

The *Trip Result Set* $R_q = \{\overline{T}(u, d)\}$ such that for each $T(u, d) \in T$ for which $\overline{T}(u, d) \subseteq T(u, d)$ and each $t \in \overline{T}(u, d)$ is geo-located within $\overline{R}$.   □

In order to address the two above stated problems, we developed tools described in Sect. 3.

2.2   Analysis Dimensions

What kind of analysis can be performed on trips? Certainly a graphical representation on the Earth map is straightforward, but the way trips are represented is not obvious.

We identified several *Analysis Dimensions*.

- *Path.* For each user, the analysis of the path followed during the trip could reveal unexpected knowledge. For example, discovering that a tourist attraction is often visited after the visit to a museum, could suggest local governments to better organize public transportation services.
- *Origin Airports.* The origin airport of trips could let administrators to understand for which countries the governed region is more attractive. This could lead to marketing actions to consolidate the attraction factors, or to understand how to become more attractive for other countries.

- *Time Slots*. Depending on the daylight time, travelers do different activities. In particular, in the morning or in the afternoon they go around visiting places; in the evening usually they look for a restaurant where to have dinner; in the night they probably are in their hotel room. Thus, tweets could be grouped and analyzed based on precise daylight time slots, to discover, e.g., where they mostly spend nights.
- *Week Days*. Another important dimension concerning time is the week day. In fact, it is likely that the specific week day can influence the places visited by tourists. For example, this could suggest to open a Museum on Sundays.

Tweet Alignment. In order to make effective path analysis and, in general, to enable intermediate aggregations, each tweet in a trip is aligned based on the distance between its date and the date of the beginning tweet of the trip. Tweet Alignment is performed by computing the *Tweet Trip Day t.td* as $t.td = (t.date - h.date) + 1$, where h is the hang tweet of the trip (the tweet posted in the origin airport).

Daylight Time Partitioning. In order to enable the dimension analysis based on daylight time slots, each tweet is extended with the proper time slots. We decided to adopt the following mapping:

1. $TS1$: 22:00am – 05:59am, Night;
2. $TS2$: 06:00am – 11:59am, Morning;
3. $TS3$: 12:00pm – 17:59pm, Afternoon;
4. $TS4$: 18:00pm – 21:59pm, Evening.

In particular, $TS1$ can provide information about where travelers sleep. Instead, likely, $TS4$ can provide information about where travelers have dinner. Finally, $TS2$ and $TS3$ can provide information about the activities of our travelers within the region of interest.

3   The *FollowMe* Suite

The *FollowMe* suite is an open pool of tools, each one devoted to a specific task. In fact, at the current stage of development of the project, we only gather messages from *Twitter*, but the long term goal of the project is to collect posts coming from various social networks. Consequently, new components must be easily added and the data storage service must flexibly deal with semi-structured and text-based documents. Hereafter, we describe in more details the software tools currently in the suite, which are depicted in Fig. 2.

- *MongoDB*. The storage service is responsibility of *MongoDB*, a recent and very famous No-SQL DBMS. It is designed to deal with collections of documents, where each document is represented as a JSON object. The main advantage in using MongoDB is the ability to manage documents with different structures within the same collections, this way overtaking the concept of schema in tables, that obstacle the adoption of traditional relational technology where documents with variable structures must be stored.

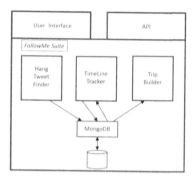

Fig. 2. Architecture of the *FollowMe* suite.

- *Hang Tweet Finder.* This component is responsible to query the *Twitter* API to look for tweets posted in the area of the monitored airports. In fact, *Twitter* API provides the capability to search for geo-located tweets, given the coordinates of the center and the radius of an area of interest.
  These tweets are called *hang tweets*, because they are the hang to identify users to follow in their trip.
- *Timeline Tracker.* For each user identified by means of hang tweets, the *Timeline Tracker* follows his/her timeline, i.e., the history of tweets posted by the user. In particular, the *Timeline Tracker* considers only geo-localized tweets posted in the next 8 days after the date of the hang tweet.
- *Trip Builder.* While the *Hang Tweet Finder* and the *Timeline Tracker* collect potentially interesting tweets from *Twitter*, the *Trip Builder* actually reconstruct trips by querying the storage area. In particular, the *Trip Builder* is launched by specifying the bounding box of the geographical area in which we want to discover trips.
- Finally, the *FollowMe* suite is completed by a *user interface*, that allows analysts and administrators to manage the gathering process and start queries. Furthermore, services provided by tools within the suite can be exploited by applications through suitable APIs.

Output Data Formats. The *Trip Builder* represents trips as sequences of tweets. In order to allow an easy exploitation by external tools, such as Mat-Lab, Excel, etc., trips are generated as CSV (comma separated value) files. For each tweet the user identifier, the data and time, the latitude and longitude are reported; furthermore, for each identified trip the origin airport (i.e., the airport where the hang tweet was posted) the date of the last tweet in the monitored area and the duration of the stay in the same area are reported, among all. Table 1 describes above attributes.

Geographical Layer. When geographical data are concerned, visualization on a map is an important issue. This is even more important in our project, where analysts need to understand where travelers mostly spend their time in the area. For this reason, we also generate several KML representations of the trips.

Table 1. Attributes for each tweet

Attributes	Description
SNet	Identifier of each social network
TweetId	Identifier of each tweet
UserName	Identifier of each user (traveler)
Date	Date of tweet publication
Time	Time of publication of tweet
Latitude	Latitude at which the tweet was posted
Longitude	Longitude at which the tweet was posted
OriginAirport	Departure airports for each user (traveler)

KML is the input format accepted by *Google Earth* and by Google Maps API; in particular, in Google Maps API-based web applications information layers described as KML files can be added to maps. However, for analysis tasks, *Google Earth* is a very powerful tool, because it permits to select information item to show. In particular, KML files can contain (possibly nested) folders, that can be very useful to partition information items based on a specific property. For example, an analyst could interested in partition trips based on the airport where trips originated from. Since the analysis needs could be manifold, several KML files are generated. They are reported in the following list.

– Locations partitioned by origin airport.
– Locations partitioned by time slot.
– Trips depicted as polylines and partitioned by users.

In this way, the analyst can view the trips by several perspectives, and better understand the dynamics of trips.

4   Case Study: The EXPO 2015 in Milan

In order to illustrate the effectiveness of our approach, we built a simple case study on the basis of a small set of geo-located tweets gathered by the *FollowMe* suite. The goal of the case study is to discover travelers coming to Lombardy, the region in the center of northern Italy where the main city is Milan, that in these days is world wide famous due to EXPO 2015. Therefore, we identified a pool of 30 European airports; they were chosen based on the presence of flights to airports in Lombardy and such that the number of posted tweets in a single day is not huge (Madrid and Lisbon were discarded because more than 1500 tweets a day were posted in the area of the two airports).

We collected hang tweets and timelines in the period between April 20, 2015, and May 11, 2015. By performing a query to discover trips in the bounding box of Lombardy, the *Trip Builder* generated a result set of 50 trips, formed by a total of 168 trips.

Table 2. Number of tweets and travelers for origin airports

Origin airport	Trips	Posted tweets
Athens	8	32
Barcelona	16	65
Beauvais	1	2
Berlin	3	5
Bucharest	1	1
Charleroi	2	8
Copenhagen	7	27
Frankfurt	1	6
Munich	3	6
Stansted	7	14
Stansted	1	2

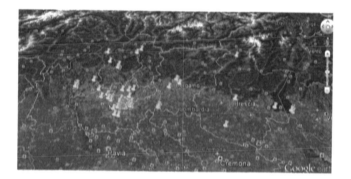

Fig. 3. Tweets distribution on the Lombardy region.

Discovered trips originated in 11 different airports, reported in. In Table 2 we show the 11 Origin Airports. Besides each airport name, we report number of trips that originated from that airport (column *Trips*), as well as the total number of tweets that constitute those trips (column *Posted Tweets*). For example, the 8 identified trips originated in Athens are composed of 32 tweets. It is possible to notice that Spanish travelers use to post a more tweets than travelers coming from other countries: the system detected 16 trips from Barcelona, that is, more than the sum of trips from Athens and Copenhagen.

The KML layers describing the discovered trips, were analyzed by means of *Google Earth*. Figure 3 shows the distribution of tweets that travelers posted within the Lombardy region. It is possible to note that these tweets are mainly concentrated in Milan area. The presence of travelers in this area are likely conditioned by EXPO 2015.

Figure 4, that represents the dimension *Origin Airports*, shows the distribution of tweets with respect to travelers coming from Barcelona. It is possible to

Fig. 4. Tweets distribution with respect to travelers come from Barcelona.

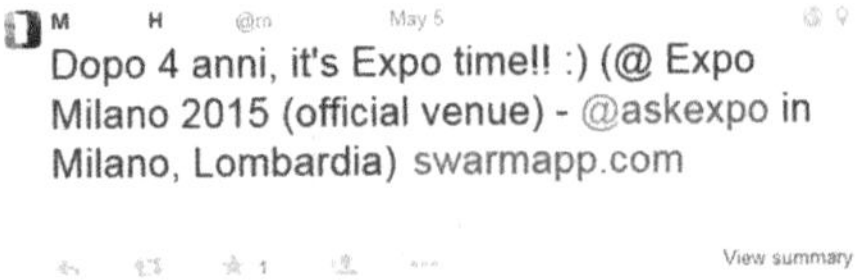

M   H   @m   May 5
Dopo 4 anni, it's Expo time!! :) (@ Expo
Milano 2015 (official venue) - @askexpo in
Milano, Lombardia) swarmapp.com

View summary

Fig. 5. Tweet of a Spanish traveler.

note that Spanish travelers concentrate their tweets mainly in the area of Milan
and beyond.

Moreover, some travelers that posted these tweets arrived in Lombardy after
EXPO started. For example, in Fig. 5 we report a tweet posted by a Spanish
traveler in which the writer talks about EXPO 2015.

Figure 6, that represents the *Path* dimension, shows the full trip of the same
Spanish traveler, that is, his/her route in Lombardy region. It is possible to note
two interesting things. The first one is that the traveler posted his/her tweets
mainly in the city of Milan. The second one is pushpin 5, that represents the post
reported in Fig. 5; the pushpin shows that the traveler was actually in EXPO
2015 area.

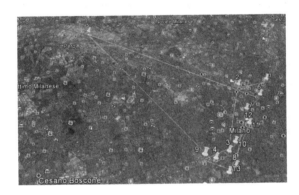

Fig. 6. Path of one traveler.

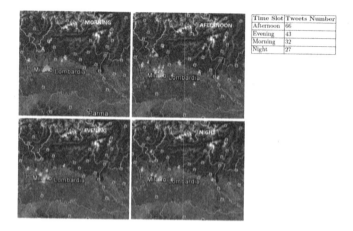

Time Slot	Tweets Number
Afternoon	66
Evening	43
Morning	32
Night	27

Fig. 7. Tweets distribution in time slots.

Finally, Fig. 7 represents the distribution of tweets with respect to the four Daylight Time Slots defined in Sect. 2 and, moreover, represents the *Time Slots* dimension. It is possible to note how the distribution of tweets is geographically more sparse in the Afternoon than in the others time slots, where the tweets are concentrated in the Milan area. There are many reasons that explain this behavior, but one possible cause of this is that the travelers have their base in city of Milan and prefer to visit the Lombardy area after lunch.

5 Conclusions and Future Work

As stated at the beginning, tourists are an important asset for the economy of the regions they visit. In particular, for public administrations is very useful to understand how tourists travel on the region they govern.

Therefore, in this work, we developed an original approach that permits to follow traveling *Twitter* users by tracking their geo-located messages they post on *Twitter* during their trips. Tools in the *FollowMe* suite generate several outputs for the result set of reconstructed trips, so that several analysis dimensions (*Time Slot, Origin Airport, Path*) can be exploited to analyze results.

As far as future work is concerned, we have to consider that the project is only at the beginning steps. The main efforts will be devoted to connect with other social networks and gather posts from them. This way, we should obtain a wider spectrum of information, by integrating several sources of information. For this purpose, the main problem is that users use different ids on different social networks, so the hardest, yet exciting challenge, will be to find techniques to recognize different ids belonging to the same user.

References

1. Bora, N., Chang, Y.-H., Maheswaran, R.: Mobility patterns and user dynamics in racially segregated geographies of US cities. In: Kennedy, W.G., Agarwal, N., Yang, S.J. (eds.) SBP 2014. LNCS, vol. 8393, pp. 11–18. Springer, Heidelberg (2014)

2. Cuzzocrea, A.: Analytics over big data: Exploring the convergence of dataware-housing, OLAP and data-intensive cloud infrastructures. In: 37th Annual IEEE Computer Software and Applications Conference, COMPSAC 2013, Kyoto, Japan, 22–26 July 2013, pp. 481–483 (2013)

3. Cuzzocrea, A.: Big data mining or turning data mining into predictive analytics from large-scale 3Vs data: the future challenge for knowledge discovery. In: Ait Ameur, Y., Bellatreche, L., Papadopoulos, G.A. (eds.) MEDI 2014. LNCS, vol. 8748, pp. 4–8. Springer, Heidelberg (2014)

4. Cuzzocrea, A., Bellatreche, L., Song, I.-Y.: Data warehousing and OLAP over big data: current challenges and future research directions. In: Proceedings of the Sixteenth International Workshop on Data Warehousing and OLAP, DOLAP 2013, San Francisco, CA, USA, 28 October 2013, pp. 67–70 (2013)

5. Cuzzocrea, A., Saccà, D., Ullman, J.D.: Big data: a research agenda. In: 17th International Database Engineering & Applications Symposium, IDEAS 2013, Barcelona, Spain, 09–11 October 2013, pp. 198–203 (2013)

6. Cuzzocrea, A., Song, I.-Y.: Big graph analytics: The state of the art and future research agenda. In: Proceedings of the 17th International Workshop on Data Warehousing and OLAP, DOLAP 2014, Shanghai, China, 3–7 November 2014, pp. 99–101 (2014)

7. Grabovitch, I., Kanza, Y., Kravi, E., Pat, B.: On the correlation between textual content and geospatial locations in microblogs. In: GeoRich 2014, Snowbird, Utah (USA), 23 June 2014, June 2014

8. Hawelka, B., Sitko, I., Beinat, E., Sobolevsky, S., Kazakopoulos, P., Ratti, C.: Geo-located twitter as proxy for global mobility patterns. Cartography Geogr. Inf. Sci. **41**(1), 260–271 (2014)

9. Lee, R., Sumiya, K.: Measuring geographical regularities of crowd behaviors for twitter-based geo-social event detection. In: ACM LBSN 2010, San Jose, CA, (USA), November 2010

10. Stephens, M., Poorthuis, A.: Follow thy neighbor: connecting the social and the spatial networks on Twitter. Comput. Environ. Urban Syst. **41**(1) (2014). doi:10.1016/j.compenvurbsys.2014.07.002

11. Walther, M., Kaisser, M.: Geo-spatial event detection in the twitter stream. In: Serdyukov, P., Braslavski, P., Kuznetsov, S.O., Kamps, J., Rüger, S., Agichtein, E., Segalovich, I., Yilmaz, E. (eds.) ECIR 2013. LNCS, vol. 7814, pp. 356–367. Springer, Heidelberg (2013)

12. Widener, M., Li, W.: Using geolocated twitter data to monitor the prevalence of healthy and unhealthy food references across the us. Appl. Geogr. **54**, 189–197 (2014)

Requirement and Systems Engineering

Understanding User Requirements Iceberg: Semantic Based Approach

Zouhir Djilani[1](✉) and Selma Khouri[1,2]

[1] LIAS/ISAE-ENSMA, Poitiers University, Poitiers, France
[2] National High School of Computer Science, Algiers, Algeria
{djilaniz,khouris}@ensma.fr

Abstract. The proliferation of extended enterprises requires softwares to support heterogeneous and autonomous users partners' sub-systems. In this context, early studies have neglected *users requirements* definition step in the development process, which was considered as the cause of a large failure rate of the developed softwares. To address this deficiency, considerable research has been devoted to software development life-cycle by adding a new phase called *users requirement collection and analysis*, which delivers the requirements document ($\mathcal{RD}$). However, in the context of Global Information System ($\mathcal{GIS}$), the grouping of partners $\mathcal{RD}$s in one global $\mathcal{RD}$ suffers from three drawbacks: the unification of vocabularies including the used *terms* and *concepts* (universe of discourse) and the unification of the used *formalisms*. Additionally, relationships between requirements must be efficiently defined and identified. We propose in this paper a complete requirements framework that manages the cited issues, offering a scalable approach for $\mathcal{RD}$ definition in the context of $\mathcal{GIS}$ development. The feasibility and effectiveness of the approach is tested using $\mathcal{LUBM}$ (http://swat.cse.lehigh.edu/projects/lubm/) ontology benchmark, *EuroWordnet* (http://www.illc.uva.nl/EuroWordNet/) and the courses management system ($\mathcal{CMS}$) (http://wwwhome.cs.utwente.nl/~goknila/sosym/) requirements document.

Keywords: Information system · Requirements engineering · Ontology

1 Introduction

Nowadays, the proliferation of extended enterprises which can be geographically distributed contribute to the emergence of Global Information Systems ($\mathcal{GIS}$) in several fields like scientific research, trade, business, etc. The development of ($\mathcal{GIS}$) requires a thorough analysis of *users' requirements* ($\mathcal{UR}$) at the local and the global level. This analysis is performed based on $\mathcal{UR}$ of different partners and actors of the project, which may have different skills and trainings. Consequently, this situation leads to heterogeneous requirements that influence the construction of the $\mathcal{GIS}$. Unfortunately, most important studies related to $\mathcal{UR}$ analysis for $\mathcal{GIS}$ consider $\mathcal{UR}$ as a black box that provides a *uniform* set

© Springer International Publishing Switzerland 2015
L. Bellatreche and Y. Manolopoulos (Eds.): MEDI 2015, LNCS 9344, pp. 297–310, 2015.
DOI: 10.1007/978-3-319-23781-7_24

of requirements. To overcome the integration issue in software systems, various efforts proposed integration techniques and approaches of data, applications and platforms. Less effort has been made for $\mathcal{UR}$ integration. $\mathcal{UR}$ integration represents a real challenging issue in industry, where several partners interacts. Each partner expresses his requirements in a local *Requirement Document* ($\mathcal{RD}$) using his own *terms* (the jargon), his own *formalism* (the modeling language) and has his own *concepts* (universe of discourse). This issue is actually observed in $\mathcal{GIS}$s of big companies with whom our laboratory[1] is collaborating like Airbus airplanes construction company and Areva nuclear company. A large number of studies point out a high failure rate in operational implementations of $\mathcal{GIS}$, due to the lack of $\mathcal{UR}$ understanding [4]. Some attempts have been made to address requirements integration issue in software engineering applications [5,9,15], but no comprehensive solution has been found so far to manages the three levels of heterogeneity cited. Furthermore, few attention is paid for pairing requirements with other requirements [6].

The fact that the heterogeneity of $\mathcal{UR}$ is due to the diversity of their owners (they are expressed by different partners), requirements integration can easily borrow a solutions used to integrate a $\mathcal{GIS}$ project which concerns the data sources. Integrating data sources has been largely studied in the 90's, and several projects propose to use ontologies to explicit their sense and then facilitate their integration. Two main types of ontologies are used [2]: (i) *MultiLingual Ontologies* ($\mathcal{LO}$) used to define the lexical meaning of terms that appear in a given domain, and relationships between terms such as *synonym* or *antonym*. *MultiWordnet*, *EuroWordNet*,..etc. are a well-known examples of such ontologies. (ii) *Conceptual Ontologies* ($\mathcal{CO}$) used to define concepts of a domain. A concept may be associated with different terms in the $\mathcal{LO}$ layer. Two main ontological concepts are distinguished [7]: canonical concepts (primitive) and non-canonical concepts (defined), which use expression languages in their definition. These ontology layers can be seen as the $\mathcal{GIS}$ global dictionary, where each designer picks her/his terms and concepts. Another characteristic of conceptual ontology is their capability of reasoning that can be used to identify conflicts and inconsistencies in requirements. These two types of ontologies have been usually used in isolation way for data sources integration. If we perform a finer analysis of requirements integration, we can identify two components: a used vocabulary (which is similar to the concepts and proprieties in the context of source integration), a used modeling language (which is equivalent to the physical models of data sources: relational model, XML, etc.), the expression language (equivalent to the query language). In this situation, the use of conceptual ontologies will contribute in unifying the used concepts, whereas the multilingual ones contributes on expressing requirements in a uniform an multilingual way.

In this paper, we propose an approach (illustrated in Fig. 1) which provides a uniform, integrated and consistent set of $\mathcal{UR}$ through: (1) the unification of vocabularies (terms and concepts) and formalisms heterogeneities, (2) the automatic identification of direct and indirect requirements relationships, (3) the

---

[1] http://www.lias-lab.fr/?lang=en.

definition of a reasoning system on requirements to identify hidden relationships, and to provide a consistent $\mathcal{RD}$. This paper is organized in five sections: Sect. 2 presents related works of our study. Sect. 3 provides a detailed description of our approach. Each step is formally defined and illustrated. Section 4 evaluates the performances of our approach. Section 5 summarizes our contributions and sketches some perspectives.

2 Related Work

Several studies in requirements engineering community tried to deal with the main difficulty of unifying partners $\mathcal{RD}$ in one global $\mathcal{RD}$, that we classified in three categories: (1) Studies that unify requirements formalism in one global formalism, using model driven engineering approaches [5,11]; (2) Studies that propose to eliminate semantic and syntactic conflicts by giving a formal specification of requirements using: ontological approaches in requirement specification or reasoning [9,10,15], mathematical specification of requirements [5]. The majority of these studies treat semantic and syntactic conflicts, but they ignore the heterogeneity of modeling languages and formalisms; (3) Studies that use reasoning techniques to identify requirements relationships and check their consistency. These studies use mathematical frameworks [3] or model driven approaches [13]. In these studies, relationships among requirements are often inadequately captured and are often limited to binary relations, and requirement conflicts are identified too late or not at all. Additionally, the scheduling and containment relationships between requirements are ignored. In our approach, requirements have a complete and unique representation. Different types of conflicts are eliminated. Requirements relationships are semantically and formally defined and new relationships can be inferred. We believe that our approach satisfies all requirements qualities required for software systems: *completeness*, *correctness*, *consistency* and *non − redundancy*. As illustrated in Fig. 1, the approach covers all the stages of requirements definition phase.

3 Proposed Approach

Before detailing our approach, some hypotheses related to global enterprises are needed. Each partner involved in the $\mathcal{GIS}$ has its own designers team, that defines his requirements in a local $\mathcal{RD}$ using his proper vocabulary (terms and concepts) and modeling language. Developing a $\mathcal{GIS}$ requires one validate global $\mathcal{RD}$ that contains all partners $\mathcal{RD}s$. Our approach is based on the hypothesis of the existence of : a domain ontology ($\mathcal{DO}$) that defines the domain of interest and a multilingual Ontology ($\mathcal{LO}$), that consensually defines all terms used in the $\mathcal{GIS}$. This hypothesis is weakened by the development of several large ontologies in various domains. We illustrate our approach using $\mathcal{LUBM}$ domain ontology and *EuroWordNet* multilingual ontology. In parallel, each partner has its own requirements formalism, eg. UML use case, Goal formalism, etc. A pivot model in second defined to unify all partners formalisms. Our scenario allows

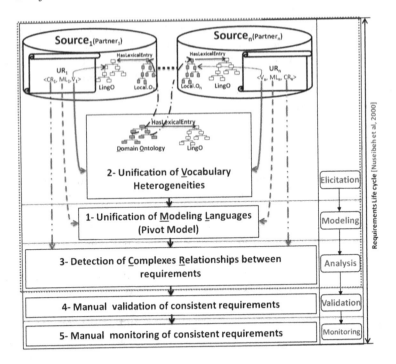

Fig. 1. Approach steps

each partner to define his local $\mathcal{RD}$ using his own vocabulary (Fig. 1). The $\mathcal{LO}$ plays the role of the $\mathcal{GIS}$ dictionary, and each partner chooses the most relevant terms that defines his local requirements. Each requirement terms correspond to a set of concepts in the $\mathcal{DO}$, where the local ontology $LocalO$ can be extracted from the $\mathcal{DO}$ to define formally each partner local requirements, and to unify the universe of discourse used by partners. The pivot model is connected to the ontologies meta-models and the multilingual model adopted by the general lexi-con $EuroWordnet$ (Fig. 2). The relationships between requirements are modeled using the $\mathcal{DO}$, $\mathcal{LO}$ and the precedence graph ($\mathcal{PG}$). Where in our case, the $\mathcal{PG}$ give the possibility to modeled a specific two types of relationships: require-ments that *require* the achievement of other requirements, and requirements that *contain* other requirements. To identify all requirements relationships and check their consistency, we have proposed an semi-automatic reasoning tool. The details of the approach are explained in what follows:

3.1   Unification of Formalisms

As explained previously, each partner formalizes his requirements with his own modeling language using informal, semi-formal or formal formalisms. We have proposed in [1] pivot model, which is defined to integrate three semi-formal widespread formalisms: UML use case formalism, goal oriented formalism and process-oriented formalism (we chose the treatment conceptual model of the French methodology Merise). In the first version of our pivot model, each requirement is defined by: *Actions*, *Results* and *criterion*. We noticed that this formalization does not allow the definition of all requirements details, which are necessary to have a unique requirement representation. In order to remedy this shortcoming, we proposed an enriched pivot model ($\mathcal{EPM}$) as illustrated in Fig. 2 (part "pivot Model"). We formalize mathematically our $\mathcal{EPM}$ as follows: $Pivot_{model}$:$<Actor, Requirement, Relationships>$, in which:

- $Actor = \{act_1, act_2, .., act_N\}$, a set of actors who interact with the system. We distinguish two actor types: it can be an actor who defines the requirement (*actor system*) or an actor in the requirement (*subject*). An actor can be a person, a company unit or an autonomous system.
- $Requirement = \{Req_1, Req_2, ..., Req_n\}$, requirements expressed by an actor. We define a Req_i by the quadruplet: $< TASK, R, C, T >$, such as:
  - $TASK = \{task_1, task_2, ..., task_m\}$, a set of tasks that a requirement performs. Each $task_i = < Subject, Action, Object >$, where:
    * *Subject*: is an actor who uses the requirement to achieve a result ;
    * *Action*: is an action represented by a verb that a system performs to yield to an observable result;
    * *Object*: is the concept (mental or physical) concerned by the requirement action (verb);
  - $R = \{r_1, r_2, ..., r_p\}$: is the results realized by the system;
  - $C = \{c_1, c_2, ..., c_k\}$: a set of criteria which quantify a result;
  - T: type of requirements, in our case $T \in \{ Goal, Usecase, Treatment \}$.
- $Relationships = \{relation_1, .., relation_n\}$, set of relationships between requirements. For each $relation_i \in Relationships$, $relation_i \in \{ Equal, Contain, Refine, Require, Conflictswith, partiallyRefine, Include, Extend, NOT, AND, OR \}$.

For instance, the parsing of Req_{17} from the $\mathcal{CMS}$ requirements document: "The system shall allow students to create teams" with our $\mathcal{EPM}$, defines: *create* as the *Action*, *students* as the *subject*, *teams* as the *object*, no result and no criterion is defined. The transformation of the input requirements model to the pivot model is automatic and is fully described in [1].

3.2   Unification of Vocabularies

Unification of Vocabularies: is defined by the unification of terms and concepts involved in the $\mathcal{UR}$:

a- Unification of Terms: In the $\mathcal{GIS}$, partners $\mathcal{RD}s$ are often defined in natural language. They contain terms that may have similar or opposite meanings in the same or different languages, which generates vocabulary heterogeneous. To explain the lexical meaning of terms heterogeneities let's take the same requirements Req_{97} and $Req_{97'}$ defined in above. The parsing of Req_{97} and $Req_{97'}$ with our $\mathcal{EPM}$ gives that, the two requirements are different but in reality the fulfillment of the two requirements have the same influence in the $\mathcal{GIS}$, so they have no result, no criterion but they have respectively an *equal* tasks: $\mathcal{TASK} = \{ < \text{administration, manage, courses} > \}$, $\mathcal{TASK} = \{ < \text{administration, gérer, cours}> \}$.

In order to resolve heterogeneity of terms, $\mathcal{UR}$ are projected on the $\mathcal{LO}$. Each partner chooses or picks her requirements terms (structured using the pivot model) from the $\mathcal{LO}$. The $\mathcal{DO}$ layer is linked to the $\mathcal{LO}$ where each concept of $\mathcal{DO}$ may correspond to a set of terms in $\mathcal{LO}$ [2]. This is illustrated in Fig. 2 by the link between the pivot model, the conceptual ontology meta-model and the $\mathcal{LO}$ model. The links between a $\mathcal{LO}$ and a $\mathcal{DO}$ are used in different projects like multilingual model adopted by *EuroWordNet* [12,16] and the Linguistic Information Repository (LIR) [14]. After eliminating vocabulary(lexical meaning) conflicts using the LO, the parsing of requirements Req_{97} and $Req_{97'}$ using our framework (Fig. 2) deduces that the two requirements are *equal*.

b- Unification of Concepts (Universe of Discourse): In the $\mathcal{GIS}$, partners can define their requirements using their own specific concepts defining the universe of discourse. This situation leads to various conflicts between partners requirements: semantic conflicts (naming, Scaling, objects representation, Confounding or context); syntactic conflicts (data types and representation). As example, let's take the following requirements from the $\mathcal{CMS}$ document which are collected from two different partners participating in the same $\mathcal{GIS}$ (Req_{97}: *England Partner*; $Req_{97'}$: *French Partner*):

- Req_{97}: The system shall allow only the administration to manage courses.
- $Req_{97'}$: Le systéme doit permettre uniquement a l'administration de gérer les cours.

This requirement can be defined by two partners that participate in the same $\mathcal{GIS}$ differently. As instance, the concepts: *Course* defined by proprieties (ID, $Name$, $DateCreat$) by $Partner_1$ and *Cours* defined by proprieties (ID, Nom, $DatCreat$) by $Partner_2$. This representation presents a naming conflicts between the two concepts *Course* and *Cours*, We use the domain ontology to identify these types of conflicts.

The domain ontology is composed of concepts which belong to part of the world, it is defined as a conceptual ontology that contains the concepts of a given domain. For example, the $SNOMED$ ontology could be considered as the medical domain ontology. They are extensively used to eliminate these kind of conflicts [1,9]. We propose in our approach the use a domain ontology ($\mathcal{DO}$) as a shared ontology. As explained previously, each term in the $\mathcal{LO}$ layer is linked to its corresponding concepts in the $\mathcal{DO}$ layer. Each partner can thus extract his own $LocalO$ that allows partners to formally define their requirements. This extraction can be achieved automatically. In order to eliminate this requirements heterogeneities, we connect our $\mathcal{EPM}$ with the domain ontology elements (*Classes*, *Individual*, *Proprieties*). Consequently, the use of a sharing

$\mathcal{DO}$ eliminates concepts conflicts and unifies their definition between the $\mathcal{GIS}$ partners.

In our approach, each partner $\mathcal{RD}$ is formally defined by a *LocalO* extracted as a module from $\mathcal{DO}$. Ontology modularity is a well-known issue in ontology engineering field, where an ontology is extracted from a given ontology using a *signature*. In our approach, the signature corresponds to the set of local terms of the multilingual ontology used for defining local requirements. Three extraction scenarios are possible: (1) *LocalO* $\subseteq \mathcal{DO}$: The $\mathcal{DO}$ contain all concepts and proprieties of the *LocalO*, (2) *LocalO* $\supseteq \mathcal{DO}$: *LocalO* contains all $\mathcal{DO}$ concepts and proprieties, (3) *LocalO* $= \mathcal{DO}$: The *LocalO* contain exactly the $\mathcal{DO}$ concepts and proprieties. This is illustrated in Fig. 2 by the link between the pivot model and the $\mathcal{DO}$ meta-model. The $\mathcal{DO}$ model is inspired from $\mathcal{OWL}$ meta-model (the W3C standard for defining ontologies).

3.3 Detection of Requirements Relationships

Once the set of requirements unified (i.e. formalism, vocabulary and concepts conflicts are eliminated), it is possible to reason on requirements in order to extract hidden relationships between them. These relationships are defined in our proposed framework formalization as: $OntoDLPivot_{model}:< \mathcal{DO}, \mathcal{LO}, Pivot_{model} >$where:

- $Pivot_{model} :< Actor, Requirement, Relationships >$, represent our $\mathcal{EPM}$;
- *Relationships*: will be defined as $Relationships = \{relation_1, .., relation_n\}$, set of requirements relations. For each $relation_i \in Relationships$, $relation_i \in 2^R$. R is a set of *roles* defined from $\mathcal{DO}$ and $\mathcal{LO}$ proprieties.

a- Requirements Relationships in Literature: In the Requirement Engineer ($\mathcal{RE}$) community, the informal definition of requirements relationships that existed in literature [5], are presented bellow: Let $(R_1, R_2, .. R_n)$ set of requirements:

- Equal Relation: R_1 equal to R_2, if the fulfillment of R_1 have the same influence for the system as the fulfillment of R_2, and vice-versa;
- Conflicts Relation: R_1 conflicts with R_2, if the fulfillment of R_1 excludes the fulfillment of R_2 and vice versa;
- Contain Relation: R_1 contains $R_2,..., R_n$, if $R_2,..., R_n$ are parts of the whole R_1(part-whole hierarchy);
- Refine Relation: R_1 refines R_2, if R_1 is derived from R_2 by adding more details to its properties;
- Partially refine Relation: $R1$ *partially refines* R_2, if R_1 is derived from R_2 by adding more details to properties of R_2 and excluding the unrefined properties of R_2;
- Require Relation: R_1 requires R_2, if R_1 is fulfilled only when R_2 is fulfilled. The *require* relation can be seen as a precondition for the requiring requirement.

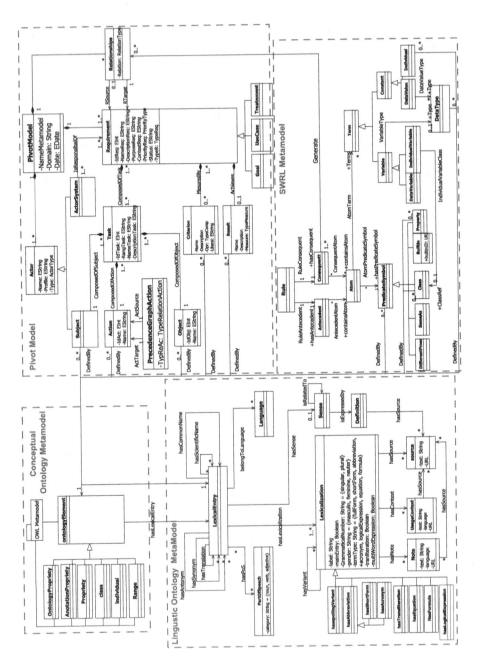

Fig. 2. Linking pivot model, $\mathcal{SWRL}$, conceptual and multilingual ontologies meta-models

b- Formalization of Scheduling and Contain Relationships: Two types of relationships that require special attention: *contain* and *require* relationships. Our proposed framework must be capable of representing scheduling and containment between requirements. We have thus enriched our proposed framework by the *PrecedenceGraphAction* class (Fig. 2), that defines relationships (*contain*, *require*) between requirements actions. Our approach includes the possibility to formalize the scheduling and the containment between two requirements using a precedence graph ($\mathcal{PG}$). The $\mathcal{PG}$ is a grammar graph, defined as $(\mathcal{A}, \mathcal{U})$, where:

- $\mathcal{A} = \{a_1, a_2 \dots a_n\}$ is the set of nodes that represent in our case a set of *actions* (verb) that define tasks in requirements;
- $\mathcal{U} = \{u_1, u_2, \dots, u_n\}$ represent the edges that represent the precedences constraints (*ContainAction*, *RequireAction*) between actions. As instance, there is an edge from a_i to a_j if the *action* of a_i have a precedence constraint with *action* of a_j. In our work $\mathcal{U} = \{ContainAction, RequireAction\}$.

Our requirements framework is extended after linking the $\mathcal{PG}$ model as follows: $PGOntoDLPivot_{model} :< \mathcal{DO}, \mathcal{LO}, \mathcal{PG}, Pivot_{model} >$: The $\mathcal{DO}$ and $\mathcal{LO}$ represent respectively the domain and multilingual ontologies; the $Pivot_{model} :<$ *Actor, Requirement, Relationships* $>$, where *Relationships* represent the set of Relationships that are defined from the $\mathcal{DO}$, $\mathcal{LO}$ and $\mathcal{PG}$. As example let's take the following requirements:

Req_{97}: The system shall allow only the administration to manage courses;
Req_{99}: The system shall allow only the administration to delete courses;
$Req_{99'}$: The system shall enable only the administration to create courses.

Based on our framework, we can identify that : the two requirements Req_{97} and $Req_{99'}$ have a contain relationships between *manage* and *delete* actions. Consequently, the fulfillment of Req_{97} contain the fulfillment of $Req_{99'}$. So we can conclude that Req_{99} *contain* $Req_{99'}$. If we take the example of the two requirements $Req_{99'}$ and Req_{99} defined in above, in the same manner, we can deduce that $Req_{99'}$ *require* Req_{99}. We show in the next section that this formalization is useful for reasoning on requirements in order to identify hidden relationships between them.

c- Reasoning Process. We extend our framework by a reasoning model that allows: an automatic identification of direct and indirect requirements relationships, automatic identification of direct and indirect requirements relationships, automatic check the consistency of identified and inferencing relationships. Note that each requirement in the $\mathcal{EPM}$ is defined as follows: $Req_i =< TASK, R, C, T >, 1 \leq i \leq n$, where $TASK, R, C$ and T, represent respectively a set of tasks, results, criterion and types of Req_i.

In our approach, the connection between the requirements and the ontology models allows the definition of each requirement *semantically* by a set of *ontological concepts* used for defining the requirements (from $\mathcal{DO}$). This set of concepts is called the *domain* of the requirement, it is defined as follows: Domain(Req_i)= Domain ($\mathcal{TASK}$) $\cup$ Domain ($\mathcal{C}$), where:

- Domain($\mathcal{TASK}$) = { Domain($task_1$) $\cup$ .. $\cup$ Domain($task_m$) } a set of tasks that define the requirements Req_i where, $task_m$ =< $Subject_m$, $Action_m$, $Object_m$ >, then we define the Domain($task_m$) = Domain($Subject_m$) $\cup$ Domain($Action_m$) $\cup$ Domain($Object_m$);
- Domain ($\mathcal{C}$)= { $c_1 \wedge .. \wedge c_k$ };

We defined reasoning rules for each type of requirements relationships (direct and indirect) and check their consistency. These relationships are formalized using $\mathcal{SWRL}$ language in our framework. $\mathcal{SWRL}$ meta-model extends thus our proposed model in Fig. 2. We explain bellow the different types of rules that we defined in order to provide our tool the possibility to automatically reason on requirements and detect relationships between them:

- Identification rules: this semantic formalization allows to automatically identify complex relationships. As instance, *Equal* relationship is identified using the following rule: let Req_1, Req_2 be requirements; Req_1 equal to Req_2 if: (1) $\wedge$ (2) is true, where: (1)- ((Domain($Subject_i$) $sameAs$ Domain($Subject_j$)) $\vee$ (Domain($Subject_i$) $similarTo$ Domain($Subject_j$)))$\wedge$ ((Domain($Object_i$) $sameAs$ Domain($Object_j$)) $\vee$ (Domain($Object_i$) $similarTo$ Domain($Object_j$))) $\wedge$ ((Domain($Action_i$) $sameAs$ Domain($Action_j$)) $\vee$ (Domain($Action_i$) $similarTo$ Domain($Action_j$))), where ($i, j \geq 1$); (2)- ($\forall c_i \in$ Domain(C) of Req_i, $\forall c_j \in$ Domain(C) of Req_j) : (c_i equal c_j)) where ($i, j \geq 1$).
- Inferencing rules: the automatic inferencing process consists in deriving new relations based on the complexes relations that the ($\mathcal{RE}$) defined. We give an example of inferencing rules by transitivity relations: Let requirements Req_1, Req_2, Req_3, if $refine(Req_1, Req_2) \wedge refines(Req_2, Req_3)$ then, $refine(Req_1, Req_3)$.
- Consistency checking rules: our system has additionally the possibility to automatically identify among existing relationships, those that cause a contradiction. As instance, let Req_1, Req_2 be requirements, if $equal\ (Req_1, Req_2) \wedge conflict\ (Req_1, Req_2)$, then Req_1, Req_2 having a consistency problem.

3.4 Manual Validation of Requirements

After the detection of complexes relationships the global designer can analyses the complex relationships (identified, inferenced and checked), then validate the consistent requirements and eliminate the inconsistent requirements. This validation aims to provide a $\mathcal{RD}$ of quality. The global designer can manually use relationships in order to delete or neglect some redundant requirements from the $\mathcal{RD}$ (equal or contained ones). As instance, let R_i and R_j be requirements: (1) if R_i $refine/PartiallyRefine$ R_j, the designer can keep R_j and eliminate R_i; (2) if R_i equal R_j, the designer can keep one of the two requirements and eliminate the other one; (3) if R_i contain R_j, the designer can keep R_i and eliminate R_j; (4) if R_i in $conflicts$ with R_j, the designer must choose one of the two

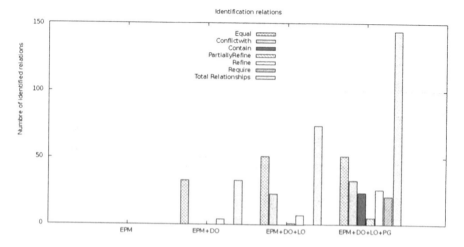

Fig. 3. Relations detected in each formalism.

requirements by defining a strategy of elimination. As instance, a requirement has a priority attribute, which can be used to eliminate requirements having the lowest priority. (5) if R_i *require* R_j, the designer must consider requirements scheduling (R_j first then R_i in second).

3.5 Monitoring of the Consistent Requirements

In the $\mathcal{RE}$ life cycle the last step in treatment of user requirements is the monitoring step, it gives the actual situation of requirements (proposed, Realized, analyzed, accepted, rejected, replaced). In our work, we propose to realize this step manually by the global designer, who can monitor the set of requirements during the DW design-life cycle.

4 Performance Evaluation

Our environment is implemented using *Protégé* framework[2], a free open-source ontology editor, which is strongly supported by the developers and academic communities. We have used: (1) the Lehigh University BenchMark ($\mathcal{LUBM}$) ontology [8], as the $\mathcal{DO}$. The ontology is formalized in $\mathcal{OWL}$ language; (2) the plug-in ProSé[3] for ontology modularity in order to extract *LocalO* from the $\mathcal{DO}$; (3) 100 requirements from $\mathcal{CMS}$ requirements document, defined in different formalisms : goal-oriented (35), Merise (25) and UseCase (40); (4) the *Eclipse* plug-in, *ATLAS Transformation Language* (ATL)[4], to describe mapping rules from sources requirements models to the target pivot requirements

---

[2] http://protege.stanford.edu/.

[3] http://krono.act.uji.es/people/Ernesto/safety-ontology-reuse.

[4] http://www.eclipse.org/atl/.

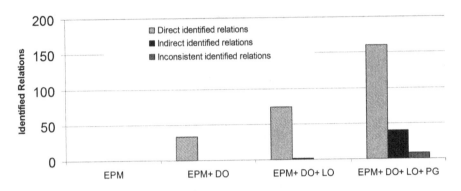

Fig. 4. Identified and inconsistency relations.

model; (5) and (*EuroWordNet*) multilingual ontology. We then extended the $\mathcal{OWL}$ meta model of $\mathcal{LUBM}$ ontology by our defined pivot model, multilingual model then by the $\mathcal{PG}$ model. Our reasoning system uses $Jess$[5] rule engine. The effectiveness of our approach is tested on the following aspects: (i) the rate of requirements relations detected; (ii) the execution time and (iii) the scalability of the approach. The experiments are executed in a workstation with $Intel(R)$ processor, $Core(TM)$i7-4770 CPU 3,40 GHz, 8 GB of RAM, under the operating system $Windows$ 7 $professional$ 64 bits. Figures 3 and 4, demonstrate that our proposed framework formalization ($\mathcal{EPM}$ connected to $\mathcal{DO}$,LO and $\mathcal{PG}$) identifies more requirements relationships compared to a conventional requirements analysis approach, and our proposed reasoning system is executed in several steps. The scalability and execution time aspects are verified by reasoning on 20 sets s_1, s_{20} of requirements, where the size of each set $s_i, 1 =< i <= 20$ is 5*i requirements. Figure 5 shows that our approach is executed in a reasonable time and can scale.

5   Conclusion

In this study, we defined a complete requirements framework that: unifies vocabularies(terms and concepts) and formalisms heterogeneity and identifies various requirements relationships at the intentional and extensional levels. For managing the formalism heterogeneity, we have defined the *pivot model*, that allows an easy transition from partners' $\mathcal{RD}$s to a formal specification in the global $\mathcal{RD}$. For managing lexical, syntactic and semantic heterogeneities, we hypothesize the availability of a *multilingual ontology* and a *domain ontology* that each partner designer can reference to extract his own local ontology. Concerning the relationships between requirements, we use: (i) the multilingual ontology (*EuroWordNet*) that extracts the *disambiguation, synonyms* and *antonyms* relations between requirements components and also increase their

---

[5] http://www.jessrules.com.

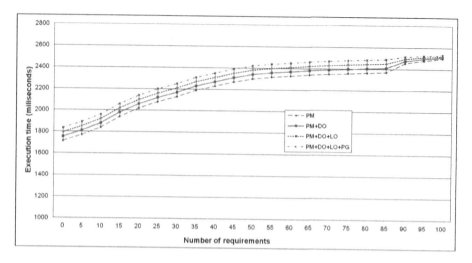

Fig. 5. Scalability and execution time.

linguistic expressiveness; (ii) the Precedence graph to detect the *scheduling* and *containment* between requirements; (iii) a reasoning system which is able to automatically deduce direct and indirect requirements relationships as well as their consistency checking. As perspectives, this approach still needs to be tested on large $\mathcal{RD}s$ and to measure the impact of requirements evolution on the $\mathcal{GIS}$ design architecture. We also intend to *manage (delete, update, insert)* automatically requirements and monitoring of requirements in time by exploring the reasoning results.

References

1. Boukhari, I., Bellatreche, L., Jean, S.: An ontological pivot model to interoperate heterogeneous user requirements. In: Margaria, T., Steffen, B. (eds.) ISoLA 2012, Part II. LNCS, vol. 7610, pp. 344–358. Springer, Heidelberg (2012)
2. Fankam, C., Jean, S., Pierra, G., Bellatreche, L., Ameur, Y.A.: Towards connecting database applications to ontologies. In: First International Conference on Advances in Databases, Knowledge, and Data Applications, 2009, DBKDA 2009, pp. 131–137. IEEE (2009)
3. Giorgini, P., Mylopoulos, J., Nicchiarelli, E., Sebastiani, R.: Formal reasoning techniques for goal models. In: Spaccapietra, S., March, S., Aberer, K. (eds.) Journal On Data Semantics I. LNCS, vol. 2800, pp. 1–20. Springer, Heidelberg (2003)
4. Giorgini, P., Rizzi, S., Garzetti, M.: Goal-oriented requirement analysis for data warehouse design. In: Proceedings of the 8th ACM International Workshop on Data warehousing and OLAP, pp. 47–56. ACM (2005)
5. Goknil, A., Kurtev, I., van den Berg, K., Veldhuis, J.-W.: Semantics of trace relations in requirements models for consistency checking and inferencing. Soft. Syst. Model. **10**(1), 31–54 (2011)

6. Gotel, O.C., Finkelstein, A.C.: An analysis of the requirements traceability problem. In: Proceedings of the First International Conference on Requirements Engineering, 1994, pp. 94–101. IEEE (1994)

7. Gruber, T.R.: A translation approach to portable ontology specifications. Knowl. Acquisition 5(2), 199–220 (1993)

8. Guo, Y., Pan, Z., Heflin, J.: Lubm: a benchmark for owl knowledge base systems. Web Semant. Sci. Serv. Agents World Wide Web 3(2), 158–182 (2005)

9. Kaiya, H., Saeki, M.: Ontology based requirements analysis: lightweight semantic processing approach. In: Quality Software (QSIC 2005), pp.223-230. IEEE (2005)

10. Körner, S.J., Brumm, T.: Natural language specification improvement with ontologies. Int. J. Semant. Comput. 3(04), 445–470 (2009)

11. López, O., Laguna, M.A., Peñalvo, F.J.G.: Metamodeling for requirements reuse. In: WER, pp. 76–90 (2002)

12. Montiel-Ponsoda, E., Aguado de Cea, G., Gómez-Pérez, A., Peters, W.: Modelling multilinguality in ontologies (2008)

13. Perrouin, G., Brottier, E., Baudry, B., Le Traon, Y.: Composing models for detecting inconsistencies: a requirements engineering perspective. In: Glinz, M., Heymans, P. (eds.) REFSQ 2009 Amsterdam. LNCS, vol. 5512, pp. 89–103. Springer, Heidelberg (2009)

14. Peters, W., Montiel-Ponsoda, E., Aguado de Cea, G., Gómez-Pérez, A.: Localizing ontologies in owl (2007)

15. Saeki, M., Hayashi, S., Kaiya, H.: A tool for attributed goal-oriented requirements analysis. In: ASE, pp. 674–676 (2009)

16. Vossen, P., Bloksma, L., Rodriguez, H., Climent, S., Calzolari, N., Roventini, A., Bertagna, F., Alonge, A.: The eurowordnet base concepts and top ontology. Deliverable D017 D **34**, D036 (1998)

User Stories and Parameterized Role Based Access Control

Ścibor Sobieski$^{(\boxtimes)}$ and Bartosz Zieliński

Department of Computer Science, Faculty of Physics and Applied Informatics,
University of Łódź, Ul. Pomorska nr 149/153, 90-236 Łódź, Poland
{scibor,bzielinski}@uni.lodz.pl

Abstract. There are two established techniques for describing user requirements: User Stories and Use Cases. In this paper we describe a new semi-formalized, constrained natural language format for user stories. The format uses variables to correlate precisely various parts of the story and mixfix format to express strictly defined operators in an (almost) natural language form. We demonstrate how to extract from this format access control information for role based access control.

1 Introduction

There are two established techniques for describing user requirements: *User Stories* and *Use Cases*. In this paper, we will build a new semi-formal format for one of them — user stories. As an application of the new format we will demonstrate how to generate from it a fine-grained role based access control policy.

There exist several more or less formal standards for writing *User Stories*:

- "As a ⟨*role*⟩, I want ⟨*goal/desire*⟩ so that ⟨*benefit*⟩" (see [8]).
- "As a ⟨*role*⟩, I want ⟨*goal/desire*⟩", where "so that" is optional (see [7]).
- "In order to ⟨*receive benefit*⟩ as a ⟨*role*⟩, I want ⟨*goal/desire*⟩" (see [4]).
- "As ⟨*who*⟩ ⟨*when*⟩ ⟨*where*⟩, I ⟨*what*⟩ because ⟨*why*⟩" (see [3]).

All of these have their merits but share the feature of using natural (though constrained) language, which makes them comfortable to use for humans, but, at the same time, difficult to use directly as a computer verifiable formal specification of the system requirements, allowing for automated code generation. Of course, an appropriate formal specification can be created based on user stories, but usually the customer will be unable to understand it and hence to verify that it expresses the intended user requirements, leading to misunderstandings.

We were partially inspired by the computer language Maude [5,6] often used to express and test formal specifications (see e.g., [9,20,21]). The language uses the so-called mixfix format for user defined operations to allow emulation of almost any syntax (even SQL, see [21]). Operators in mixfix format can have multi-word names with slots for arguments, e.g., the operator send _ to _ with subject _ has three slots for arguments: the message body, recipient address and mail subject, e.g.,

© Springer International Publishing Switzerland 2015
L. Bellatreche and Y. Manolopoulos (Eds.): MEDI 2015, LNCS 9344, pp. 311–319, 2015.
DOI: 10.1007/978-3-319-23781-7_25

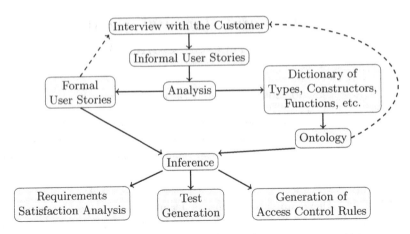

Fig. 1. Workflow for formalized user stories

```
send "Hello" to user@mail.com with subject "Greetings".
```

Thus, the mixfix format allows for an unambiguous, machine readable syntax, at the same time easily interpretable by non-specialists.

Figure 1 describes an intended workflow for our formalized user stories. As an outcome of the meeting with a customer we obtain the requirements, which resemble user stories but really aren't. Those informations are then analyzed by bussines analysts and converted into formalized ones. At the same time, the entities participating in the stories — the users, data elements, activities, etc. — are dictionarized, and relations between them are explicated leading to the creation of the domain ontology. This ontology defines symbols and operations used within formalized user stories and facilitates reasoning about the stories.

Because of their accessibility to non-specialists, the formal user stories and ontologies can be discussed with the customer which leads to their (iterated) corrections. At the same time, the stories can be formally analyzed to find inconsistencies. Finally, one can use the formal stories together with the ontology to generate tests, formal requirements checkers, as well as access control rules. In the present paper we study only the last of these applications.

1.1 Prior Work

A model-driven approach to security policies in Java applications was proposed in [16]. Their framework involves a security metamodel generic enough to express a variety of access control models including RBAC [19] and OrBAC [12]. The model instantiation can be automatically converted into a XACML description of the policy, which is then used to generate Java code for access control weaved into the application as aspects. Our approach is less generic as we use the particular security language designed with the specification of the row level access control in relational databases in mind (cf. [15,17,20,22]). Our approach is also not based on UML metamodeling but rather on first order logic and term algebras.

A paper [14] presents a tool for building ontology from user stories expressed in natural language. The user stories the authors have in mind are completed with links to other stories and code. A state of the art in automatic ontology generation is presented in [2]. The presented methods can be relevant for generation of ontology describing terms appearing in our formal stories.

2 A Format for User Stories

Each user story describes a single task performed by some person. A single formal User Story consists of the following four parts:

Subject — describes a person performing given task.

Operation (verb) — a verb describing what the subject wants to do.

Argument(s) [opt.] — "things" on which the operation acts. An argument is an **object of the operation** if accessing it is a part of the rationale of the operation. It is a **parameter** if it is accessed read only and it only provides auxilliary information to the operation.

Condition [opt.] — it must be satisfied if the operation is to be performed.

The grammatical format of the elements should fit the sentence template:

[Subject] wants to [Operation] [Argument(s)] if/whenever [Condition]

In the following examples we will present several user stories for a system for managing student enrollment for the university.

Example 1. Variables are marked by "@", as @X in the following user story:

@X as a <u>Candidate</u> wants to <u>view</u> @X<u>'s account data</u>

The phrase "@X as a <u>Candidate</u>" serves as a subject description corresponding to a more verbose expression such as: " Let X be any candidate. X wants to [...] ". "<u>Candidate</u>" is a role, which can be understood as a type of person. Hence the expression "@X as a <u>Candidate</u>" can be alternatively interpreted as a declaration of variable @X of type <u>Candidate</u>, and written more formally and concisely as @X:<u>Candidate</u>.

The operation in the above story is "<u>view</u>" which is applied to a single argument (object) "@X<u>'s account data</u>", a complex expression consisting of a call to a single argument function <u>_'s account data</u> in a mixfix format (the underscore denotes the slot for an argument) applied to @X. The function <u>_'s account data</u> returns account data for the person registered in the system passed as an argument, in this case @X.

Example 2. The operation <u>create</u> in the following user story:

@X as an <u>Operator</u> wants to <u>create</u> a <u>list</u> @Y <u>of</u> <u>candidates</u>

is applied to the argument "<u>list</u> @Y <u>of</u> <u>candidates</u>" having a form of a variable introduction. The expression <u>list</u> @Y <u>of</u> <u>candidates</u> introduces @Y as a variable of type <u>list of candidates</u>, i.e., some collection (<u>list</u>) of elements of type <u>candidate</u>.

Example 3. Expression "@Y<u>'s degrees</u> <u>are false</u>" in the following user story:

@X:<u>Operator</u> wants to <u>disqualify</u> a <u>candidate</u> @Y if @Y<u>'s degrees</u> <u>are false</u>

is a condition for the operation of the story (disqualification of some candidate @Y) to happen. It consists of a call to a mixfix predicate "<u>_are false</u>" which is passed a single argument, in this case a call to a function <u>_'s degrees</u> bound to a variable @Y.

2.1 Variables

Variables denote individuals of a given kind. Each user story is implicitly universally quantified with respect to all free variables appearing in the user story. Variables allow correlating roles and different arguments of operations.

Variables may appear in subject, arguments and conditions. Conditions must not introduce new free variables, though they may introduce local variables bound by a local quantification (universal or existential) with range of values limited to the elements of some collection. Another limitation is that variables should not correlate different arguments of operation. This limitation is justified by our procedure for passing from Formal User Stories to access control policies.

When a variable first appears in the User Story it should be given a type (e.g., `@X:Type` or a mixfix version). The scope of a free variable is the whole user story. The scope of a bound variable is limited to the scope of its quantifier.

2.2 Types

Types abstract common features of individuals. Types are either atomic, like `Document`, `Message`, etc., or complex, built, e.g., with collection constructors such as `set of Type`, e.g., `set of Document`. To improve readability we abbreviate `set of Type` as `set of Types` or even `Types`. Other collection constructors may be specified in the ontology, e.g., `List of _s :: Collection` declares `List of _s` to be a constructor of collection type for an arbitrary type substituted for an underscore (e.g. `List of Students`). The types can be also parameterized, e.g. "`List of Students of Faculty`", where `Faculty` is a parameter which should be instantiated, e.g. "`List of Students of English`". In the context of subject description such parameterized types are called *parameterized roles* (e.g. "`Dean of Faculty`"). The usefulness of such parameterized roles is demonstrated by the following user story:

`@D:Dean of @X:Faculty wants to view  the grades of the students of @X`

The most important relations between types are "subtype of" and "is a synonym of" relations. Thus, if any individual of type A is also an individual of type B we will write $A \sqsubseteq B$. If A is another name for a type B (i.e., A is a synonym of B) then we will write $A \equiv B$. Note that $A \sqsubseteq B$ and $B \sqsubseteq A$ implies $A \equiv B$.

Example 4. `Candidatate`, `Operator` and `Administrator` are subtypes of `User`. This we specify by writing `Candidate ⊑ User`, `Operator ⊑ User`, `Administrator ⊑ User`.

2.3 Values

Values can be used as objects, subjects and parameters. Values are constructed using *value constructors* and *functions*. Functions do not construct new values, but rather return existing features based on the arguments. For instance, a constructor "`password('a')`" constructs a new value of type `password` from the string `'a'`. On the other hand, the function "`Password of @X:User`" returns the (existing) password of the user bound to @X. Functions and value constructors can also use mixfix notation (e.g. message(@X:MessageBody) to @Y:Address). Signatures of constructors and functions are defined similarly:

```
f :: Function T₁, T₂, ..., Tₙ -> [ref] T
H :: Constructor T₁, T₂, ..., Tₙ -> T
```

Arguments of functions and constructors are read only. We use functions with "ref" modifier to access values which are to modified by operations.

Example 5. The first function declared below returns, for a given user, a reference to the user's password, which can be then passed to the operation of a password change:

```
_'s password :: Function User -> ref Password
_'s subjects :: Function Student -> List of Subjects
```

The second function returns a list of subjects chosen by a given student. The list will be accessed read-only, hence the function returns it as a value.

Example 6. The following is a declaration of a constructor supposed to create a new message with a body given by a string and addressed to a given user:

```
message _ to _ :: Constructor String, User -> Message
```

Function and constructor calls are composable. Formally we have:

Definition 1. *Functional terms of type T are defined recursively: A variable of type T is a functional term of type T. If f is an n-argument function/constructor with signature f :: Function/Constructor T_1, T_2, ..., T_n -> [ref] T and, for all $i \in \{1,\ldots,n\}$, ϕ_i is a functional term of type T'_i such that $T'_i \sqsubseteq T_i$ then $f(\phi_1, \phi_2, \ldots, \phi_n)$ is a functional term of type T. We write $\psi : T$ if ψ is a functional term of type T. Free(ψ) denotes the set of variables appearing in the term ψ.*

Ontology can also declare some functions in terms of others, e.g.,

$$f(X_1 : T_1, X_2 : T_2, \ldots, X_n : T_n) \equiv \psi(X_1, X_2, \ldots, X_n).$$

Example 7. The code below identifies the function _'s Phone returning a phone for a given user with the composition of a function _'s Phones returning list of all phone numbers of a given user with the function First returning the first element of a list.

```
_'s Phone :: Function User -> Phone
_'s Phones :: Function User -> List of Phone
@X:User's Phone ≡ First(@X's Phones).
```

2.4 Conditions

The (optional) condition part of the given user story restricts the applicability of the operations of this user story to the situations when it is satisfied. Conditions have the form of logical expressions build from atomic predicates, standard logical connectives, and existential and universal quantification over members of collections. The atomic predicates are opaque from the point of view of user story, though they can be related to other predicates or even defined in the additional ontology. A signature for an atomic predicate is declared as follows:

P :: Predicate T_1, T_2, ..., T_n

A predicate name P can be given in mixfix format.

Definition 2. *A* condition *is defined recursively as follows:*

- *If P is an n-ary predicate with signature P :: Predicate $T_1, \ldots, T_n$ and if for all $i \in \{1, \ldots, n\}$, ϕ_i is a functional term such that $\phi_i : T\phi_i$ and $T\phi_i \sqsubseteq T_i$ then $P(\phi_1, \ldots, \phi_n)$ is a condition and $Free(P(\phi_1, \ldots, \phi_n)) = Free(\phi_1) \cup \cdots \cup Free(\phi_n)$.*
- *If ϕ and ψ are conditions then $(\phi$ and $\psi)$ as well as $(\phi$ or $\psi)$ are conditions and $Free(\phi$ and $\psi) = Free(\phi$ or $\psi) = Free(\psi) \cup Free(\phi)$.*
- *If ϕ is a condtion then $(not \; \phi)$ is a condition and $Free(not \; \phi) = Free(\phi)$.*
- *If ψ is a condition then also $(\underline{For \; all} \; X_1 : T1, \ldots, X_n : T_n \; \phi)$ and $(\underline{Exists} \; X_1 : T1, \ldots, X_n : T_n \; \phi)$ are conditions and $Free(\underline{For \; all} \; X_1 : T1, \ldots, X_n : T_n \; \phi) = Free(\underline{Exists} \; X_1 : T1, \ldots, X_n : T_n \; \phi) = Free(\phi) \setminus \{X_1, \ldots, X_n\}$.*

2.5 Operations

The ontology for User Stories must define the signatures for all the operations. We allow the overloading of operation names if they have a different number and/or types of arguments. The signature of an operation is declared as follows:

Operation name :: Operation m_1 $Type_1$, m_2 $Type_2$, ..., m_n $Type_n$

where Operation name is operation name in mixfix format with n slots for arguments. $Type_1$, ..., $Type_n$ is the list of types of arguments, in the order they appear in Operation name, and m_1, ..., m_n are the modes of arguments which can be either w (modified only), r (read only) or rw (both modified and read).

Example 8. The operation declared below accepts two read only arguments:

Send the _ to the _ :: Operation r Message, r User.

Example 9. In the operation declared below, the single argument (the password to be changed) is passed in the rw mode. The "w" part of is obvious, but the operation needs also to read the password (or its shadow) in order to authorize its change.

Change the _ :: Operation rw Password.

3   From User Stories to PRBAC

Roles [10,18,19] are now the standard administrative help directly supported by majority of databases and other systems such as application servers. Parameterized RBAC [1,11,13] introduces role templates (constructors), the arguments of which define some partition of data. Instantiation of such templates with actual parameters creates the usual roles.

The language for security policies which we use is a modified PRBAC with some shades of OrBAC [12]. We assume that we have a collection of user types called roles and that we can instantiate roles using appropriate constructors.

A security policy is a collection of rules. Each rule is a 5-tuple consisting of: a subject description, a context provided by an operation name, a mode of access (e.g., r, w, or rw), an object or a collection of objects which are accessed during the operation, and an optional condition. The security policies can be now implemented in many ways. We do not go into details but we will comment here on a certain general aspects of implementation.

For the finest level of control, any activity of the user (having a given role) should happen in the context of an operation performed — this means that from a point of view of RBAC the operation is another component of the current (parameterized) role of the user. In practical terms, this means that before performing first operation of User Story operation "A" the application should make a call, e.g., setContext("A") which informs the security subsystem (both in the application and in the database) that the subsequent activity should have access only to those data elements which are necessary for the operation "A".

Each rule describes an allowed data access and any data access that is not allowed by some rule is forbidden. We do not use rules which forbid access. A data access is allowed when there is a rule such that:

- the data access is executed on behalf of the user whose role matches the role in the rule and within the same context as in the rule.
- the data element and its access mode are matched by the object and mode in the rule and the condition in the rule is satisfied.

Essentially, the rules are analogous to the first four components of User Stories. The rules are also similar to those for user stories: the free variables are universally quantified and they must be declared when first used. Also the condition cannot introduce any new variables. Hence, they can be trivially extracted from User Stories. Some care must be taken only in case of multi-argument operations, as each rule explicitly deals only with a single data element: each argument of a user story's operation gives rise to a separate access control rule.

Example 10. Consider the following two user stories:

```
@X:Administrator of @Y:Department wants to
   edit @Z:Employee's personal data if @Z is employed in @Y.
@X:Employee wants to edit @X's personal data.
```

completed by the ontology (semicolons separate declarations in the same line):

```
Department::Type; Administrator of _ ::Role Department
Employee::Role; PersonalData::Type; edit _ ::Operation rw PersonalData
_'s personal data::Function Employee -> [ref] PersonalData
_ is employed in _::Predicate Employee, Department
```

Note that the _'s personal data returns a reference to an appropriate data elements, so that it can be used as a principal function symbol in the term passed to the `edit` operation which modifies its argument. From the above user stories completed with the ontology we can derive the following policy tuples:

```
(@X:Administrator of @Y:Department, edit::PersonalData,
         rw, @Z:Employee's personal data, @Z is employed in @Y)
(@X:Employee, edit::PersonalData, rw, @X's personal data, true)
```

This policy means that after the application executing on behalf of user U sets the context to "`edit::PersonalData`" it can access only personal data of either

- any employee of department D whenever U has role "`Administrator of D`"
- or the personal data of U if U has the role "`Employee`"

Those two choices need not be exclusive, e.g., if the ontology also declares the role `Administrator of @Y` to be a subrole of `Employee`.

4   Conclusion

We have described a new constrained natural language and formal format for User Stories and we have shown how this format assists in developing access control policy for application data. In the future we need to develop a tool, which performs the conversion automatically. This is also the first of the papers in which we describe applications and advantages of the new User Story format.

References

1. Abdallah, A., Khayat, E.: A formal model for parameterized role-based access control. In: Dimitrakos, T., Martinelli, F. (eds.) Formal Aspects in Security and Trust. IFIP International Federation for Information Processing, vol. 173, pp. 233–246. Springer, Boston (2005). doi:10.1007/0-387-24098-5_17
2. Bedini, I., Nguyen, B.: Automatic ontology generation: State of the art. PRiSM Laboratory Technical report. University of Versailles (2007)
3. Bulsuk, K.G.: An introduction to 5-why. http://goo.gl/uhWRnR
4. Chris Matts, G.A.: Feature injection: three steps to success. http://goo.gl/eY2LJ0
5. Clavel, M., Duran, F., Eker, S., Lincoln, P., Marti-Oliet, N., Meseguer, J., Talcott, C.: Maude Manual (Version 2.6) (2011)
6. Clavel, M., Durán, F., Eker, S., Lincoln, P., Martí-Oliet, N., Meseguer, J., Talcott, C.: The maude 2.0 system. In: Nieuwenhuis, R. (ed.) RTA 2003. LNCS, vol. 2706. Springer, Heidelberg (2003)
7. Cohn, M.: Advantages of the "as a user, I want" user story template. http://goo.gl/jAQNS0
8. Connexstra: Connexstra story card. http://goo.gl/5nssK9
9. Denker, G., Meseguer, J., Talcott, C.: Protocol specification and analysis in Maude. In: Proceedings of the Workshop on Formal Methods and Security Protocols (1998)
10. Ferraiolo, D., Kuhn, D., Chandramouli, R.: Role-Based Access Control. Artech House computer security series. Artech House, Boston (2003)
11. Ge, M., Osborn, S.: A design for parameterized roles. In: Farkas, C., Samarati, P. (eds.) Research Directions in Data and Applications Security XVIII. IFIP International Federation for Information Processing, vol. 144, pp. 251–264. Springer, Boston (2004). doi:10.1007/1-4020-8128-6_17

12. Kalam, A.A.E., Baida, R., Balbiani, P., Benferhat, S., Cuppens, F., Deswarte, Y., Miege, A., Saurel, C., Trouessin, G.: Organization based access control. In: Proceedings of the IEEE 4th International Workshop on Policies for Distributed Systems and Networks, POLICY 2003, pp. 120–131. IEEE (2003)
13. Kuhn, D.R., Coyne, E.J., Weil, T.R.: Adding attributes to role-based access control. IEEE Comput. **43**(6), 79–81 (2010)
14. Landhausser, M., Genaid, A.: Connecting user stories and code for test development. In: 2012 Third International Workshop on Recommendation Systems for Software Engineering (RSSE), pp. 33–37, June 2012
15. Miodek, K., Pychowski, J.: Elastyczny system uprawnien uzytkownikow w systemie zarzadzania baz danych PostgreSQL. In: Bazy Danych - Modele, Technologie, Narzedzia, pp. 309–314. WKL Gliwice (2006)
16. Mouelhi, T., Fleurey, F., Baudry, B., Le Traon, Y.: A model-based framework for security policy specification, deployment and testing. In: Czarnecki, K., Ober, I., Bruel, J.-M., Uhl, A., Völter, M. (eds.) MODELS 2008. LNCS, vol. 5301, pp. 537–552. Springer, Heidelberg (2008)
17. Rizvi, S., Mendelzon, A., Sudarshan, S., Roy, P.: Extending query rewriting techniques for fine-grained access control. In: Proceedings of the 2004 ACM SIGMOD International Conference on Management of Data, SIGMOD 2004, pp. 551–562. ACM, New York (2004)
18. Sandhu, R., Ferraiolo, D., Kuhn, R.: The NIST model for role-based access control: towards a unified standard. In: Proceedings of the Fifth ACM Workshop on Role-based Access Control, pp. 47–63 (2000)
19. Sandhu, R.S., Coyne, E.J., Feinstein, H.L., Youman, C.E.: Role-based access control models. IEEE Comput. **29**(2), 38–47 (1996)
20. Sobieski, Ś., Zieliński, B.: Modularisation in maude of parametrized RBAC for row level access control. In: Eder, J., Bielikova, M., Tjoa, A.M. (eds.) ADBIS 2011. LNCS, vol. 6909, pp. 401–414. Springer, Heidelberg (2011)
21. Sobieski, Ś., Zieliński, B.: Using Maude rewriting system to modularize and extend SQL. In: Proceedings of the 28th Annual ACM Symposium on Applied Computing, pp. 853–858. ACM (2013)
22. Stonebraker, M., Wong, E.: Access control in a relational data base management system by query modification. In: Proceedings of the 1974 Annual Conference, ACM 1974, vol. 1, pp. 180–186. ACM, New York (1974)

A Reusable Software Architecture for Geographic Information Systems Based on Software Product Line Engineering

Nieves R. Brisaboa[1], Alejandro Cortiñas[1], Miguel R. Luaces[1(✉)], and Matias Pol'la[2,3]

[1] Databases Lab, University of A Coruña, A Coruña, Spain
{brisaboa,alejandro.cortinas,luaces}@udc.es
[2] Giisco, Facultad de Informática, Universidad Nacional del Comahue, Neuquén, Argentina
matias.polla@fi.uncoma.edu.ar
[3] Concejo Nacional de Investigaciones Científicas y Técnicas, Buenos Aires, Argentina

Abstract. In the last years there has been a continuous growth in functionality of geographic information systems (GIS) resulting in many different software artifacts. Even though each GIS is used in different areas with different objectives, they all share many features and requirements and therefore it is possible to apply techniques based on intensive software reuse, such as software product line engineering (SPLE). Although there has been much research on software product line engineering in the last years, the definition of a software product line for the domain of geographic information systems has not been undertaken.

In this work we identify the requirements and functionalities of a generic product for a web-based geographic information system, grouping them into commonalities that allow us to reuse many software artifacts, and variabilities that allow use to configure different products. Then, we define the functional and technological architecture of a software product line that uses current technologies for web-based application development. Finally, we design a tool to configure and assemble the components to generate the possible products. The resulting platform is flexible enough to adapt each product to the specific needs of each customer.

Keywords: Geographic information systems · Software product line engineering · General-purpose software architecture · Variability management

1 Introduction

The field of Geographic Information Systems (GIS) has received much attention in the last years. Many disciplines such as cartography, biology, ecology,

Partially funded by MINECO ref. TIN2013-46801-C4-3-R (PGE & FEDER) and Xunta de Galicia ref. GRC2013/053 (FEDER) for authors in UDC.

© Springer International Publishing Switzerland 2015
L. Bellatreche and Y. Manolopoulos (Eds.): MEDI 2015, LNCS 9344, pp. 320–331, 2015.
DOI: 10.1007/978-3-319-23781-7_26

transportation and warehouse logistics use GIS to store, query and visualize geographic information. The improvements in communication technologies, together with the increased penetration of Internet access, have enabled the use of GIS technology with mobile equipment to visualize and manage data stored on remote computers accessible over the Internet. Clear examples of this trend are the success of applications like Google Maps, the inclusion of location-based functionality on a large number of web applications (e.g., Flickr, Facebook, Twitter), and the emergence of different types of GIS applications for municipal management, urban planning, tourism or property management.

Even though GIS applications have always had many common features and requirements such as storing and indexing geo-referenced data, displaying information as a set of layers, or grouping layers into different maps, the software artifacts used to implement the applications used different and incompatible conceptual, logical and physical data models (e.g., different definitions for the data type *polygon*, or different semantics for the predicate *overlaps*). Hence, it was very difficult to build interoperable applications because even the simplest task (e.g., data migration) was an arduous one. To solve this problem, a collaborative effort to define standards for GIS has been carried out by two organizations: ISO (through ISO/TC 211 and the 19100 set of standards) and the Open Geospatial Consortium (OGC). Nowadays, the application of techniques based on intensive software reuse such as software product line engineering (SPLE) is possible and relevant in the GIS domain. A software product line is a set of software-intensive systems sharing a common, managed set of features that satisfy the specific needs of a particular market segment or mission and that are developed from a common set of core assets in a prescribed way [12]. Software product lines enable systematic reuse in cases where there are families of products, i.e. similar products differentiated by certain characteristics. This new paradigm enables companies to improve the quality of software produced as well as reduce costs and launch times, thereby promoting the industrialization of software development.

Starting from the experience of our previous work in geographic subdomains such as marine biology [4,5] or the development of GIS applications [2,11] and geographic information retrieval algorithms [3], we have designed a software product line for GIS. The products of this SPL are web-based GIS that can be used to browse, query, analyze and manage geographic information. In Sect. 2 we present background concepts on SPLE. Then, in Sect. 3 we define the features of the product and we group them into components. After that, in Sect. 4 we define the platform architecture in the functional and technological levels. Then, in Sect. 5 we present the architecture of the tool that allows us to configure and assemble the software assets to generate the final products. Finally, future work and conclusions are discussed in Sect. 6.

2 Related Work

The traditional approach to software development performs the elicitation of requirements, design, implementation, testing and maintenance for each individual according to the specific needs of each customer. The disadvantage of this approach is that it requires high development and maintenance costs in order to produce high quality products. For this reason, new methodologies have emerged to apply mass-production and reuse strategies to the software development process. One such methodology is Software Product Lines Engineering (SPLE) [1,12,15], which focuses on separating the development of core, reusable software assets (i.e., the *platform*), and the development of the actual applications (i.e., the *products*). The platform is modeled as a set of *features* that represent a characteristic of a system relevant for some stakeholder (e.g., a requirement, a technical function or function group or a non-functional characteristic) and a set of *variation points* that represent the commonalities and variabilities of the different products. Individual products are modeled as a concrete selection of features and alternatives for the variation points in the platform. Finally, the product is built by adapting and assembling software artifacts from the platform.

The scope and range of products that a product line can deliver is determined by the flexibility of the platform, which in turn is determined by the variability of the platform features. Therefore, variability management, which involves the tasks of identifying and defining the platform features, defining the functional and technological architectures of the product, and defining the product line configuration and derivation processes, is one of the main tasks in SPL development. There are many modeling techniques to identify and define the platform features, such as FODA (Feature Oriented Domain analysis) [8], FORM (Feature Oriented Reuse Method) [9], FM (Feature Modeling) [7], DM (Decision Model) [14], or OVM (Orthogonal Variability Model) [12]. There are also some approaches centered on the product architecture and the configuration and derivation process, which can be classified into annotative [10] (i.e., adding annotations in the source code to indicate the variant point and the different variants) or compositional (i.e., implementing the variants with different software assets). A metadata model that follows a mixed approach, taking into account the main advantages of both of them such as traceability (compositional) and fine-grained adjustments (annotative), has been defined in [6,13].

Furthermore, we have presented in [4,5] a methodology that extends the framework presented in [12] to create a product line in the marine ecology subdomain. This product line has been used in a case study that includes the work with biologists from two institutes and that resulted in the instantiation of two products within this subdomain. However, although there has been much research on software product line engineering in the last years, the definition of a software product line for the domain of geographic information systems has not been undertaken.

3   Identifying Features and Components for GIS Products

In this section, we identify and define all the functional and non-functional features for web-based geographic information systems analyzing several existing GIS applications with different scopes and features. Then, we determine which software assets are required by the platform to provide all the features identified.

3.1 Feature Variability

We use the variability management model presented in [6,13]. It defines four types of variability for each feature (Mandatory (M), Optional (O), Alternative (A) and Variant(V)), and three types of dependencies between features (Uses, Requires and Excludes). The graphical notation is depicted on Fig. 1.

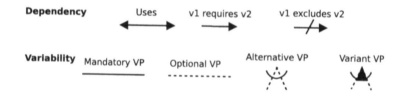

Fig. 1. Variability Management - Graphical Notation. Extracted from [6]

In addition to the variability types and dependencies described above, it is necessary to add a new element to the variability management model, called *variability scope*, which represents whether the scope of variability for a feature is *global* (notated as *VG*) and the variant is chosen once and applied every time the functionality is selected, or the scope is *specific* (notated as *VS*) and a concrete variant must be chosen every time the functionality is selected. For example, the architecture selection is *global* feature because it only has to be selected once and it is applied in all variation points. However, the visualization type of map viewers is a *specific* feature because an application can have multiple map viewers with some of them being *embedded* within a web page, some others being displayed in a *full page*, and some others being *detachable* (i.e., they start embedded but they can also be displayed in a full page).

Table 1. Table feature variability - subset

Id	Feature	M	O	A	V	Scope
1	Architecture selection	●				VG
2	Data model definition	●				VG
3	Maps definition	●				VG
3.a	Layers definition	●				VG
3.b	Styles definition		●			VG
4	Map viewers	●				-
4.a	Visualization type	●				VS
4.b	Geographics cope	●				VS
4.c	Mapviewer tools		●			VS
5	Geodata edition		●			VG
6	User management		●			VG
...						

In Table 1 we show a subset of the features identified (the full table includes more than 90 features). We have grouped them into different variant points according to their function and we have established the variability type and scope of each one. From the various GIS applications studied, we have not only defined functional features like *user authentication*, but we have also defined many non-functional features such as *map viewer library selection*. While the former will turn out in new functionalities added to the product, the latter only represents a design decision that changes the technology used to view the maps in the web application. Some of the main features identified in our platform are the following:

- **Architecture Selection.** The technology used for some functions of the products may vary (e.g., the DBMS or the map visualization library). We give more detail regarding this feature on Sect. 4.
- **Data Model Definition.** Each product may have an specific data model that must be defined as the first step in the configuration tool, as we can see on Sect. 5.
- **Managing Maps, Layers and Styles.** Each product may define its own collections of map layers, visualization styles, and maps (i.e., a named collection of ordered map layers with default styles). Furthermore, another feature enables users of the product to manage them on runtime. The definition of layers and maps is a mandatory feature because it has no sense to build a GIS application without them.
- **Configuring the Map Viewers.** Every GIS application has one or more map viewers, each one with its own configuration. Therefore, the scope of these features is specific. Some of the features in this variation point are the selection of the visualization type (i.e., the map viewer may be embedded in some other content or shown in full page mode) or the selection of the different tools that can be enabled (zooming and panning the map, opening modal views with info of the selected elements, getting the permanent link of the current view, etc.).
- **Editing the Geographic Data.** We can optionally enable the edition of the geographic data on our GIS product. This allows the user to import data from shapefiles or a WMS service, or even update the geographic data directly on a map viewer.
- **Enabling User and Authentication Management.** As in any web-based system, we can control the people who has access to the application and to each feature of it. We can see this feature is optional, since we may want the application to be totally open.

In Table 2 we present a subset of the dependencies that we have found between each feature. For example, if we choose not to use a *Map Cache Server* in our application, we force the layers to be generated each time by our *Map Server*. For example, feature *Maps definition* (3) has a *requires* dependency with the feature *Layers definition* (3.a), and this one has a *uses* dependency with the feature *Styles definition* (3.b). Also, the *Map viewers* feature has a *requires*

Table 2. Table feature dependencies - subset

Id	Name	Use	Requires	Excludes
...				
3	Maps definition		3.a	
3.a	Layers definition	3.b		
3.b	Styles definition			
4	Map viewers	4.c	3, 4.a, 4.b	
4.a	Visualization type			
4.a.1	Embedded map			
4.a.2	Full page map			
4.a.3	Switching type allowed		4.a.1, 4.a.2	
4.b	Geographic scope			
4.c	Map viewer tools			
...				

dependency with *Maps definition*, *Visualization type* and *Geographic scope*, and a *uses* dependency with *Map viewer tools*. Furthermore, the subfeature of *Visualization type*, *Switching type allowed*, has a *requires* dependency with both subfeature *Embedded map* and *Full page map*.

After defining all dependencies and variabilities, the relationships and constraints between features can be shown graphically in a variability model. Figure 2 shows the features described in Table 2. In the model we can see all variation points (places where the variability occurs) represented by light gray squares with the annotation VS or VG, according to their scope.

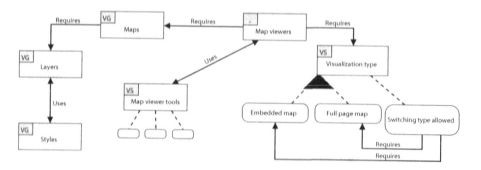

Fig. 2. Portion of the variability model

3.2   Functional Components

Starting from the collection of features identified and defined in the variability model described above, we have identified and defined a set of software components that will implement all the possible features of the resulting products. The components implementing any mandatory variant are called *core components* and they will be included in all the generated products.

- **Data Model.** The software engineer that uses the SPL to create a product must provide a complete definition of the GIS application data model. The software engineer may use alphanumeric and geographic data types, relationships between entities with concrete cardinality, and simple restrictions like the non-nullity of any element. This component is in charge of implementing the data model in a specific architecture.
- **Data Access.** This component is responsible for all the functionality that involves creating, reading, updating and deleting elements from the data model.
- **Map Viewer.** This component implements the functionality related to viewing and interacting with geographic information using maps.
- **Data Viewer.** The functionality related to browsing and interacting with text-based data (e.g., lists, editing forms, etc.) is implemented by this component.
- **Menu.** Nearly all web applications have a menu component to access all sections and features thereof. Thus, our generated GIS application should have also this component.
- **Database Management System.** The DBMS chosen will affect many other components, especially in the low level layers (Data model and Data access components). The configuration of this component will include the definition of the database, as well as the credentials used to connect to it. We provide various options to choose between them.

The rest of the components are called *optional components* and may be or not in the final products. Some of these components are totally isolated from the rest, but there are many functionalities that require certain relationship and interoperability between them.

- **User Manager.** Some GIS applications will require authentication, different user roles and the common functionality provided for any user-related web product.
- **Map Manager.** Maps, layers and styles are defined during the configuration of the product. Furthermore, this component allows the product administrator to manage these elements on runtime. Otherwise, the initial configuration will be static.
- **Map Data Importer.** If the GIS produced should be able to import new geographic data (i.e., from shapefiles), this component will allow it. The new data can be added from different sources, besides the mentioned one.
- **Map Data Exporter.** Component used to export any to map to several type files, like PDF or PNG. It also allows the user to print the visualized maps.
- **Map Server.** Most GIS applications use a map server to produce the cartography images. We have decided to make this component optional because a map server is particularly costly in terms of hardware and configuration.

Therefore, some GIS applications may use an internal map server to draw cartography whereas other applications may rely on external map servers (e.g., OpenStreetMap) and display all geographic elements only at the client side.

– **Map Cache.** Some GIS applications that require an internal map server may not require the cartography to be generated in real-time. Therefore, this component implements a map cache so that static maps are displayed instead of being generated each time they are required.

– **Static Pages Manager.** Not all the content displayed on the GIS application can be generated automatically. Some content may depend on specific and product-related information. To provide this flexibility on the user interface, we have defined a component that handles the creation of customized content using static web pages. These pages will be able to use other components of the SPL (such as embedded maps) to enrich the interface.

4   Platform Architecture for GIS Products

The software architecture plays an important role in any information system. Particularly, in SPL the definition of the platform architecture is a major task because it must support the entire product range and scope previously defined. For this reason, the platform architecture must be general and flexible enough to capture both commonalities and variabilities. On the other hand, the platform architecture must be concrete and efficient in order to support the creation of products that can be used in real-life problems.

In this sense, we have defined a three-layer architecture composed of a user interface, responsible for the interaction with the user; a processing layer which contains all the functionality defined for the GIS; and a model management layer, responsible for physical data storage and data management. In Fig. 3 we have classified the major components described in Sect. 3.2 according to the layer where their activity takes place. We can see that there are three types of components: *user interface-layer* components, *data-layer* components and *transverse* components, which belong mostly to the processing layer but that also affect the other two.

Regarding the technological architecture, web-based GIS applications usually have simpler or less functionalities than desktop-based ones. However, thanks to the late improvements in communications, server-side and client-side processing, and web-based frameworks, we believe that a web-based GIS product can be built. Figure 4 presents the platform architecture in terms of technology. It also shows a feature model of the architectural variation points, which are annotated with the legend *VG* and all the variants associated to each one are represented with light gray boxes. We have decided to define only five variation points to avoid an unmanageable number of alternatives that add unnecessary complexity.

In the user interface layer we have decided to use an open-source web application framework called AngularJS because it presents a modular design which enables us to define a flexible configuration and to implement the different variants with different software artifacts. In this layer, we have also decided to define

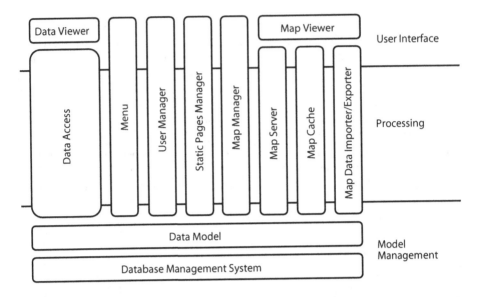

Fig. 3. Platform architecture with functional components

a variant point with two alternatives to visualize the geo-referenced data in the user interface: OpenLayers and Leaflet. These libraries have different scopes and therefore provide different advantages to the final product.

The processing layer is based on Spring MVC. The REST services used to communicate the user interface with the processing layer are implemented with Spring controllers, and the services that provide communication with the model management layer are built using the dependency injection pattern of Spring. We also use Spring Security to support user authentication and access-control. Finally, as described in Sect. 3.2, the functional architecture defines a variation point to include an internal map server (GeoServer) and a map cache (Tile-Cache).

Finally, the model management layer a variant point with two alternatives for the data access technology: Java Database Connectivity (JDBC) or Hibernate. This layer also has a variant point with three alternatives for the Database Management System: PostgreSQL and PostGIS, MySQL or Oracle Spatial.

5   Configuration and Derivation Tool for a SPL in GIS

The process for the generation of products in a software product line consists of two main activities: *product configuration*, where the selection of the desired features occurs; and *product derivation*, where the final product is assembled. Figure 5 presents the tool that we have designed that enables both tasks. The left side of the figure shows all the components of the product configuration tool. On the right side of the figure we show the product derivation tool that receives the product configuration and assembles the final product using the software

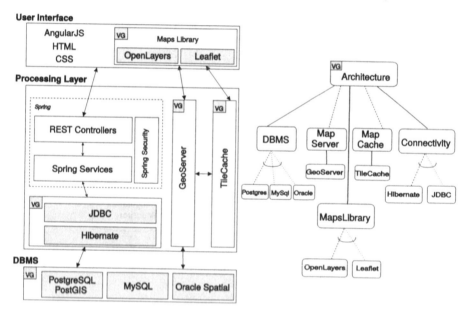

Fig. 4. Technological platform architecture and variability model

assets from the asset repository. The configuration of each product is stored in the configuration repository and can be loaded in the tool in any moment, so we can derive the exact same product again or update a product starting from a previous configuration. We also maintain version control over the products and their evolution.

The configuration tool is composed of several modules that allow us to tailor the product to the user's needs. In this task, all the variability present in the shared platform should be instantiated according to specific needs within the defined range. For this, first the data model of the application must be provided. Once the tables are described, the set of maps that provide the geographical context as well as the layers and the styles must be described. Then, the product features must be selected in the variability configuration and feature selection module. The module receives as input the variability model in XML format as defined in [6]. This model is composed of different tags that represent the variabilities, constraints and relationships defined in Sect. 3. Then, the module generates an instance of the model with the functionality and actions selected by the software engineer. This module also controls the validity of the selection of features, according to the constraints and dependencies in the variability model. In addition to the selection of features, the software engineer can optionally provide static content such as text and pages in the applications, as well as the details of the web aspect. The software engineer can also configure the application menu using the menu configuration module.

The input of derivation tool is the configuration generated with the config-uration tool in the previous step. The task of the derivation tool is performed

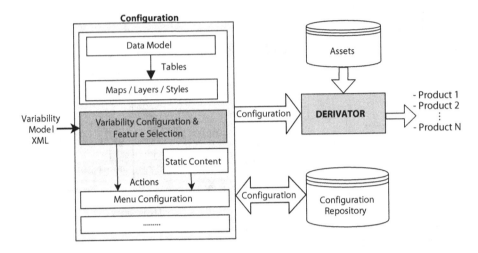

Fig. 5. Configuration and derivation tools

without user interaction. First, the configuration is parsed and after that the product is built using the software assets extracted from the asset repository.

6   Conclusion and Future Work

In this paper we have presented a software product line for web-based geographic information systems. We have first identified and defined functional and non-functional requirements for such systems based on the analysis of the characteristics of a set of GIS applications. Then, we have defined a platform for these products as a set of features, their variation points, and their restrictions following the model introduced in [6]. After that, we have grouped the features identified into two set of components: core and optional. This allowed us to define the functional and technological architecture of the platform taking into account the current trends in web-based technology for GIS applications. Both are highly-modular, which facilitates the assembly of products and their maintainability. Finally, we have designed the configuration and derivation tools that are used to build the final products.

Regarding future work, we are currently implementing all the components, working with three different products to validate and evaluate the benefits of the software product line. We are also testing and analyzing other technologies such as Yeoman, in addition to those described in [6,13], in order to be able to deal with the high level of variability proposed for the software product line.

References

1. Bosch, J.: Design and Use of Software Architectures: Adopting and Evolving a Product-Line Approach. ACM Press/Addison-Wesley Publishing Co., New York, USA (2000)

2. Brisaboa, N.R., Lema, J.A.C., Fariña, A., Luaces, M.R., Parama, J.R., Viqueira, J.R.R.: Collecting and publishing large multiscale geographic datasets. Softw., Pract. Exper. **37**(12), 1319–1348 (2007)

3. Brisaboa, N.R., Luaces, M.R., Places, A.S., Seco, D.: Exploiting geographic references of documents in a geographical information retrieval system using an ontology-based index. GeoInformatica **14**(3), 307–331 (2010)

4. Buccella, A., Cechich, A., Arias, M., Pol'la, M., Doldan, S., Morsan, E.: Towards systematic software reuse of gis: Insights from a case study. Comput. Geosci. **54**, 9–20 (2013)

5. Buccella, A., Cechich, A., Pol'la, M., Arias, M., Doldan, S., Morsan, E.: Marine ecology service reuse through taxonomy-oriented SPL development. Comput. Geosci. **73**, 108–121 (2014)

6. Buccella, A., Pol'la, M., Cechich, A., Arias, M.: A variability representation approach based on domain service taxonomies and their dependencies. In: XXXIII International Conference of the Chilean Society of Computer Science (SCCC 2014), Talca, Chile. IEEE Computer Society Press, 08–14 November (2014)

7. Czarnecki, K., Grunbacher, P., Rabiser, R., Schmid, K., Wäsowski, A.: Cool features and tough decisions: a comparison of variability modeling approaches. In: Proceedings of the Sixth International Workshop on Variability Modeling of Software-Intensive Systems, VaMoS 2012, pp. 173–182. ACM, New York (2012)

8. Kang, K., Cohen, S., Hess, J., Nowak, W., Peterson, S.: Feature-Oriented Domain Analysis (FODA) Feasibility Study. Technical report CMU/SEI-90-TR-21, Software Engineering Institute, Carnegie Mellon University Pittsburgh, PA (1990)

9. Kang, K.C., Kim, S., Lee, J., Kim, K., Shin, E., Huh, M.: Form: A feature-oriented reuse method with domain-specific reference architectures. Ann. Softw. Eng. **5**, 143–168 (1998)

10. Kästner, C., Apel, S., Kuhlemann, M.: Granularity in software product lines. In: Proceedings of the 30th International Conference on Software Engineering, ICSE 2008, pp. 311–320. ACM, New York (2008)

11. Places, A.S., Brisaboa, N.R., Fariña, A., Luaces, M.R., Paramá, J.R., Penabad, M.R.: The galician virtual library. Online Inf. Rev. **31**(3), 333–352 (2007)

12. Pohl, K., Böckle, G., van der Linden, F.J.: Software Product Line Engineering: Foundations Principles and Techniques. Springer-Verlag New York Inc., Secaucus (2005)

13. Pol'la, M., Buccella, A., Cechich, A., Arias, M.: Un modelo de metadatos para la gestión de la variabilidad en líneas de productos de software. In: Proceedings of the ASSE 2014: 15th Simposio Argentino de Ingeniería de Software, Buenos Aires, Argentina (2014)

14. Schmid, K., Rabiser, R., Grünbacher, P.: A comparison of decision modeling approaches in product lines. In: Proceedings of the 5th Workshop on Variability Modeling of Software-Intensive Systems, VaMoS 2011, pp. 119–126. ACM, New York (2011)

15. van der Linden, F., Schmid, K., Rommes, E.: Software Product Lines in Action: The Best Industrial Practice in Product Line Engineering. Springer-Verlag New York Inc., Secaucus (2007)

SPL Driven Approach for Variability in Database Design

Selma Bouarar[1]($\boxtimes$), Stéphane Jean[1], and Norbert Siegmund[2]

[1] LIAS/ISAE-ENSMA - Poitiers University, Poitiers, France
{bouarars,jean}@ensma.fr
[2] Department of Informatics and Mathematics, University of Passau,
Passau, Germany
Norbert.Siegmund@uni-passau.de

Abstract. The evolution of computer technology has strongly impacted the database design. No phase was spared: several *conceptual* formalisms (e.g. ER, UML, ontological), various *logical* models (e.g. relational, object, key-value), a wide panoply of *physical* optimization structures and *deployment* platforms have been proposed. As a result, the database design process has become more complex involving more tasks and even more actors (as database architect or analyst). Getting inspired from software engineering in dealing with variable similar systems, we propose a methodological framework for a variability-aware design of databases, whereby this latter is henceforth devised as a Software Product Line. Doing so guarantees a high reuse, automation, and customizability in generating ready-to-be implemented databases. We also propose a solution to help users make a suitable choice among the wide panoply. Finally, a case study is presented.

Keywords: Database design · Software Product Line · Variability

1 Introduction

The proliferation of information systems (e.g. decisional, statistical, and scientific) has led to the development of different systems for storing data. These latter are called databases (DB), and they have been becoming increasingly fundamental for every sector. Once the DB technology became mature, a design life-cycle has emerged, mainly composed of three phases: *conceptual, logical,* and *physical* designs.

The growing use of databases and the upward diversity in nowadays applications, more powered by the *big data era*, have revolutionized the DB technology. These facts (i) have subjected the design life-cycle to a continuous evolution: heterogeneity of data sources, diversity of conceptual/logical models, storage layouts, wide panoply of optimization structures and even the integration of new phases such as the *ETL* phase, (ii) have led to new careers related to DB management besides the usual designer and DBA, like DB architect, analyst, and

© Springer International Publishing Switzerland 2015
L. Bellatreche and Y. Manolopoulos (Eds.): MEDI 2015, LNCS 9344, pp. 332–342, 2015.
DOI: 10.1007/978-3-319-23781-7_27

developer. Every actor has his/her own variables (sphere of operation) through which he/she can configure the design. A such high degree of variety and collaboration shows the increasing complexity of nowadays DB design process. This observation has motivated us to closely analyze the latter and spot the main variables that control the life-cycle as well as their dependencies.

Originally, the idea of developing similar complex products belonging to a specific family, and based on a set of variables (assets) is a well known process in Software Product Line (SPL) Engineering, as *Variability management*. It is defined as the ability of a product or artifact to be changed, customized or configured for use in a particular context. It has proved very successful in many domains, through improving productivity, product maintainability, quality, and tailoring products so as to meet, as specific as possible, customers' needs. Our proposal can be summed up in how to adopt the SPL approach in managing variability in DB technology.

By exploring the major state-of-art, we figured out that this issue has been partially addressed (i) using different techniques inspired from software engineering, and (ii) has been concerned with only parts of separate phases of DB design process, despite their interdependence. For instance, Rosenmuller et al. [11] proposed *FAME-DBMS*, a prototype of a DB management product line, focusing only on a part of the physical layer of the design process, but leaving out other important phases in the life-cycle, such as conceptual and logical ones. In a parallel line of research, they developed means to tailor the DB conceptual scheme according to the application [15]. However, these approaches present isolated solutions indicating even more the need for a holistic variability-aware development of DB systems. In this paper, we propose an *SPL-inspired* methodological framework for a variability-aware design of databases. The framework allows developers to both (i) derive ready-to-be-implemented DB applications, by composing features related to the whole design of DB, and (ii) evaluate the design process so as to help users make better choices.

Our paper is structured as follows: Sect. 2 surveys existing research related to *variability management* and the current vision of DB research community on it. Section 3 presents our SPL-inspired methodology to manage the variability of DB design. Section 4 presents its evaluation process. Experiments are conducted in Sect. 5.

2   State of the Art

Originally, DB design process was limited to the physical step, and more particularly the DBMS that was relatively static and uniform (e.g. hierarchical DBMS). Over time and giving the upward diversity in DB application, developers strive for general-purpose solutions (like *Oracle*). Unfortunately, generality often introduces functional overhead and it is inappropriate for use in high constrained environments (e.g. embedded systems). As a result specific-purpose solutions have appeared to exactly fit to the special application scenarios. *PicoDBMS* [9], a lightweight DBMS for smart-cards, and *TinySQL*, a tailor-made query-language

Table 1. Classification of customization solutions to design DB.

Phase	Target	Input	Technique
Conceptual Design	Conceptual Schema	Global Schema	Modeling Tools[14] SPL[7, 15]
Logical Design	Query Language	Requirements of a specific logical schema	SPL [12]
	Query Optimizer	Requirements of a specific physical schema	SPL [16]
Physical Design	Deployment Layout	Requirements of a specific data layout	Grammar [18]
	DBMS	Requirements of a specific DB type	Component-based[5],FOP[1] Preprocessors,AOP[17],SPL[11]
Whole DBLC	DB Design	Requirements of the DB application	SPL

for sensor networks, best illustrate this type. Specialized solutions often redeveloped huge parts of systems from scratch leading to duplicated implementation efforts and time. Between the two extremes of piling-up a broad range of functionalities and reinventing the wheel for each scenario, both of the above approaches present limited capabilities for managing variability as they do not provide a general approach for reusing functionality to similar systems of a domain.

Customizable solutions are thus the alternative, since they can be used to provide extensible architectures or to generate tailor-made DB that attain high customizability and reuse. They can be built with a number of different techniques [10] as summarized in Table 1. Most of them correspond to the physical layer. Presumably, this is motivated by the complexity and the diversity present in that phase and performance requirements of DB applications. DBMS is the most studied part in the physical phase, and the conceptual scheme in the others. In the DB design area, Broneske et al. [3] have shown the superiority of SPL in mastering variability compared with other design methodologies. That said, SPL and model driven engineering techniques are complementary since the latter looks promising to automate the production chain in SPL [13]. Our approach is unique since it tackles the whole design process in one stroke so as to consider the interdependence of the phases whatever the environment is (ordinary as well as high-constrained environments). At first glance, our tool can be assimilated to DB modeling tools like *PowerAMC* [14], since this latter can also generate a script corresponding to some design choices. However, *PowerAMC* deals solely with the **modeling aspect** of the DB design, while omitting the other design matters as well as their dependencies like the normalization of the logical schema, the physical optimization and so forth.

3   DB Design as an SPL

Our first contribution aims at defining a variability-aware methodology, that devises DB design process as an SPL, and hence taking full advantage of this approach. Dealing with the DB design process as a whole allows users to have an overall vision, consider life-cycle interdependencies, and tackle all DB design steps while increasing process automation. Moreover, in contrast to the classic DBMS-to-DB vision, according to which, comes the DBMS selection before the logical step, we will see that our SPL-based approach can add more independence by delaying the DBMS selection to a later point in the process. On the other hand, our modeling is far from being unique or exhaustive. However, we believe that we have defined the basic level of granularity, that is sufficient to reach our objectives, namely to perform and evaluate the performance of the design process. Moreover, users can easily extend our feature models to additional needs. We first discuss our SPL framework.

3.1   Identifying Variability

Conceptual design (CD) in this stage, the design is mostly a matter of data modeling, so variability concerns (Fig. 1) the formalism, and the model itself [7,15] whereby the elements can be divided into two categories: the core ones which must be present whatever the application is, and the variable ones, which depends on the application/client.

Logical design ($\mathcal{LD}$) the variability inside the logical design can emerge mainly at two different levels: data model and normalization (Fig. 1). Mapping rules variants is merged with the data model for the sake of clarity.

Physical design ($\mathcal{PD}$) variability can emerge at different levels (Fig. 2).

3.2   Constraining Variability

Two types of dependencies are considered in our framework: (i) strict constraints expressed through the couple of relations: *require/exclude*, and (ii) flexible constraints that can be defined as helpful suggestions expressed through the couple *recommend/recommend-not*, and do intervene in order to advise and assist the designer during the configuration process. They are collected from designers' experience, and they can be enriched over time thanks to the designers collaboration. Dependencies are an important element for the configuration process held by users, since they reduce inconsistency and possible configurations number. Below, some few examples of our SPL integrity constraints:

multidimensional **recommend** *vertical-layout, MySQL-DBMS* **exclude** *MV, semantic* **require** *deployment-architecture, flash-device* **recommend-not** *MV*.

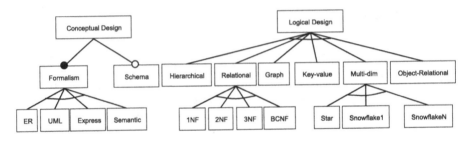

Fig. 1. Excerpts of $\mathcal{CD}$ (Left) and $\mathcal{LD}$ (Right) feature models.

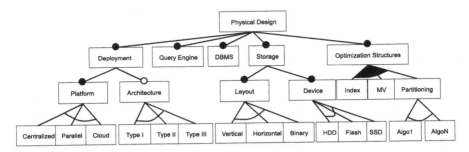

Fig. 2. Excerpt of the $\mathcal{PD}$ feature model.

3.3   Implementation of DB SPL Framework

We have chosen the *FeatureIDE* tool, an eclipse-based IDE, and one of the most complete and open source plugins that we have found in literature [4]. We have implemented our framework using the *AHEAD* composer that supports composition of *Jak* files. *Jak* extends Java with keywords for Feature Oriented Programming (FOP). First, features and constraints are modeled via the editor. *FeatureIDE* creates two directories: *features* that contains a directory for each defined feature, and *configs* that can contain different configurations (valid combination of features). For instance, if the user wants to implement the *UML* feature, aiming at transforming the ER model into an UML diagram, he/she must implement the corresponding algorithm in the *UML* directory. Note that our features can be one of three types: (i) ordinary ones that contain binary code, (ii) interactive that require an input from the user, and (iii) neutral that contain only parameters used either for evaluating the design or for a further data deployment.

Once all features are implemented, the user can configure a desired product (DB instance), by selecting a valid combination of features. While checking some boxes (features), other following boxes can either be: (i) highlighted as a symbol of hints, i.e. recommended choices related to the present feature, (ii) disabled in case of *exclude* dependency, or (iii) automatically checked in case of *require* dependency. We have implemented the basic features and dependencies, that should be enriched by the users by dint of much using. Finally, the user executes the configuration to derive the final script. This latter corresponds to the functional requirements of the current application. The DBA can enrich it thereafter, so that non functional requirements could be also taken into consideration (stored procedures, triggers, etc.) before the real deployment. This script can be accompanied with additional useful informations as it will be discussed in the next section. SPL input will be defined in Sect. 5.1.

4   DB Design Evaluation

The final DB design is the result of the different selected features summarized in the script which can also be seen as the path devised by the designer throughout the DB design feature models. Indeed, it would be much more interesting if a value is assigned to the final script in order to help the user to choose between different designs (scripts). Evaluating design process requires two parameters: the criteria of evaluation, and the evaluation tool which can be metrics or cost models to calculate the value. Generally, the criteria used in DB are performance, energy consumption, and the required size to the implementation. In our proposal, we are interested in *query performance criterion*, for which, cost model specifications are as follows:

Cost-model Input:
- DB schema.
- Queries.
- Data statistics (table sizes, attribute domains, etc.).
- Storage characteristics (Page size, memory size, etc.).
Cost-model Output: an estimation of the input/output number, between the disk and the main memory while executing each query.

A cost model is a tool designed to evaluate the performance of a solution without having to deploy it on a DBMS, and to compare different solutions. We recall that we are in the design phase, hence the above inputs of the cost model are not set up yet, except the schema. However, designers can always have an idea about the frequent queries (considering Pareto principle), and data statistics while analyzing users' requirements.

It is important to note that our feature model was conceived with in mind, performance evaluation, that's why we have ignored other aspects as privacy and recovery.

DB Design Query-Performance Estimation

In practice, the cost model depends on the execution plan of the query, i.e. the order of the algebraic operators in the query tree. These operators are determined by the selected *Logical model*, and thus the query language. Each operator has its own algebraic formula to calculate its cost. This latter formula, in turn, differs according to the used optimization structures. In a nutshell, each selected feature has an impact on the calculus of the cost model, as follows (according to the chronological order):

- *Conceptual-Formalism* allows users to set up their conceptual DB schema. This latter has no direct measurable impact on query performance, since it is requirement-oriented, and a modeling matter more than anything else. It will be of great value if the evaluation criteria was the *security* or *understandability* (*usability*). The former defines which subjects (users, groups, roles) can or cannot access each object. The latter involves metrics for measuring the quality of a conceptual schema from the point of view of its understandability [6].
- *Conceptual-Schema* determines which query to be considered from the whole workload, since it provides the "local" and data constraints.
- The *Logical-Modeling* features determine the algebraic operators to be used.
- *Storage-Layout* features serve to provide a final rewriting of the queries. In fact, queries have to be rewritten according to the final deployment of data.
- *Deployment-Platform*, *Deployment-Architecture*, and *Storage-Device* feed the cost model with necessary parameters, such as storage information: memory size, block size.
- *Optimization Structures* determine the mathematical formula for each algebraic operator.

Allowing designers to evaluate their design choices summarized in the script, implies adding the layer of the above roles in the corresponding features. Algorithm 1 shows the process of evaluating the performance of DB design process.

Now that tools are ready, the best solution is to automatically provide the optimal script value, by choosing from all possible combinations. However, this is a very long and complex task. For the first version of our proposal, we provide a manual solution, that relies on user experience and whereby he/she has to select the most appropriate paths to his/her application, and then compare their costs.

5   Use Case and Experiments

Below, we explain how to use our SPL, and how helpful is the evaluation process.

5.1   DB Design as an SPL

Figure 3 gives a high-level view of the activities involved in our SPL operation (DB design). Our starting point is the ER *Conceptual Model*(CM), because this formalism can be mapped to any logical model (with user intervention when mapping to *NoSql* models). Moreover, it can handle different data types thanks to its extended releases (XML). The user can either create the CM (including data constraints) or provide it. The other formalisms, whenever selected, allow mapping the ER CM to the target formalism. If *Schema* selected, then the user can tailor an existing global conceptual model to specific needs. Note that normalization features are interactive, since they need an extra-input [2] about some design parameters like

Algorithm 1. Calculation of the DB design query-performance cost.

Input: - The DB schema (*Logical Model*);
- The query workload $\mathcal{Q} = \{Q_1, Q_2, ..., Q_m\}$ (*Requirement Analysis*);
- DB statistics (*Requirement Analysis*);
- Deployment & Storage characteristics (*Neutral* features)

Output: Design performance cost.

begin

Select the appropriate queries (*Conceptual Schema*);
Generate the query trees from the workload (*Logical Model*);
Adjust (rewrite) query trees according to the deployment (*Storage layout*) ;
Apply the cost model on the final execution plan (*Optimization Structures*);

end

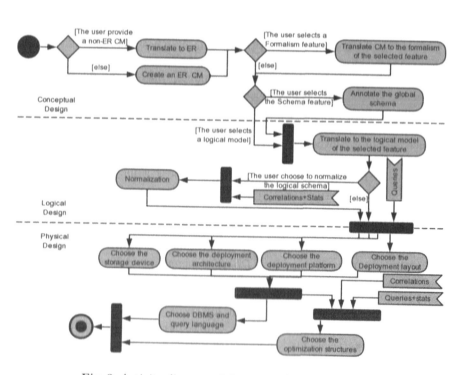

Fig. 3. Activity diagram of the usage of DB Design SPL

attribute size, number of tuples, functional dependencies for the different normal forms of the relational model, in addition to hierarchies for the multidimensional case. The designer has definitely at least an approximate idea about these values determined from requirements. Likewise, *Optimization Structures* are interactive features, because they depend heavily on additional parameters like the workload. In practice, some indexes can be derived right from the logical model, partitioning depends on the query workload, materialized views depend on both queries and correlations [8]. As for *Deployment Platform, Storage Device*, and *Deployment Architecture* features, they are neutral since they only allow to set some parameters without an application layer.

After doing these choices, the set of the proposed DBMS shrinks according to the selected features. They can be standard DBMS such as *Oracle, PostgreSQL*, or *MySQL*. As they could be, in high-constrained applications, core features of tailor-made DBMS such as those of *FAME-DBMS* for embedded systems [11].

5.2   DB Design Cost Estimation

In order to show the importance of evaluating the performance of the design process, we instantiate the approach described above using as input the Star Schema Benchmark (SSB), with a scale factor of 100, and a workload of 12 queries. Experiments are conducted on Oracle DBMS with 8192 as block size, hosted on a server machine with 32 GB of RAM. The user has made 6 configurations (scripts). They concern a multidimensional application with different (i) normalization forms: star and a snowflake variant, and (ii) different optimization structures: none (No-OS), materialized view (MV), and horizontal partitioning (HP). As already mentioned, conceptual design has no direct measurable impact on performance, and we will take the overall schema. Figure 4 shows the total performance cost of executing the SSB workload using the six configurations. The designer would choose the one having the lowest performance cost, in this case, it is the one corresponding to a materialized snowflake schema.

6   Conclusion

In this paper, we have been interested in managing variability of the DB design which is the most critical step of the *DB development life-cycle* (analysis, design, implementation, testing, and tuning). This was motivated by the large functionality and complexity of today's DB applications. Studying variability in the design phase affect the whole DB development life-cycle, and its scope can be easily extended to cover the remainder. In fact, our second contribution falls under the testing phase. Also, we are further going to address the evolution issue responsible on the *tuning* phase, that can be well handled thanks to the development overview provided by the variability study of the design step.

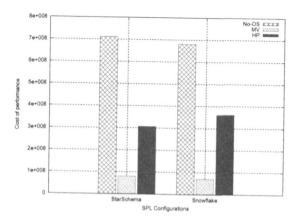

Fig. 4. The performance cost of selected scenarios.

References

1. Batory, D., Barnett, J., Garza, J., Smith, K., Tsukuda, K., Twichell, B., Wise, T.E.: Genesis: an extensible db management system. IEEE Softw. Eng. **14**, 1711–1730 (1988)
2. Bouarar, S., Bellatreche, L., Jean, S., Baron, M.: Do rule-based approaches still make sense in logical data warehouse design? In: Manolopoulos, Y., Trajcevski, G., Kon-Popovska, M. (eds.) ADBIS 2014. LNCS, vol. 8716, pp. 83–96. Springer, Heidelberg (2014)
3. Broneske, D., Dorok, S., Köppen, V., Meister, A.: Software design approaches for mastering variability in database systems. In: GvDB, vol. 1313 (2014)
4. El Dammagh, M., De Troyer, O.: Feature modeling tools: evaluation and lessons learned. In: De Troyer, O., Bauzer Medeiros, C., Billen, R., Hallot, P., Simitsis, A., Van Mingroot, H. (eds.) ER Workshops 2011. LNCS, vol. 6999, pp. 120–129. Springer, Heidelberg (2011)
5. Geppert, A., Scherrer, S., Dittrich, K.R.: Kids: construction of database management systems based on reuse. Technical report (1997)
6. Golfarelli, M., Rizzi, S.: Data warehouse testing: a prototype-based methodology. Inf. Softw. Technol. **53**(11), 1183–1198 (2011)
7. Khedri, N., Khosravi, R.: Handling database schema variability in software product lines. In: 20th Asia-Pacific Software Engineering Conference, APSEC (2013)
8. Kimura, H., Huo, G., Rasin, A., Madden, S., Zdonik, S.: Coradd: correlation aware database designer for materialized views and indexes. PVLDB **3**, 1103–1113 (2010)
9. Pucheral, P., Bouganim, L., Valduriez, P., Bobineau, C.: Picodbms: scaling down database techniques for the smartcard. VLDB J. **10**, 2–3 (2001)
10. Rosenmller, M., Apel, S., Leich, T., Saake, G.: Tailor-made data management for embedded systems: a case study on berkeley db. DKE **68**(12), 1493–1512 (2009)
11. Rosenmüller, M., Siegmund, N., Schirmeier, H., Sincero, J., Apel, S., Leich, T., Spinczyk, O., Saake, G.: Fame-dbms: tailor-made data management solutions for embedded systems. In: Proceedings of Software Engineering for Tailor-made Data Management (2008)

12. Rosenmüller, M., Kästner, C., Siegmund, N., Sunkle, S., Apel, S., Leich, T., Saake, G.: SQL à la Carte - toward tailor-made data management. In: Proceedings of the 13. GI-Fachtagung Datenbanksysteme für Business, Technologie und Web (BTW), pp. 117–136 (2009)

13. Royer, J.C., Arboleda, H.: Model-driven and software product line engineering. Iste Series, Wiley (2013). http://books.google.fr/books?id=ws5RnwEACAAJ

14. SAP, S.: Sap sybase powerdesigner (2013). http://www.sybase.com/products/modelingdevelopment/powerdesigner

15. Siegmund, N., Kästner, C., Rosenmüller, M., Heidenreich, F., Apel, S., Saake, G.: Bridging the gap between variability in client application and db schema. In: Proceedings of the 13. GI-Fachtagung Datenbanksysteme für Business, Technologie Web (BTW) (2009)

16. Soffner, M., Siegmund, N., Rosenmüller, M., Siegmund, J., Leich, T., Saake, G.: A variability model for query optimizers. In: Proceedings of DB&IS, pp. 15–28 (2012)

17. Tesanovic, A., Sheng, K., Hansson, J.: Application-tailored database systems: a case of aspects in an embedded database. In: Proceedings of the International Database Engineering and Applications Symposium, IDEAS 2004 (2004)

18. Voigt, H., Hanisch, A., Lehner, W.: Flexs a logical model for physical data layout, vol. 312, pp. 85–95 (2014). http://dx.doi.org/10.1007/978-3-319-10518-5_7

Author Index

Printed in the United States
By Bookmasters